The Process of Composition

The Process of Composition

Third Edition

Joy M. Reid
University of Wyoming

Process of Composition, Third Edition

Pearson Education, 10 Bank Street, White Plains, NY 10606

Editorial director: *Allen Ascher*
Executive editor: *Louisa Hellegers*
Acquisitions editor: *Laura LeDréan*
Development manager: *Penny LaPorte*
Development editor: *Janet Johnston*
Director of design and production: *Rhea Banker*
Associate director of electronic production: *Aliza Greenblatt*
Production manager: *Ray Keating*
Senior manufacturing manager: *Patrice Fraccio*
Manufacturing buyer: *Dave Dickey*
Associate technical production manager: *Steven D. Greydanus*
Interior design: *Steven D. Greydanus*
Associate art director: *Carey Davies*
Realia: *Wendy Wolf*

Library of Congress Cataloging-in-Publication Data

Reid, Joy M.
The process of composition/Joy M. Reid—3rd ed.
p. cm.
ISBN 0-13-021317-9 (alk. paper)
1. English language——Study and teaching—Foreign speakers. 2. English language—Rhetoric—Study and teaching. 3. Academic writing—Study and teaching. I. Title

PE1128.A2 R449 1999
808'.042dc21 99-038017

10 9 8 7 6 5 4 3 2

Contents

Chapter 3
Planning the Essay: Explaining an Academic Topic 65

Chapter 4
Introduction to Academic Research: The Investigating Report 99

GUIDELINES

FIGURES

STUDENT ESSAYS

Explaining Papers

Arguing Papers

Analyzing Papers

Preface to the Third Edition

Since I completed the first edition of *The Process of Composition* (*POC*), the teaching of ESL academic writing has changed, in some ways dramatically. Dozens of writing books for all levels of ESL language proficiency have been published; teachers are better prepared in their graduate programs to teach writing, in some cases taking full semester courses in teaching ESL composition. The TOEFL Test of Written English (TWE), as well as college and university gate-keeping placement and exit examinations in writing, have demonstrated the need for competence in academic writing. Moreover, the backwash from such examinations, coupled with increased dissemination of composition techniques throughout the world, has resulted in students who, regardless of their language proficiency, recognize the benefits of writing competence and know more about their academic writing needs than they have in the past.

Much research in both native English speaker (NES) and ESL writing has further informed teachers and teacher-trainers. Several areas of study have sought to answer the fundamental question **How best to prepare ESL students to become successful, efficient, effective academic writers?** To answer this question, researchers have investigated

- what ESL students have to write in college/university courses,
- what subskills are common to most writing assignments across the curriculum, and
- how to design a writing program, a writing course, a daily syllabus to give ESL students the opportunity to achieve linguistic, rhetorical, contextual, and content competence.

In addition, research in learning and teaching theories has influenced classroom approaches, methods, materials, and techniques as teachers consider

- how students learn,
- what students already know about writing, what they think they know, and what they can demonstrate that they know,
- how ESL writers develop their skills (and how to measure that "development"),
- which writing skills are cognitively more complex, and
- which skills are transferable (will follow students out of the writing class and into their academic careers).

Theory and the Teaching Philosophy of POC3

This edition of *POC* reflects my ongoing classroom experiences in teaching ESL writing courses, the increase in ESL writing teacher awareness and knowledge, the changes in student preparation and motivation, and the results of high-quality ESL composition research. The approach in this edition is Kinneavian: James Kinneavy (1966) focused his theory of writing on *aims* and *means*:

- Knowing the purposes (that is, the *aims*) for the writing, which are determined by the person who designs, assigns, and assesses the writing, is essential.
- Understanding and implementing appropriate ways to organize and present ideas for the reader will result in effective communication.
- Multiple modes (e.g., extended definition, comparison/contrast, cause-effect) are often used as *means* to the end in fulfilling academic writing assignments.

- The major purpose of the composition class is to engage the students in proactive rhetorical problem-solving.

In addition, more than thirty years of teaching ESL writing have led me to the following assumptions about ESL composition students:

- Most students do not really want to be in the class, but they are willing to learn, and they want to perform at potential.
- No student deliberately turns in writing assignments that are poorly done or error-ridden.
- For many students, every writing assignment seems like a "brand new ball game." That is, they are not aware of useful strategies and processes for all academic writing tasks, and they need to understand and practice how to apply those skills and strategies across writing assignments.
- Most students have only extremely limited strategies for decoding a writing assignment; consequently, they need practice in analyzing authentic writing tasks and audience expectations from across the disciplines.
- ESL students are often unaware of the linguistic, rhetorical, and content differences among disciplinary genres and, just as important, of the similarities.
- A great majority of ESL students are in the fields of science, technology, and business; therefore, class assignments should reflect the subskills used in writing in those fields.
- Students know a lot about what they need, so teachers need to communicate often, to *ask* students, to *listen*, and to make necessary adjustments.
- Each class comprises individuals, and so the needs of the course change, more or less, each time it is offered.

Practice-Based Changes in POC3

Research in such areas as discourse analysis, discipline-based rhetorical genres, and analysis of cognitive complexity in rhetorical problem-solving has led me to distinguish between sequencing—the organization and presentation of materials in an orderly way so that students can use "old knowledge" as the basis on which to build new knowledge—and spiraling: the need to re-present, in differing situations and increasingly sophisticated renditions, concepts and skills that need to be practiced and practiced again.

Spiraling grows out of (a) sequencing and (b) analyzing what students demonstrably do (or do not) know. The more cognitively complex and the more "foreign" the material, the more the need for spiraling. Simple repetition is not spiraling, however. Instead, the teacher must find different ways to introduce the complicated or alien concepts and to draw students into (a) trying again, (b) improving, (c) practicing more sophisticated applications, (d) succeeding, and (e) transferring the skill to other writing tasks. Indeed, real spiraling doesn't happen by chance: a course, a syllabus, daily lesson plans, and writing assignments must be constructed with sequencing and spiraling in mind.

In this third edition of *POC*, three major areas of cognitive complexity are spiraled:

1. Focus on audience
   - identification
   - analysis of audience expectations
   - strategies to fulfill those expectations
2. Use of support/evidence
   - showing (use of detail) vs. telling

- specific detail vs. generalized "evidence"
- how much detail/evidence is adequate
- what kinds of evidence are effective

3. Citation (and plagiarism)
   - what needs citing
   - how to cite
   - use of multiple sources
   - synthesis of multiple sources

POC3 spirals these problem areas by

- presenting audience analysis exercises in every chapter, with increasingly complex and task-focused criteria.
- providing authentic writing assignments from across the college/university curriculum in every chapter, and by reminding students often *not to write the assignments* but rather to analyze the purpose(s), audience expectations, and processes for fulfilling those expectations.
- sequencing cognitively complex writing skills:
  - formats: memo, essay, report, review
  - grammar: clusters for specific aims and means
  - citation: from a single citation of available information to a complete reference sheet for a research paper.
- focusing on the use of specific detail and evidence in every chapter:
  - in-class exercises, analysis of student samples
  - design and implementation of surveys and interviews
  - use of library resources and the World Wide Web
  - appropriate use of nontext materials (diagrams, photographs, charts)
  - evaluation of sources.
- offering frequent metacognitive exercises for student reflection and writing.

Moreover, *POC3* seeks to better prepare ESL students for writing tasks in their major fields by

- teaching strategies and then providing assignments that require some technical writing skills, such as
  - the formats and functions of memos and résumés
  - the design and use of nontext materials
  - the writing conventions, language, and purposes of progress reports and business cover letters.
- assigning writing tasks that require authentic audiences, relevant purposes, and primary research sources:
  - an Explaining paper that requires an interview with an authority
  - an Investigating paper that focuses on Internet proficiency and an oral report to the class (the audience)
  - a Problem-Solving paper to be sent to an authority who can solve the problem.
- asking students to be reader respondents to their peers' writing, not to act as critics, but rather to be an interested, encouraging, suggesting audience in pair and small group work.

- providing the necessary tools to access Internet sources and online library catalogs, to identify and locate those sources, and to evaluate and synthesize the material.
- weaving and spiraling the use of research throughout the textbook, thereby allowing students to become familiar, and even comfortable, with citation styles, rules, and formats.
- collecting materials for ease of access and use in three Appendices: (A) Citation, (B) Surveys, and (C) Résumés and Application Letters.

What Remains the Same in *POC3*

Although *POC3* contains many innovations, several of the basic assumptions about the teaching of ESL writing remain the same as in the first and second editions.

- The focus is on academic writing skills, particularly those skills that are used across academic disciplines.
- The concepts of audience and purpose continue to be the basic scaffolding of the book.
- The inclusion of relevant student samples has proved to be an excellent, motivating teaching approach (now widely used by other authors). Students continue to appreciate reading effective academic writing by others who have successfully completed the course. In this edition, nearly 40 percent of the student samples have been replaced with more current examples, which were submitted (and often voted on) by students.
- The overall goal of the course is to adequately prepare ESL students to function with self-confidence when they encounter writing assignments in future academic classes.

Finally, *POC3* continues my commitment to write the textbook *for students*. A Teacher's Manual is also available.

Acknowledgments

For the earlier editions of *POC,* I remain grateful to Colorado State University colleagues Peggy Lindstrom and Katie Knox for their suggestions and support; to (now former) graduate students Maryann O'Brien, Jim Griswold, and Linda Stratton for their willingness to experiment; to Tony Lueck, Betty Hacker, and Evelyn Haynes for their tutoring about the library; to Martha Pennington, Margie Swindler, Ilona Leki, Lin Grissith, and Mark Sawyer for their careful reviews of the manuscript and textbook; and to Andy Roney of Prentice Hall for his encouragement. I continue also to be especially thankful to the many students who have regularly given their permission to use their writing and their feedback on exercises and assignments.

Then and now: so many things change. For this third edition, I am particularly grateful for the care, the guidance, the expertise, and the support of Janet Johnston and Laura LeDréan of (now) Pearson Education, and I am grateful to Jamie Hayes Neufeld and Steven D. Greydanus for their generosity in providing information about (now) research and the Internet. Reviewers Esther Robbins, Margaret Sullivan, Mary Wong, Joyce Wulff, and Georgu Xu, most of whom had used *POC* in its previous edition, offered valuable insights and suggestions. Finally, (now) the University of Wyoming English Department provided class release time for my research, and (now, with Shelley teaching at Oklahoma State University and Michael organic farming in Idaho), only Steve has had to persevere.

To the Student

This textbook has been written for students, not for teachers (I write a detailed "Teachers' Manual" for them). I have taught academic writing to ESL students more than thirty years, and during that time, the students in my writing classes have contributed their writing, their suggestions, and their evaluations of the material in this book.

The general advice of those students is that *before you begin* your work to improve your academic English writing in this course, you should make a list of *your* goals for the course. Because each student has different strengths and weaknesses, different ways of learning, and different academic needs, each individual must be responsible for analyzing his or her writing problems, making decisions about his or her commitment to learning, and pursuing his or her specific goals.

Here are my general objectives for students in the course, which are based on my teaching experiences.

Pre-writing processes (before writing the essay): Students will be able to

- understand the assignment *or* choose a subject they are interested in,
- identify and analyze the audience (often the course instructor),
- decide on the purpose(s) of their writing,
- narrow the subject so that it can be covered adequately within the limits of the assignment, and
- begin to collect ideas and details.

Organizing and drafting: Students will be able to

- begin and end the paper clearly, using the conventions of academic writing,
- write a thesis statement of intent and/or opinion,
- use topic sentences in the body paragraphs to help guide the reader, and
- use coherence and cohesion devices to demonstrate the relationships between sentences and paragraphs.

Developing the essay: Students will be able to

- support ideas and/or opinions,
- investigate sources and resources to use in the development of their ideas, specifically
  - past knowledge and experience
  - observing and recording
  - books, magazines, videos, and other published material
  - the World Wide Web and other computer resources
  - authorities about the topic (by interview)
  - others (by survey),
- use specific details to explain their general ideas,
- use facts, examples, physical description, and personal experience to develop and support their ideas, and
- use citations to give credit to sources and resources.

Revising processes (re-reading, changing, and strengthening the essay): Students will be able to

- reconsider the expectations of the audience,
- reflect on the purpose(s) of the paper,
- consult with another "pair of eyes" (a classmate, a tutor, their teacher), and
- add, delete, and/or substitute supporting materials.

NOTE: These writing processes (selection, planning, presentation, and revision) do not usually occur in the linear form above. Instead, experienced writers may revise as they draft, add evidence as they revise, and continue to collect materials throughout the writing process.

The Advantages of Partner and Group Work

Educational research shows that college/university students often learn more from each other than from a teacher's lecture. Moreover, students in previous writing classes have agreed that working with other students in the writing course was valuable in their development as academic writers.

However, working with a partner or a small group of classmates can be disastrous, especially if the partners or group members do not understand clearly the purpose(s) of the tasks. Therefore, it is necessary to understand how cooperative work functions successfully in U.S. college/university composition classrooms.

- Partner or small group work usually involves a short-term task.
- The partner or the group members may change frequently rather than remain the same for the semester. That is, the teacher may form new partnerships or groups within the class daily, weekly, or monthly. In that way, you will have opportunities to work with most class members by the end of the course.
- Working with many of your classmates helps to form a "writing community;" that is, as you get to know your classmates, you will be more able to ask advice and to learn from one another. Moreover, reports from U.S. and multinational employers indicate that a major criterion in their hiring process is the ability and willingness of employees to work together.

In some of the exercises in this book, students work together because two or more minds are often more creative, more efficient, and more effective in solving problems and finding answers than just an individual mind. In addition, students respond to each others' written work because the comments of an authentic audience can often help the writer.

As you work with different partners and small groups of classmates, you might be interested in what research in the field of group dynamics has shown to be the essential roles of different group members.

The Facilitator	The Harmonizer	The Initiator
The Encourager	The Recorder	The Negotiator
The Reflector	The Confronter	The Compromiser

Each of these roles can add to the effectiveness of group work. Notice that some roles direct the partnership or group forward through the process and to the product. Others focus on the necessary discussion of alternatives. Still others have strengths in maintaining the harmony of the partnership or group.

The five rules for successful partner or group work are simple, and they apply to many areas of life outside of class:

1. **Respect** the dignity of others in word and deed. That is, practice ABC (**A**lways **B**e **C**ourteous).
2. **Participate**: without the mind and input of each person, the task is more difficult.
3. **Listen** carefully. Ask questions to get information, not to place blame or make speeches.
4. **Argue about issues**. Differences of opinion are usually integral to the work. If you argue about issues and not about people, the discussions will be more productive, and harmony will be preserved.
5. Be willing (a) to help others resolve disagreements, and (b) to **compromise**.

Authentic Academic Assignments

Throughout this textbook, I have included assignments that have been given by college and university instructors at several U.S. institutions and in academic disciplines from A to Z: from introductory art and biology classes to graduate courses in water resources and zoology. The purpose of these assignments is not to intimidate you, but rather to help you develop essential strategies that will enable you to (a) analyze real academic writing assignments, (b) determine ways to fulfill each assignment, and then to be able to (c) apply your knowledge to writign assignements you will receive in college/university courses in the future.

You will not write any of the assignments. Instead, you will complete a series of increasingly more complex assignments that ask you to identify keywords and writing tasks in each assignment, to discuss the writing conventions—such as organization and use of evidence—required by the assignment, and to decide the most appropriate method(s) of presenting materials that will fulfill the expectations of each academic reader/evaluator.

By the end of this course, you should feel confident not only about your ability to analyze writing assignments but also to determine information that is missing in an assignment, information that you will ask the instructor to complete.

Chapter 1

The Fundamentals of Writing: Audience and Purpose

I am surprised to say that I learned a lot in this course that I thought I knew before. For example, before this class, I had never really thought about my audience. Now I cannot write anything without asking myself "What should I say for ____? What will interest ____?" I have improved my writing strategies from prewriting to paragraph hooks. Overall this class made me improve my writing, reading, and also my English speaking.

Leng Heng Goh, Malaysia

THIS TEXTBOOK FOCUSES on academic essay writing.* There are two essential rules for successful academic writers: write about what you know (and investigate what you don't), and always write for an audience.

To write competent college/university essays, writers must be able to make appropriate decisions and to apply techniques—writing conventions—by which academic writers are expected to communicate with academic audiences. Therefore, the goal of this textbook is to provide student writers with information that will allow them to demonstrate a command of academic writing skills when they complete the course.

The Audience

In order to communicate ideas that have interest and value, writers must decide

- who the audience is: the instructor? classmates? parents? the editor of a newspaper? an admissions officer?
- who the writer of the essay is: a student? a son or a daughter? a subscriber to a magazine? an expert about the topic?

The audience is an essential concept because writers must make decisions about topics, evidence, methods of presenting material, and even grammar (vocabulary, sentence structure, and verb tenses) according to who will read the finished product. For most academic writing, the audience will be the instructor who assigns the writing. Sometimes, however, students write for other audiences, or instructors assign specific audiences for written work. Writers must consider the following:

- What are the needs, the interests, and the expectations of the audience?
- What does the audience know about the topic?
- What do the readers *not* know about the topic?
- What might the readers want to know; that is, what will engage their interest?

Who the *writer* is (i.e.,† what role the writer will play in communication with the audience) is also important. As writers consider their topics, they will also need to learn

- what they know about the topic,
- what else they need to know,
- how they will find that information, and
- how they will best communicate that information to the audience.

EXERCISE 1-A

1. Plan (but do not write) an informal paragraph on "How I Spent Last Saturday Night." Think about yourself as the writer of this paragraph (a granddaughter or grandson, or a student, or a friend), and about your audience. Notice how your selection of ideas and language will be different as you write for these three audiences:

   a letter to your grandmother
   a memo to your advisor
   an e-mail to your best friend

2. Plan (but do not write) an academic paragraph that describes a tree. Notice that you remain the same writer in terms of knowledge about the topic, but that as your audience changes, the way you present the material differs for each of the three audiences:

---

* Before you begin reading this chapter, please read the "To The Student" (in the front matter) for the objectives of the course.

† The term "that is" is often abbreviated "i.e." when it is used inside parentheses ( ) to define other words. Do not use the abbreviation outside of parentheses in academic essays.

an elementary school child
a classmate
a professor of botany

3. Share your plans with a small group of classmates. What differences do you notice in the plans for different audiences?
4. Discuss the ways that your role as a writer changed as you presented the material to different audiences.

FULFILLING AUDIENCE EXPECTATIONS

All audiences have expectations, and when those expectations are not met, readers can become confused, irritated, and even resentful. Professors in the U.S. also have expectations: when they design and assign writing, they *expect* their students to write in very specific ways. If a student does not fulfill the expectations of the instructor (who is the audience for most academic papers), the results could include a lower grade on the paper.

Many native English speakers are familiar with the expectations of U.S. professors. One of the major objectives in this course is to help student writers discover those expectations and to learn how to fulfill them.

These ways of presenting written material are called "writing conventions." For example, a personal letter in English follows a specific form. Student Sample 1 below demonstrates the writing conventions for a personal letter. Student Sample 2 demonstrates the conventions for a business letter. The writing conventions of each form are identified in brackets [ ].

PERSONAL LETTER

[Date]	September 20, 1998
[Informal salutation—at the margin]	Dear Chelagat,
[Introduction] *[Indent the beginning of each paragraph]*	→ How are you doing? I'm doing OK here in the States and am beginning to adjust. Things here are different, though—from the American accents to the (UGH!) dorm food, but I guess different is good in some ways.
[Body of the letter] *[Single-spaced]* *[Conversational language]* *[Personal experience]*	→ One thing that really surprised me is the class and learning atmosphere. You know how back home we have to be completely alert and sit upright in class? Well, here students sit in any manner they choose. Some talk, read the newspapers, and even sleep during class! Can you imagine drinking and eating in class? I can't stand it when the student sitting next to me is chewing out loud while the teacher is lecturing! I'm sure we'd be banned from class or even suspended from school in Kenya.
[Informal drawing] *[Informal punctuation]*	→ When I first saw these behaviors in my classes I was shocked, but after a few days I got used to it. Nowadays I actually have a sip or two of my Pepsi during class, and I must say I enjoy it (:-). However, I still think talking during a lecture is disturbing and rude. Don't worry—that's a practice I don't intend to adopt!
[Closing]	→ Send me a letter soon, OK? I'm looking forward to hearing from you. Please pass my regards to your family.
[Complimentary close]	See yah!
[Hand-written signature]	Beatrice Kilach
[NOTE: country is not part of the personal letter]	**Kenya**

[Writer's address] 801 Downey Hall
University of ________
______________ 65621

[Date] April 24, 1998

[Reader's name, title] [Reader's address] Professor Janet Constantinides
Chair, English Department
University of ________
______________ 65621

[Formal salutation] Dear Professor Constantinides:

[Single-spaced] [Reason for writing] I am an international student enrolled in ENGL 1210 (English as a Second Language), and I am writing you this letter as part of an assignment. In this first-year composition class, we were required to write a paper about a problem on the campus, and to suggest solutions to that problem. The final part of our assignment is to send a copy of our paper to a person on the campus who is in a position of authority to solve the problem.

[Double-spaced between paragraphs] [Body of letter: explanation] The problem I chose concerns the inadequate training of replacement Residence Halls Assistants (RAs) in the dormitories at the University of __________. My paper emphasizes the problems that result when RAs are hired at mid-semester who have no training or experience. The enclosed essay suggests a solution that seems logical and is easy to implement.

[Formal language] However, because I am at present one of those RAs, and because I hope to continue being an RA next year, I am hesitant about sending this paper to the Director of Resident Housing. Therefore, my instructor spoke with you, and you suggested that I send the paper directly to you. In that way, you can communicate the problem and the solution to the appropriate person without indicating the authorship of the paper.

[Formal conclusion] Thank you very much for offering a solution to my problem, and for reading this letter and the essay. If you are able to communicate with the Director of Resident Housing, I would appreciate hearing from you about his response to my recommendations.

[Formal complimentary close] Sincerely,

[Hand-written signature: first and last name] Emmanuella Sotiropoulou

[Typed name] Emmanuella Sotiropoulou

[NOTE: country is not part of letter] Greece

EXERCISE 1-B

1. For Beatrice's personal letter (Student Sample 1), who is the audience? What makes the letter "personal"?
2. In what ways is Emmanuella's letter more formal? Who is the audience for her letter?
3. With your classmates, discuss the differences between the forms of the personal letter and the business letter. Be specific.
4. Why has the name of the university been deleted in the business letter?

Writing Assignment I This is an exercise in creative writing. To fulfill the assignment, you must (a) become a different person and (b) persuade your audience to send you money by creating information. That is, *truth is not necessarily a part of this assignment.*

Note: You will not mail this letter. Instead, you will share it with your classmates. Therefore, you can entertain your readers with your persuasive story.

Situation: You have been gambling in Las Vegas and have lost all the money you were going to use to pay your college/university tuition this semester. Plan and then write a letter to one of these audiences.

your favorite rich uncle	a close friend
Bill Gates, Chair of Microsoft	your college/university financial aid officer

1. You will write either a business letter or a personal letter, depending on your audience.
2. For your letter, follow the writing conventions of the student samples above.
3. Share your letter with 3 or 4 of your classmates, and read 3 or 4 letters written by your classmates.
4. Which letter entertained you most? Why? Which was most persuasive? Why?

Some Differences Between Written and Spoken English

All languages have different levels of informality and formality. The level of formality depends on the audience, the purpose, and the situation. For example, when you tell a child how to cross a street when the streetlight is green, you use shorter and simpler words, simpler sentences, a higher tone of voice, and even different body language (i.e., hand gestures and facial expressions) than you would use with a classmate when you instruct her about registration processes at your college/university.

In general, academic written English is more formal than spoken English. First, because the writer does not know the readers personally, the writer must write words and sentences that are clear for a variety of readers. Second, because the audience for written English usually is not immediately present, the writer is unable to "see" what the reader does not understand (i.e., by looking at the facial expressions or by having the listener interrupt with a question). Therefore, the writer must explain ideas and opinions in more detail. Third, because the writer cannot guess the audience's attitude toward the ideas or opinions in the written material, the writer must choose a more formal voice.

Characteristics of the differences between academic written English and less formal spoken English are listed in Figure 1-1.*

• more-formal vocabulary	*children*	instead of	*kids*
• less-colloquial language	*The restaurant was excellent*	instead of	*Well, dude, it was gnarly.*
• fewer, but longer, words	*Mount Rainer is exquisitely beautiful*	instead of	*Mount Rainer is, well, more or less a pretty outstanding mountain in terms of beauty.*
• complete sentences	*I wanted to go home*	instead of	*Because I wanted to.*
• fewer questions and exclamation sentences	*This paper will define X*	instead of	*What do you think X means? You're right!*
• fewer personal pronouns	*Most consumers prefer Brand A*	instead of	*I love Brand A, and you will too!*

* Figure 1-1 means that the figure that follows is in Chapter 1 and is the first figure.

• more complex sentences	*My parents came to America for their children's education, leaving behind their lives in Pakistan.*	instead of	*My mother and father came to America. They came for their children's education. So they left their lives in Pakistan.*
• more specific evidence (more detail)	*Two recent research studies (Anderson, 1998; Li, 1997) report that . . .*	instead of	*Ya know what I mean?*

Figure 1-1 *Differences Between Written and Spoken English*

"VOICE" IN WRITTEN ENGLISH

In writing, "voice" is defined as the ways in which the writer's personality and attitude toward the topic are revealed to the audience. The decision about what voice to use depends on the audience and the purpose of the writing. In a personal letter, for example, the writer's voice is personal, conversational, and informal. In much academic writing, however, writers strive for a "neutral" voice, which is formal and objective.

However, not all academic writing is extremely formal. The choice of language and structure in a paragraph or essay may be deliberately less formal to facilitate communication with the reader. In the paragraph below, the writer is communicating directly with his classmates. He uses a personal, conversational voice to persuade his readers.

When the cold Colorado December weather sets in, and you are yearning for sunshine and beaches, come with me to Venezuela. When the snow is a depressing three feet deep, and the roads and sidewalks are icy and dangerous, the temperature is about 80 degrees (Fahrenheit) in Caracas. For us, December means parties, vacations at the seashore, clear skies, and fun. In the capitol, my hometown, we shop during the day, stopping at an outside cafe for lunch, and then go dancing in the evenings under the stars. The next day we drive to the beaches with their snow-white sand and warm blue water. I know that Colorado is popular for skiing, but you can ski until May in the high country, so why should you endure the terrible cold in December? Don't miss this opportunity! Come to Venezuela this December as soon as your finals are over, and return to Colorado for the spring semester with a beautiful tan.

***Ivan Hernandez,* Venezuela**

In contrast, the next paragraph is written in a more formal, objective, scientific voice.

Structural Safety for a Handicap-Accessible Fishing Dock at Sibly Lake

The magnitude of the total load is a combination of the dead load (weight of the structure), live load (people and moveable objects), and environmental load (wind and snow). Using the ASCE Standard (1990), the maximum load calculated for the walkways and the fishing bays was 179.2 pounds per square foot (for calculations, see Appendix A). The possibility of the use of the railing as a diving platform led to the calculation of a point load of 506 pounds per 8 feet of railing. The walkways and fishing bays were modeled for load application as shown in Figure __. The walkways and fishing bays had tributary areas of 48 square feet and 112 square feet respectively.

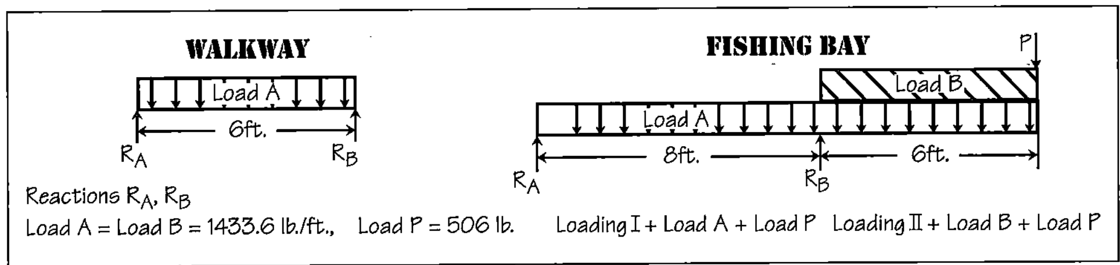

Figure __ *Load Applications*

<u>Reference</u>

American Society of Civil Engineers. (1990). *Minimum design loads for buildings and other structures* (Rev. of ANSI A58.1-1982). New York: ASCE.

***James Palmer,* U.S.**

EXERCISE 1-C

1. In Ivan's paragraph about Venezuela (Student Sample 3), underline the language that is informal and conversational: personal pronouns, colloquial language, use of questions and exclamations, simpler sentences, and less-formal vocabulary.
2. Compare and contrast the voice in Ivan's paragraph and in Beatrice's personal letter (Student Sample 1). Which is more informal? How do you know? <u>Suggestion:</u> use the list that demonstrates the differences between speaking and writing in English (pp. 5–6).
3. In Student Sample 4, identify the language and the structures that make the voice more formal and objective.
4. In Student Sample 4, what does "Appendix A" mean?

Writing Conventions: The Paragraph Form

Academic writing has many rules, called "writing conventions," about the appearance and format of the writing, and academic readers will expect student writers to use those conventions.

For example, U.S. academic audiences expect that a paragraph is a series of sentences that develop *one* idea. In academic writing, that idea is usually stated in a general form in a single sentence, called the **topic sentence**. The topic sentence tells the *audience* about the *purpose* of the paragraph. That is, the topic sentence tells the audience what ideas to expect in the paragraph.

Figure 1-2 displays the paragraph form that academic readers will expect.

[Indent 5 spaces] →Main idea about the topic (called the "topic sentence")
[Information about the main idea: facts, examples, description] ______
[Conclusion] ______

Figure 1-2 *Paragraph Form*

Writing Assignment II

1. Choose one of the topics from Exercise 1-A (i.e., "How I Spent Saturday Night" <u>or</u> "A Tree"). Next, choose two of the audiences from Exercise 1-A.
2. Then write two paragraphs—one for each of the two audiences—about your chosen topic.
3. Exchange paragraphs with a partner. As you read your partner's paragraphs, take notes about the differences in the paragraphs in

   ideas (*what* was written in each) — vocabulary
   grammar structures (*how* each was written) — voice

4. Which piece of writing do you think would be most successful for its audience? Why? Discuss your discoveries with your partner.

Purposes for Writing

There are three general purposes for writing, and they can all occur in a single essay, although usually one of the purposes is dominant:

1. to explain (educate, inform)
2. to entertain (amuse, give pleasure)
3. to persuade (convince, change the reader's mind)

Within each of these general purposes, writers select one or more specific purposes. Some purposes are external to (outside of) the actual writing: to fulfill an assignment, to receive a good grade, or to demonstrate knowledge to an instructor. Other purposes are directly related to "3 **A**s":

- **A**ssignment (or selected topic)
- the intended **A**udience
- the **A**vailable (collected) material

The following examples demonstrate purposes for writing authentic assignments given in college/university classes.

I **Instructor's Assignment:**
Write a paragraph about "pets as therapists."

Audience: Your classmates

Available material: What you know from past knowledge or experience

General Statement of Purpose: to educate (inform, explain to) my classmates

Statements of Specific Purposes:
- to explain to my instructor three ways that pets can help disabled people
- to inform my classmates about how visits to the hospital by a friendly dog or cat are being used to help patients forget their suffering
- to educate my friend Mario about how elderly people live longer and better lives when they own a pet

II **Instructor's Assignment:**
Should people have the legal right to be tested for hereditary (that is, genetically inherited) diseases—such as Huntington's disease or breast cancer—and be told the results?

Audience: The instructor who will evaluate the essay

Available material: Library and computer-based research, interview(s) with authorities (doctors, medical ethicists)

General Statement of Purpose: To persuade (convince, change the mind of) my instructor

Statements of Specific Purpose(s):

- to persuade my teacher that every person has the right to be tested for genetic weaknesses and be told the results
- to convince my teacher that the disadvantages of genetic testing outweigh the advantages
- to change Mr. Gilroy's mind to agree with me that genetic testing should be not only be a right but also a requirement for all people

EXERCISE 1-D Choose three writing topics from each of the list of titles below (a total of 6 topics, 3 from the first list and 3 from the second). Select a general purpose and one or more specific purposes for each topic.

Topic List 1

The Causes of an Ice Cream Headache
My Favorite Fast-Food Restaurant
The Advantages of Close-Captioned TV
Underage Drinking: What's the Solution?
Should the Amount of Time 8–12 Year Olds Spend on the Computer Be Limited by Their Parents?

Topic List 2

Vitamin C and Health
Dormitory Food: Help!
Bioengineering: What Is it?
What Is a Horoscope?
How Does a Volcano Become Active?

General and Specific

As writers plan their paragraphs, they need to know the difference between a general idea and a specific detail. Between the two, many levels may exist. In the next example (in which the words answer the question "Where are you?"), each word or phrase (i.e., idea) is more specific than the word or phrase above it. The answer begins with the most general ("in the universe") and ends with the most specific ("in a classroom at UW"). Each of the words between has a *sub*ordinate (i.e., less general) relationship to the word above it. You can indicate this subordinate relationship by indenting (→) each word or phrase.

Subordinate Relationships

[most general (least specific)]

↓

[less general (more specific)]

↓

[least general (most specific)]

universe
→ solar system
→ planet
→ earth
→ North America
→ United States
→ Wyoming
→ Laramie
→ University of Wyoming
→ a UW classroom

In the following examples, some words are *co*ordinate (*co* means equal). That is, they are equal in their level of generality or specificity. Coordination between words or ideas is indicated by *not* indenting.

Subordinate Relationships

essay
→ sentence
→ syllable
→ letter

Subordinate and Coordinate Relationships

researching a topic ("Injuries in Soccer")
→ doing an experiment
using library sources — *[coordinate]*
→ locating books
locating magazines — *[coordinate]*
→ locating *Sports Illustrated*
locating *Soccer* — *[coordinate]*
→ reading an article in *Soccer*

EXERCISE 1-E Choose 2 of the general words (i.e., categories) below, and list 3–5 subordinate and/or coordinate words or phrases. Indent (→) to indicate the subordinate relationships, but do not indent to indicate the coordinate relationships.

trees *children* *books* *insects*

In the following examples, each subject for writing is followed by several more specific words. Notice that the words or phrases in each of the *sub*ordinate "sets" are coordinate. Notice also that a more specific word can become a word with even more specific topics.

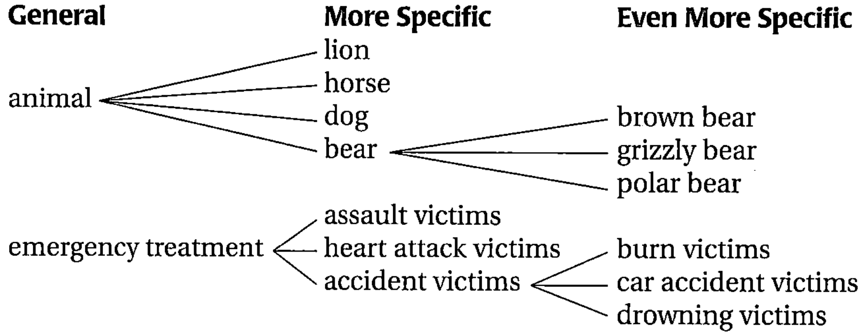

EXERCISE 1-F Look at the **Even More Specific** column above. Choose 2 of the topics and make them even more specific. Use the example below to help. Notice that narrowed topics can be narrowed again and again.

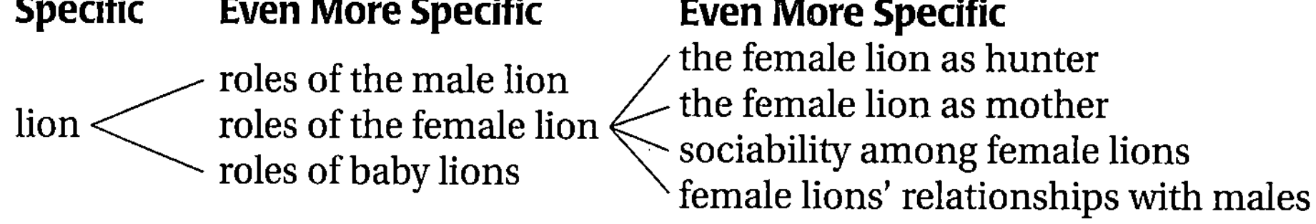

FOCUS: Choosing "A Piece of the Pie" (General and Specific)

When writers are assigned a general subject like "Democracy," they usually narrow that subject to a more specific topic, such as

- The Differences Between Democracy and Socialism
- The Disadvantages of Democracy in Establishing a Medical System
- Three Characteristics of Democracy
- Does Technology Promote Democracy?

Although the titles for the more specific topics are longer, they allow writers to *focus*—as they might focus with a camera, from a wide view of the landscape to a single flower. *Focusing* attention on a smaller "topic" that can be discussed in depth allows writers to use examples and details rather than just general (superficial) statements.

The subjects below have been narrowed to topics (and could be narrowed further).

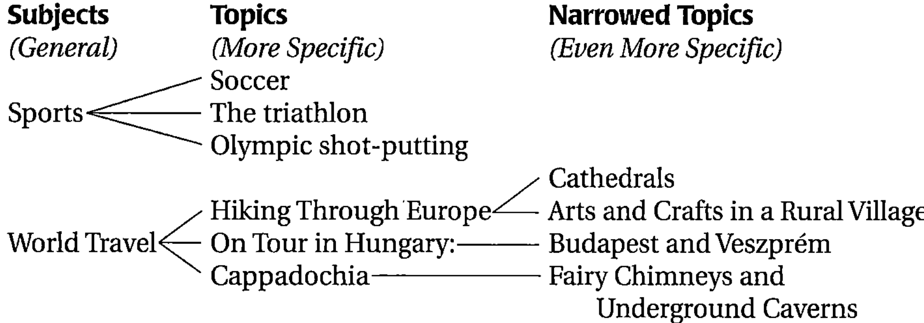

Writers might also think of the subject "Soccer" as a whole pie. Writing a paragraph about everything about soccer would probably result in a paragraph that was filled with *general* statements about soccer that the audience already knows. Instead, writers might make the subject more specific by selecting just a "piece" of the pie:

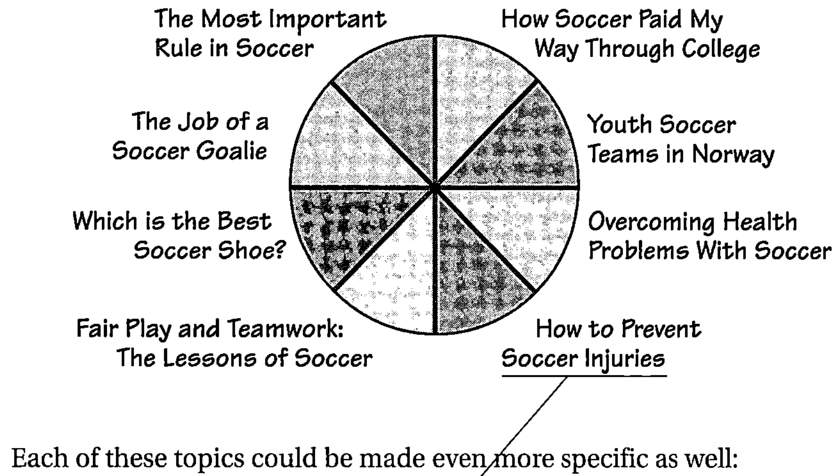

Each of these topics could be made even more specific as well:

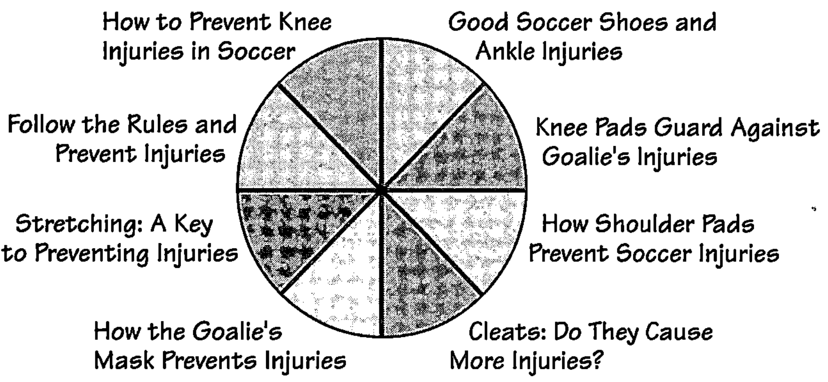

EXERCISE 1-G

1. Draw a circle, using the subject of your major field of study. Then divide your major field into 6–8 possible topics. Four of these topics might be:

   Why I Am Majoring in ____   My Area of Interest in ______
   Important Issues in the Field of ______   Three Important Terms in _____

2. Choose two of your possible major-field topics. Divide each of those topics into an even more specific list of 3 or 4 topics.
3. Select one of those topics and divide it into a list of 3 or 4 even more specific topics.
4. Share your major-field exercise with a partner or with a small group of classmates.

USING MEMORABLE DETAIL

The short, general paragraph below was written in response to the assignment "Write a paragraph about your mother." Notice that the student wrote about the "whole pie" instead of "a piece of the pie." The result is a paragraph that could describe almost anybody's mother.

> My mother can handle just about anything that life can throw at her. She is overflowing with love, and she gave me the best care any child could have gotten. She has taught me more than any teacher in school. Usually she's the most excitable person in our house. I just can't imagine what it would be like without her.

The student writer needs to use specific detail and examples so that readers will learn more about a specific mother and so that they will accept the ideas and opinions in the paragraph. For this student's paragraph, each general sentence could be followed with specific memorable examples and detail. To help this student, a classmate might ask her questions about each of the sentences:

1. *My mother can handle just about anything that life can throw at her.*
   - Show me, with examples and specific details.
   - What has life "thrown at her"? How did she "handle" each of these?
2. *She is overflowing with love.*
   - Show me, with examples and specific details.
   - What example can you write about that shows "overflowing with love"?
3. *She gave me the best care any child could have gotten.*
   - What kinds of care did she give you?
   - Specifically, how did she show her care?
   - Can you give two examples of "best care"?
4. *She has taught me more than any teacher in school.*
   - What examples can you give that show me what she taught you?
   - In what specific ways did she teach you "more than any teacher"?

Notice that if this student writer had answered *any* of the questions, she would have had a more interesting and memorable paragraph. Then she could have eliminated the last quality of her mother ("the most excitable person in our house") since it does not focus on the loving and teaching qualities of the mother, as do the other general sentences. She might also write a different concluding sentence, since the one she has written ("I just can't imagine what it would be like without her") is not about the mother, but about the writer. If writers learn and practice the strategy of asking questions about the ideas they use, they will be able to use examples and specific details in their writing that will interest their audience and make their writing memorable.

Writing Assignment III Write a paragraph about your mother.

Before Writing

1. Divide the subject (your mother) into 4–6 "pieces" and list those topics.
2. Choose two of those topics and write a list of three even more specific topics.
3. Exchange your "even more specific" topics with a partner.
4. Read your partner's topics and choose two that you find most interesting.
5. Write 2 or 3 questions about each of those topics.

Writing

6. Choose one of the topics for which your partner has written questions.
7. Write the paragraph, answering the questions (and any others that you can ask) with examples and specific details about your mother.
8. Reread your paragraph, making any changes that will improve the paragraph.
9. Rewrite the paragraph with the changes you made.

After Writing

10. Read three of your classmates' paragraphs about their mothers. Take notes.
11. Choose the paragraph you liked best and be prepared to say why: "I liked X's paragraph because . . ."

EXERCISE 1-H

1. Read only the first sentence of each paragraph below.
2. What questions do you expect will be answered in the paragraph that follows each first sentence? Write those questions.
3. Read the paragraphs. Were your questions answered? With a small group of classmates, discuss the questions that were not answered. Should they have been answered? If so, in what ways?
4. One "piece of the pie" in each of the paragraphs is in italics; it might be the focus for that paragraph. Suggest some specific details the writer might have used to support that focus in each paragraph.

I My mother is caring, thoughtful, understanding, and most important of all, loving. She is a beautiful 39 years young, 5' 2" tall and 110 pounds. She is a postal supervisor for the Dallas Bulk Mail Center. She has three healthy boys, and all of them excel in some sport. She's divorced now and remarried to a man she loves dearly. *My mother loves to keep her body in shape, so she works out three times a week,* and she still stays devoted to her children. She is a very friendly and outgoing person who loves to give to charity.

II *My mother has been the bookkeeper for my father's company* and a housewife *since I was a child.* She is a very responsible and good housewife for her three children. One day she asked me to help her bookkeep. As a junior high school student, I was very glad to help her work. She gave me a good opportunity to learn about her work. Through helping her, she taught me the importance of her work with her. This is a memory for me.

III It started nineteen years ago when she brought me into the world. Maw gave me the best care any child could have gotten. *She has taught me more than any teacher in school* and is overflowing with love. Always understanding and easy to communicate with and there when needed. She's the best: my "Maw."

EXERCISE 1-I Read the comments of the students below about pair and group work in a writing class. Then, with a partner, write a list of the advantages and disadvantages of group work discussed by these students.

I like working in groups because my classmates can help me to solve problems. For example, my problem-solving paper was much more difficult than I had thought, but with my group's suggestions, I selected the best solution. Also, we speak English to each other, and so my language improves with the practice.

Zaini Basri, **Indonesia**

One reason I value group work during class is that my classmates are like mirrors; they reflect my weak points so that I can revise my writing before I turn it in to my teacher. Sometimes a classmate is too stubborn and sharp, but that just reminds me not to be so.

Berit Fahnsen, **Norway**

For my arguing paper, it was good to ask for the opinions of my group because I needed to see the topic from many different angles. Only then could I develop counter-arguments and support my own ideas with strength.

Landu Kalemba, **Zaire**

1. With your partner, list additional advantages and disadvantages of pair/group work from your personal experience.
2. Reread "To The Student," p. xivv, and discuss the roles listed for successful pair/group work (e.g.,* Facilitator, Harmonizer). Consider your individual strengths in each of these areas: what might be your most successful role in a small group?
3. Some educators have discussed the roles of group members in terms of animals. For example, they suggest that the following characteristics of animals will not be beneficial for group work:

   the fish: sits with a cold, glassy stare, not responding to anyone or anything
   the frog: croaks on and on about the same subject in a monotonous voice
   the monkey: plays games and chatters, preventing the group from concentrating on serious business
   the ostrich: put its head in the sand and will not listen to others' ideas

   Have you ever worked in a pair or group with one of these "animals"? Discuss your group experiences with your partner.

---

* The term "for example" is often abbreviated "e.g." when it is used inside parentheses ( ). Do not abbreviate "for example" outside of parentheses in academic essays.

4. These same educators have indicated that pairs/groups function well when members include students with some of the characteristics of the owl, the turtle, the shark, the bear, and the fox. With your partner, discuss which characteristics of these animals might be used successfully in group work. Which might be disadvantages for pair/group work?
5. Share your discussions with another pair of partners and then with the class.

Writing Assignment IV Write a paragraph about one experience, either positive or negative, that you have had while working with a group. In the first sentence, state whether the experience was positive or negative. Then describe the experience so that the readers (i.e., your instructor and your classmates) can understand why your experience was positive or negative.

EXERCISE 1-J

1. Read 3 paragraphs about group work written by your classmates.
2. At the end of each paragraph, write "What I remember about this paragraph is ________________." (List one or more specific memorable details.)
3. Which of your classmates' paragraphs did you like best? Be prepared to say: "I liked X's paragraph because ______________."

TELLING AND SHOWING

The difference between general statements (telling) and specific detail (showing) is often the difference between ineffective and effective academic writing. Simply telling a reader general ideas or opinions may be easy, but it is rarely memorable or pleasing or persuasive. U.S. academic readers expect their students to produce writing that demonstrates (i.e., shows) the students' ideas and provides evidence for their opinions. Compare these statements:

[Telling] I saw a snake.

[Showing] I saw a snake in the park today. It was about a foot long, dark brown with a yellow stripe down its back. When I picked it up, it was warm and smooth. And here it is!

The next four paragraphs were written by students in response to an assignment to write about the meanings of their names. The students tried to *show,* using facts, specific details, personal experiences, and examples, what their names mean. Read the paragraphs and do the exercise that follows.

My complete name is Lili Margarite Chan Gonzalez. My first name, Lili, was the name of a famous ballet dancer. She was my grandfather's fiancée. They never got married because one night after her show she was killed with a knife in the street where she lived. In my country, most of my friends call me Lilian because they say that Lili is a diminutive of Lilian. My second name is the name of a flower and also the name of a saint. In the Catholic religion, our second name must have a Catholic meaning. Chan, my third name, is a Chinese name. I really don't know anything about it. My real last name is Gonzalez, and it is a very common Spanish name.

Lili Gonzalez, **Brazil**

My full name is Adel Addeb Ali Hassan Ali Ebram O'hide Salamah Faraq Al-Hadad. These ten names are my name plus my father's and my grandfather's names from my father's side. It is a custom in Arabia that every child has to be called by his father's side. We also have a tradition of calling each male child Mohammed when he is born for the first seven days. So I would actually have twenty names if we add Mohammed before each of my other names, as it is common to do back home. My family name is supposed to be Al-Hadad, but for some reason my sixth grandfather was famous, so his sons and grandsons took his name to be a family name. All of these names are Arabian. Of course, I just use three of these names at school, and in most of my daily life I just like to be called by my first name, Adel. But I remember all of these names because it is believed that we should be proud of our grandfathers.

Adel Salahah, **Saudi Arabia**

My name is Sin Sing Chiu, Henry. Anyone who looks at my first and second names will be puzzled by the meaning that they convey in English: that I have committed so many crimes (Sin) that I have come to "Sing" them out! However, Sin and Sing have completely different meanings in the Chinese language. In my family, every male generation is assigned a definite first name; mine happened to be Sin, which means "kind" in Chinese. The second name was given by my grandfather. He thinks that kindness should be wide-spread over the lands and seas. It is for this reason that I received the name Sing, which means "voice." Chiu is my last name, and I am proud of it, because it is one of the names of the dynasties in China, and it includes a very large family. We even have generation books dated back to our great-great-great grandfathers. My English name, Henry, was chosen by my brother; it is for convenience that I have adopted this name. Since my Chinese name is not easy for non-Chinese speakers to pronounce correctly, I can be remembered by my English name.

Henry Chiu, **Hong Kong**

Most people in the U.S. know me by the Chinese name given to me by my friends from Taiwan: "Ai-Sen," which means "love-forest," or forest lover, a fitting name for a forestry major. But my full name is Malik Muhammad Ehsan-ur-Rashid Khan. In Arabic, Ehsan means favor and Rashid is another name for God, so when put together, it means "God's favor," and it implies that God did a favor for my parents by sending me to them. Malik is my family name; my father's name is Muhammad Khan. Notice how it surrounds my (unique) name. This is to show that my father will take care of me and will protect me from anything that might try to harm me.

***Ehsan Khan,* Malaysia**

EXERCISE 1-K

1. Without looking back at the paragraphs, list 5 details that you remember. Then discuss these details with a small group of classmates. What made these details memorable?
2. Without looking back at the paragraphs, select the one you liked best. What did the writer show in that paragraph?
3. In the first paragraph, Lili's second (Margarite), third (Chan), and fourth (Gonzalez) names need more detail for the reader. What details could she add? (An example might be: "A margarite is a small, sweet-smelling blue flower that blooms in the early spring; my mother hoped that I would be as delicate and beautiful as that flower.")
4. In Student Sample 9, in sentence 4, Adel discusses the history of his "family name." What question(s) could you ask Adel that would make that history clearer for the reader? What other question(s) might help Adel show more in his paragraph?
5. In Henry's fourth sentence (Student Sample 10), he states that every male generation is assigned a definite first name. What do you think this means? What question(s) might you ask Henry about it? What other question(s) might help Henry show more in his paragraph?

Writing Assignment V Write a paragraph that explains your name for your instructor and your classmates.

Before Writing

1. Ask yourself questions about your name. Write some notes about your answers to those questions.
2. Consider what is interesting for your instructor and your classmates about your name.

Writing

3. Write the paragraph, with specific examples and memorable details, about your name.
4. Reread your paragraph, making any changes that will improve the paragraph.
5. Rewrite the paragraph with the changes you made.

After Writing

6. Read three of your classmates' paragraphs about their names. Take notes.
7. Choose the paragraph you liked best and be prepared to say why: "I liked X's paragraph because . . ."

The Topic Sentence and Controlling Ideas

Every paragraph students write in this course will have a topic sentence that introduces the main idea of the paragraph. The topic sentence informs the reader what the paragraph will be about. The topic sentence

- is the most general sentence in the paragraph; all the sentences that follow it are less general, more specific.
- states the purpose of the paragraph for the audience.
- is the most important sentence in the paragraph; it acts as an "umbrella" that "covers" all of the ideas in the paragraph.
- contains controlling ideas that control the information in the paragraph.

Controlling ideas (sometimes called "key words") are words or phrases that give the main ideas in the paragraph. The sentences that follow the topic sentence will then

explain *define* *clarify* *illustrate.*

That is, the sentences will support and/or prove the controlling ideas in the topic sentence.

After the topic sentence appears, the readers expect that the sentences that follow will answer questions about the controlling ideas such as:

Who?	*What?*	*When?*	*Where?*
How?	*How much?*	*Why?*	*In what ways?*

The answers to these questions are the specific details and examples that follow the topic sentence.

In the topic sentences below, the controlling ideas are circled, and the questions a writer (or reader) might ask follow each topic sentence.

1. It is very (difficult) to be (alone) in a (foreign) country.

   Questions: Why? In what ways? How do you know?

2. There are several (unusual superstitions) in my (country) about (death.)

   Questions: What are they? In what ways are they unusual? When are they used?

3. The most (serious problem in higher education) in Venezuela is the growing (number of students) who (fail courses) several times.

   Questions: Why is the problem so serious? How many students fail? What are the causes of this problem? What are the effects?

4. Most (people) have the (wrong idea) about the (definition of statistics.)

   Questions: What idea is wrong? What is the right definition? Why?

EXERCISE 1-L

1. In the topic sentences below, circle the controlling ideas.
2. Write specific questions about the controlling ideas in each topic sentence that readers might expect will be answered in the paragraph that follows.

   A. There are differences in shape, color, and taste between the two most popular varieties of dates in Saudi Arabia.

   Questions: ______________________________

   ____

   B. One of the most recent technical advances in the use of water is the development of hydroelectric power.

   Questions: ______________________________

   ____

   C. The creativity of the preschool child can be developed with special activities.

   Questions: ______________________________

   ____

   D. Audience violence at soccer games is destroying the game.

   Questions: ______________________________

   ____

E. There are four major transportation problems in my country.

Questions: ______________________________

____

3. Which of the topic sentences in #2 interests you? Why?

Writing Assignment VI

1. Write an "authority list": a list of 4–8 subjects that you know about, that you could communicate about to your classmates and/or instructor, and that would be interesting for that audience.
2. Make a circle (a "pie") for four of the subjects on your authority list. Divide each circle into 4–8 sections. Write more specific topics for each of these "pieces of the pie."
3. Choose 2 of the more specific topics and make them even more specific so that you could write a paragraph about each for your audience.

Writing the Topic Sentence

Writing a successful topic sentence is the first step to an effective paragraph. Inexperienced writers often make two errors as they construct topic sentences.

1. A topic sentence cannot be a simple statement of fact because there would be no controlling ideas that need development. These are *not* topic sentences:

   You can buy these socks at K-Mart.
   My birthday is July 26th.

2. Weak topic sentences are often stated as simple personal opinions, with the controlling ideas "I like" or "I feel" that are difficult to support. Instead, remove "I think" or "I feel" and restructure the topic sentence without those phrases.

Weak Topic Sentences	**Better Topic Sentences**
I can't help liking this book.	This book is exciting and reader-friendly.
I feel that spanking a child is physically abusive.	Spanking a child is physically abusive.
I like cats better than dogs.	Cats make better house pets than dogs.

Further, a successful topic sentence usually contains one or both of the following:

- **a statement of intent** that tells what the writer will explain in the paragraph. These topic sentences will not use the writer's opinion, and they often begin with statements such as "This paper explains . . ." or "The purpose of this essay is to . . ."
- **a statement of opinion** that the writer will prove or support in the paragraph. Topic sentences of opinion often use value words (e.g., *better, more beautiful, worst*)

These topic sentences have a statement of intent or opinion.

[Intent] This paper demonstrates the *advantages and disadvantages* of living off-campus.

[Opinion] Smoking by a pregnant woman is *evil* because it will cause genetic defects in the unborn child.

[Intent] To see Europe on $50 a day, try *hiking*.

[Opinion] Competing in the "Iron Man" race is *good* for the soul as well as body.

[Intent] Building a room that utilizes passive solar energy *can reduce* eating costs.

Often a topic sentence will contain both a statement of intent and a statement of opinion. In these examples, each opinion and controlling idea for intent is underlined.

[Opinion and intent] Ethnobotany is a major field specialization that can be <u>satisfying</u> for the student because of its <u>benefits</u> to the medical community.

[Opinion and intent] Censorship of art—movies, books, and music—is <u>unfair</u> to the people because it is in <u>opposition</u> to the democratic government.

[Opinion and intent] Learning mathematics by memorization gives children <u>better understanding</u> of the science of math than learning with calculators or computers.

Note: Distinguishing between topic sentences of intent and opinion is less important than understanding that the value words of opinion need more support to persuade an audience than a more objective topic sentence of intent.

Writing Assignment VII

1. Write a paragraph for your classmates and your instructor about one of your focused (i.e., even more specific) "authority list" topics from Writing Assignment VI. Be sure to write a topic sentence (of opinion or intent or both) for your audience. Then answer the questions about the topic sentence with details, examples, and your own experience.
2. During class, read three paragraphs written by your classmates. Take notes about each paragraph, then decide which you like best and why.
3. Below are three student comments about why they liked writing by their classmates. Read these comments, and be prepared to state why you preferred one of your classmates' paragraphs: "I liked X's paragraph about Y because . . ."

I liked Eddie's essay about the New Year's celebration in Malaysia because it brought back memories about Chinese New Year in my own country.

***Fan Zhang,* People's Republic of China (PRC)**

I liked José's paper about snow fences because its highly detailed explanation and his diagram helped me really understand how snow fences "work."

***Sura Gautam,* India**

I liked Emmanuella's essay about voodoo because it was so vivid; when she described the rituals with the chickens and the pin-stuck dolls, she sounded like a vodun herself!

***Brenda Alpízar,* Puerto Rico**

Writing a Point Paragraph Outline

Each paragraph written in this course will contain a topic sentence and four to eight supporting sentences that are more specific than the topic sentence. Writers can diagram such a paragraph by indenting the ideas (i.e., the points) for the more specific ideas, and indenting again for the even more specific examples and details in the paragraph. Here is a diagram of a balanced, detailed paragraph.

[Topic sentence of opinion] *Riding a bicycle is preferable to driving a car.*

[Point 1] It costs less (compared to driving)

[Examples and details about Point 1]
- to buy (compared to a car)
- to repair and maintain.

[Point 2] It's healthier (compared to driving)

[Examples and details about Point 2]
- better exercise (compared to a car)
- causes less pollution.

[Point 3] It's more satisfying (compared to driving)

[Examples and details about Point 3]
- to enjoy the scenery
- to become part of nature
- to save the environment.

[Concluding sentence] In all but the most inclement weather, the bicycle is a pleasurable means of transportation.

The resulting paragraph:

Riding a bicycle is preferable to driving a car. First, a bicycle is relatively inexpensive to buy and to maintain. While a car may cost thousands of dollars to buy and hundreds of dollars annually in maintenance, a good bicycle costs about two hundred dollars, and its yearly maintenance cost is very small. Biking is also healthier. Not only does the biker get more physical exercise than the driver; bicycles are also nonpolluting. The consequence is a biker with strong legs and a strong heart whose lungs are polluted only with the exhaust of the cars that share the road. Finally, bicycling is, unlike driving, personally satisfying. Instead of being a robot inside a machine, the biker pedals along, enjoying the scenery, becoming part of nature. Moreover, bicycling helps us to tread lightly on the earth, thereby helping to preserve our environment. In all but the most inclement weather, the bicycle is a more pleasurable means of transportation.

Read Student Samples 15–18. Then do the exercise that follows.

Amazing Devil-Fish

[Topic sentence] In the minds of many people, the octopus is considered an animal of hell, a devil-fish; however, this strange creature has amazing powers. First, the octopus has excellent, human-like eyesight; their eyes, like those of vertebrates, have lids, irises, crystalline lenses, and retinas. When a predator appears, the orange-brown eyes, which are mobile and so can be turned in different directions, flash in the sea like the sun in the sky. Similarly amazing is the octopus's facility for changing shape. Generally, *[Specific details]* its favorite hiding place is a small cavity in a rock; the octopus, usually a round marine animal, can make itself entirely flat like an envelope, or it can stretch itself like India rubber in order to enter the small crevice.

Figure __ *Octopus*

This remarkable animal can also transform itself by changing color: white, black, and even red! The agents for these color changes are the chromatopheres, the color cells; the octopus has two different kinds of cells, one for the dark colors and another for the light ones. Why does the octopus have all these transforming abilities? Because he has lost the protective shell of his ancestors and must therefore have alternative ways to survive in the sea.

Annick Burkhalter, **Switzerland**

16 STUDENT SAMPLE

[Topic sentence] It is hard for foreign student wives to be able to make many American friends since most of their husbands go to school full time while they have to stay home taking care of the children and the house. First, finding transportation and paying for a baby-sitter can be overwhelming problems; this situation makes it impossible for wives to go out often and to meet people. Furthermore, most foreign wives don't speak English at all when they first come, and this keeps them from *[Specific examples]* having a conversation with an English speaker, even in the laundry room of an apartment building. Finally, foreign students usually live in student housing, and generally the Americans who live there go to school. In many cases, if only the husband is going to school, the American wife will be working. Consequently, the American couple does not have time to socialize, and so the foreign wives have very few American friends.

Carmen Ortiz, **Venezuela**

Playing Soccer and Taking a Math Test

[Topic sentence] Maybe it seems impossible to compare these two ideas because a soccer game has nothing in common with a math test, but they are more similar than we think. First, if you want to get a good score on a test or win a soccer game, you have to be prepared. The best way to prepare is to practice, for when you are on the field or in the classroom, the only thing you have is the capabilities you acquired by training. Second, after each *[Specific reasons]* practice, you have to rest and reflect in order to put your ideas and plans in order. In both the soccer game and the math test, you need to be able to focus, to concentrate, so you will be exact in what you do. In both situations, one mistake could mean that everything is wrong, either in the goal you are trying to score or in the math equation you are trying to solve.

***Kleber Niza,* Ecuador**

What Engineers Write

The world of engineering has changed dramatically in the past fifty *[Topic sentence]* years; engineers now produce more papers than projects. Today they write technical reports detailing every aspect of various technical ideas or designs as well as research papers for publication. In addition, working engineers spend at least a third of their time, and sometimes as much as 60% of their time writing such documents as

- short reports such as a plan to test equipment or software, a test report presenting and analyzing test results, or a document analyzing a design tradeoff and recommending a decision
- user manuals, including the how-does-it-work part of an equipment manual, specification documents, and requirements documents
- progress reports every week or month, along with revised plans
- grant proposals for research that must contain preliminary design documents (i.e., overview of the design) and detailed design documents (exactly what is in it and how it works)
- one-page or even one-paragraph summaries of a whole project: why do it, how you are doing it, what results you expected, what results you are getting, and what your continuing plan is
- one-page or even one-paragraph notes explaining a complex technical project to the non-technical person or to managers

In the past, engineers spent much of their professional time creating highways and bridges and dams and railroads. For engineers today, however, the tools of writing are at least as important for professional growth and development as are the tools of technology.

***Rob Christenson,* U. S.**

EXERCISE 1-M 1. With a partner or in a small group, make a point paragraph outline for two of the paragraphs, using the format of the example on page 21.

2. In Student Sample 15, how does Annick's use of the nontext material (i.e., the drawing) help the reader?
3. In Student Sample 18, how does Rob's list help the reader?
4. In your opinion, which paragraph is the most interesting? Why? Discuss your choice with your classmates.

The Function of Second Sentences

Although topic sentences are essential for clear academic paragraph writing, the sentence that follows the topic sentence is often equally important for the reader. Sometimes the topic sentence of a paragraph is clear and narrowly focused. In that situation, the audience can easily predict (i.e., guess) the main ideas of the paragraph from that single sentence. For example, in the next sentences, the writer goes directly from the topic sentence to the points in the paragraph. The topic sentences below are italicized.

[Writer continues with the first example]

My mother has taught me more than any teacher. For example, when I was trying to be brave after my father's death, she taught me that it was all right for men to cry.

[Writer sets the scene—the time, the situation—and summarizes the incident]

My most embarrassing moment happened at the airport. As I was running down the concourse to catch my plane, my suitcase suddenly flew open, and all of my underwear spread across the carpet.

[Writer continues with the first of two or three reasons]

Doing class exercises in groups helps me learn better. One reason is that my classmates often know more than I do.

EXERCISE 1-N Each topic sentence below is simple and well focused. Therefore, the writer can immediately begin with the points in the paragraph.

1. With a partner, write the next sentence in each paragraph.

   A. My mother, unlike most mothers, is a terrible cook. ______________

   ____

   B. There are three healthcare problems in my country. ______________

   ____

   C. Burning fields for shift cultivation is a simple process. ______________

   ____

   D. In my language, there are several words for *warrior*. ______________

   ____

   E. There are three unique funeral rituals in Sri Lanka. ______________

   ____

2. For each sentence, did you use a signal for the reader? These might be
   - an introductory word such as *First, . . .* or *The first is . . .*
   - a pronoun such as *These are . . . .* or *They represent . . .*
   - the repetition of a key word from the topic sentence, such as *The most serious <u>problem</u> is . . .* or *The <u>rituals</u> are . . .*
3. If you did not, add one of the signals to help the reader.*

---

* For additional information about these signals, see Chapter 4, page 117.

SECOND SENTENCES FOR MORE FOCUSED PARAGRAPH TOPICS

The more complex or the more vague or abstract the topic and the topic sentence, the more difficult it is for the writer to focus the paragraph with a single topic sentence. For example, two of the sentences on page 24 could benefit from the use of a second sentence that helps the reader focus the paragraph:

[Writer focuses specifically on the emotional lessons]

> *My mother taught me more than any teacher.* While I learned facts from teachers, I learned about feelings from my mother. For example, . . .

[Writer focuses only on problem-solving with classmates.]

> *Doing class exercises in groups helps me learn better.* That is, working with several classmates to solve a problem helps me remember the lesson. One reason is . . .

For these topic sentences, and others that seem vague to a reader, a second sentence helps to more clearly focus the paragraph for the reader. Usually the second sentence is more specific than the topic sentence. The specificity of the second sentence often enables the reader to predict what will follow in the paragraph.

Unfortunately, students learning to write second sentences for U.S. academic prose often write second sentences that puzzle and even irritate their readers. Therefore, studying the second sentences of paragraphs can help students discover the expectations of the U.S. academic audience. Remember these recommendations about second sentences (each second sentence below is underlined):

1. Do not simply restate the topic sentence. Make the second sentence more specific. Save the restatement of the topic sentence for the concluding sentence in the paragraph.

   Going to the movies is a nice way to spend leisure time. <u>It offers a pleasant social event with others as well as the relaxation of being able to watch the entertainment rather than to provide it.</u> For example, . . .
   Concluding sentence: Therefore, when I finish work, I often look forward to going to the movies with friends.

2. Choose the main controlling idea of the topic sentence as the main idea of the second sentence.

   The Cambodian New Year (celebration) is the most important holiday in my country. <u>The celebration lasts a week, and it takes months of preparation.</u> Preparations for the celebration begin . . .

3. Think about the audience. As the audience reads the topic sentence, what questions will they expect to be answered in the paragraph that follows?

   Spelling is one of the most frustrating skills to learn in English.

   Questions: (Why is spelling frustrating? In what ways is it frustrating?)
   <u>The main reason for spelling frustration is that English rules are so arbitrary.</u> For example, . . .

EXERCISE 1-O

1. Work with a partner or in a small group. Write an appropriate second sentence for each topic sentence. For some of the topic sentences, the second sentence can begin the paragraph immediately. For others, the second sentence is necessary to clarify the focus of the paragraph for the reader.

   A. Two components make up any textile: the fiber and the weave. ________

   ____

   B. Injuries have hurt the football team's success. ________

   ____

C. In Kentucky, we have a tobacco culture. ______________________

____

D. In many hospitals, visits from specially trained dogs are used to help cheer children with cancer. ______________________

____

E. The religious rituals in Sumo wrestling are invisible to non-Japanese.

____

2. With a partner or small group of classmates, write the third sentence for each paragraph and discuss what the other paragraph sentences will be.

GUIDELINES
for Writing a Paragraph

- Choose a subject that you know about. *Studying Abroad*
- Identify your audience. *Classmates*
- Narrow your subject to a topic that will interest your audience.

  Advantages and Disadvantages of Being a University Student in the U.S.
  → *Problems of Living Alone While Studying at a U.S. University*
  → *Most Serious Problem of Living Alone . . .*

- Collect and take notes about some ideas about your topic.

cleaning the apartment	*living an irregular schedule*
missing classes because of my schedule	*shopping and cooking for myself*
spending my money too quickly	*having to do the laundry*
having no one to help me with discipline	*not completing my studying*
having no one to wake me in the morning	*loneliness*

- Consider the general and specific purposes of your paragraph.

  To entertain my audience with my problems

- List details about ideas that will interest your audience and fulfill your purposes.

  waking up late: late for class, no breakfast
  housework: wastes time, tedious, looks nice when finished
  laundry: embarrassment, incompetence, tediousness
  loneliness: no American friends

- Limit the ideas to the most important ones you want to communicate.

  housework or loneliness (choice: *housework*)

- State the main idea of the paragraph in your topic sentence (with controlling ideas).

  Since I began (living) in an (apartment) and going to school, I have experienced many (problems).

- Write an appropriate second sentence for the paragraph.

  The most irritating has been housework.

- Make a point paragraph to ensure a paragraph that is detailed and balanced.

[Topic sentence] *[Controlling ideas]* *Since I began living in an apartment and going to school, I have experienced several problems.*

[Second sentence] The most irritating has been housework.

[Point 1] Cleaning the apartment

[Examples and details]
- takes time from my studies
- makes the apartment look nice

[Point 2] Shopping for food is also difficult.

[Examples and details]
- don't know the English names
- takes extra time to ask for help

[Point 3] Cooking my food is often frustrating.

[Examples and details]
- uncooked or overcooked
- sometimes made incorrectly

[Point 4] Doing my laundry is embarrassing.

[Examples and details]
- far away—wastes time
- instructions are complicated
- have to sit with the women

[Concluding sentence] If I did not have to do these jobs, I would have many more hours to concentrate on my studies.

Writing Assignment VIII Use the second of your "authority list" subjects that you narrowed to a topic in Writing Assignment VI (p. 19). Follow the steps given in the **Guidelines for Writing a Paragraph** (p. 26) to decide on a topic, select a purpose and audience, narrow the focus of your topic for your audience, and develop ideas for your topic.

EXERCISE 1-P

1. Exchange paragraphs with a classmate. Use this **Revision Checklist** to analyze the paragraph.

Revision Checklist

   - Read just the first sentence of your partner's paragraph. Write 2 or 3 questions that you expect will be answered in that paragraph.
   - Read the whole paragraph. Were your questions answered?
   - Underline the topic sentence of your partner's paragraph. Circle the controlling ideas.
   - Did your partner use a second sentence to help focus the paragraph?
   - What is the best part of the paragraph? Why?

2. Reread your own paragraph and think about the discussion with your partner. How can you improve your paragraph?
3. Rewrite your paragraph and turn it in to your instructor.

The Paragraph and Academic Examinations

This course begins with a review of paragraph writing not only because less experienced academic writers often find the "building" of essays from paragraphs a successful development process, but also because effective paragraph writing can be useful to students when they encounter short-answer questions on academic examinations. These examination questions require students to demonstrate their knowledge in a clear, organized paragraph. In other words, academic readers of the answers to short-answer examination questions expect that the answers will follow the same writing conventions as the paragraphs described above: a general topic sentence followed by specific supporting details.

EXERCISE 1-Q Below are 6 authentic short-answer examination questions from undergraduate college/university courses. The course for which each question was written is in parentheses. With a partner or in a small group, select 2 of the questions and plan (*but do not write*) a one-paragraph answer for each. To plan each paragraph, do the following:

A. identify the audience
B. describe the expectations of that audience
C. state the purpose
D. discuss the specific detail needed
E. review the writing conventions
F. think about a topic sentence

1. (Business Management) Property tax is often considered a bad tax. Do you agree or disagree? Present your argument—for or against—on the grounds of equity and efficiency.
2. (Agriculture) Describe the wheat rust cycle.
3. (Political Science) If you were in charge of the armed forces, how would you handle the role of women in the military? Support your opinions.
4. (Nutrition) Discuss the risk-benefit ratio of red meat in the diet.
5. (Natural Resources) Discuss the process involved in testing pollution that is caused by carbon monoxide.
6. (Sociology) If you were awarded a grant of one million dollars, which problem in your community would you select to solve? Why?

Writing Strategies

Strategies are steps that we take to achieve a goal more quickly, more easily, more effectively. For example, some ESL students develop language learning strategies of asking questions, guessing intelligently, taking notes, or using their first language in order to learn a second language. Other students may prefer such strategies as repeating ideas or reading aloud, memorizing, and reflecting about ideas. Analyzing individual strategies and practicing those strategies can make students more active learners; they become responsible for their own learning. The results include not only successful learning but also increased self-confidence.

Students also use a variety of strategies as they plan and write their academic assignments. Some students begin taking notes and writing those assignments immediately; others need to think about the ideas before they begin to write. Some students prefer the pre-writing strategy of making an outline; others find that brainstorming their ideas first helps them to write (see Chapter 2 for more about pre-writing strategies). Some students find that working with small groups of classmates helps to produce ideas; others prefer to work alone, or to seek help in the campus Writing Center.

One student wrote the humorous list below to demonstrate his (ineffective!) writing strategies.

How Not to Write a Paper

1. Sit in a straight, comfortable chair in a well-lighted place with plenty of freshly sharpened pencils.
2. Read over the assignment carefully, to make certain you understand it.
3. Walk to the vending machines and buy some coffee to help you concentrate.
4. Stop to visit with a friend on the way back.
5. When you sit at your desk again, remember that you need to call your mother.
6. Go look at your teeth in the bathroom mirror.

7. Listen to your favorite CD to help your writing motivation.
8. Check the newspaper to make sure you aren't missing something on TV.
9. Plan your future.
10. Scoot your chair across the room to the window and watch the sunrise.
11. Lie face down on the floor and moan.
12. Leap up and write your paper.

EXERCISE 1-R The survey that follows is designed to gather information about successful strategies used by academic writers and to provide the survey takers with insights into their studying/writing preferences about their surroundings. Complete the survey.

What Environmental Factors Help You Write?

Directions: As you prepare to write an assignment, which of the following environmental factors do you prefer? Which are important for you? For each factor, (a) circle the answer(s) that you prefer, or (b) write another answer on the lines, or (c) circle NI (Not Important).

Please answer the survey quickly; that is, do not reflect, just answer. Then discuss your preferences with your classmates.

Place	formal (desk, straight-backed chair, ______________) informal (bed, floor, soft chair, ______________) NI
Surroundings	clean messy ______________ NI
Time	morning (early, late) afternoon (early, late) evening (early, late) NI
Tools	pencil pen yellow pad spiral notebook computer ______________ NI
Clothing	formal informal ______________ NI
Light	bright soft dark ______________ NI
Temperature	warm cool ______________ NI
Sound	quiet noisy radio television music *(type)* ______________ NI
Sustenance	food *(specify)* ______________ drink *(specify)* ______________ NI
Rewards	Do you promise yourself a reward for getting started? If so, what? ______________ ______________ Do you promise yourself a reward for finishing? If so, what? ______________ ______________
Other	What other "rituals" do you have that make your writing more comfortable or effective? ______________ ______________

EXERCISE 1-S With a small group of classmates, discuss the results of your survey:

1. How do your results differ from those of your classmates?
2. In what ways are they similar?
3. Do you agree or disagree with your survey results? Why?
4. What did you learn about your writing habits from taking the survey?

Writing Assignment IX Follow the **Guidelines for Writing a Paragraph** (p. 26) to write a paragraph about the results of your survey. Which environmental factors are most important for you when you write? Which are not so important?

EXERCISE 1-T

1. Exchange paragraphs with a classmate. Use the **Revision Checklist** (p. 27) to analyze your classmate's paragraph.
2. At the end of the paragraph, write what you think is the best part of the paragraph.
3. Reread your own paragraph and make any changes that will improve it.
4. Rewrite your paragraph.

The Paragraph and the Essay

Paragraphs are the most important building blocks of academic essays. The functions of the paragraph are the same: to state an idea and then to support that idea with specific detail.

Below is a student essay. The introduction and the conclusion of the essay have functions (i.e., different writing conventions) that will be discussed in Chapter 3. Each of the middle paragraphs, however, has the same form and function as the paragraphs you have written in this chapter: a topic sentence, followed by supporting detail.

Coffeehouses in Turkey

[Introduction]

[Thesis statement, controlling ideas]

Perhaps there are many places in Turkey that would amaze foreigners, but undoubtedly visiting the coffeehouses is one of the most interesting cultural experiences. These prominent parts of Turkish society are very different from coffeehouses in the western world. In spite of the fact that most of them consist of only one room, a small world exists there which reflects the different aspects of Turkish life. *Coffeehouses in Turkey are really extraordinary places because of their historical importance, their functions, and their customers.*

[Topic sentence, controlling ideas]
[Second sentence narrows focus]
[Examples and supporting details: facts]

<u>Even before the Turkish republic was established, the coffee houses existed and were important to the culture</u>. They were called *Kiraothane*, an Arabic word which means "reading houses," because they were meant to be places where the educated men could go to read their newspapers while having their tea or coffee and smoking the Hubly-bubly—a special instrument used for a special tobacco found in Asia. In past times, only the wealthy men were educated, and they were the only customers. As time went on, however, a lot of coffeehouses were opened, and various kinds of people began to visit them. The purpose of the coffeehouse changed; the Arabic name disappeared, and they began to be called simply *Kahuehane*: "coffeehouse."

[Topic sentence, controlling ideas]
[Supporting details: physical description]

<u>Today almost every neighborhood has a coffeehouse; typically it is very simply decorated, but it has a special atmosphere</u>. In the single room are a lot of chairs and tables where patrons talk and play card games as they enjoy their coffee or tea. A bar is usually situated in one of the corners where the tea and coffee is made, soft drinks are kept, and the Hubly-bublies are prepared. In most coffeehouses, a big mirror hangs on one of the walls, and in some of them a pool table is put in the middle of the room. Frequently, a very old-fashioned radio on the bar plays continually in the smoke-filled room.

[Topic sentence, controlling ideas]

<u>Nowadays, coffeehouses are shared by all kinds of men who come to spend free time playing cards, to meet friends, and to have a quick cup of coffee, in the morning to begin a new day or in the evening before</u>

[Second sentence narrows focus] returning home. These coffeehouses are often the only places where different kinds of men come close and meet each other. Thus, one must not be surprised to notice that while two young men play cards at one table, [Supporting details: examples] two retired lawyers at the next discuss politics. It is also possible to see an aged doctor playing cards with three young university students while several taxi drivers watch the game as they wait for customers. Indeed, it [Concluding sentence] is not unusual to see a clerk having a cup of coffee at one table while a bank manager does the same at another.

[Topic sentence, controlling ideas] Although coffeehouses are comfortable and leisurely places, they also have some very strict rules. For example, women are not allowed inside because these places are for men only. Naturally, if a woman goes into a [Supporting details: examples, facts] coffeehouse, she will lose the respect of the men there. In addition, boys under 18 years cannot enter because it is illegal; as a matter of fact, they cannot enter any place in Turkey where gambling is held. Curiously enough, customers in the coffeehouses play all kinds of card games except poker, which is forbidden because it is counted as serious gambling. However, most of the card games are very similar to poker and are usually [Concluding sentence] played for money. A final restriction in coffeehouses is the prohibition of alcohol; serving alcohol is against the law and against religious principles.

[Conclusion] Because of the camaraderie that exists in the neighborhood coffeehouses, most men in Turkey go there frequently. Some people think that the coffeehouses are unhealthy because of the smoke, and others think they are bad because of the gambling. However, they remain a popular and important part of Turkish life.

Jamal Asaad, **Turkey**

EXERCISE 1-U

1. With a partner, discuss the ways in which the writer fulfilled readers' expectations about U.S. academic writing conventions in each of the middle paragraphs in this essay.
2. Who is the audience for this essay?
3. What is the general purpose for this essay? What are the more specific purposes?
4. Two of the middle paragraphs in this essay have a second sentence. In what way does each help direct the focus of the paragraph for the audience?
5. In your opinion, which of the middle paragraphs is the most interesting? Why? Discuss your selection with your partner.

Writing Assignment X

Write a paragraph that describes what you have learned as you read about and practiced academic writing in this chapter. Use some of the questions below to help you begin writing, or think of other ideas you can choose to write about.

What was the easiest learning experience you had?
What was the most difficult? Why?
What are the differences between what you thought you already knew about academic writing and what you learned in this chapter?
What questions do you still have about the learning experiences in this chapter?
How will your experiences help you with future academic writing tasks?
What else do you need to learn about academic writing?

Use the **Guidelines for Writing a Paragraph** (p. 26) to narrow your topic and to support your ideas with specific details from your personal experience.

Chapter 2

Making Decisions in the Writing Process: Developing and Supporting Ideas

When I learned how to choose just "a piece of the pie," my essays became more interesting because I had more room for details, the key to reader interest. Of course, these details don't do any good if they come in a merry and unstructured order. I also need a clear organization to guide my reader down the page.

Jon Boeckman, Norway

ALL EFFECTIVE WRITING is based on choices and decisions made by the writer, decisions such as

Which topic should I choose?
Who is my audience?
What is my main idea?
What ideas and details best support my topic sentence?
What examples and experiences will best convince my audience?
What is my purpose?
How should I present my ideas?
How should I collect my material?

As writers learn more about selecting and making decisions, their writing improves. First, selection of the sentences and ideas to support the topic sentence depend on the 3 **A**s: the **A**ssignment (the purpose), the **A**udience, and the **A**vailable material. This chapter focuses on the many decisions academic writers must make as they collect information, develop supporting details, and present material in response to academic writing tasks.

Strategies for Collecting Information

Collecting details to explain and support an idea can be a time-consuming task. Yet these details are essential for successful academic writing. In fact, the details are usually more interesting for the reader than the main idea of the paragraph because the audience is usually familiar with the "skeleton," the main idea. It is through the details—the muscles, the tendons, the ligaments—that the main idea is demonstrated or proved for the audience. Therefore, using *memorable details* is a goal for any academic writer.

Fortunately, several helpful strategies can be used to collect details that will help writers develop main ideas. Not all of these strategies will prove equally useful for every writer; students must experiment and then decide which are effective. Some students prefer to use the computer as they develop their strategies. Some even black out the screen on the computer and type whatever thoughts come into their minds. Other students use a prewriting software program that leads them through the development process. Still other writers prefer to use a pen (or pencil) and paper, or to speak into a tape recorder. Finally, decisions about how to use collecting strategies may depend on the writing assignment as well as on individual preference.

The following examples demonstrate some successful collecting strategies.

LISTING

List main idea categories. Then add examples and detail beneath each.

Topic Sentence: There are several words that mean "to eat" in Thai culture, but one should know how to use them correctly.

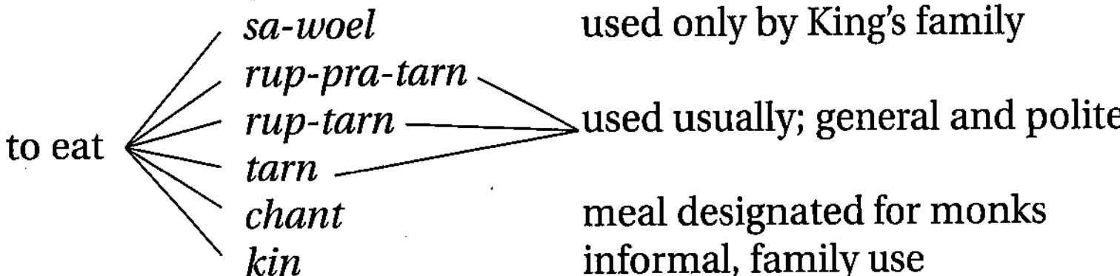

Concluding Sentence: However, there are a lot more local words that mean "to eat" which are dependent on each section of the country.

1 STUDENT SAMPLE

"TO EAT"

[Topic sentence] There are several words that mean "to eat" in Thai culture, but one should know how to use them correctly. For example, Thailand is one of the few countries in the world that has a monarch system. To show our respect to the king's family, we always use some special words when we want to discuss them. For instance, the word *sa-woel** is one that means *[Specific facts and details]* "to eat" for royalty. In terms of Buddhism, we also have lots of words for the monks. The word *chant* means "to eat" for them. We will use it only if we want to invite monks to have a meal. In addition, the Thais will say *rup-pra-tarn* or *rup-tarn* or *tarn*, which are polite ways of saying "to eat." We also use the word *kin* to ask anyone to eat who is close to us, such as our family or friends. There are a lot more local words that mean "to eat" that depend on the part of the country.

***Chakan Theerasatiankul,* Thailand**

BRAINSTORMING [AND REVISING]

Write steadily and quickly for 2–10 minutes about your topic. Do not pause. Do not worry about grammar or sentence structure.

We have several discriminate slang terms for a single woman who can't get married until in her late 20's in Japan. In Japan career women increasing and marriageable age is going to be high, on the contrary, many women still try to get married until 25 years old, otherwise, they are often hurt by the discriminate words.

"old Miss" is the most widespread word. "Miss" is a title used before the name of an unmarried woman, but in Japanese it means a young unmarried woman, hence, a single woman who is not young is called "old Miss"—second, (urenokori) is also a discriminate word for unmarried woman. Original meaning is the unsold thing like a woman who is left on the shelf. Finally, Christmas cake is a metaphor for a woman who can't get married until her late 20's—near the Christmas thousands of Christmas cakes are display in the stores, but they are never sold out and become old and go stale.

SLANG TERMS FOR A SINGLE WOMAN

[Topic sentence] We have several discriminatory slang terms in Japanese for a woman who doesn't get married until her late twenties. In Japan, the number of career women is increasing and the marriageable age is getting older; however, many women still try to get married before they are twenty-five years old. Otherwise, they are often hurt by embarrassing labels. First, an older unmarried woman may be called an "old miss," the most widespread slang word. Every Japanese person knows that phrase. "Miss" is a title

* Words that are foreign are usually *italicized.*

[Specific details] used before the name of an unmarried woman in English, but in Japanese it means a *young* unmarried woman, so a single woman who is not young is called an "old miss." Another discriminatory word is *urenokori*. The original meaning is "an unsold thing," and it means a woman who has been left on the shelf. Finally, the term "Christmas cake" has the same meaning. Like the leftover Christmas cakes that grow old and stale after the Christmas season has passed, the older single woman is labeled in this derogatory manner. In Japan, getting married is more important for a *[Concluding sentence]* woman than having a job and being independent, so many discriminatory words for an unmarried woman exist.

Kaori Tomisawa, **Japan**

CLUSTERING

Start with your topic in the middle of a page. Link ideas about your topic with circles and lines. Look for cross-connections between the ideas.

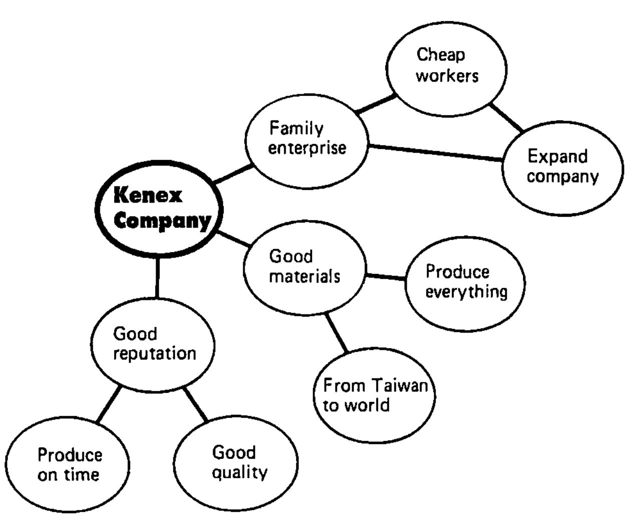

THE KENEX COMPANY

[Topic sentence] There are three reasons that the Kenex Tennis Company is so successful in Taiwan. First, the company was started as a family enterprise. The family all worked, so they saved a lot of money in salaries. That money allowed them to expand the company rapidly. Second, the Kenex Company buys good raw materials, so the products—tennis *[Specific reasons]* shoes, tennis balls, and tennis racquets—are high quality. That quality makes Kenex's products marketable all over the world because the company has a good reputation. Third, the company produces on time, and it delivers the products quickly and efficiently. For these reasons, I *[Concluding sentence]* believe that the Kenex Company will grow even bigger and better in the future.

Mickey Chyu Kwang-Jiu, **Taiwan (R. O. C.)**

OUTLINING

Divide your topic into three or four points that you think are important. For each point, list 3 or 4 examples. For each example, list several details.

How I Prepared to Come to the U. S.

In a refugee camp—wrote letters to countries

I Immigration interview
   A. difficult to complete history
      1. very young
      2. couldn't remember
   B. frightened

II Waiting

III Immigration called
   A. found parents for me
   B. arranged my trip

IV Worrying
   A. about my English
   B. about my new family

V Arrived—nice family

How I Prepared to Come to the U. S.

In 1980, I spent two years in a refugee camp in Thailand, and I decided to write letters to all the countries in the world, asking them if they would accept me into their country. Finally, the Immigration Office of the United States interviewed me. That test was very difficult for me because I had to complete a history about my parents, my family, and my relatives. Since I was very young, I didn't remember very much. After my interview, I waited for a response. I knew that the Immigration Office would decide whether or not I should come to the U.S. I waited for about four months; then they called my name, and they made a photograph for my passport. I was so excited about the trip, but during that time I was worried, too, because I didn't speak English, and I wondered who my new parents would be. I didn't prepare anything for the trip because I didn't know I was going to go to the U.S. until the last minute. When I arrived, my new parents made me feel welcome in their home.

***Farid Soeu,* Cambodia**

FLOW CHART

Use for cause-effect planning. Work both backward (for causes) and forward (for effects) from your topic.

Subject: Automobile Accidents (causes/effects)
Topic: Alcohol: The Major Cause of Auto Accidents

SUBJECT: Automobile Accidents (causes/effects)

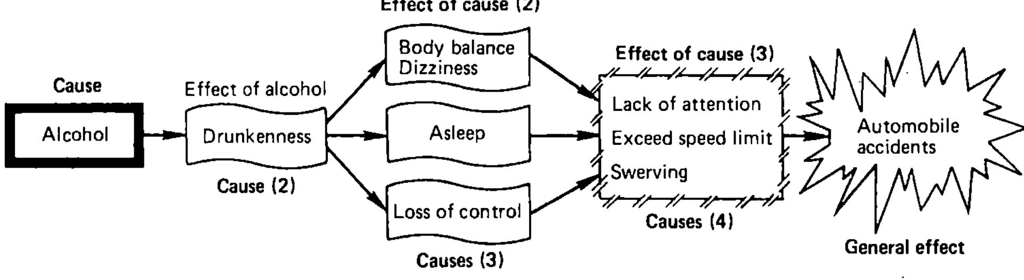

Automobile Accidents

[Topic sentence] The majority of automobile accidents in Nigeria result from alcohol. A person who has drunk too much beer gets into a strange state called drunkenness. This state is marked either by an unpleasant feeling of loss of balance, or by falling asleep. Either of these problems is dangerous for drivers. On the road, a drunk driver is too dizzy to pay attention to traffic signs, and his lack of control may lead him to run a STOP sign, exceed the speed limit, or swerve his car. As a result, he may either hit another car or a person. It is very likely that he will crash his car, and often he will kill or injure himself and others. Therefore, the government of Nigeria has established stricter laws against drunk drivers.

***Kombu Elukessu,* Nigeria**

DOUBLE-ENTRY NOTES [OR TRIPLE-ENTRY]

Divide your details into two lists (e.g., observations and feelings; similarities and differences) or three lists (e.g., product, target audience, evidence) and write your details according to those categories.

Subject: Halloween
Topic: My First Halloween Celebration

Observation of Details *(facts, data)*	**Feelings about Observed Details** *(impressions, reactions, ideas, questions)*
– life-sized paper dolls painted red	– like blood; when I touched one, I was so startled I fell down!
– carved pumpkins with lit candles inside	– why are pumpkins part of Halloween? I felt eerie inside.
– ghosts everywhere	– we also have celebrations for our ancestors, but they are not frightening

6 STUDENT SAMPLE

My First Halloween Celebration

[Topic sentence] Halloween is an important ceremony for American people, like Christmas in Japan. On this night (October 31st), American people believe that the dead return to the real world, so they disguise themselves as witches, vampires, or Frankenstein to frighten the ghosts away. Then, they decorate their dorm rooms a lot to welcome the "ghosts" of the dead. In my *[Specific facts and details]* dormitory, the residents made our floor into a ghost house to scare the children who came to "trick-or-treat." Imagine the dark and deserted floor with only flashing lights on big silver balls—it was scary! Also, some dolls were painted red like blood; their heads were made of carved pumpkins with creepy smiles, and on the wall there were painted skeletons. In addition, plastic spiders and bats hung from the ceiling and sometimes clung to us! We played weird music loudly and we made up our faces like ghosts. Then we frightened the kids by hiding behind pillars to attack them all of a sudden, catching their legs from behind and chasing them. The children screamed and ran desperately, laughing all the while. It was so much fun!

***Ryoko Kobayashi,* Japan**

JOURNALISTIC QUESTIONS

Use the "5 Ws and 1 H" questions that newspaper reporters use to discover what you know and what you do not know about your topic.

Topic: My trip to the U.S.

Who? me—how I felt and what I did
What? travel to the U.S.
When? September 21, 1997
Where? From Seoul, Korea, to Corvallis, Oregon
Why? To study English so I could get employment in Korea
How? By plane and then by bus

7 STUDENT SAMPLE

Il Jo Goes to the USA!

[Topic sentence] On September 21st, 1997, I began a difficult day. I arrived at Kim-Po airport with my family and friends, but I couldn't believe I was leaving Korea. I couldn't express my heart to other people; my girlfriend was shedding tears. When I parted, I couldn't say anything because I was holding back my tears. At last, I got on the airplane. I was afraid of everything, so I couldn't sleep; those long hours were like hell. I was more afraid than I had been when I joined the army four years before. At last, I arrived at the Portland airport, but I was at a loss. I felt very strange, and my English was very poor. Fortunately, I met a Korean man by chance. He was the same age as I, and he had come to study English at Oregon State University, too. He had a friend who was already an OSU student, and his friend came to pick him up at the airport, so I came to Corvallis comfortably. That was a pleasant end to my difficult day. *[Specific details of personal experience]*

Choi Il Jo, **Korea**

EXERCISE 2-A

1. With a small group of classmates, discuss the collecting strategies seen above.

   Which have you used before? Which have you never used?
   Which do you think will be helpful for you? Why?

2. Without rereading the 7 student samples above, choose 2, and make a list of details that you remember from each of them. Share your list with your small group.

   Why did you choose the paragraphs you chose?
   Did you choose different paragraphs from the others in your group?
   If you chose the same paragraphs, did you choose different "memorable details" or the same?
   Why did you remember the details you used? That is, why did you find them "memorable"?

3. For Student Samples 1–7, decide with your group on the following:

   Who is the audience?
   How do you know?
   What are the general and specific purposes for each?

4. Discuss the "voice" of the writers in Student Samples 4, 5 and 6. Which uses more formal language and sentence structures? Give specific examples.

5. Which of the 7 paragraphs did you find the most interesting? Why? Discuss your selection with your classmates. Be prepared to state: "I liked X's paragraph because . . ."

Writing Assignment 1

1. Choose a subject or a topic from your authority list. Use the general-to-specific strategies from Chapter 1 to narrow that subject and focus your topic for an audience of your classmates and your instructor. That is, decide on "a piece of the pie."
2. Decide and then write the general and the specific purposes of your paragraph.
3. Use 1 or 2 collecting strategies (listing, brainstorming, clustering, outlining, flow charting, double-entry notes, or questions) to develop examples and details for your paragraph.
4. Consult the **Guidelines for Writing a Paragraph** (p. 26) as you write a topic sentence of opinion and/or intent for your paragraph.

EXERCISE 2-B

1. Exchange topic sentences with a partner. Read your partner's topic sentence and circle the controlling ideas.
2. Write 2–4 questions that you expect will be answered in the paragraph.
3. Return your partner's topic sentence. Then discuss your questions with your partner.

Supporting Techniques

After you have chosen a topic, an audience, and a purpose, and you have collected some information about your topic, you will select the supporting techniques that will help you achieve your purpose(s) for writing. Four important techniques of support are

facts   *examples*   *physical description*   *personal experience.*

Usually your decision will be based on the details you have collected:

Have you developed an outline or a flow chart based on *facts*?
Have you made clusters of *examples* about your topic?
Have you brainstormed or drawn a picture from *personal experience*?
Have you listed details of *physical description*?

Of course, you can use more than one supporting technique in your paragraph. You might, for example, use a physical description of a personal experience, or you might use facts in an example.

FACTS

Using facts to support a topic sentence requires a writer to be certain that the facts are accurate and relevant. Using an authoritative source for the facts makes the support more believable to the audience. For example, a student writer might interview a surgeon who specializes in knee replacement about the newest techniques in her field, or consult a book about gardening to discover what insects attack roses. Chapter 3 will explore the use of authoritative sources and the citations for them.

The main ideas in the following paragraphs are supported by facts: numbers, statistics, and other pieces of information that can easily be verified. Read the paragraphs and do the exercise that follows.

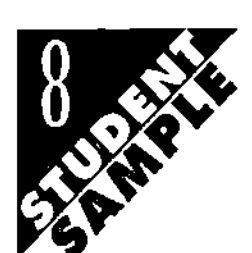

The Three Basic Food Groups

[Topic sentence] In Lesotho, a country in South Africa, nutritionists developed a food chart that is simple and easy to follow. Each of the food groups is labeled with a number at the center of the "pot" that contains the pictures of various foods. The chart, depicted in Figure __, is divided into three equal parts, one for each food group, so that Lesotho citizens can see that each

food group is equally important and that eating from each group every day is a good way to stay healthy.

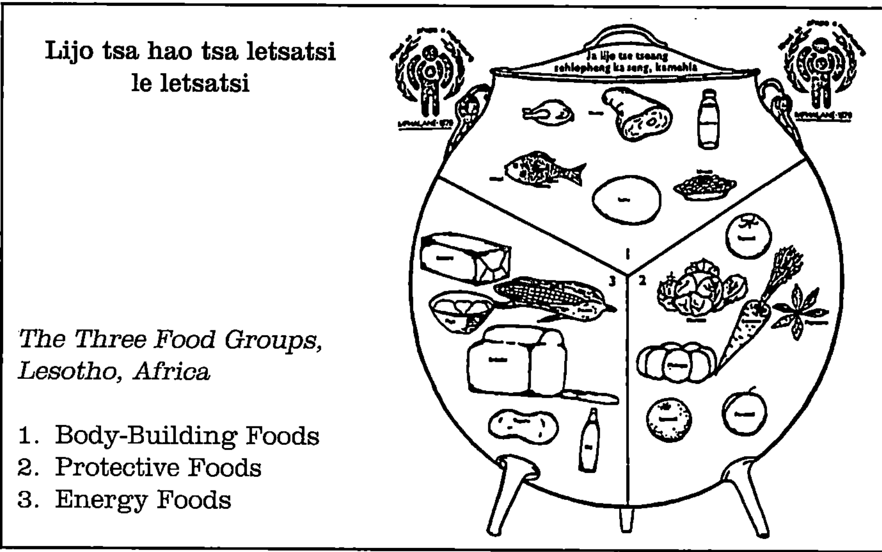

Lijo tsa hao tsa letsatsi
le letsatsi
The Three Food Groups,
Lesotho, Africa
1. Body-Building Foods
2. Protective Foods
3. Energy Foods
1
2
3

Figure __ *Lesotho Food Chart*

[Specific facts] Food Group 1, translated at the bottom of the chart as "Body-Building Foods," consists of high-protein eggs, dairy products, fish, and meat. Group 2 comprises fruits and vegetables and is labeled "Protective Food"; Group 3 includes starches: bread and corn, potatoes and other carbohydrates. However, the chart is so clearly made that even a person who does not speak the language of Lesotho, who therefore cannot read the title and the headings of the chart, can easily understand what each food group includes. The simplicity of this chart is, in my assessment, its greatest virtue, and the information it provides has the possibility of strengthening the health of the entire country.

Jennifer Anderson, **Nutrition Extension Agent (U.S.)**

The Beautiful Norwegian Hardanger *Bunad*

For local and national celebrations, women from the Hardanger district in western Norway wear their hand-made national costumes, called the *bunad*, to the festivities. Like most daughters in the Hardanger district, I learned to make my *bunad* from my mother. Figure __ shows the Hardanger *bunad*.

[Specific facts] The white embroidery on the white linen shirt and apron of the *bunad*, and the home-woven red wool vest with rose-patterned ribbons, contrast with the long black wool skirt. The belt, made of red wool with intricate beaded patterns, is the most valuable part of the costume; the buckles and ornate jewelry are made of silver and gold. The costume also has two or more brooches and two buttons decorated with beads, pinned to the front of the shirt. I am not married, but married women also wear a brooch twice the size of the others on their *bunads*, with a five-inch long silver chain that symbolizes the bond of marriage. They also wear a headpiece of white linen, and long, wide ribbons with symmetrical patterns that hang from the belt over the apron and add color to the black skirt. All dressed up in our *bunads*, we women sing, dance local folk dances, and wave the Norwegian flag.

Figure __ *The Hardanger Bunad*

Gulla Burke, **Norway**

EXERCISE 2-C

1. Underline the topic sentences in Student Samples 8 and 9 and circle the controlling ideas.
2. What *facts* are given in each paragraph?
3. Academic writers often use nontext materials (charts or graphs, photographs or drawings) to add interest and to help their readers. In what ways does the chart in Student Sample 8 help the audience?
4. In Student Sample 9, the writer uses a hand-drawn picture to demonstrate the Norwegian Hardanger *bunad*. Without the drawing, how difficult would the description of this costume be to "see"?
5. In both of the student samples, the writers are authorities. That is, they are experts about their topics. In what ways does the use of authoritative authors help the readers?

PHYSICAL DESCRIPTION

Our five senses—sight, hearing, smell, taste, and touch—are a source of detail about the world around us. Writers can use one or more of the senses to "paint a picture" for their readers about what they are describing, and they can compare one sense with another when they communicate impressions and "pictures" to their readers. Below are some of the categories of detail associated with each physical sense.

Sight: shape—round, square, flat
size—large, small, huge
color—red, azure, sunny yellow
brightness—light, dark

Sound: quality—clear or muffled, harmonious or harsh
volume—loud or soft

Smell: quality—sharp, sweet, clean, stale
effect—suffocating, intoxicating

Taste: quality—bitter, flat, sweet, sour
effect—sickening, lip-pursing

Touch: texture—smooth, rough, sharp, dull
temperature—hot, cold, lukewarm
weight—heavy, light

EXERCISE 2-D Identify the sense(s) used in each of the following sentences and discuss the ways these physical descriptions help the reader.

1. The fat lady looked like a beach ball in that multi-colored cape.
2. As we sat in the house trailer, the heavy rain pounded like a thousand ping-pong balls on the tin roof.
3. In the humid summer, the dirty apartment smelled like a dead goat.
4. The strange fruit tasted like a sour cucumber.
5. The kitten licked my hand; her tongue felt like sandpaper.

Writing Assignment 11 Write 10 sentences, each using one or more of the physical senses. Then exchange sentences with a partner. Identify the sense(s) used by your partner in each of the sentences. Then choose two sentences you especially liked, and read them for the class.

EXERCISE 2-E Read the paragraphs below. Underline the topic sentence in each paragraph. Circle the words or phrases of physical description.

[Support: physical description]

A hike I once took with a group from my school to the mountains near Riyadh gave me wonderful memories. Before we started the hike, the sunlight was shining brightly. When we went into the woods it was quite dark, like the sun was no longer in the sky. We felt that we were walking in hallways because the trees were so big and tall that they prevented sunlight from coming through. It was absolutely quiet and silent, like a sad and grim night. In the distance, we heard some birds cackling and some turkeys gobbling as if they didn't want us to be in this place. Also, small brooks were bubbling here and there. Although the weather was extremely hot, the water of the brooks was almost too cold to touch. After hiking four miles, we became exceedingly tired. We felt we had accomplished a great journey.

***Shams Othman,* Saudi Arabia**

My Favorite Place

The best place for me to forget all my worries is under a palm tree at dusk. When I am worried about a problem, or I just want to be alone, I go to the beach around six in the afternoon and sit in the shade of a palm

[Support: physical description]

tree. The sand is a little hard to sit on, but this does not bother me. As the wind blows like a whistle, and the waves become softer as they reach the shore, the air has a slight smell of the sea. The pelicans pass by in groups of seven before they disappear behind the horizon. Others float on the water, hoping to catch a fish before leaving. As time passes, there is an immense silence; the sun begins to descend, and the sky changes from tones of dark blue to canary yellow and finally to deep orange. As the sun slips below the horizon, I leave behind my worries.

***Luana Pereira,* Venezuela**

Word Choice

Using physical description to support a topic sentence requires that writers be precise in their choice of words. Using the right word to describe or explain a point will affect readers' responses as well as their understanding. In contrast, a general or vague term will often confuse rather than clarify the point. To practice precision in diction and to expand vocabulary, writers use a monolingual English dictionary to check the exact meaning of words. They also consult a thesaurus (a dictionary of synonyms) that not only gives the synonyms of words but also gives information concerning the different shades of meaning and the meanings associated with those words.

Learning associative meanings is one of the most sophisticated language skills for English as a second (or third or fourth) language student. For example, in a thesaurus, these synonyms are given for "laugh": *snicker, roar, titter, guffaw, giggle, chortle, cackle, chuckle.* Most native English speakers know that *giggle* and *titter* are small laughs used to describe girls' or young women's laughter (not boys' or men's, or old women's); *snicker* is a term that has a negative feeling—often the laugh is about someone else's misfortunes; *roar* and *guffaw* are usually male words that indicate a less formal, perhaps even rural, setting and social status. *Cackle* is related to but not exactly a *laugh*; it is usually an unpleasant laugh associated with a very old woman, sometimes a witch. Clearly, the associated meanings that surround many synonyms demonstrate that no word is exactly the same as another.

EXERCISE 2-F

1. Examine each of the following sets of words from a monolingual English dictionary or a thesaurus. Decide which of the words is closest in meaning to the original word. Then discuss whether each of the synonyms has an associated meaning that is

   positive or negative
   masculine or feminine
   stronger or weaker in meaning
   formal or colloquial
   high or low in social status.

   intelligent: *clever, smart, shrewd, ingenious, knowing, astute, bright*
   love: *admire, cherish, approve, adore, idolize, passion, affection, attachment, devotion, fondness, ardor, amour*
   distasteful: *repugnant, repellent, abhorrent, obnoxious, unlikeable, disgusting*
   pale: *pallid, ashen, wan, colorless, blanched, doughy, waxen, weak, faint*

2. For the following words, do not think of synonyms. Instead, think of the feelings you associate with these words. What are the first thoughts that enter your mind when you see each word? For example, the word *green* might make you think of trees or of jealousy ("green with envy").

   red | *Mary* | *politician* | *capitalist*
   New York City | *pig* | *mother* | *TOEFL*

3. Discuss your associations with your classmates.

Writing Assignment III

1. Use the topic sentence and details that you developed in Writing Assignment I (p. 39). Write a paragraph that uses facts and/or physical description to develop that topic sentence.
2. Exchange paragraphs with a partner. As you read your partner's paragraph, underline the facts and circle the words or phrases of physical description.
3. Return your partner's paragraph and discuss the memorable details you liked most in that paragraph.

EXAMPLES

Supporting a topic sentence by the use of examples often makes a general topic sentence understandable in more specific ways. Academic writers frequently use examples that contain facts and physical description to explain their ideas to the audience.

How many examples are enough? In the next student sample, a single typical example with many details is sufficient. In the second sample, two examples with fewer details support the topic sentence effectively.

12 STUDENT SAMPLE

[Topic sentence, controlling ideas] *[Single example, many specific details]* *[Concluding sentence]*

The assumption that the children of divorced parents prefer to remain with their mother, and indeed that the mother wants them, may sometimes be false. For instance, one divorced man exhausted the courts, the lawyers, his finances, and himself while attempting to regain custody of his four children. The mother had been an alcoholic and had shown little interest in the children's welfare even prior to the divorce, yet it was not until the children reached their teens that their custody was reconsidered. The drug and truancy problems of these youngsters were brought to the attention of the juvenile judge, who discovered that they had been unhappy at home for some time. Their love for their mother had long since disappeared, and they asked to be placed with their father, so after seven years the custody error was rectified. Undoubtedly, there are many similar cases that have not been resolved. While the child custody laws seem fair in theory, they are not always fair in practice.

Roberta Scott, **U. S.**

13 STUDENT SAMPLE

Agrarian Reform in Venezuela

[Topic sentence, controlling ideas] *[Example 1, details]* *[Example 2, details]* *[Concluding sentence]*

Agrarian reform in Venezuela has had positive and negative effects on agriculture. For example, some farmers have obtained loans from the government which they have invested in their land. For example, many of those farmers have bought machines to work on their land. They have cultivated the land very quickly. Therefore, they have already obtained benefit from their land, and Venezuela has too. But many farmers have not spent the loan money on their land. Instead, they have bought houses or cars, and the majority have used this money to go to the capital because they want to live there. The result is that many farms are abandoned, and nobody wants to cultivate them.

Morella Andrade, **Venezuela**

EXERCISE 2-G

1. After reading just the topic sentence in each student sample, what questions did you expect would be answered in the paragraph? Were you correct?
2. Who is the audience for each of the samples above? Be specific. How do you know?
3. What are the general and the specific purposes for each of the paragraphs?
4. In your opinion, which is the more interesting paragraph? Why? Discuss your selection with your classmates.

PERSONAL EXPERIENCE

Sometimes the most effective support in a paragraph is a story from the writer's experience or from an experience the writer knows about. By telling the reader a brief story of an actual incident that supports the topic sentence, the writer strengthens and supports the main idea(s) of the paragraph.

When writers use personal experience, they must decide how much detail is necessary. First, the amount of detail depends on the attitude of the audience. If the audience will be persuaded easily, only limited detail is necessary. But if the opposite is true, more detail can add persuasiveness. In addition, only those details that relate directly to the topic sentence are essential. For example, in the second student sample below, what the writer wore to the play, who else attended the play, or who the actors were would not be necessary to support her topic sentence.

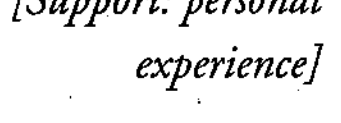

[Support: personal experience]

The reason I don't drink whiskey very often is because I had a bad experience with it. Eight months ago, I went drinking with my friends after a graduation ceremony at my university in Japan. The day was our last day as students. Everyone was aware that we wouldn't be able to meet each other after this day, so we intended to enjoy this night drinking liquor. While reminiscing about our university times, I drank considerable whiskey. When I started to go home with some friends, I became aware that I had drunk too much. I don't remember anything about getting home. On the following day, my friends said that I fell from the train platform when I was walking at the edge of it. At just that time, a train was coming to that platform, so my friends tried to help me, but they couldn't help because they were also drunk. I asked why I was living now. Their response was that the train came to the opposite side of the platform. I swore never to drink too much after I heard this story.

***Hiro Yabuki,* Japan**

15 STUDENT SAMPLE

[Support: personal experience]

Why don't I like plays? When I was only twelve years old there was a play shown about the Algerian revolution during French Colonialism. That was a time in my country's history when the French stayed in Algeria for 130 years. The play was written about a true story; it was written by a French reporter who lived with the French army in Algeria. The play was about how the French treated the Algerian people until the liberation. In the middle of the play, we saw two French soldiers coming out of a tavern. Suddenly, they saw an Algerian woman who was pregnant. One of them said, "I bet she has a baby boy." The other said, "No I swear it's a girl." Then, after an argument, they bet some francs and followed the woman. They caught her, and one of them took a dagger and pushed it into her belly. How cruel it was! I really could not stand the sight and went out of the theater, swearing not to see any more plays in my life.

[Concluding sentence]

Rhoma Mohamed, **Algeria**

Warm Breast

When I was ten years old, I experienced pain and comfort in one day. I was playing in a brook, in spite of my father's warning, and I treaded on a piece of broken glass and felt a terrible pain. I was fearful, too, since I was alone and an hour's distance from home. I pushed on the wound with my thumb to stop the bleeding and hopped unsteadily home. When I arrived I stole into my grandma's room; only then could I cry with pain on my grandma's comfortable breast. She dressed my cut and sheltered me from my father's scolding. She was always my refuge, but that was the last time. Soon she went to my uncle's home in Seoul, and several months later, she died there. I still have the scar on my foot, and whenever I see that scar, I remember my grandma's warm breast.

[Support: personal experience]

Kwen-Woo Lee, **Korea**

EXERCISE 2-H

1. Circle the controlling ideas in each topic sentence in Student Samples 14–16.
2. Each writer uses a second sentence in his or her paragraph. How do those second sentences help the reader? (You may review second sentences on p. 24.)
3. Without rereading the student samples, make a list of memorable details for each. Why did you remember those details especially? What can you learn about listing memorable details?
4. Each of these paragraphs has a personal "voice"; each uses some informal language. Why? Which do you think is written in the least formal voice? How do you know? Discuss your choice with your classmates.
5. In your opinion, which paragraph is the most interesting? Why? Discuss your choice with your classmates. Be prepared to state: "I liked the paragraph about X because . . . "

Writing Assignment IV

1. Choose a subject or a topic from your authority list. Use the general-to-specific strategies from Chapter 1 to narrow that subject or topic for an audience of your classmates and your instructor. That is, decide on "a piece of the pie."
2. Write the general and the specific purposes of your paragraph.
3. Use two of the collecting strategies (listing, brainstorming, clustering, outlining, flow charting, double-entry notes, or questions) to develop examples and/or personal experiences for your paragraph.
4. Write the topic sentence for your paragraph. Do you need a second sentence to guide your reader?
5. Exchange topic sentences with a partner. Read your partner's topic sentence and circle the controlling ideas. Then write 2–4 questions that you expect will be answered in the paragraph.
6. Return your partner's topic sentence; discuss your questions with your partner.

Writing Assignment V

1. Write a paragraph that uses examples and/or personal experience to develop that topic sentence.
2. Exchange paragraphs with another (not your first) partner. As you read your partner's paragraph, answer the questions on the **Revision Checklist** (p. 27).
3. Return your partner's paragraph and discuss your answers to the questions on the **Revision Checklist,** as well as the memorable details you liked most in your partner's paragraph.
4. Reread your paragraph. Consider your discussion with your partner and decide how to improve your paragraph. Then rewrite it.

Methods of Development

Another decision that student writers must make is how to organize their ideas. In academic writing, five methods of development are conventionally used to organize supporting material in a paragraph, and academic readers expect students to use these conventional development methods to organize their paragraphs.

Process	*Classification*
Extended Definition	*Cause(s) or Effect(s) (or both)*
Comparison or Contrast (or both)	

These methods of development are used in academic writing to inform, explain, entertain, persuade, and educate the audience. Choosing a method of development depends on the 3 **A**s: the **A**ssignment (purpose), an analysis of the **A**udience, and the **A**vailable supporting material you have collected.

PROCESS

Explaining HOW ("How to . . .")

Describing a process for an audience requires students to think about the exact steps in that process. For example, putting on a coat or tying shoes can seem easy, but trying to describe each step of the processes for a novice audience may be extremely difficult. Process paragraphs can give readers directions or explain how something happened (e.g., photosynthesis, a Hollywood stunt for a movie). All the paragraph titles below are for process paragraphs; the overall purpose for each is underlined, and the type of writing assignment is in italics.

How We Did This Experiment	an <u>inform</u>ative biology laboratory *report*
How to Win a Sumo Wrestling Match	an <u>inform</u>ative *essay*
How to Fall Off a Ski Lift	an *explanation* of an <u>amusing</u> process
How to Redesign the TOEFL	a <u>persuasive</u> *memo* of a solution

To explain a process, writers first separate the parts of the process into steps, then describe each step chronologically (in time): first step, then second step, and so forth. Precise descriptive words are used that will not confuse the audience. **Chronological connectors** can help the audience understand from one step to the next.

[Note commas]

First,	*Second,*	*The third step is*	*Fourth,*
Next,	*Then,*	*After that,*	*Finally,*

How do writers choose the steps for a process? And how do they choose the amount of detail to include for each step? If, for example, the writer is giving elementary school students directions to plant a seed, each step must be discussed in clear detail, with drawings or photographs that accompany the process. If the writer is describing to first-year students the steps to register for classes at the college/university, these steps need to be written in extensive and precise detail. On the other hand, if the writer is describing the changes in the registration process for third-year students, who already know the registration system, the description can focus only on the steps that have changed, not on the entire process.

Read these process paragraphs written by students and do the exercise that follows.

How I Prepare for a Canoe Trip

[Development: process] It is not only the canoe trip itself that pleases me; I also like the preparation for the trip. First, I enjoy shopping for the food. When I go away for the whole weekend, I buy quite a lot of fresh groceries instead of canned ones because I like cooking in a real sense. I buy dairy goods, eggs, meat, vegetables and potatoes. Next, I enjoy packing the tent, which I usually set up to dry and air during the week previous to the excursion. Although I have gone through this particular routine many, many times, the simple taking down, folding, and packing of the equipment always fills me with hopes and expectations. Finally, checking the marine chart, which I generally do the night before I leave, thrills me. Looking over the chart for alternative water roads and camping places almost enables me to make the trip in my mind ahead of time. The chart shows the archipelago outside Stockholm, a vast area with thousands of small islands and straits. It really takes some planning to choose a route for a weekend trip. Despite the fact that I have paddled in this Baltic archipelago for many years, I have so far succeeded in selecting different routes each time.

Tommy Hansen, **Sweden**

Becoming an Acupuncturist

[Development: process] A rigid system of examinations is used to accredit acupuncturists in China. The first part of the exam is a day-long oral scrutiny of a student's knowledge by his professors. According to Dr. Jiu Li, an accredited acupuncturist from Taipei, each student is questioned about his familiarity with the principles of acupuncture, diagnostic techniques, and the classic texts. The professors require near-perfection in the answers. A single error often means failure. On the second day, if the student has passed the oral examination, he demonstrates his ability with the needles of acupuncture on a life-sized wooden statue of a man which is covered with wax and filled with water. As Dr. Li explained, tiny holes have been drilled through the wood at approximately 165 acupuncture points on the body. There are no markings on the wooden figure, and the holes are invisible under the wax. The examiner poses a situation to the student; the student then names a point on the body for the treatment of a specific situation. If it is the correct location, he is asked to demonstrate how to insert the needles. The student chooses the right kind of needle and pushes it through the wax, using the proper technique. If he is right, water streams through the hole. [Concluding sentence] If he is wrong, he never becomes an acupuncturist.

Reference

Li, J. (1996). Personal Interview, February 13.

Kelly Cobb, **U. S.**

EXERCISE 2-I

1. Underline the topic sentence and circle the controlling ideas in each topic sentence in Student Samples 17 and 18.
2. Identify the techniques of support used in each paragraph (fact, examples, physical description, personal experience).
3. With a small group of classmates, discuss the steps in each of the samples. Is each step in the process of Samples 17 and 18 clear for the reader? Does a step need to be added, or does a step already in the paragraph need to be explained further in greater detail?
4. In the first sample, put brackets [. . .] around each chronological connector used by the writer to help his audience.
5. In the second sample, notice the use of an interview with an authority. How is the expert (Dr. Li) used by the author? In what ways does the interview help the writer of this paragraph? the reader?
6. Write a point outline for Student Sample 17.

EXTENDED DEFINITION

Explaining WHAT
("The meaning of . . .")

Formal definitions of words are found in a dictionary. They usually have three parts: the word itself (the term), its general category (class), and the detail that distinguishes it from other members of its class. For example:

term	**class**	**distinguishing detail**
A triangle is	*a plane figure*	*with three sides.*

Words such as *apple, pencil,* and *dictionary* can usually be defined similarly, in a short sentence, because they are concrete. That is, we can perceive them with one or more of our senses (sight, hearing, smell, taste, and/or touch). In contrast, an abstract word is usually about an idea or a feeling, something not perceptible by the senses.

The more abstract a word is, the more difficult for a writer to define it simply. Think about words such as *knowledge, love, courage,* and *democracy* (which we cannot perceive with our senses); try to define them in a single sentence. These words might require extended definitions. Academic writing assignments often ask students to define a word (or a piece of equipment, or a concept) that requires a complete paragraph of information and perhaps even a drawing, a chart, or a photograph.

A paragraph of extended definition usually begins with a short statement that contains the term, its class, and its distinguishing features. Then it uses several techniques of support (facts, examples, physical description and/or personal experience) to define, describe, classify, and perhaps even explain what the term is *not*, or how the term differs from another closely related term.

Read the following student samples of extended definition. Notice that in each case an abstract word or term is defined by using more than one supporting technique. Then do the exercise that follows.

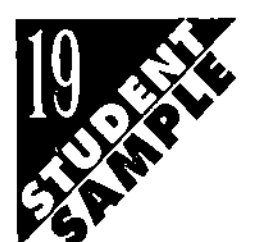

Definition of a Taiwanese Saying

[Development: extended definition]

A saying can interpret a situation in a culture, often more clearly and quickly than formal language can. For example, *Fat dog* and *skinny pig* are comprehensible phrases, and we can "see" them in our minds. However, they have a surprisingly different meaning in a (translated) Taiwanese saying: "The weight has been gained by the dog rather than by the pig." To explain this saying, one must understand that pork serves as the main source of meat for Asia. In our ancient agricultural society, most Asian families raised pigs. When you have a *skinny pig,* you will not have enough meat for you family. A worse problem is to have a *fat dog* because that means the dog is too lazy to chase away wild animals that look for food in your backyard. In more direct words, either of these situations means that you are not a worthy person because you have been irresponsible about your animals. Today, the saying is used in less agricultural ways. For example, if you have been gardening, and you have taken special care of your roses but no care of your daisies, yet the daisies bloom beautifully by themselves, you might use this saying about yourself. In another example, perhaps you studied your brains out for economics, a required course, and gave up on accounting, an elective course. However, when you get an A in accounting and a C in economics, you might use this saying to express your feelings: "The weight was gained by the dog rather than the pig!"

***Li Sun,* Republic of China (ROC)**

Kachina Dolls

Kachinas are not gods; as their Hopi Indian name denotes, *ka* for respect and *china* for spirit, they are respected spirits of the dead, of mineral, plant, bird, animal, and human entities. A kachina doll is a small, carved, wooden human-like representation of the supernatural beings worshipped by the Hopi Indians. Kachina dolls are the visible intermediaries or messengers to the gods. In the polytheistic Hopi society, all plants and animals, as well as some inanimate things, have spirits which the Hopi visualize in human form. For instance, when a Hopi goes to gather yucca roots to use as shampoo, he prays to the spirit of the first plant he finds and passes it by, gathering the second one. When he goes hunting, he prays to the spirit of the game and apologizes for having to take its life. Thus, the spirits of men, animals, and plants are the kachinas most often carved into kachina dolls.

[Development: extended definition]

[Concluding sentence]

***LaDean McConahay,* U. S.**

Bananas and Status in Guatemala

The banana (the most abundant tropical fruit) is called different names by different groups in my country, and each name reflects a different social class. People in the upper class call the fruit *banana*, which is also the way it is known internationally. This social class includes more educated people who have been overseas and in touch with other societies. If they referred to the banana in any other way, they would know that others viewed them as lower class citizens, and they would not want that to happen! Another name for banana is *minimo,* the Spanish name for the fruit, which middle-class society calls it. This group is formed mostly of people who have a strong identification with their own culture, and who believe in the preservation of values and traditions in a very patriotic sense. Finally, the same fruit is called *guineo* by the people who actually grow it. This social class is populated by farmers and people living in

[Development: extended definition]

[Concluding sentence]

small towns. They have used the word *guineo* for centuries, and they prefer it to the more foreign-sounding *banana*.

***Sergio Velasquez,* Guatemala**

EXERCISE 2-J

1. Identify the term, class, and distinguishing details of the formal (dictionary) definition of the main word(s) being defined in Student Samples 20 and 21.
2. Underline one place in Student Samples 20 and 21 that states what the term does *not* mean.
3. Locate and label the techniques of support used by the author of each sample.
4. Is the term being defined in each paragraph described completely? Do you have any questions about the term that you might ask the author?
5. Which paragraph did you prefer? Why? Discuss your choice with your classmates.

Writing Assignment VI

1. Write a paragraph of extended definition using one of the following abstract words (or choose another abstract word, perhaps from your authority list). Your purpose is to make the term clear to an audience of your classmates.

prejudice	*horror*	*diplomacy*
normal	*euphemism*	*patience*

2. Collect details by experimenting with one of the strategies demonstrated earlier in this chapter that you have rarely (or never) used. Then decide whether that strategy was effective for you.
3. Use the **Guidelines for Writing a Paragraph** (p. 26) to plan and then write the paragraph, beginning with a dictionary definition and then explaining the word further by using more than one technique of support to define and explain the term. Use the **Guidelines for Writing a Paragraph** to help you.
4. Exchange paragraphs with a partner. As you read your partner's paragraph, use the **Revision Checklist** (p. 27). Write the techniques of support you see in the margins, and underline the detail(s) you believe are most interesting and/or memorable. Then, at the end of the paragraph, write questions to help your partner with revision. Discuss your notes and comments with your partner.
5. Reread your paragraph and consider your partner's comments. Then decide how to improve your paragraph. Rewrite your paragraph and give it to your instructor.

COMPARISON-CONTRAST

Explaining
IN WHAT WAYS:
("X is like Y" and/or "X is different from Y")

Comparison and/or contrast are methods of development that show likeness and/or difference between two persons, places, things, or ideas. Academic writing frequently uses comparison and/or contrast to explain a concept or to evaluate an idea.

The purpose of comparison is to show how persons, places, things, or ideas that are usually considered very different are alike in some way or ways. For example, a comparison paragraph may begin with how *X* and *Y* are commonly seen as different, and then describe the ways they are uncommonly alike.

The opposite is true of contrast. The paragraph is written to show how persons, places, things, or ideas that are often considered alike are different in some way or ways. A contrast paragraph may begin by stating how *X* and *Y* are usually seen as alike, and then describe the unique ways in which they are different.

Note: The word *comparison* is sometimes used in academic writing assignments to mean both comparison and contrast. For example, "Compare the ideas in these two journal articles" might mean to both compare and to contrast the ideas. To be certain, check with the instructor who gave the assignment.

Two Ways of Organizing Comparison and/or Contrast Paragraphs

The two basic organizational plans for a comparison and/or contrast paragraph follow the point paragraph outline presented in Chapter 1. The choice of one or the other organizational plan depends on the 3 **A**s: the **A**ssignment, the **A**udience, and the **A**vailable material.

Plan A: Discuss first one (*X*) and then the other (*Y*)
Topic sentence about X and Y
1. All of X, point by point
2. All of Y, point by point that parallel X's points (i.e., they are arranged in the same order)

Plan B: Discuss one point about both *X* and *Y*, then another, and another, about *X* and *Y*
Topic sentence about X *and* Y
1. Point 1 about *X* and *Y* + details
2. Point 2 about *X* and *Y* + details
3. Point 3 about *X* and *Y* + details

For either of these plans, to write effective comparison and/or contrast paragraphs, writers should

1. analyze the audience carefully.
- Are readers interested in X and Y? Why?
- What do they already know about X and Y?
- What do they want or need to know?
- How can the writer best present your information for them?

2. be clear about purpose: why compare and/or contrast *X* and *Y*?
- to explain the little-known similarities and/or differences?
- to entertain by using amusing details about unique features?
- to persuade your audience that, for example,
  - one is preferable to the other?
  - what happened in one case may happen in another?
  - while both are different, both are acceptable?

3. use comparison and/or contrast connectors to help the readers.

Some comparison connectors	**Some contrast connectors***
Similarly,	*In contrast,*
Compared to X,	*However,*
Likewise,	*Conversely,*
In much the same way,	*On the other hand,*

In the comparison and /or contrast student samples below, notice the organization and the connectors.

COMPARISON

Parenting House Plants

Raising house plants involves nearly as much care and knowledge as raising children. First, both plants and children are sensitive to their environments. For example, a plant will grow faster and be much healthier if it is raised in an atmosphere of tender care. The same is true for a child, who will be happier and healthier if her parents love and nurture her. Similarly,

* For more information about connectors, see Chapter 4, page 117.

proper care of house plants requires the owner to have a basic knowledge of plants. He must know, for instance, which of his plants need direct sunlight and which need to be kept in shady places, and how much water each plant requires for optimum growth and appearance. Parents, too, must have knowledge of their children's needs in order to provide what is necessary for their best physical and mental development. Finally, the owner of house plants must be willing to provide the best possible care for his plants. A child also needs time and energy from her parents, to play with her, to talk to her, and to care for her. Generally speaking, happy, healthy plants and children are the result of extra time, knowledge and energy.

***Arden Boyer-Stephens,* U. S.**

COMPARISON AND CONTRAST

Paris: Past and Present

Even though the skyline and the cityscape of Paris has not changed very much during the last decade, my enjoyment of my first visit to Paris ten years ago was a hundred percent greater than that of my recent visit. In 1987, I visited Paris as a member of a high school tour group. I met my new friends on the airplane, and they provided me with security for my first trip abroad. However, my recent visit was a solitary, lonely trip; I traveled alone and had to protect myself all the time. In 1987, I had friends to talk with and share the new sensational atmosphere. We spent a night at a five-star hotel and talked all night about our adventures, and we often stopped at a café for a cup of coffee and a piece of cake. In contrast, in 1997, I had to share a room with strangers, so I had no one to talk with. Consequently, wherever I went was no longer exciting. I visited many of the same places—the Eiffel Tower, the Seine, the West Bank—but although they still looked and seemed the same, I could not express my feelings to anybody. I saw many people sitting in cafés, and I even stopped at several that I remembered, but even a cold glass of beer no longer fascinated me. I finally realized that my friends in 1987 had made Paris lively and memorable for me.

***Shinei Tsukamo,* Japan**

CONTRAST

Harvesting

Unlike the United States farmer, who harvests rice by using machines, Indonesian farmers use human power. Generally, American farmers drive expensive machines that pick, separate, and bind the grain. These men use plows, combines, and harvesters to get their grain from field to market, and they are paid good salaries for their work. In contrast, Indonesian harvesters are women. Their equipment consists of a single tool called *anai-anai,* a small blade attached to a bamboo stick. The women cut the stems of the rice handful by handful and put the bundles into a basket which they carry on their backs. As soon as the basket is full, the harvester goes to the owner, who loads the grain for market. The "salary" of the women is not money, but grain. Their wages depend on how many bundles they cut, but normally they get one bundle of every eight.

***Endah Frey,* Indonesia**

EXERCISE 2-K

1. Underline the topic sentence in Student Samples 22–24, and circle the controlling ideas.
2. Put brackets [. . .] around the comparison and/or contrast connectors that you find in each sample.
3. In the margin of each paragraph, write the techniques of support used as evidence (facts, examples, physical description, and personal experience).
4. With a partner or a small group of classmates, identify whether the writer of each sample used Plan A or Plan B. How do you know?
5. Which of the writers uses the most formal "voice"? Which has the least formal? How do you know? Review the characteristics of voice in Chapter 1, page 6.
6. For each sample, write what you think the author's general and specific purposes were for writing. Share your statements of purpose with your group, and discuss any differences you discover.

CLASSIFICATION

Explaining WHAT ("Kinds of . . .")

Classification paragraphs are the result of the writer grouping information into categories (classes). A single topic can be classified in various ways according to the author's purpose(s) and audience. For example, under the general subject "television advertising," different categories might include

- *products* advertised: cars, deodorant, running equipment, aspirin
- *products not permitted* to be advertised: cigarettes, pornographic films, illegal drugs, liquor
- *advertising techniques* used: young beautiful women, testimonials from ordinary people, rock music with advertising lyrics, famous cartoon characters.

In the categories below, notice that a category can be made even more specific.

Subject: College Students
Categories:

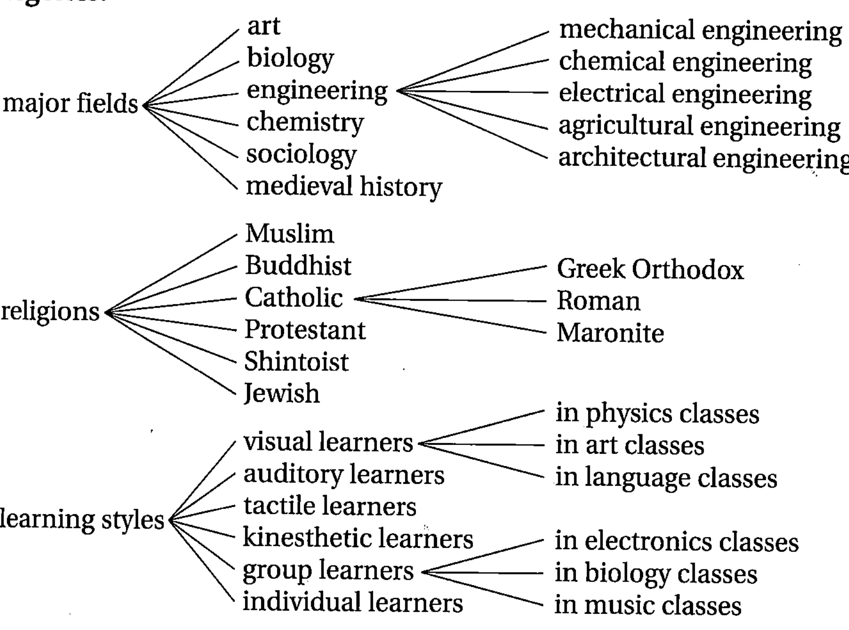

A successful classification occurs when the members of each group

- are arranged under a clear category (e.g., "words for rice," "kinds of errors," "learning styles").
- are arranged logically and explained clearly in the paragraph.
- are a relatively complete description of the category (class) (e.g., college students arranged by class—freshmen, sophomores, juniors, and seniors—includes nearly all students).
- do not overlap (i.e., students are usually not both Jewish and Catholic at the same time).

Effective classification paragraphs have a clear purpose: to inform the audience, not to bore the readers with information they already know. Therefore, writers must analyze their audiences carefully and provide new information or perceptions about the topic, particularly in their explanation of the classification. Below are examples of effective classification topics.

Unusual pets in the U.S.: ferrets, wolves, boa constrictors
Some effects of the El Niño tide on California's weather: substantially more rain, increase in mud slides and flooding, and colder temperatures
Demographic characteristics used by linguists investigating language change: age, gender, ethnicity, education, and social status of their subjects
Four ways that biometric devices use physical characteristics for identification: fingerprint, voice print, retinal or iris pattern of the eye, and DNA "signatures"

Read the paragraphs below that are developed by classification. Notice the techniques of support—*examples* in the first paragraph, and *facts* and *physical description* in the second paragraph—that are used to *explain* the classes (categories) and the members of those classes. Then do the exercise that follows.

25 STUDENT SAMPLE

[Topic sentence] *[Development: classification]* *[Support: examples]*

Since I began to study English, I have noticed three kinds of persistent errors in my speech; I think these errors are also the most common mistakes made by other Spanish-speaking students. The first is that I speak sentences which are similar to Spanish. For instance, I will say, "I have bought *a blouse nice*" instead of *a nice blouse*. Another mistake is that I often translate directly from Spanish, forgetting the characteristic idiomatic expressions in English like "getting along with." Some vocabulary words cannot be translated literally: *silverware*, for example, is a common name in English for eating utensils which aren't necessarily made of silver. My final mistake in spoken English is the grammatical problem of verb endings. I will often say "She *do* the shopping" instead of *does* or "It is possible *solve* your problems" instead of *to solve*. If I can correct these three problems in my English, I think Americans will be able to understand me much better.

Esther Gencel, **Peru**

26 STUDENT SAMPLE

RICE

[Topic sentence] In my native language, there are six words for *rice*. We use different words to describe (a) where the rice seed is planted, (b) the color of the harvested rice, and (c) whether or not the rice is cooked. For example, *padi* refers to the rice seed. If the rice is planted in a field, we call it *padi* [Development: classification] *sawah*, and if it is planted on a hill, we call it *padi huma*. In my country, farmers who live in the higher regions of Malaysia produce *padi huma*, while those who live in the lower elevations produce *padi sawah*. We can differentiate these two by their color: *padi sawah* is gold, while *padi huma* [Support: facts, physical description] is reddish brown. Moreover, *padi sawah* needs more water to grow than *padi huma*. Both *padi huma* and *padi sawah* only refer to the rice grain. We call uncooked rice *beras*, and the cooked rice *nasi*. For example, my mother tells me to cook the *beras* so that we can have *nasi* for dinner. *Pulut* is another name for *nasi* or uncooked rice; the difference between these two is that *pulut* is more starchy compared to *nasi*, and it is naturally sweeter when cooked. Having more than one word for *rice* in our language indirectly reflects our culture, because in Malaysia, rice is our staple food. We have rice everyday, and maybe that is the reason we have [Concluding sentence] so many words for *rice*.

Zainah Muhamed, **Malaysia**

EXERCISE 2-L

1. Write the general category and the members of that group for each Student Sample.
2. Write a statement of specific purpose for each sample paragraph. Share your statement with a small group of classmates, and discuss any differences you discover.
3. Without rereading the paragraphs, write 3 memorable details from each. Share your details with your classmates, and discuss any differences you discover.
4. Make a point outline for one of the paragraphs.
5. Student Sample 26 uses a second sentence. How does it help the reader?
6. Which sample did you prefer? Why? Discuss your choice with your classmates.

EXERCISE 2-M With a partner or in a small group, choose two of the following academic subjects (or another academic subject). Divide the subject into 2 or 3 possible categories (classes). List 5–7 members of each group that could be classified under each of these categories. Use the example to help your choices and categorization.

Assignment subjects:

- chemical elements
- video games
- Greek philosophy
- insects
- dormitory dinners
- famous biologists
- causes of war
- nonverbal communication
- 20th-century inventions

Example:

Subject: Abstract Art

Possible categories:

Kinds of art (e.g., sculpture, painting, architecture)
Artists (e.g., Pollack, Dove, Kandinsky, Warhol)
Modern art museums in the U. S.

Writing Assignment VII For an audience of your instructor and your classmates, write a paragraph of classification by choosing

A. three kinds of errors that you make in your spoken (or your written) English
B. 4–8 words in your native language that have similar meanings
C. another topic from your authority list

1. Collect details and examples for your paragraph by experimenting with two of the collecting strategies demonstrated earlier in this chapter. Then evaluate the effectiveness of each of those collecting strategies for you.
2. Write a topic sentence of intent that informs your readers about the *purpose* for your paragraph.
3. Use the **Guidelines for Writing a Paragraph** (p. 26) to plan and write the paragraph. Use at least two techniques of support (facts, examples, personal experiences, or physical description).

EXERCISE 2-N

1. Exchange paragraphs with a partner. Use the **Revision Checklist** (p. 27) as you read your partner's paragraph.
2. In the margins of the paragraph, write the techniques of support you find, and underline the detail(s) you believe are most interesting and/or memorable.
3. At the end of the paragraph, write 2 questions to help your partner with revision.
4. Discuss your notes and comments with your partner. Listen to your partner's comments carefully.
5. Rewrite your paragraph, using your own ideas and any of your partner's comments that seem important to you.
6. Read three of your classmates' paragraphs. Take notes about each paragraph.
7. Be prepared to say which of those paragraphs you liked best: "I liked X's paragraph about Y because . . ."

CAUSE[S] AND/OR EFFECT[S]

Explaining WHY X happened and/or the effects of X

Cause and/or effect paragraphs investigate why things are as they are, or why something happened, or the effects of an event or a situation. Students are often assigned a cause and/or effect paper in academic classes; the audience for the paper is almost always the instructor of the class, and the purpose of the assignment is usually to demonstrate the writer's knowledge of the situation, to show the cause(s) and/or the effect(s) of that situation.

Below are three authentic cause-effect short-answer tasks given on undergraduate examinations by college/university instructors. Each field of study is in parentheses, and additional information is enclosed in brackets [. . .].

1. (*Business*) Explain the **effects** that comparable pay for comparable work would have on the U.S. economy.
2. (*Nutrition*) Analyze the relationship [i.e., the **causes** and **effects** of the relationship] of fatty acids and/or cholesterol to heart disease.
3. (*Natural Resources*) What are the **effects** of aquaculture technology on the genetic diversity of the wild fish population?

EXERCISE 2-O

1. With a partner, underline the "key words" in each assignment. That is, which words give information about how the test-taker should respond?
2. Discuss possible answers to the short-answer examination tasks. As you plan (*but do not write*) the answers, consider the expectations of the audience, the purpose of the task, and the supporting detail needed to answer each task appropriately.
3. Share your ideas with other partners in your class.

Links Between Causes and Effects

Figure 2-1 demonstrates the processes (the multiple causes) involved in a single event (effect), a fire in a building. Notice that

1. there can be three or more types of causes:

Immediate:	the first, visible cause(s) for the effect(s)
Remote:	the reason(s) for the immediate cause(s)
Underlying:	the cause(s) that took place before the immediate cause, but that were ultimately responsible for the effect(s)

2. an effect can sometimes become the cause of another effect.

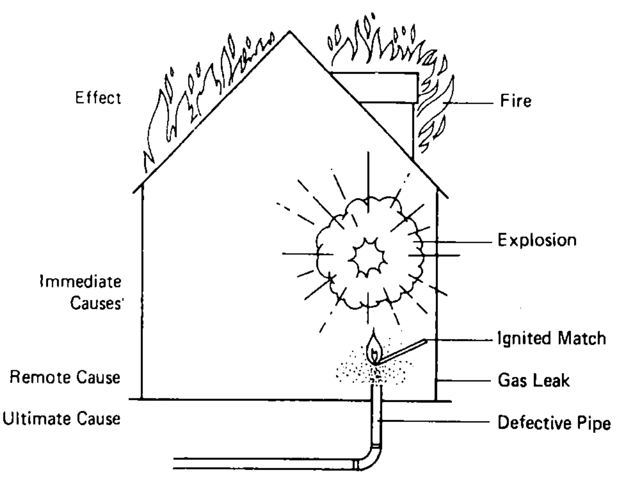

Figure 2-1 *Cause-Effect Chain*

In Figure 2-1, a fire (the effect) may have been caused by an explosion (the immediate cause) that was ignited by a match being lit (another cause of the explosion). The gas leak that caused the explosion (a remote cause) was the result (the effect) of a defective gas pipe (the underlying cause), which was installed several years ago. Thus, in the more complex explanations, the causes and effects form a *chain of events.*

Forms of the Cause (Reason)-Effect Paragraph

There are several ways to organize a cause-effect (*or* cause *or* reason *or* effect) paragraph. One form of the *cause* (or *reason*) paragraph

- begins with a statement of the *effect*
- explains the immediate cause(s) (*or* reason[s] for) that effect
- explains the underlying cause(s) (*or* reason[s] for) that event
- concludes with an explanation of the relationship(s) between the cause(s)/reason(s) and the effect

One form of the *effect* paragraph

- begins with a statement of the *cause*
- discusses the short-term (immediate) effect(s) of the cause
- describes the intermediate-term effect(s) of the cause
- explains the long-term (future) effect(s) of that cause
- concludes with a statement of the relationship(s) between the cause and the effect(s)

Read the following cause(s)/reason(s) and/or effect(s) paragraphs. Then do the exercise that follows.

[CAUSES]

Possible Causes of Ball-Lightning

Ball-lightning is a rare natural phenomenon. According to eyewitnesses, it is usually a perfectly ball-shaped, red, yellow, or white object that ranges from a couple of inches up to six feet in diameter (Egely, 1988). It floats in the air with the speed of a fast-walking person, following a curved path and lasting up to ten seconds. It is electrically charged, just like ordinary lightning. While in motion, the ball gives a hissing, buzzing sound, but it stays away from good conductors, including the human body. It can disappear silently, slowly decreasing in size, or by an explosion, in which case a smell resembling sulfur or ozone remains (Berry, 1990).

What causes ball-lightning? Serious scientific research has many theories. Some scientists think that it occurs from a mixture of chemical substances that become electrically charged; others view ball-lightning as the result of radioactive particles formed from atmospheric gases. The most widely accepted explanation is that ball-lightning is a form of electrical discharge (Singer, 1991). According to this theory, when dry air passes through an electrically charged cloud during a storm, and conditions are not adequate to form ordinary lightning (because dry air is a good insulator), the so-called "brush discharge" occurs in a spherical shape between the cloud and the earth's surface. The ball-shaped electrical discharge is called ball-lightning.

References

Berry, J. D. (1990). *Ball lightning and bead lightning*. New York: Plenum Press.

Egely, G. (1988). Hungarian ball-lightning observations in 1987. In Ohtsuki, Y.H. (Ed.), *Science of ball lightning*, pp. 131–143. Singapore: World Scientific Publishing.

Singer, S. (1991). *The nature of ball lightning*. New York: Plenum Press.

***Csaba Rozgonyi,* Yugoslavia**

[REASONS]

Why Did the Aztecs Believe in Human Sacrifice?

In the 13th century, the Aztec Indians of Mexico sacrificed humans to their gods, but this was not an act of hatred, revenge, or murder. Instead, it was a valuable religious offering to a god. One reason the Aztecs believed in human sacrifice was a story about their gods: when the "fifth world" was founded without light, the gods congregated and decided that one of them had to be sacrificed to the sun. One god "immediately closed his eyes and leaped into the flames" (Bradley, 1992, p. 22), feeding the sun god, Huitzilopochtli, with his own blood. This was the main precedent for sacrifice in the Aztec religion. Second, the Aztecs believed that "every night the sun god would fight with the stars and the moon, and armed with sunshine, would bring the new day; only by providing the sun with nourishment, in the form of human blood, would the sun and life prevail" (Duran, 1975, p. 161). Therefore, the practice of human sacrifice became the most significant ritual in the Aztec religion. Finally, when the Aztecs warred with other tribes near their town of Tenochtitlan, their objective was not to kill but to capture their enemies. According to their beliefs, their captives belonged to the gods and therefore their hearts were "the most acceptable sacrifices" (Vaillant, 1950, p. 205).

References

Bradley, J. (September 20, 1992). Q & A on cultured empire of 20 million. *The Denver Post,* C-3.

Duran, F. D. (1975). *Book of the gods and rites of the ancient calendar.* Oklahoma City: Pan American Series.

Valliant, G. (1950). *Aztecs of Mexico.* Garden City, NY: Doubleday & Co.

Luis Ramirez, **Mexico**

[EFFECTS]

If I Could Make One Change . . .

My decision to live in an apartment during my first year of college had several negative effects. First, I lived with three girls from my country, so I did not improve my English because I spoke Malay most of the time. Moreover, we took exactly the same classes, so I did not have a chance to meet or study with my other classmates. Instead, I tended to spend more time studying with my roommates. Furthermore, since I did not have many American friends, I did not learn very much about American culture; I did not celebrate Halloween or Thanksgiving or Christmas. Finally, I did not share experiences with people. I did not attend parties or go skiing or even spend leisure time in the Student Center. So although my life during my first year of college was secure and pleasant, if I could change one thing about my first year of college, I would choose to live in a dormitory; I think my life would have been more interesting and more fun.

Norlela Othman, **Malaysia**

EXERCISE 2-P

1. Underline the *causes* in the second paragraph of Student Sample 27, the *reasons* in Student Sample 28, and the *effects* in Student Sample 29. Share them with a small group of classmates, and discuss any differences you discover.
2. Who is the audience for each of the paragraphs? How do you know? Discuss your decisions with your classmates.

3. Which techniques of support (facts, examples, physical description, personal experience) did the writers use? Label those techniques of support in the margins of each paragraph.
4. Which of these writers used a second sentence to help the reader with the focus of the paragraph? In what ways did the second sentence help the audience?
5. In the third sample, about "effects," Norlela writes about a chain of events that results in "negative effects." Underline two effects that became causes for her problems.
6. Use the scale below to identify the level of formality in the language for the three paragraphs. Discuss your decisions with your group, giving reasons for your choices.

   more formal ◄──────────────► less formal

7. In your opinion, what kind(s) of pictures, line drawings, charts, or other forms of visual materials might interest the readers of each of the three samples above? Discuss your choices with your classmates.

Decision-Making for Writers

Because decision-making is the heart of successful writing, students often find it helpful to see a summary of the decisions they make before they write, as they write, and as they rewrite. In the last two chapters, you have learned about these processes for making writing decisions:

Before Writing
(Pre-Writing)

- choosing a subject or understanding a writing assignment
- selecting the purpose and the audience (usually the instructor) for the writing or understanding the assigned purpose and audience (almost always the instructor)
- narrowing the subject to a topic: choosing "a piece of the pie"
- deciding on the most effective strategies for collecting examples and details, and collecting those examples and details

During Writing
(Drafting and Revising)

- selecting those details and examples that are most interesting and relevant to explain, clarify, or illustrate the ideas
- constructing a clear, focused, precisely worded topic sentence to state the main idea of the paragraph
- using a second sentence, if necessary, to clarify and focus the paragraph
- selecting **technique(s) of specific support and detail** to better explain the ideas
- choosing which **method of development** will best present the material and fulfill the writing purpose
- deciding what "voice" to use, including the choice of words, sentence structures, and grammar in the paragraph

After Writing
(Peer Response and Writer Revision)

- asking for feedback on the topic sentences and the paragraphs from peers and teacher
- revising and rewriting the paragraph, based on the writer's own ideas and the feedback from "other eyes"

Note: Of course, these decisions are not usually made in the linear way they appear on this page. Instead, without much consideration, some of these decisions are made as they "come up" in individual writing processes.

Writing Assignment VIII

1. Choose one of the topics below (or a different topic from your authority list) that you can write a cause/reason and/or effect paragraph about. Select an audience that is neither your classmates nor your teacher: perhaps a brother or sister? an expert in the field? a child whom you do not know?

TOPICS:

Cause(s) of	**Effect(s) of**
headaches	student fatigue
automobile accidents	fast food
the success of a sports team	the failure of a sports team
choosing a major field	studying for the TOEFL

2. Experiment with a strategy you have not used previously to collect details and information about your topic.
3. Use the **Guidelines for Writing a Paragraph** (p. 26) to plan and to write the paragraph.

EXERCISE 2-Q

1. Exchange paragraphs with a partner. Try to become the audience for your partner's paragraph. Answer the questions in **Revision Checklist** (p. 27); then share your answers with your partner.
2. Use the discussion with your partner to improve your paragraph as you rewrite it.
3. Read three of your classmates' paragraphs. Be prepared to state which of the paragraphs you liked best and why: "I liked X's paragraph about Y because . . ."

EXERCISE 2-R With a partner or in a small group, review the differences between oral and written styles of communication (p. 5). Then read (or reread) the student samples listed below and discuss the "voice" in each of those paragraphs. Some of the paragraphs are informal and conversational; others have a more formal voice. Indicate (by writing the number of the chapter, 1–4) on the formality scale where you think each sample belongs. If your opinion differs from your partner's or your classmates' opinions, discuss the differences.

Student Sample (SS)	**Topic**	**Writer**	**Page**
Chapter 1, SS 18	What Engineers Write	Rob Christenson	23
Chapter 2, SS 15	Personal Experience	Rhoma Mohamed	45
Chapter 3, SS 15	Snow Fences	José de la Llave R.	86
Chapter 4, SS 13	The Cost of TV Ads	Myung Engle	122

FORMALITY SCALE

more formal ◄——————————————► less formal

Expanding a Paragraph into an Essay

Sometimes readers feel that the information in a paragraph is incomplete; they want more detail, more examples. In this case, the paragraph may have too broad a focus. Instead of a paragraph, it could become an essay. In the paragraph below, the writer could easily add facts, examples, physical description, and personal experiences to inform, entertain, and persuade the reader that Thailand is the best place in the world for a vacation. Lines within the paragraph indicate places where additional information could be added; indentations indicate where a new paragraph might begin.

Thailand: A Wonderful Resort Area

If I had a two-week vacation, I would go to Thailand because it has everything I need to relax and to enjoy myself. First I would go to Pattaya, ______________________________, where there are beautiful beaches with coconut trees and white sand that lasts for miles and miles. At the beach, I could smell the fresh breeze from the sea, and the sand is so fine that it slips through my fingers. ______________________________. When the sun is too hot, I could jump into the blue water which is so clear that I can see some tropical fish swimming around. ______________________________.

If I wanted to see some of the Thai culture, there are many temples in Bangkok, which are charming and sparkling under the sun. ______________________________. Their windows and doors are usually made of colorful glass, crystal, and gold. ______________________________. After admiring the exterior, I could go inside. ______________________________. Then I might worship Buddha, ______________________________, wishing him to bring me good fortune.

Besides the culture, every tourist would like to shop. Thailand is a great place for shopping. There are many traditional handicrafts and ornaments made of shells that sparkle in the golden sunlight; ______________________________. It is also entertaining to bargain. ______________________________.

After a day's touring, I would look forward to enjoying a great Thai dinner in a restaurant built of coconut trees. ______________________________. The traditional Thai food is so different from the food in other countries. ______________________________. Finally, I would return to my hotel, full of memories and food, all my troubles flown away.

***Chui Ho,* Thailand**

EXERCISE 2-S

1. Who is the audience for this paragraph? How do you know?
2. What is the general purpose of the paragraph? What might the more specific purposes be?
3. With a partner or small group of classmates, discuss the supporting details that the writer might add to this paragraph to make it into an essay. What questions could you ask Chui Ho? Be specific!
4. Reread the paragraphs listed below. With a small group of classmates, discuss the ways in which each could be expanded into an essay.
   - Mickey's paragraph about the Kenex Company (Student Sample 3)
   - Kombu's paragraph about drinking and driving (Student Sample 5)
   - Morella's paragraph, "Agrarian Reform in Venezuela" (Student Sample 13)
   - Luis' paragraph about human sacrifice (Student Sample 28)

Writing Assignment IX Write 5 separate paragraphs about the single topic of either "Escape" or "Fear." Use a different *method of development* for each paragraph: process, extended definition, comparison and/or contrast, classification, and cause(s) and/or effect(s).

Choose five of the titles below. Then experiment with 1 or 2 collecting strategies to gather information for each paragraph.

Titles

How to Escape *or* How to Overcome Fear
Extended Definition of Escape *or* Fear
Cause(s) of an Escape *or* a Fear
Effect(s) of an Escape *or* a Fear
Two Similar Escapes/Fears
Two Contrasting Escapes/Fears
Three/Four Kinds of Escapes/Fears

1. Follow the process in the **Guidelines for Writing a Paragraph** (p. 26) to consider your audience and purpose, to construct 5 topic sentences, and to select two or more techniques of support for each paragraph.
2. Write the paragraphs. Reread each paragraph and revise it to make it better.

EXERCISE 2-T

1. Exchange paragraphs with a classmate. As you read your partner's paragraphs, take notes on

   A. the audience: Do all the paragraphs have the same audience?
   B. the purpose(s): Do all the paragraphs have the same purpose(s)?

2. Answer the questions in **Revision Checklist** on p. 27. Share your answers with your partner.
3. Could all or some of the paragraphs become an essay? How? Discuss the possibilities with your partner.
4. Based on your discussion with your partner, rewrite your paragraphs.

Chapter 3

Planning the Essay: Explaining an Academic Topic

What Was Easy About This Course?

Nothing in this class was easy for me, but I believe that learning about paragraph and essay structure will help me in all of my university courses. This structure is very different from Japanese. We do not use thesis statements or topic sentences in our academic writing. However, I will not forget about the structure, and with the practice in this course I feel more confident about writing.

***Kuni Oshitani,* Japan**

IN ADDITION TO audience and purpose, academic writers must also learn about **writing conventions** in order to fulfill the expectations of the U.S. academic audience. Writing conventions include patterns expected by the academic reader in such areas as

- the overall organization,
- the functions of the paragraphs,
- the amount and kinds of evidence,
- the appropriate use of word-signals to help direct the reader, and
- the use of citations (i.e., references).

This chapter considers writing conventions for writers who plan essays that **explain** *what, how,* and/or *why.*

Drafting

Most experienced writers would agree that in addition to using pre-writing strategies, writing, revising, and rewriting drafts is the basis for successful writing. Academic writing is no different; student writers must be prepared to write a "rough" draft, revise it, then continue to draft and revise until the essay (or technical report, or research paper, or software review) is ready for the audience.

The processes of drafting are not necessarily linear (i.e., first we write, then we revise, then we rewrite). Some writers draft and revise simultaneously; others "write" by thinking about and mentally "rehearsing" the sentences and paragraphs of their papers before actually typing those thoughts into a computer. Still other writers compose short sections of their essays (perhaps beginning in the middle of the essay) and then revise them, one at a time. But all these writers understand that they need time, effort, and multiple drafts before they can turn in an effective essay.

Overall Organization of the Academic Essay

In general, academic writing assignments share similar writing conventions in their overall organization (although the lengths of the parts of the paper depend on the actual assignment). Many academic assignments require a two-page essay; because most word-processed pages contain approximately 250 words, the length of the essays will be about 500 words. Such essays are sometimes called "the five-paragraph essay" because they usually contain an introduction, three body paragraphs, and a conclusion. The parts of the essay are the focus of this chapter.

An academic essay is a series of paragraphs about one topic; each paragraph has specific functions.

1. The beginning, or the **introduction**, is the first paragraph in the essay. The functions of the introduction are

    - to introduce the topic to the reader in an engaging way,
    - to orient the audience by giving a little background information about the topic, and
    - to state the thesis of the essay (the main idea, the focus, the purpose) for the reader.

2. The middle is called the **body** of the essay. The functions of these **body paragraphs** are to

   - explain,
   - define,
   - clarify, and
   - illustrate the main idea of the essay, and to persuade the audience that the writer's ideas and opinions are worthwhile.

   Note: The number of body paragraphs in an academic essay depends on the length and complexity of the writing assignment.

   Each body paragraph has the same writing conventions and functions as the paragraphs you have written in previous chapters. That is, each begins with a topic sentence that contains controlling ideas; the topic sentence is followed by several supporting sentences that use

   facts *examples* *description* *experience*

   to prove (i.e., strengthen, give evidence for) the topic sentence.

   Body paragraphs in essays are developed by the methods you studied in Chapter 2:

   1. process
   2. extended definition
   3. classification
   4. comparison and/or contrast
   5. cause(s) or effect(s) or both

   Note: In an academic paper, each body paragraph may have a different method of development.

3. The end, or **conclusion**, is the paragraph that completes the essay by one or more of the following:

   - by summarizing the main ideas in the essay
   - by making recommendation(s) about ideas presented in the essay
   - by offering a solution to the problem discussed in the essay
   - by making a prediction about ideas or issues discussed in the essay

The Explaining Essay

Almost all academic essay assignments require that student writers *explain* ideas and opinions, and often persuade the audience that the ideas are worthwhile. In an explaining essay, writers answer one or more of the following questions: *What? How? Why?* For example, an academic explaining assignment could ask students to

- explain *what:* write an extended definition of

  what a word such as "reflexology" means
  what a term in their major field means
  what a concept such as "prejudice" is

- explain *how:* describe a process (i.e., what steps are used), such as

  how to do a laboratory experiment
  how to make a successful oral presentation
  how to pass an examination successfully

- explain *why:* use cause and effect to discuss

  why an automobile accident occurred (causes)
  why global warming is destructive (effects)
  why soccer injuries occur (causes and effects) and the permanent injuries that result (effects).

The authentic academic assignments below ask students to write papers that explain *what, how,* and/or *why.* The first (most complicated) assignment is explained for you. Read each assignment, and then do the exercise that follows. Explanations are in brackets [ ].

I Health Sciences

(6–10 page paper, written outside of class, with references)

[*Explain* what, how, why]

Should adult cloning of human genes be prohibited by law? *Describe* the cloning process, then *explain* the ethical questions involved in this issue. Give and *support* your opinion.

Explanation: For this assignment, students will

1. answer the question *what* by [*Extended definition*]
   defining *cloning*
   listing and defining the ethical questions
2. answer the question *how* by [*Chronological process*]
   describing the basic steps of the cloning process
   using signals such as *First, Second, Next, Then, After that,* and *Finally,* to direct the reader through the process [*Transitions*]
3. give their opinion about whether or not adult cloning of human genes should be prohibited by law [*NOT explaining*]
4. answer the question *why* by [*Causes and effects*]
   detailing (giving evidence of) causes that support opinion(s)
   detailing (giving evidence of) effects that support opinion(s)

II Agriculture

(in-class examination, two-page essay)

[*Explain* what, how]

Explain three significant events or inventions that make our milk today the best ever.

III Mechanical Engineering

(in-class examination, short answer: 1 or 2 paragraphs)

[*Explain* why]

Discuss three reasons why the "infrastructure crisis" is so apparent in the U.S. highway system.

IV History

(3-page paper, written outside of class)

[*Explain* what, why]

Periods in history bear names such as The Age of Anxiety or The Industrial Revolution or The Elizabethan Age. What name would you give to the 1990s? Using specific examples, explain why you chose that particular name.

EXERCISE 3-A

1. With a partner or in a small group, make each academic assignment above into 1 or 2 questions that ask *what, how,* or *why* (e.g., What are three significant events . . .?).
2. With your group, decide how best to explain each of the assignments.

3. Discuss the methods of development (i.e., process, extended definition, comparison/contrast, cause-effect, classification) that student writers might use in each assignment.
4. For one of the Explaining assignments, write one topic sentence for one body paragraph.

Selecting a Topic

Often the instructor of an academic class chooses the subject for the academic writing assignment. Sometimes the student must write about the entire subject in the assignment. Many assignments, however, suggest that students select a "piece" of the subject, that is, narrow the subject to a topic (see pp. 10–11 to review narrowing).

Note: In the case of longer or more important writing assignments in a college/university course, it is appropriate for students to see the instructor outside of class to explain their limited experience with U.S. academic writing, and to request more information about the purpose and the writing conventions for the assignment. It is also appropriate for students to ask the instructor to provide a successfully completed assignment for that course from a previous class and/or for a different subject.

Selecting a topic for an academic essay is similar to choosing a topic for a paragraph. The same initial process applies:

- Write about what you know.
- Identify and analyze your audience.
- Decide on the general and the specific purposes of the essay.

In addition, writers try to avoid topics that are (a) abstract, (b) based on religious beliefs, or (c) based on political beliefs. These topics are often difficult to explain clearly and/or to use to persuade an audience unless the writer is an authority and is writing for an audience of other "believers." Examples:

Avoid: *Abstract Topics*
The Virtue of Patriotism
How to Be Happy
Love

Avoid: *Religious Topics*
Should Abortion Be Illegal?
Capital Punishment
Which Religion Should You Choose?

Avoid: *Political Topics*
Capitalism Is Best!
Should Taiwan Become a U.N. Member?

Choose: *Concrete Topics*
Four Types of E-Mail "Flaming"
How to Install a Roof Vent in a Van
Getting Married vs. Staying Single
Should International Students Pay More for University Health Insurance?
The U.S. Infrastructure in Crisis: Why?
Milk: The Perfect Food
My Major Learning Style Preference
Characteristics of First-Borns
The Advantages of Food Additives

EXERCISE 3-B The authentic academic assignment below asks students to write an Explaining paper. Although the topic is unfamiliar, we can analyze what kind of explaining the assignment requires. With a partner or in a small group, read and discuss the assignment analysis.

[*Explain* what, why]

Philosophy
(2 or 3 page paper, written outside of class)
Beauchamp and McCullough argue that the conflict generated by the "beneficence" and the "autonomy" models of the physician–

patient relationship is an inescapable dimension of medical practice. Define and explain the "beneficence model" and the "autonomy model" of the physician-patient relationship. Which model best fits your desires as a patient? Why?

Explanation: For this assignment, students will

[Extended definition]

1. answer the question *what* by
   defining the two models (Beneficence and Autonomy)
   using specific, perhaps personal examples to further explain.

[NOT explaining]

2. give their opinion about which model they prefer personally.

[Causes and effects]

3. answer the question *why* by
   detailing (giving evidence of) reasons that support opinion(s)
   using personal examples to support their reasons.

Below are two more authentic explaining assignments. Read them and do the exercise that follows to analyze the assignments.

[*Explain* why] **I** **Political Science**

(5-page paper, written outside of class, with references)

Using the public opinion data on the 1996 presidential election contest between George Bush and Bill Clinton, explain why Clinton won the election.

[*Explain* what, how, why] **II** **Food Science**

(5–8 pages, not including references, tables, and figures; written outside of class)

Explain the advantages and disadvantages (for manufacturers and for consumers) of the use of food additives by companies who produce dry cereal. Use a minimum of ten references (at least 7 referenced journal articles of the past two years).

EXERCISE 3-C

1. Using the processes from Exercises 3A and 3B, work with a small group of classmates to identify the audience and the general purpose for each assignment. How might student writers in each of these courses fulfill the expectations of their instructors?
2. Decide what questions you expect might be answered in the body paragraphs of each essay.
3. For one of the assignments, discuss which methods of development the writer might use. Be specific.
4. Each of the assignments needs clarification. What questions might you ask the instructor about each of them?

Pre-Writing for the Essay

Collecting Ideas

Gathering information for the large subject of an essay may help writers narrow the subject to a topic. That is, by using one or more of the "collecting strategies" discussed in Chapter 2—*brainstorming, listing, clustering, outlining, flow-charting, double-entry notes,* and/or *questioning*—student writers may discover an appropriate "piece of the pie." Another way to begin to plan an Explaining essay is to begin with a general subject and then narrow to more specific details. Asking questions about the general subject may lead to an interesting topic, as the following example shows.

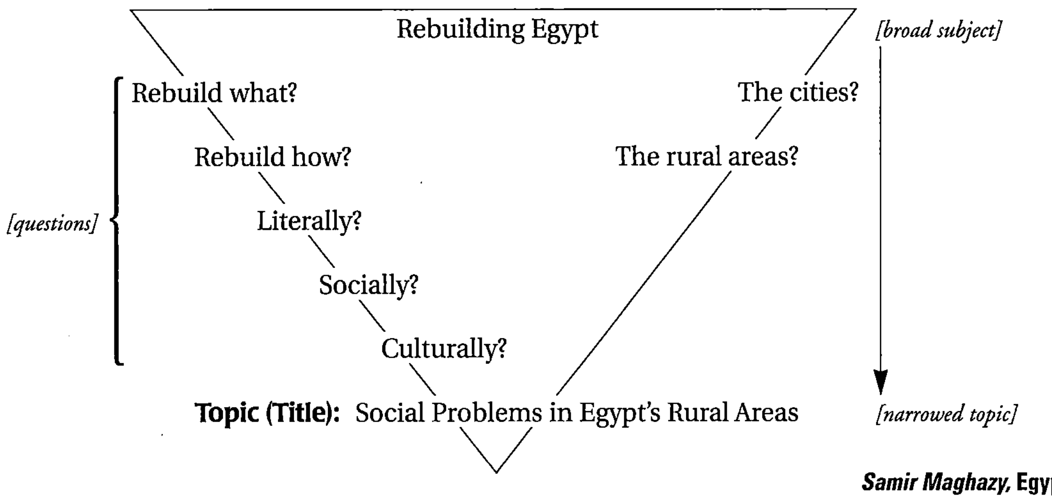

***Samir Maghazy,* Egypt**

Still another way to begin planning an academic essay is to begin with a single idea (perhaps a fact) and then, by asking questions, to discover the narrowed topic to communicate to the audience. The example below demonstrates that process.

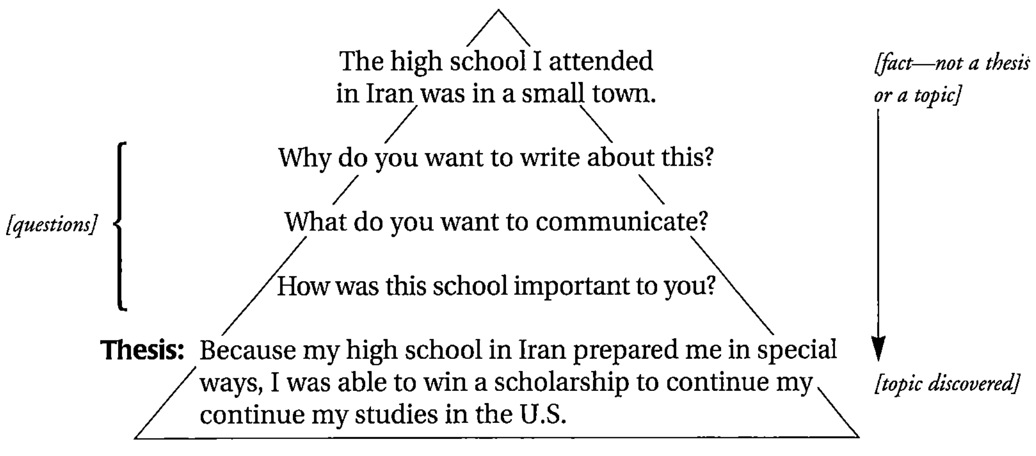

The high school I attended
in Iran was in a small town.
[fact—not a thesis
or a topic]
Rebuilding Egypt
[broad subject]
Rebuild what?
The cities?
Rebuild how?
[questions]
Why do you want to write about this?
What do you want to communicate?
How was this school important to you?
Thesis: Because my high school in Iran prepared me in special
ways, I was able to win a scholarship to continue my
continue my studies in the U.S.
[topic discovered]

***Moshen Harivandi,* Iran**

Writing Assignment I

1. Choose one of the subjects below, each of which has been used successfully by students who have taken this course. Or choose a subject from your authority list. Use your chosen topic to write an essay of approximately 500 words (2 word-processed, double-spaced pages).

Suggested Topics

sumo wrestling	S.A.D. (Seasonal Affective Disorder)
proxemics	food additives
feng shui	Hollywood stuntmen (or women)
fireworks design	nonverbal language

2. Because each of these subjects is too large for your assignment, narrow the subject to a topic. That is, select a "piece of the pie" as a topic.

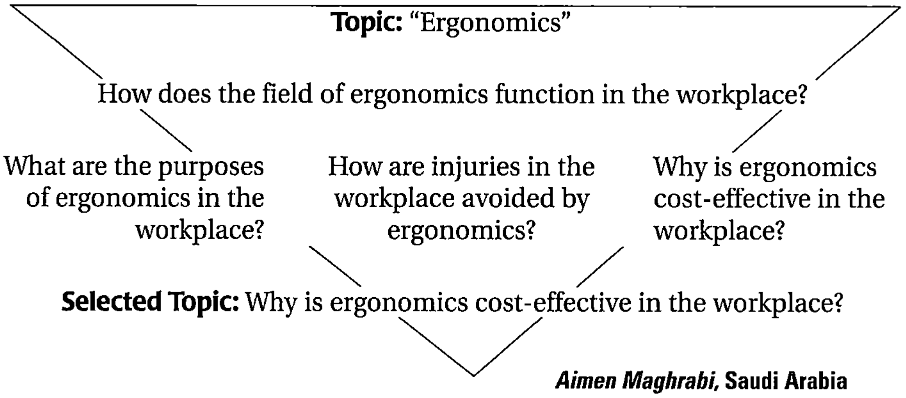

Topic: "Ergonomics"

How does the field of ergonomics function in the workplace?

What are the purposes of ergonomics in the workplace?

How are injuries in the workplace avoided by ergonomics?

Why is ergonomics cost-effective in the workplace?

Selected Topic: Why is ergonomics cost-effective in the workplace?

***Aimen Maghrabi,* Saudi Arabia**

3. This essay will require a background paragraph (see p. 73) that will explain the topic to your audience.
4. Collect ideas for your essay, using one of the Collecting strategies in Chapter 2 and/or one or more of these questions.

   What information do you already have about the topic?
   What additional information will you need to complete the essay?
   What source(s) can (might) you use to collect this information?

5. Carefully analyze the audience for your essay. Use the **Guidelines for Audience Analysis** below.
6. Using the **Guidelines for Composing** (on the inside front cover of this book), plan your essay.

Audience Analysis

For every academic writing assignment, students must identify and analyze their audience as they plan the purpose of the essay and develop their ideas. Usually the instructor will be the audience because she or he will be assigning the grade for the writing. However, sometimes the audience will include others: classmates, other students, or others outside the classroom. The following guidelines assist audience analysis.

GUIDELINES
for Audience Analysis

- Who is the audience? (age, education, interests, economic and social status)
- What is the audience's attitude about the topic?
- What does the audience already know about my topic?
- What will interest my audience, engage their attention, and encourage them to continue reading?
- What does the audience need/want to know?
- How can I best provide that information?
- What questions must (might) I answer about the topic?
- What is my expectation about the audience's reaction(s) to the essay?
  - What do I expect the audience to think? to do? to feel?
  - How do I expect the audience to change as a result of reading my essay?

The Optional Background Paragraph

Whether students are writing a short, two-page essay or a twenty-page research paper, they will consider whether their essays need a background paragraph: a paragraph that follows the introduction and contains additional background information for the reader. For example, if a student is writing about whether or not his classmates should live in the dormitories or off-campus, a background paragraph probably will not be needed because the audience knows about the topic. If, however, a student is writing an essay entitled "Hand Reflexology" for the same audience, the readers need additional information immediately after the introduction.

The decision about a background paragraph is based on the 3 **A**s:

- The **A**ssignment (the purpose): Does the instructor expect the writer to demonstrate background knowledge about the topic?
- The **A**udience: Do the readers know enough about the topic already?
- The **A**vailable Material: Does the writer have interesting material that the audience will enjoy reading that will also help them understand the essay that follows?

Note: Even if the writer believes that the instructor fully understands the background about the topic, using a background paragraph can demonstrate the writer's ability to communicate the background information concisely and well.

Background paragraphs can give some of the following information:

- definitions of key terms
- a brief history of the issue or the problem (depending on the audience)
- political or social background essential for reader understanding
- current relevant information about the topic from books, magazines, Websites, interviews, and surveys
- information about the way(s) information was gathered, such as how and to whom a survey was administered or how an authority about the topic was selected and interviewed

Often, writing a background paragraph in the academic essay gives student writers the opportunity to demonstrate that they have researched the topic. They will, therefore, be able to use citations (references) in that paragraph, and to add a reference list to their essay. Below are background paragraphs from two student essays. Each follows the thesis statement of the essay (that last sentence in the introductory paragraph). The citations in the first are **bold-faced** for ease of reading.

1 STUDENT SAMPLE

Birth Order and Music Preference

[Thesis statement] *According to my survey results, birth order does have an effect on a person's music preference.*

Background Paragraph

[Topic sentence] Researchers have studied birth order to discover whether or not the sequence in which children are born affects their personalities and their *[History, research]* lives **(Kinsmen, 1990)**. According to this research, first-born children are more often achievers in school and in their careers, probably because their early, formative lives were spent with adults. Paul Mussen, professor of *[Direct quotation, in-text citation]* child psychology, states that "First-born children tend to have very high standards for themselves and are highly motivated to achieve the best they can" **(1997, p. 69)**. In contrast, middle children make sure that others are taken care of first. They usually have great interaction with their peers,

and they tend to have many friends. They are usually very optimistic adults **(Sutter, 1997)**. Finally, youngest children are usually less cautious about their behavior. As Dr. Meghan Dinkins, my Child Psychology professor, says, "They [youngest children] tend to participate in more dangerous activities and are more likely to take risks" **(1997)**.

[In-text citation]

References

Dinkins, M. (1997). Personal Interview, October 10th.

Kingsmen, L. (1990). *Effects of birth order.* New York: Soloman.

Sutter, L. M. (1997, October 1). Birth order: *Factsheet.* 1. [Online article]. Retrieved March 8, 1998 from the World Wide Web: http://www.ag.ohio-state.edu/~ohioline/hyg-fact/5000/5279.html

Amy Hubble, **U.S.**

2 STUDENT SAMPLE

My Learning Style

[Thesis statement] *From the survey results, my major earning style is visual, but although my score is too low, I believe that I am also an auditory learner.*

Background Paragraph

[Topic sentence] *[Definition]* *[Direct quotations]* *[In-text citation]* *[Survey process]*

The Learning Style Preference Survey (Reid, 1984) contains 30 questions, evenly divided into six areas: visual, auditory, tactile, kinesthetic, group, and individual learning. By definition, visual learners are people who learn most from their eyes, "from seeing words in books, on the chalkboard, in workbooks," and who benefit when they "take notes of lectures and oral directions." Students who are auditory "learn from hearing words spoken and from oral explanations"; they also "benefit from hearing audiotapes, lectures, and class discussions" (Reid, 1984, p. 4). To qualify as a "major learning style," the student must have a survey score of 38 to 50. I answered the survey questions, and my auditory score (36) was very close to my visual score (38); therefore, I believe that I possess both learning styles. Figure __ depicts my learning styles scores.

[Chart]

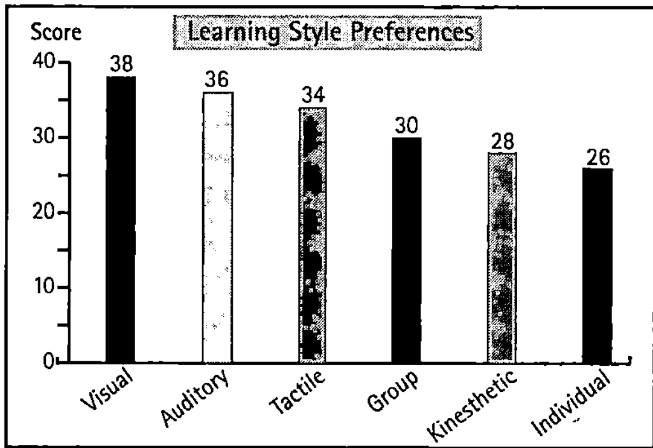

Figure __ *My Learning Styles Scores*

Reference

Reid, J. (1984). The Perceptual Learning Style Preference Survey.

Wu Gu, **People's Republic of China (PRC)**

EXERCISE 3-D

1. For each background paragraph, circle the word(s) in the thesis statement that are repeated in the topic sentence that follows.
2. In both Student Samples, notice the use of in-text citations (in **boldface** type) and end-of-text references. How does the use of other authors' ideas and words strengthen the information in these paragraphs?
3. Does either of the background paragraphs use a second sentence? If so, in what way does the second sentence help to direct and focus the reader?
4. On the scale below, write the number of the Student Sample background paragraph where you believe the level of formality of the language is on the formality scale. Discuss your decisions with your classmates.

   more formal ◄——————————————► less formal

5. The first paragraph could become an entire essay. Where could Amy divide the material into several paragraphs? What information could she add?

Writing Assignment:

The Background Paragraph

1. After you have narrowed the subject and selected your essay topic, ask a partner or a small group of classmates what they know about your topic, and what they need to know.
2. As you begin to gather information about your topic, consider the information that you need to include in your background paragraph.
3. Draft the background paragraph of your essay.

Titles for Academic Essays

Often the selection of a topic (or the narrowing of a writing assignment in a course) will lead to the title for your essay. The purposes of titles are

- to attract the reader,
- to give the reader an idea of what the essay is about, and
- to provide focus for the essay.

The title is usually a phrase, not a complete sentence, and all extra words should be excluded. Sometimes a title can be a question; then it is followed by a question mark (?). Titles should be clear, concise, and precise. Other guidelines for titles:

- Do not use quotation marks to surround the title.
- Do not put a period (.) at the end of a title.
- Center the title on the top of the first page or the center of the cover page.
- For capitalization, either capitalize *all* the letters in the title or capitalize the first letter of all the *important* words.

Note: If only the first letters of important words in a title are capitalized, do not capitalize small words like "in" and "a" except at the beginning of the title. To highlight titles, do one of the following (*but not more than one*):

- Underline the title: Social Problems in Mali
- Italicize the title: *The Crisis in Donor Organs*
- Boldface the title: **Should the Olympics Be Reorganized?**
- Capitalize the entire title: COFFEEHOUSES IN TURKEY

Finally, for most academic writing tasks, the title for an assignment should be on a cover sheet, a piece of paper that contains only the information shown in Figure 3-1:

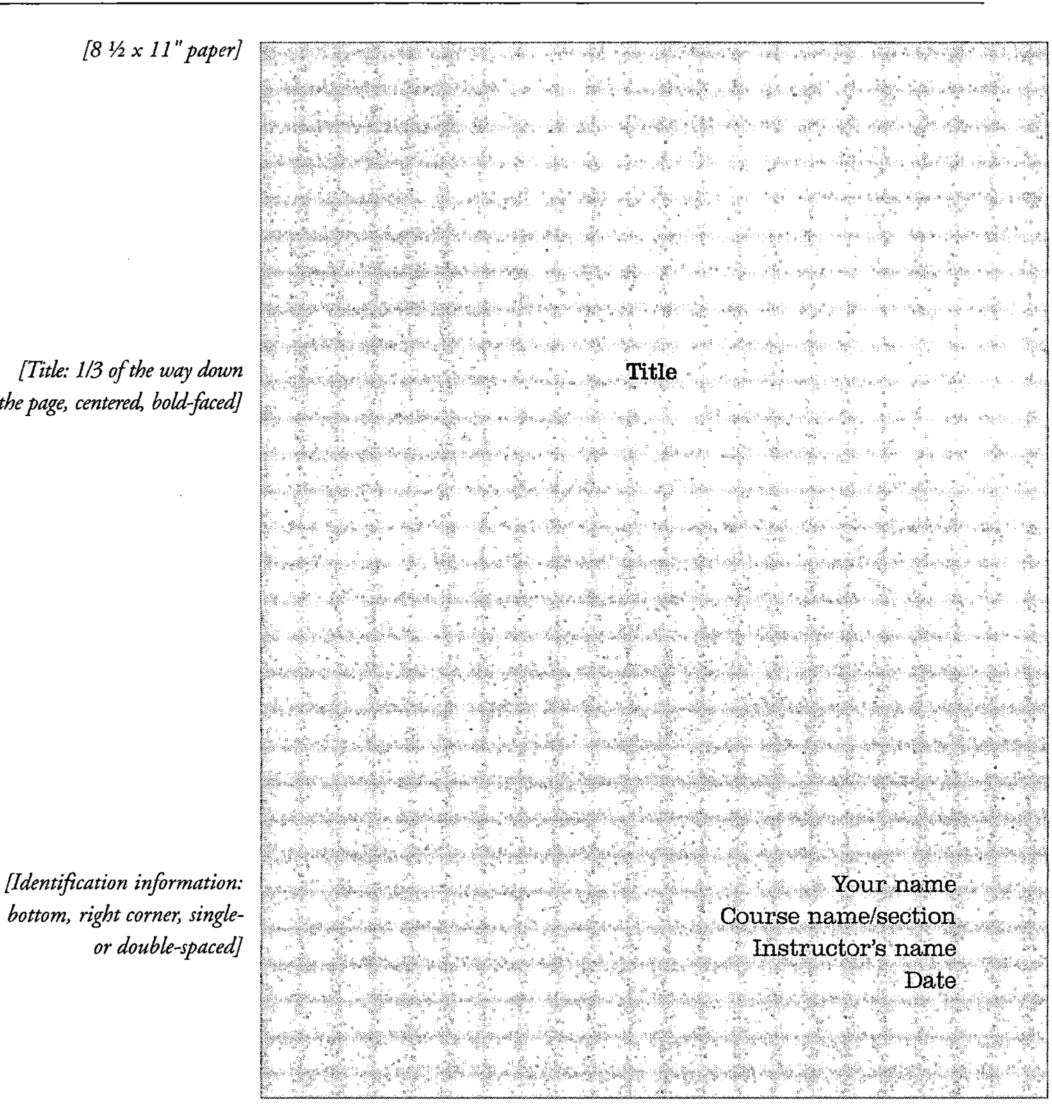

Figure 3-1 *Cover Sheet for Academic Writing Tasks*

EXERCISE 3-E With a partner, discuss possible titles for the essay you are writing. Then evaluate each other's titles.

- Will it engage the reader?
- Does it focus the essay for the reader?
- Does it clearly describe the main idea in the essay?
- Has it followed the punctuation and capitalization writing conventions?

The Thesis Statement

Each academic essay contains a **thesis statement**. This statement is usually one sentence that gives the writer's purpose for the essay. The thesis statement

- is the most general, most important sentence *in the essay*. It acts as an "umbrella" over the essay. All ideas in the essay must fit under this umbrella.

- is the strongest, clearest statement in the essay.
- usually comes at the beginning of the essay, usually at the **end** of the introductory paragraph.
- must *not* be a simple statement of fact that requires no development.
- will probably not be expressed as a question because a question contains no intent or opinion. The answer to that question is the thesis statement.
- will contain controlling ideas that "control" the content of the essay and guide the reader.

Note: In many ways, the thesis statement of an essay is similar to the topic sentence of a paragraph (see Chapter 1, pp. 17–18).

THESIS STATEMENTS OF OPINION AND/OR INTENT

Thesis statements usually have two functions. First, thesis statements of intent state just the purpose of the essay, without evaluative words.

[controlling ideas circled]

A soccer coach must have four qualities.

In contrast, thesis statements of opinion usually contain the purpose of the essay and evaluative words such as *best, worst, valuable, unpleasant, boring,* and so on.

[evaluative words underlined]

My neighbor owns four cats; these animals present a serious health hazard in our neighborhood.

A successful thesis statement results from selection, qualification, and specificity. In the example below, the writer narrowed his original thesis statement as he narrowed his topic for a 500-word Explaining essay about the Koran.

The Koran is wonderful.

[The evaluative opinion wonderful *is too vague to be supported in the essay.]*

The Koran is the perfect book for everyone.

*[*Everyone *is still too general, and* perfect *is difficult to support.]*

The Koran is one of the best religious books in the world.

[Somewhat qualified, but brings in a bigger topic: other religious books.*]*

The Koran is an important religious book.

*[*important *is more qualified, more objective, but the sentence needs an additional idea to help direct the essay.]*

The Koran is the basis for the lifestyle of millions of Muslims.

[Reasonable, specific, supportable opinion and clear intent for the essay]

EXERCISE 3-F Below are student samples of thesis statements, followed by their proposed organization for each essay. With a partner or in a small group,

- circle the controlling ideas in each thesis statement,
- discuss how each of these essays could be developed,
- decide whether you would use different methods of development, and
- decide whether you would use different techniques of support.

Essay Plan A

[*Explain* what, why] Thesis statement of opinion and intent:
In El Salvador, uneven distribution of wealth, overpopulation, and political corruption are major problems. (assigned subject)
Audience: instructor, political science class
Purpose: to explain the major problems in El Salvador so that my professor will know that I understand the material
Methods of development: extended definition (background paragraph), cause(s) and effect(s) of each problem
Techniques of support: facts, examples, physical description

Alfredo Chorro, **El Salvador**

Essay Plan B

[*Explain* why] Thesis statement of intent:
The reasons I came to the U.S. to study were to educate myself and then to return to Libya to apply my education.
Audience: classmates and instructor
Purpose: to explain my reasons for studying in the U. S.
Methods of development: classification (and explanation) of my reasons, the cause(s) and effect(s) of my decision
Techniques of support: personal experience, examples, facts

Mohamed Yacob, **Libya**

Essay Plan C

[*Explain* how, why] Statement of intent and opinion:
Michelangelo's three famous sculptures—the Pieta, David, *and* Moses—*demonstrate his artistic genius throughout his life.* (assigned subject)
Audience: professor of my art history class
Purpose: to explain my opinion of Michelangelo's sculpture and to demonstrate for my professor what I have learned in class about evaluating sculpture
Methods of development: compare and contrast the sculptures, and give the cause(s) and effect(s) of their similarities and differences
Techniques of support: facts, physical description, examples

Sergio los Santos, **Mexico**

Diagram of the Academic Essay

Many students learn more quickly if they can study a model or a diagram of the academic essay. Figure 3-5 depicts the academic essay in diagram form. Students may use this diagram for essays they write during this course, and for essays they write in other college/university classes.

Title of the Essay

The introduction begins with a general statement about the topic, to engage and interest the reader.

The thesis statement is the most general, most important sentence in the essay.

Approximate length of the Introduction: 50–75 words in a 500-word essay.

Introduction

- introduces the topic
- gives limited background information to orient the reader
- states the thesis (the purpose) of the essay, with controlling ideas that direct the essay

The topic sentence is the most general, most important sentence in the paragraph.

Sometimes the first body paragraph functions as a "background" paragraph that gives the reader additional essential information about the topic.

Body paragraphs are longer than the introduction or the conclusion because they contain support and/or explanation for the controlling ideas.

Approximate length of body paragraphs in a 500-word essay: 125 to 175 each.

Use transitions within and between body paragraphs to demonstrate relationships between words and sentences, and to guide the readers.

Body Paragraphs

- begin with a topic sentence directly related to a controlling idea in the thesis statement
- topic sentence has controlling ideas that direct the paragraph
- contain supporting sentences of *facts, physical description, examples,* and/or *personal experience*
- are organized according to a method of development that is used to present and explain the ideas: *process, extended definition, comparison and/or contrast, classification, cause* and/or *effect*
- paragraph hooks "link" paragraphs and help to guide the reader: repetition of word(s) in the last sentence of one paragraph in the first sentence of the next

The conclusion begins with body paragraph, then broadens to "reflect" (but not repeat) the introduction.

Approximate length: 40–60 words

Conclusion

- contains concluding "hook" to the last word/phrase
- brief summary of main idea(s) of the essay
- prediction, solution, recommendation, and/or suggestion

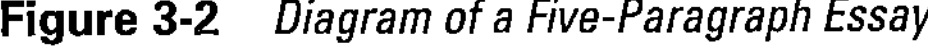

Figure 3-2 *Diagram of a Five-Paragraph Essay*

Writing Assignment:

A Thesis Statement for the Explaining Essay

1. Use the topic you chose and the ideas you collected in Writing Assignment I to write a thesis statement for the 5-paragraph essay you are developing. Consider your purpose and audience as you construct your thesis statement.
2. Exchange thesis statements with a partner and discuss the following questions with your partner:
   - Is each thesis statement one of opinion and intent *or* of intent? How do you know?

- What do you expect to read in the body paragraphs of your partner's essay?
- What do you think the audience for this essay will be most interested in? Why?

3. Discuss your ideas with your partner. Then revise your thesis statement to improve it.

Paragraph Relationships

In academic essays, the thesis statement is directly related to the topic sentences in the body paragraphs. It is the "umbrella" statement that covers the ideas in the essay; it focuses the readers' attention on the main point of the essay.

Each topic sentence in the body paragraphs relates to and focuses on one or more of the controlling ideas in the thesis. Then each set of supporting sentences that follows a topic sentence relates directly to the controlling ideas in that topic sentence. In this way, all ideas in the essay are related; no idea "outside the umbrella" should occur. The essay will be unified and consequently easier for the audience to read. Figure 3-3 demonstrates the paragraph relationships in a typical five-paragraph essay of approximately 500 words.

Note: The introduction and the conclusion in the essay are short because they have different functions in the essay. While the body paragraphs need facts, examples, physical description, and/or personal experience to support the topic sentence, the functions of the introduction and the conclusion do not. Therefore, the first and last paragraphs of an academic essay are usually short.

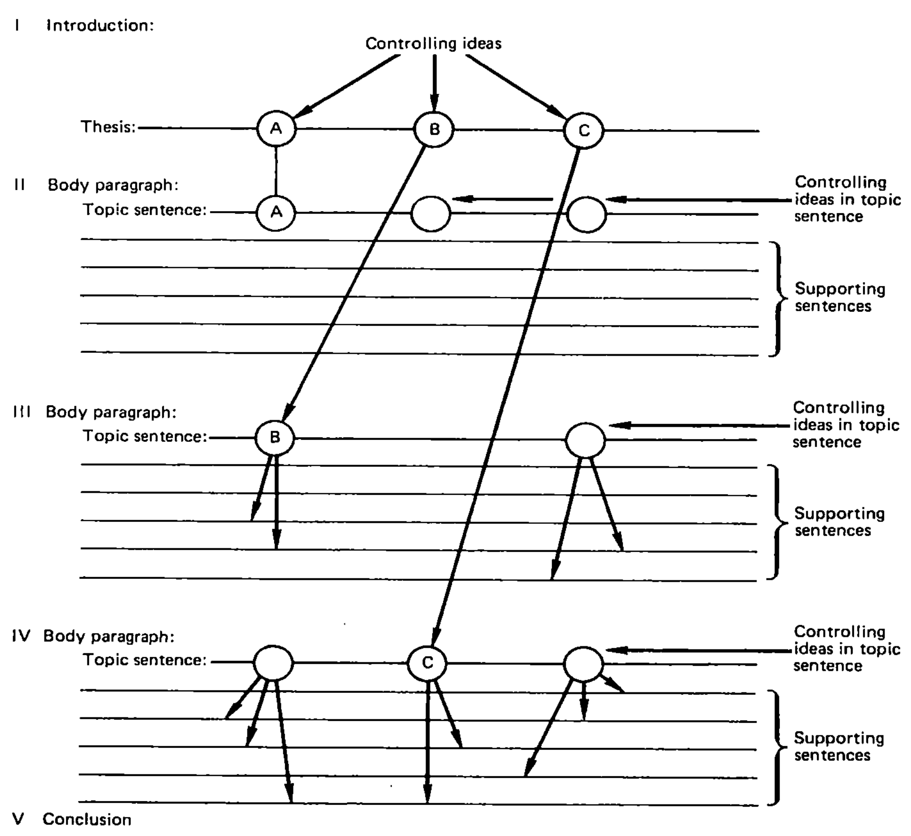

Figure 3-3 *Guide to Paragraph Relationships Within an Essay*

The Essay Map

One way to begin developing an essay is to write an "essay map," a series of sentences that includes *the thesis statement and the topic sentences in the essay.* Below are examples of the simplest form of essay mapping. Each of the essays will be about two word-processed pages (i.e., about 500 words). Each will contain an introductory paragraph, three or four body paragraphs, and a concluding paragraph.

The Head-Hunters of Borneo

Thesis: *My visit to the state of Sarawak on the Island of Borneo gave me insights on the now extinct practice of head-hunting there.*

[Topic sentences]

- The museum curator, Mr. Chin Loke Ling, outlined the history of head-hunting.
- Mr. Tai, my taxi driver, a descendant of the Bidayuhs, explained why his people by custom, killed and collected only the heads of enemy warriors.
- The Cultural Village reflected the lifestyle of the Bidayuhs.

Concluding Sentence: Now they live in peace, transformed by time to the friendliest people in the land.

Kok Yeang Chin, **Malaysia**

The Controller as the Foundation in a Successful Company

Thesis: *No matter what the size of the company, a competent controller in charge of the financial management is necessary.*

[Topic sentences]

- The controller is in charge of a variety of financial information concerning the company, and he must have complete and immediate knowledge of this information.
- An efficient and successful controller has a good work plan and a good team to work with.
- A relationship of mutual respect between the finance department and other departments in the company is essential for a successful controller.

Concluding Sentence: The value of a good controller to a corporation is immeasurable; he is the foundation of the company's success.

Marie Pecina, **Mexico**

EXERCISE 3-G

1. With a partner, for each essay map above:
   - identify the audience
   - write a statement of general and specific purpose(s)
   - circle the controlling ideas in (a) the thesis statement and (b) the topic sentences
2. Decide which method(s) of development could be used in each body paragraph.
3. Decide which technique(s) of support could be used in each body paragraph.
4. What nontext materials (e.g., charts, photographs, etc.) could each of the writers use to develop more information about the topics of these paragraphs?

Some essay maps contain more information: questions about the controlling ideas that the writer expects to answer in the essay and in the body paragraphs, a title, a concluding sentence, and/or some of the details that will be used in the body paragraphs.

Here are three complex essay maps. Read them and do the exercise that follows.

Michelangelo's Genius

Thesis statement of intent: *The greatest sculptural works of Michelangelo—the Pieta, David, and Moses—demonstrate his genius.*

Body paragraph topic sentences:

- The *Pieta* demonstrates Michelangelo's early artistic genius.
  [Questions] How? In what ways?
- Michelangelo's sculpture *David* shows his genius in middle life.
  [Questions] How? In what ways? How does it compare and/or contrast with the *Pieta*?
- Finally, the statue of *Moses* makes clear that Michelangelo's creative energies were still significant in old age.
  [Questions] How? In what ways? How does it compare and/or contrast with the *Pieta* and with *David*?

Concluding Sentence: Michelangelo's long life was filled with art; his sculptures show his lifelong artistry.

***Sergio des los Santos,* Mexico**

Marriage Preparation in Somalia

Thesis statement of intent and opinion: *Preparation for marriage in Somalia consists of very important tasks such as working hard to earn money, collecting contributions of livestock, getting money from relatives, and preparing items for the home.*

Topic sentence: *A man who intends to marry has the responsibility to have money.*

[Point #1] 1. must work to collect the money.
[Details] A. working in villages and towns (poor man)
B. selling part of livestock (rich man)
[Point #2] 2. must become a businessman
[Details] A. selling cigarettes
B. selling clothes

Topic sentence: Collection of livestock and money is another preparation for marriage.

[Point #1] 1. collect from his family
[Details] A. amount of contribution: 1–4 heads
B. contribution is a tradition
[Point #2] 2. collect from friends

Topic sentence: The woman who wishes to marry spends her time making items for the house.

[Point #1] 1. mats, wooden posts, and water containers
[Point #2] 2. collaborates with family members, relatives, and friends

Concluding sentence: Preparing for marriage is a long and tedious task in Somalia, but it is essential for the establishment of a new family.

Jamal Al-Badon, **Somalia**

Problems in Rural Egypt

[Thesis statement, controlling ideas] *Rural areas in Egypt have three serious problems: poverty, lack of education, and poor medical care.*

Audience: professor of my agricultural economics class (assigned subject)

Purpose: to demonstrate my knowledge about Egypt to my professor

- Poverty is the overriding factor in Egypt's rural areas.
  - Method of development: extended definition of poverty
  - Techniques of support: facts, examples, physical description
- As a result of this poverty, the people in the rural areas are rarely educated; almost no one goes to school past the age of twelve.
  - Method of development: cause-effect (why "rarely educated")
  - Techniques of support: facts, examples
- Because the people are so poor and so poorly educated, medical care, even when it is available, is unused.
  - Method of development: cause-effect (why unavailable, why unused)
  - Techniques of support: facts, examples, physical description
  - Conclusion ???

Samir Maghazy, **Egypt**

EXERCISE 3-H

1. With a partner, reread the essay maps above. In Student Sample 8, what methods of development and techniques of support do you think Sergio will use in his essay?
2. In Student Sample 9, circle the controlling ideas in the thesis statement. Then help Jamal clarify his thesis statement by adding the idea that both members of the engaged couple work to get ready for the marriage.
3. In Student Sample 10, what questions can you ask Samir about his thesis and about his topic sentences to help him prepare to write his essay?
4. Write two possible concluding sentences that Samir might use to end his essay.
5. Which of the essay maps do you think is most helpful for the writer? Why?

Writing Assignment:
An Essay Map for the Explaining Essay

1. Use the topic you selected and the thesis statement for your Explaining essay. Choose one of the essay map forms above and write an essay map for your essay.
2. Work with a partner to analyze both of your essay maps. For each essay map,
   - read the thesis statement; discuss questions that you expect will be answered in the essay that follows.
   - read each topic sentence. Does each relate directly to the thesis statement?
   - discuss questions that you expect will be answered in the paragraph that follows each topic sentence.
   - discuss changes that might strengthen or improve the essay map.
3. Based on your discussion with your partner, rewrite (and improve) your essay map.

Writing Conventions for the Academic Essay

The Introduction

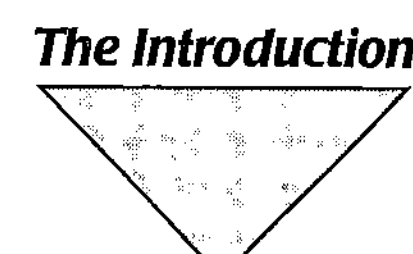

The general statement(s) with which you begin your introduction should engage your audience in your topic, orient your audience, and lead logically to your thesis statement.

THE INTRODUCTION

Effective introductions avoid two problems.

1. The *apology, complaint,* or *personal dilemma* weakens the essay because it distracts the reader and limits the credibility of the writer:

    I have now walked three times completely around the campus in a serious effort to come up with a suitable topic for this paper. When I noticed a pedestrian getting run over by a bicycle, I knew that would make a good topic for my discussion. Although I couldn't care less about the welfare of the two people involved, I went over nevertheless (I hope I never have to do it again) and asked if I could be of any assistance. That's what I'm going to talk about in this essay.

2. The *panoramic* beginning is impossible to narrow to a thesis without a break in unity.

    Since the beginning of time, . . .
    In this world of today, . . .
    War is a topic that has been handled admirably by poets throughout the course of history . . .

The following are examples of effective introductions.

11 STUDENT SAMPLE

Vitamin D Deficiency

[General statement, engages the reader] *[Limited background information]* *[Thesis statement of intent]*

Vitamin D is the sunshine vitamin, and Vitamin D is essential for good health. Until the twentieth century, however, little was known about this important vitamin, and people who lived in temperate climates tended to suffer every winter from the lack of Vitamin D. Even today, although knowledge about Vitamin D has been available for more than fifty years, many people still suffer from Vitamin D deficiencies. *This essay will describe the chemical makeup of Vitamin D, the group of diseases called "rickets" that afflict people who are deficient in this vitamin, and solutions to avoid such deficiencies.*

***Saleh Saeed,* United Arab Emirates**

12 STUDENT SAMPLE

[Scene set to interest reader] *[Limited background information]* *[Thesis statement of intent]*

Early in the 1960s, the only way to eat pigeon meat in France was by hunting. Then people began to raise this fowl to sell. At that time, the market was full of promise, but today, the market for pigeon in France is still marginal; it has not developed as expected. There is one main reason for this failure: price. *This essay examines the causes that make pigeon meat in France so expensive.*

***David Soulard,* France**

Small Town Relationships in El Salvador

[General, engaging] *[Limited background information]* Almost all of the small towns in El Salvador are similar in their general appearance. In addition, many of the people who live in these towns have a special lifestyle. In contrast to life in the larger cities, people in small towns share many cultural things and experiences. *[Thesis statement of intent/opinion]* *This unusual sharing contributes to a familial relationship among neighbors.*

Rita Saravia, **El Salvador**

EXERCISE 3-I For the introductions above, answer these questions:

1. Write one topic sentence for one body paragraph of one essay. Share your topic sentence with your class.
2. Write a title for Student Sample 12. Discuss your choice with a small group of classmates.
3. Discuss the "voice" that each writer might use for each of the essays. Which essay will be more personal? Which is the most formal and academic? How do you know?
4. What nontext materials (e.g., graphs, flow charts, line drawings) could the writers of the paragraphs use to interest their audiences?

Writing Assignment: The Introduction for the Explaining Essay

Draft the introduction for your Explaining essay. Be sure that your introduction

- interests your audience
- gives brief but necessary background information about the topic of your essay
- leads to your thesis statement (of intent and/or opinion) at the end of the introduction.

THE BODY OF THE ESSAY

The Body

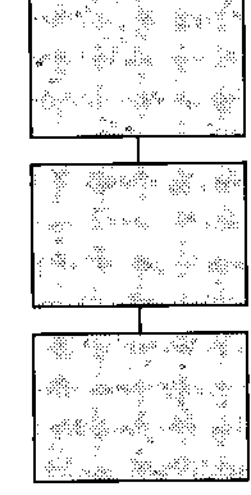

The paragraphs studied in the first chapters of this book have the overall structure of the body paragraphs of an essay:

- *a topic sentence with controlling ideas*
- *a method of development (comparison/contrast, process, classification, cause-effect, process)*
- *techniques of support (facts, examples, description, experience)*

Each body paragraph is a self-contained, fully developed unit. Like the essay itself, each paragraph has three parts: a beginning (introduction), a middle (support), and an end (conclusion). In a 5-paragraph essay, each paragraph is approximately 125 to 175 words (four to eight sentences).

Read the body paragraphs below. Then do the exercise that follows.

[Thesis statement of opinion and intent] *The tomatoes gathered in a person's garden are much more enjoyable to eat than those bought in a grocery store, not only due to their appearance and their taste, but also to the emotional feelings that they call to mind.*

Colored a dark red, the tomatoes cultivated in a personal garden are distinguishable from those with a pale skin, sometimes green-stained, that are produced by industries. The garden tomatoes have taken, day after day, the sun's light and heat. Like an egg that needs the warmth and nutrients from its mother to hatch, the tomatoes are nurtured by the sun and earth as they come to maturity. Often they are different sizes, and some are flawed, but one has only to remove that flaw. In contrast, store tomatoes are all the same size with perfect appearance, so smooth that they seem to be plastic, as though they are from an artificial world. But they are imperfect: their clear, transparent hardness and strange color reveals their true nature of unripe fruit grown without the sun.

Claire Koulinski, **France**

[Thesis statement of intent] *Snow fences are inexpensive, efficient barriers that were developed by physicists and are implemented by engineers; they control the amount of snow that blows onto major highways.*

Using complicated studies of fluids and many calculations, scientists discovered that simple wooden fences, placed at exact angles, could cause blowing snow to be deposited immediately behind the fence rather than on the roadway, thus decreasing hazardous driving conditions. Physicists call snow a fluid; they know that fluids moving at high speed have a lower pressure than fluids moving at slower velocity. Moreover, a low pressure zone is created behind the fence by the blowing snow when that fence is placed directly perpendicular to the wind flow. Hence, the blowing snow tends to fill the low pressure zone and is deposited just a few feet behind the fence, thereby avoiding the road. "The pressure in this small core area would be the minimum within the flow, and the snow

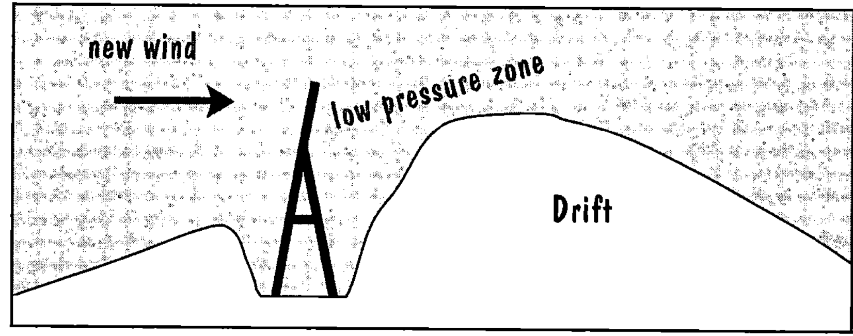

Figure __ *Side View of Snow Fence "Critical Point"*

particles from other levels would be pulled into this area of greater turbulence" (McCormick, 1966, p. 28). The figure depicts the "critical point" a few feet behind the fence where the velocity of the blowing snow becomes greater because of the fence. Because the snow falls in a pile directly behind the fence, the road remains relatively clear.

Reference

McCormick, W. B. (1996). Wind tunnel study of velocity profiles.

Unpublished dissertation, University of Wyoming.

***José L. de la Llave R.,* Mexico**

EXERCISE 3-J

1. With a partner, identify and list the technique(s) of support used in each paragraph.
2. Which method(s) of development did the writer of Student Sample 14 use?
3. Compose a title for each of the paragraphs.
4. What can you guess about the personalities of each of the writers by reading the body paragraphs? That is, what does the "voice" of each tell you about the writer?
5. What will the next (body) paragraph for each essay be about? Suggestion: reread the thesis statement.

USING CITATIONS IN ACADEMIC ESSAYS

Most major writing assignments require students to "do research," that is, to identify, locate, and read materials written by others. One reason that academic readers value the use of material outside the students' personal experience is that these references prove that student writers have examined the work of experts in their chosen topic. Another is that if the readers choose to read more about the topic, they can easily find the sources that were cited in the student's paper.

In U.S. culture, authors *own* their words and ideas. In U.S. academic prose, writers cite sources (i.e., identify the sources) for any fact or bit of information that is not general knowledge. Student writers who collect and use research material—the words and/or the ideas of another person—must (a) give credit to that person and (b) list enough information so that interested readers can find the source. **As a rule, writers should cite sources for any information they did not know before they began their research.**

In academic writing, citations must appear in two places:

- **in-text citations**: a brief reference to the author that immediately follows the author's idea(s) and/or words in the text of the student's paper.
- **end-of-text citations**: a complete reference to the author and the material (i.e., the book, the magazine, the Website) where the author's idea(s) and words are located. End-of-text citations are listed alphabetically by the last name of the author on a Reference page at the end of the student's paper.

Citation Formats

Different major fields use different citation formats.* That is, the arrangement of citation information (e.g., where the date of the publication is placed, whether or not a title is capitalized, what punctuation is used) differs. You may encounter as many as six citation formats while you are taking college/university courses.

* More information about discipline-specific citation is discussed in Chapter 5 (p. 168), and in Appendix A.

Two academic citation "styles" used in undergraduate classes are (a) the Modern Language Association (**MLA**) style, used mostly in English Departments (Style Manual: *MLA Handbook*) and (b) the American Psychological Association (**APA**) style, used widely in the humanities and social sciences (Style Manual: *Publication Manual of the American Psychological Association*). Each of these citation formats is completely described, along with numerous examples, in its Style Manual (see parentheses above).

For this writing course, students will practice **APA Style** because they will be able to use it in many undergraduate classes.*

EXERCISE 3-K

1. With a partner or a small group of classmates, discuss the value of the references used by student writers in the paragraphs listed below. In what ways did the in-text and end-of-text citations help the writer? the reader?

Student Sample (SS)	Topic	Writer	Page
Chapter 2, SS 27	ball-lightning	Csaba Rozgonya	59
Chapter 2, SS 28	human sacrifices	Luis Ramirez	59
Chapter 3, SS 1	birth order	Amy Hubble	73
Chapter 3, SS 15	snow fences	José L. de la Llave	86

2. Identify and list the information given in each in-text citation.
3. Identify the information and the sequence of information given in each end-of-text citation.
4. Discuss the sources you might consult as you write your Explaining essay.

Writing Assignment:

Drafting the Body Paragraphs for the Explaining Essay

1. Revise and rewrite the draft of your background paragraph (which will serve as the first body paragraph of your essay). Remember to use in-text and end-of-text citations as necessary.
2. Use the **Guidelines for Composing** (on the inside front cover of this textbook) to draft the other 2 or 3 body paragraphs of your essay. Make sure that
   - each topic sentence relates directly to the thesis statement of your essay:
     – do you need to modify your thesis statement?
     – do you need to modify any of your topic sentences?
   - each topic sentence has controlling ideas that control the paragraph.
   - the supporting sentences in each body paragraph relate directly to the topic sentence and the controlling ideas.

EXERCISE 3-L Exchange your body paragraphs with a partner.

- Read the background paragraph (the first body paragraph). Is the information in that paragraph helpful? If you need any more information, ask your partner. Has your partner used in-text citations? If so, are they correct?
- Read *just the first sentence of each of the other body paragraphs.* Write 2 or 3 questions you expect will be answered in the paragraph that follows.
- Read the other body paragraphs. Were your questions answered? Discuss any unanswered questions with your partner.
- Read the introduction and the thesis statement. Does each topic sentence in the body paragraphs relate directly to the thesis statement? If you don't know, ask your partner for help.

* For citation forms used in APA style, see Appendix A.

- for each body paragraph, label the techniques of support (facts, examples, description, experience) in the margin.
- which body paragraph do you like best? Why? Tell your partner: "I like this paragraph because . . ."

THE CONCLUSION

The Conclusion

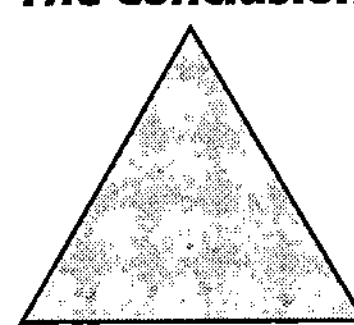

The conclusion borrows from everything that has gone before, summarizing without repeating exactly, suggesting, predicting, recommending, and/or offering a solution. It gives the essay its final shape, and it gives writers a last opportunity to show that their ideas are worthwhile.

To write strong, persuasive, graceful conclusions, follow these guidelines.

1. Begin with a concluding "connector" to help the reader (e.g., "In conclusion, ").*
2. Look at the thesis statement and make sure that the conclusion is connected to it; the conclusion reflects, but does not repeat, the thesis.
3. Begin the conclusion with a narrow statement that links it to the last body paragraph.
4. Broaden the ideas in your next sentences to summarize the main ideas from the body paragraphs; restate, but do not repeat, ideas, especially from the topic sentences; reflect, but do not repeat, those topic sentences.
5. Consider one or more of the following for the conclusion: a *prediction,* a *recommendation,* and/or a *solution.*

Avoid these problems in your conclusions:

- **Too much summary:** If the essay is short (2 or 3 pages long), the reader will probably remember most of the main points. Refer to these points only briefly. Of course, in a very long essay or in a lengthy research paper, more summary will be necessary.
- **Any completely new idea:** If a new idea occurs in the conclusion, the reader may turn the page, expecting support for the idea. If the idea is important, include it, with supporting evidence, in another body paragraph in the essay.

The following are examples of effective conclusions.

Women's Liberation in Japan

[Concluding phrase] To conclude, the role of women in Japan used to be to take care of their families; women were not educated, so they did not have jobs. *[Summary]* However, after the women's education system was improved, Japanese women became part of the job force in my country. Nowadays, many women have jobs, but there are still problems with low salaries and limited opportunities. Fortunately, these problems are being solved, so *[Prediction]* in the future there will be no difference between men's and women's jobs.

***Sumiko Ishii,* Japan**

* For more information and examples about concluding connectors, see Chapter 4, page 117.

The Beautiful Hardanger *Bunad*

[Link to previous paragraph] Last year, after I had spent four years in the United States, I celebrated Norway's Constitution Day (May 17th) in Bergen, Norway. I saw even more clearly that the Hardanger *Bunad* has a unique place in *[Summary]* Norwegian culture. Being among the thousands dressed in a beautiful *bunad*, and being part of the 500-year old history, gave me a strong feeling of pride and belonging. Suddenly I wanted to tell all my *[Recommendation]* Norwegian friends in the U.S. to come home and celebrate. I realized that such traditions are like good wines: the older they get, the better they are. . . .

***Gulla Burke,* Norway**

EXERCISE 3-M

1. With a partner, discuss what you think the thesis statement for each of these essays was.
2. What questions do you and your partner think were answered in the body paragraphs of each essay?
3. Write one topic sentence for one body paragraph for each of the essays.
4. Which conclusion do you think is the most effective? Why? Suggestion: read the summary in each of the conclusions.
5. Share your answers with another pair of partners.

Read each of the following introductions and conclusions of student essays. Then answer the questions that follow.

[Introduction] Although the Watershed Management Division in Thailand was established eighty-four years ago, watershed management has not *[Background information]* progressed as it should have. *That is because there are three major problems: the invasion of watershed areas by the populace, the lack of* *[Thesis statement of intent/opinion]* *research by the scientists, and the deficiencies of budget and personnel by the government in Thailand.*

[Conclusion] To conclude, we can see that none of the problems is easy to solve and that each is related to the others. Because of the money shortage, the *[Summary]* scientists cannot do proper research, so we cannot expand our work. The lack of data from research results in our not being able to demonstrate *[Solution]* our work to get enough money from the government. The best solution is to choose a particular area and work on the problems that exist there, gathering data and solving problems; then we can present these data to the government to make them see how very important the Watershed Management Division is.

***Arthorn Boonsaner,* Thailand**

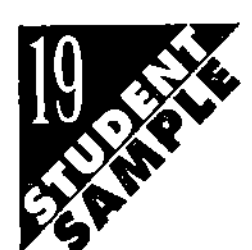

[Introduction
[Background information]
[Thesis statement of intent/opinion]

One obstacle that most foreign speakers find when they come to the United States to study at the university level is the TOEFL examination. Before permitting an international student to enroll, universities demand that they have a high score on the TOEFL exam. *Although the TOEFL has been devised to measure the students' English skills, it is not the best way to judge because of the nervousness of the students taking the test, and the luck involved in passing/failing the test.*

[Conclusion]
[Solutions]
[Recommendations]

I am just another student who plans to study in the U.S. and who wishes that the people in charge of the TOEFL examination could find a better system of testing the English skills of international speakers. Perhaps a series of tests over a period of time would reduce the anxiety of students whose university admission now rests on a single day of testing. Certainly the test-takers should be permitted short breaks between sections of the test in order to relax their minds. Finally, the TOEFL should be better standardized so that it reflects more clearly a student's English proficiency.

***Malula Moncada,* Nicaragua**

20
STUDENT SAMPLE

[Introduction]
[Background information]
[Thesis statement of intent/opinion]

There is an important discussion in Saudi Arabia about the Saudi students in the U.S. and about their progress in their studies. Some people support sending students abroad to study, but others object. However, it has been proved that the progress that graduate students have made is much better than what undergraduates have made. *Therefore, the Saudi government should stop funding undergraduate students to the U.S. and other countries, but it should continue to fund graduate students.*

[Conclusion]
[Summary]
[Recommendation]

In conclusion, there is no reasonable need to send hundreds of undergraduate students yearly to study in the western countries. But there is an actual need to help graduate students to study in well-known universities all over the world in order to give them a chance to know about the updated information in their fields.

***Mohamed Al-Yahyan,* Saudi Arabia**

EXERCISE 3-N

1. With a partner or in a small group, write a title for each of the essays.
2. Based on the thesis statement in each introduction, write 2–3 topic sentences for each of the essays.
3. Who is the audience for each essay?
   Suggestions: discuss the "voice" and the topic for each paragraph.
4. What kinds of nontext materials might each of these writers use in their essays? Be specific.

Writing Assignment: *Drafting the Conclusion of the Explaining Essay*

Write a rough draft of the conclusion for your essay. As you write, try to incorporate the concluding techniques you have learned.

EXERCISE 3-O Exchange essay drafts with a partner who has not read your essay. Read your partner's essay. In your notebook, or on your partner's essay draft, complete the **Peer Response Exercise** below.

Peer Response Exercise

1. Does the introduction begin with general information related to the thesis statement? Does the first sentence interest and engage you?
2. Circle the controlling ideas in the thesis statement. Write questions that you believe will be answered in the essay that follows.
3. Is there a background paragraph? If so, in what ways is it helpful for the reader?
4. Read the topic sentences in the body paragraphs of the essay. Are they directly related to the thesis statement? Do the paragraphs that follow each topic sentence answer the questions you wrote about the thesis statement?
5. In the margins of your partner's draft, for *each* body paragraph, identify
    - one **method of development**: *process, extended definition, classification, comparison* and/or *contrast, cause(s), effect(s)* or both.
    - one **technique of support**: *facts, examples, physical description,* and/or *personal experience*
6. In the margins of the conclusion of the essay draft, list the concluding technique(s) your partner used.
7. At the end of the essay draft, complete this sentence for your partner: "The best part of this essay draft is . . ."

Writing Assignment: *Revising the Explaining Essay Draft*

1. Reread your essay draft and consider the comments of your partner.
2. Use the **Guidelines for Revision** (on the inside back cover of this textbook) to make changes to improve your draft.
3. Rewrite your essay.

EXERCISE 3-P Read three essays written by your classmates. Take notes about each. Which did you prefer? Why? Be prepared to state: "I liked X's essay because . . ."

Writing Assignment II

1. Complete the *Perceptual Learning Styles Preference Survey* (PSLSP) and the *Multiple Intelligences Survey* (MIS) in Appendix B (p. 328).
2. Write a 2 or 3 page (double-spaced, word-processed) Explaining essay that
    - includes a background paragraph that describes 1 or 2 of your strongest learning style(s) *or* your strongest intelligence(s).
    - supports your beliefs about your major learning style(s) *or* intelligence(s) by using detailed personal experiences from your previous educational situations.

Your audience for this essay is your classmates (and your instructor). Your purposes for this essay are (a) to inform your audience about your major learning style(s) *or* intelligence(s), and (b) to demonstrate those style(s)/intelligence(s) by using personal experiences from your prior schooling.

Evaluation Criteria for This Essay
[See Diagram of Five Paragraph Essay, p. 79]

- Use of appropriate academic organization and writing conventions.
- Use of content: detailed examples and personal detail
- Use of language:* minimal errors in grammar, sentence structure, vocabulary

Writing Assignment:

Drafting the Essay

Before Writing

- Follow the directions on each survey to determine your perceptual learning strengths and Multiple Intelligences. Read the information attached to each survey to learn more about perceptual learning styles and Multiple Intelligences.
- Take some notes about your results and about the survey information.
- With a small group of classmates, discuss your results and take notes:

    Were the results of this survey a surprise for you? Why or why not?
    Are some of the results more important for you than others? If so, which, and why?
    Do you agree with your results? Disagree? Why?
    Are your results similar to or different from your classmates' results?
    Which results are most interesting for you? for your classmates?
    Will the survey results change your study habits or writing habits? If so, in what ways?

- Think about your previous classroom learning experiences in elementary school, secondary school, and college/university: What were 1–3 very successful (and/or very unsuccessful) learning experiences? Make some notes about these memories.
- Use one or more pre-writing strategies (see Chapter 2) and begin to arrange and select information and to plan your essay.

During Writing

- Using the strategies you learned in this chapter, construct an essay map.
- Begin drafting your essay, using the information about introductions, body paragraphs, and conclusions that you studied in this chapter and the **Guidelines for Composing** (on the inside front cover of this textbook).
- In your personal experience paragraphs, try to

    create specific scenes for each experience so that your reader can "see" the situation.
    use a "voice" that will engage your audience.
    focus on a main idea so that the reader is not confused about the purpose.
    use specific details in your examples to engage the reader (i.e., show, do not just tell).

- Write a title for your essay.

After Writing

- Reread your draft, making changes as necessary.
- Find "other eyes" to read your draft and make suggestions. Use the **Peer Response Exercise** (p. 92).
- Use the **Guidelines for Revising** (on the inside back cover of this book) to improve your essay.

---

* Chapter 9 contains information and exercises about language problems and sentence structures.

My Learning Styles

[Question engages audience] *[Limited background information]* *[Thesis statement of opinion and intent]*

Are surveys a good way to learn about someone's learning style? The Perceptual Learning Style Preference Survey (Reid, 1984) is designed to demonstrate how one approaches learning. Before I took that survey, I did not believe that the results would be a very accurate representation of my preferences, but after I read more about learning styles, I began to realize that some of the results did parallel my preferences. *The survey results were quite accurate in describing me as a tactile (i.e., a "hands-on") learner, but I also feel that I am equally a visual learner.*

[Background paragraph] *[Definition]* *[Process description]* *[Direct quotation, in-text citation]*

The Perceptual Learning Style Preference Survey (PLSPS) divides learning into six areas; four of these are "perceptual" (i.e., learning through the senses of seeing, hearing, touching, and full-body experiences), and the last two contrast "individual" and "group" learning. After I completed the survey and added up my score, I found that, according to the PLSPS results, I am tactile learner. This means that I "benefit from doing projects, working with objects, and moving around the learning environment" (Reid, 1984, p. 4). Table 1 shows the results of the survey.

[Table]

Table 1 *Results from the Perceptual Learning Style Preference Questionnaire*

	Visual	Auditory	Kinesthetic	Tactile	Group	Individual
Scores:	32	30	36	44	40	18

Major Learning Style Preference	38–50
Minor Learning Style Preference	25–37
Negative Learning Style	12–24

[Topic sentence] *[Techniques of support: examples, personal experiences]*

I have always been good with my hands, which would explain why I scored so high on "hands-on" learning. When I was in elementary school, I always learned more when we played with objects or moved around the room, working at different stations. I remember when I was just starting school, my teacher would recite the alphabet to us. I would do fine that day, but the next day I would have trouble recalling it. Then we started using blocks with letters on them, and I really learned it. The same occurred when it came to adding and subtracting numbers: if I could use marbles or pennies or other objects to learn, it was easy.

[Topic sentence] *[Techniques of support: examples, personal experiences]* *[Concluding sentence]*

In high school, I also learned best when my hands were involved. For example, I had a class in Environmental Chemistry. When my teacher would lecture, I would not have a clue about what he was saying. After his lecture, though, we would break into groups and, for instance, put models of molecules together at our desks to see their make-up and how they connected with other molecules. My favorite classes were ones we spent in the laboratory when we put different molecules together to see what would happen. After doing such experiments, I could finally fully understand the ideas.

[Topic sentence] *[Techniques of support: examples, personal experiences]*

However, I believe that I am a visual learner as much as a tactile learner, despite the PLSPS, and I have the school experiences to prove it. In my senior high school English class, the teacher read us a short story, and we had a quiz on it the next day. I did not do well on the quiz. The next week we read *The Adventures of Huckleberry Finn* and then took a test on it, and the following week we watched a video of *A River Runs Through It*, and again took a test. I scored higher on both the book and the video. That same year, in my engineering class, we built a model. I discovered that if I watched somebody put an object together, I could build it myself without help. However, if someone just told me how to build it, I either forgot the steps or mixed up the procedure.

[Conclusion] For me, visual and tactile learning are interconnected. When I build models, conduct an experiment, or experience an idea, I get both visually and tactilely involved. I recall having to draw a plan for a woodshop class *[Concluding techniques: summary, prediction]* in high school; as I made the plan for a cabinet, I had to visualize every joint and how it would fit. Then, as I actually built the cabinet, I had no difficulty at all. Maybe my learning style preferences are part of the reason for my major, Mechanical Engineering, where I have to read and work with my hands.

Reference

Reid, J. (1984). The Perceptual Learning Styles Preference Survey.

***Matt Mickleson,* U. S.**

Writing a Memo

Another academic form of writing with strict writing conventions is the memo. In many major fields, especially in the sciences, technology, and business, students are required to write memos that, for example, report on the progress of a major project or evaluate the participation of group members in a collaborative project.

Memos are also a form of writing common to the workplace. That is, students will probably have many opportunities to write memos after they have completed their college/university work. In general, such memos report information, remind someone (e.g., about a meeting), or invite or thank someone in the workplace.

Like other writing, the memo has a conventional beginning, a middle, and an end. The memo is usually short (a single page or less), and it is usually polite but very direct. In the guidelines below, remarks about the form and content of the memo are in brackets [ ].

GUIDELINES for Memo Writing

1. The heading of the memo distinguishes it from an informal letter or an essay. In Figure 3-4 below, notice
   - the punctuation: a colon follows each introductory word.
   - the block form: the names of the writer and the reader, and the subject for the memo, all begin at the same place.
   - the titles of the writer and the reader are optional; if you use the title, you will use
     - a very short title (e.g., Mr., Ms., Dr.) *before* the name (e.g., Mr. James Smith; Dr. Thomas Valley)
     - a short title on the same line as the name, *after* the name, and separated by a comma (e.g., Director; President)
     - a longer title on the following line, without a comma (e.g., Coordinator, Management Team; Chair, Biology Department).
   - the personal signature of the writer.

Month Day, Year

[Optional title] TO: First Last (Title)

[Note signature] FROM: First Last (Title)

[RE = "about"] RE: Title/topic of the memo

Figure 3-4 *Diagram of the Heading of a Memo*

2. The heading of the memo is double spaced. Paragraphs in the memo are single spaced, but double spaced between paragraphs.
3. None of the paragraphs is indented. Figure 3-5 shows the format of a memo.

[Date] xxxxxxxxx

[Reader] xxxxxxxxxxxxxxxxxxxx

[Writer] xxxxxxxxxxxxxxxxxxxx

[Subject] xxxxxxxxxxxxxxxxxxxx

[No indentation] xxxxxxxxxxxxxxxxxxxxxxxxxxxxxxxxxxxxxxxxxxxxxxxxxxxxxxxx
[Single-spaced] xxxxxxxxxxxxxxxxxxxxxxxxxxxxxxxxxxxxxxxxxxxxxxxxxxxxxxxx
[Double-spaced
between paragraphs] xxxxxxxxxxxxxxxxxxxxxxxxxxxxxxxxxxxxxxxxxxxxxxxxxxxxxxxx
[No indentation] xxxxxxxxxxxxxxxxxxxxxxxxxxxxxxxxxxxxxxxxxxxxxxxxxxxxxxxx
Single-spaced] xxxxxxxxxxxxxxxxxxxxxxxxxxxxxxxxxxxxxxxxxxxxxxxxxxxxxxxx
xxxxxxxxxxxxxxxxxxxxxxxxxxxxxxxxxxxxxxxxxxxxxxxxxxxxxxxx

Figure 3-5 *Format of a Memo*

4. The first paragraph of the memo states the purpose of the memo; often that is the only sentence in the first paragraph.
5. The body of the memo is often a single paragraph, and rarely more than two paragraphs. It contains the message: the purpose of the memo. It is the longest part of the memo.
6. The conclusion of the memo is also very short, usually 1 or 2 lines. Usually it restates the purpose of the memo, *or* gives the necessary information if the memo writer expects a response to the memo, *or* gives a simple farewell.
7. There is no closing or signature at the end of the memo.

[Date] October 26, 1997

[Reader] TO: Dr. Reid

[Writer] FROM: Geneé Arthur *Genée Arthur*

[Subject of the memo] RE: What I learned from writing my Explaining essay

[No indentation] [Purpose of the memo] [Single-spaced] The most important learning experiences I had were (a) how to narrow a subject to a topic so that a real audience can enjoy reading about it and (b) how not to be afraid to give too much detail.

[Topic sentence] [Body of the memo] [Single-spaced] [Explanation of the purpose of the memo] The most difficult part of my essay was narrowing my topic. I solved that problem by discussing it with a small group of classmates and picking a "piece of the pie" that I was interested in most. Because everyone in my group was writing about the same topic, we could talk about many "pieces of the pie," and we gave each other advice. Before I wrote this explaining essay, I had always thought that it was easier to write about the "whole pie," but when I started to collect information about pet therapy, I realized that my audience would be much more interested in the specific examples of disabled college students using pets for independent living than to read all of the general statements about all kinds of pet therapy.

[Topic sentence] [Techniques of support: examples, personal experience] [Details] I also learned from my group about how important detail is for the audience. We all seemed to know the general ideas: how pets are used in hospitals with sick children, how the elderly depend on pets for companionship, and how disabled people need pets. But when I listened to my classmates give examples about specific people and specific pets, I realized how much more interesting those "stories" were. So when I collected my information, I looked especially for individual examples, and I added them to my paragraphs. My favorite paragraph in my essay is the one about how Robert, the college student who was paralyzed in a diving accident, taught his dog Bear to bring him a beer from the refrigerator. For me, and for my audience, that example made Robert suddenly became a college student instead of a disabled person.

[Concluding paragraph] These writing experiences will make my next essay easier: I'll remember to narrow, to write about what interests me, and to use lots of detail!

[NOT part of memo] **Geneé Arthur, U.S.**

23 STUDENT SAMPLE

February 21, 1998

TO: Dr. Reid

FROM: Herlina Rambé *Herlina Rambé*

RE: My most effective pre-writing strategies

I have experimented with six collecting strategies. The two which are most effective for me are brainstorming and double-entry notes.

[Topic sentence] Brainstorming is my best strategy. I sit at my computer, and I write anything that flows into my mind. I do not think about making mistakes, and without that pressure, I remember more ideas. Information just comes to me. After I write everything, I read it, and I find the best ideas for my essays.

[Topic sentence] I also like double-entry notes because that pre-writing strategy shows me the difference between my thoughts and my feelings. For example, when I used it for my explaining paper, I could see how my emotions sometimes interfered with my interpretation of the nonverbal language of Americans. That helped me write my paragraph about how uncomfortable I felt when an American student stood too close to me. My mistake was not knowing that, for her, it was a comfortable distance.

[Conclusion] Before I took this course I did not practice collecting strategies, but I have discovered that these two work very well for me.

[NOT part of memo] ***Herlina Rambe,*** **Indonesia**

EXERCISE 3-Q

1. With a partner or in a small group, compare and contrast the two memos above with Matt Mickleson's learning style student essay (Student Sample 21). Consider
   - audience
   - purpose
   - the writing conventions of the memo and the essay
   - the function of each part of the memo and the essay
2. With your classmates, discuss times in your future when you might need to write a memo. What would the purpose of the memo be? Who would the audience be?

Writing Assignment III

Write a memo to your instructor that describes what you learned about academic writing from studying the material in this chapter and from writing your Explaining essay. Use the **Guidelines for Memo Writing** (p. 95) to write in a conventional memo form.

EXERCISE 3-R

1. Exchange memos with a partner.
2. As you read your partner's memo, use the **Guidelines for Memo Writing** to see whether or not your partner has followed the writing conventions for memos.
3. Discuss your findings with your partner, and listen to your partner's comments.
4. Share your memos with another pair of partners and discuss what you have learned about academic writing.
5. Reread your memo and think about how to improve it.
6. Rewrite your memo and turn it in to your instructor.

Chapter 4

Introduction to Academic Research: The Investigating Report

Oh, No! Interview!

I had never even thought about conducting an interview; I didn't know how to prepare to do so, and I was afraid—what if the person I interviewed disliked my questions? But I told myself, "You must have the courage to try." My first interview, with Professor Lee at Providence College, was not perfect. Still, I was excited about his work with cross-pollinating orchids (he owns more than two thousand pots of various orchids!), and he was courteous and full of information. After that positive experience, I prepared for and then carried out my next interview with more self-confidence because I knew that most authorities were happy to talk about their work.

Nora Huang, **Taiwan, Republic of China (ROC)**

MANY ACADEMIC WRITING assignments require students to consult sources outside of their own knowledge as they complete their papers. Therefore, as writers plan and draft their essays, they also gather information. They investigate, like detectives, the sources available to them about their topics. When students begin their search for sources, their investigations may include:

- locating information in books and other published sources (e.g., magazines/journals, maps, videotapes)
- searching for information on the World Wide Web (WWW)
- asking the opinions of others through student-made surveys
- interviewing authorities on the topic
- remembering and reflecting on past knowledge and experiences.

In this chapter, students will investigate a question that interests them, draft and revise a report that provides an answer to the question, and learn how to cite the references in the report.

Writing Assignment 1

Choose one of the investigating questions below. (Or choose another question from your authority list and narrow it to a topic question.) Write a 3 or 4 page report (double-spaced and word-processed) that answers your chosen question. Remember to use a separate page for end-of-text references.

For this report, you will:

- construct and use material from an interview with an authority,
- locate (or design) and use 1 or 2 nontext materials in your essay, and
- include 1–3 direct quotations or ideas from other authors, with appropriate in-text citations.

The first group of questions below, which asks the question *how*, calls for process analysis. The second group asks the question *what*, and calls for the investigation of a subject. The third group asks the question *why*, and focuses on causal (i.e., cause and/or effect) analysis. Some of these questions have already been narrowed to a topic for an audience of your classmates and your instructor; others will need to be narrowed.

Investigating Topics

Process Analysis

1. How does hoar frost form?
2. How do people from different cultures begin telephone conversations?
3. How do water towers work?
4. How does a Zamboni work?
5. How can you minimize jet lag?
6. How can aspirin prevent heart attacks?

Subject Analysis

7. What does a cybersnoop do? Why?
8. What is biometrics, and what does it do?
9. What is *Krahv Maga?*
10. What is an oxygen candle?
11. What are the disadvantages of artificial turf?
12. What is one new way to repair an ACL?

Causal Analysis

13. What are the cause(s) and effect(s) of road rage?
14. Why is vomit sometimes green?
15. Why do starlings have wishbones?
16. Why do flowers have a scent?
17. What caused Gulf War Syndrome?
18. Why can't we tickle ourselves successfully?

EXERCISE 4-A With a small group of classmates, discuss the topics that your classmates chose on page 100, and listen to their questions about the topics. (If you plan to choose a question from your own authority list for this assignment, introduce that question into the discussion.) Consider the **Guidelines for Audience Analysis** (p. 72).

Then select a topic for your report. Based on your small group work, write a general and a more specific statement of purpose (see p. 8) for your Investigating report.

Using Sources for Research

Student researchers may develop information they generate themselves, using previous knowledge about the topic they are investigating. They may do experiments from which they collect data—individual pieces of information (*datum* is the singular of *data*)—or interpret observations. Or they may use information gathered from surveys they design and administer and/or from interviews they conduct with authorities about their topics.

Although personal experience and observation alone are not usually sufficient evidence to present and support material for an academic audience, some academic writing assignments, such as the two below, require only the writer's experience.

I **Adult Education**
Identify something you want to learn this semester. Plan in writing how you will learn this new thing; keep a diary as you go about the process of learning, and include insights about the nature of learning in general as well as specific thoughts regarding your own learning. As you encounter problems in learning, write about the solutions you sought. At the end of the semester, write an evaluative statement that summarizes and analyzes how you believe you learn best.

II **Introduction to Sociology**
Write an autobiographical paper, 6-10 pages long, in which you (a) describe and explain the type of community where you spent your early life, (b) analyze the relationships between families in your neighborhood, (c) discuss problems that you encountered in your relationships with playmates in your neighborhood, and (d) evaluate how your life and your family's life were influenced by these various patterns of relationships.

Usually, however, academic assignments that ask for personal experience or observation also require other forms of support. For example, in the authentic biology assignment below, students are required to (a) observe and collect data, and (b) report those observed data.

Undergraduate Genetics Report
Purpose: This laboratory exercise and the subsequent report are designed to permit you to compare actual data obtained from the class, and a data sample of your own, with theoretical values obtained from the development of Punnett squares.
Procedure: A data collection sheet will be passed around to each laboratory group. You should answer each question (e.g., your blood type, do you possess a widow's peak, or dimples, attached or free ear lobes, etc.). You will also be given an individual collection sheet. At the bottom of the sheet is an area regarding color perception. Following your instructor's directions, complete this section. Tear it at the broken line and turn it in before the end of the period. All of the data for the class will be pooled and distributed in the next laboratory period.

Before the next period, obtain an independent sample of your own from about 35 persons other than members of the class—for example, your dormitory group, a club, or just the first 35 persons you encounter on the campus. Select any two traits from the data collection sheet (additional traits are not necessary).

Note: Retain your tally sheet and include it as an appendix with your report.

Report: The report should include the following sections:

A. Introduction: the purpose of the study
B. Material and methods—how were the data obtained?
C. Observations—the actual data
D. Discussion—develop Punnett squares for each of the following, and include each in your report: a dihybrid cross, a sex-linked trait, and a multiple-allele system.

EXERCISE 4-B

1. Discuss the genetics assignment above. Who is the audience for the report? What is the purpose of the report?
2. Discuss the ways in which the overall organization for the report is similar to the essay(s) you wrote in the previous chapter.
3. In what ways is the overall organization of the genetics report different from the essay(s) you wrote in the previous chapter? In what way(s) does it resemble a memo?
4. With a partner, collect data about two of the genetic markers listed in the Procedure section of the genetics assignment (i.e., blood type, widow's peak, dimples, characteristics of ear lobes) from 10 students not in your class. Then arrange these data for an audience by making a chart.

SURVEYS AND INTERVIEWS

Research Tools

Surveys and interviews are two other methods of research. **Surveys** are documents that ask a group of people (called "respondents") to complete a series of questions or statements about the topic. **Interviews** are meetings between a researcher and an expert about the topic during which the researcher questions the expert. In this chapter, you will learn about interviews.

The major differences between surveys and interviews are shown in Figure 4-1.

	Surveys*	Interviews
Purpose:	to gather information from a typical audience about the topic	to gather information about the topic from an authority
Respondents:	people chosen at random	authority about the topic
Design:	written statements or questions designed with possible answers on the document	written questions designed to be answered by the interviewee
	given to many respondents	asked of a single person
	respondents answer the survey alone and return to the designer, usually by mail	interviewee answers directly (face-to-face, on the telephone, by mail or by e-mail)

Figure 4-1 *Differences Between Surveys and Interviews*

Writing Assignment

Pre-Writing Strategies for the Research Report

Experiment with two pre-writing strategies that you rarely (or never) use to begin to collect information and to plan your Investigating report. Use the **Guidelines for Composing** on the inside front cover of this textbook to begin planning your essay.

* See Chapter 7, "Evaluating in Academic Writing," for additional information on designing surveys.

Organization of the Research Report

Most academic reports have the same overall organization as the five-paragraph essay.

- Introduction that ends with a thesis statement
- Background paragraph that defines terms, gives history, describes processes
- Body paragraphs, each with a topic sentence and supporting detail
- Conclusion with a summary, recommendation, predication, and/or solution.

The Investigating report in this chapter will follow that overall organizational plan.

Using the World Wide Web [WWW]

One of the first questions the student investigator asks is "What?" For instance, for the Investigating essay, students may need to define the topic by asking *What is biometrics? What are endorphins? What is a Zamboni? What is a wind tunnel?*

To find the answer, students can consult reference works in the library: a general encyclopedia like the *Encyclopedia Americana*, or a more field-specific encyclopedia such as the *Encyclopedia of Thermodynamics*. Or the student may find consulting a general dictionary or a field-specific dictionary more efficient. A reference librarian can direct students to these basic reference materials.

For this Investigating report, however, the most efficient and valuable resource will probably be the World Wide Web (WWW). The Web is so named because it is a collection of documents on the Internet that are "networked" (i.e., "webbed," like a spider's web). The user can "visit" any Website and "travel" from one Website to another all over the world. For example, Websites available on the Internet allow students to access libraries around the world, connect with an enormous number of databases, and visit a nearly infinite number of Webpages about millions of topics.

Note: Many WWW addresses, called Universal Resource Locators (URLs), begin the same way: **http://www.** Individual Website addresses come after the general web address:

http://www.zdnet.com/familypc/sb.html

Remember that URLs recognize both capital and lower-case letters, so be sure to type the address with the correct capitals and lower-case letters.

INTRODUCTION TO THE WEB

The process of "logging on" to the WWW depends on the available computer, the software, and telephone access. A reference librarian or the college/university technology center will provide necessary information.

To help locate information on the Web, software programs called *Web browsers* have been developed. By following the on-screen directions of a browser, students can learn to "surf" (i.e., "browse" or investigate) many Websites easily. **Netscape Navigator** and **Microsoft Internet Explorer** are two major browsers on the WWW; the computer used to access the WWW will incorporate one of these browsers.*

One note of caution: even with the help of a Web browser, using the Web can be time-consuming and irritating, especially if student researchers approach work on the Web without adequate preparation and an understanding of the limits of Web information. That is, students who log on to the Web and visit site after site may find the "surfing" approach interesting but unsuccessful and inefficient. Often they will end a long session feeling frustrated and unhappy. Without appropriate search strategies, they may believe that the Web is not a worthwhile resource.

* I am grateful to Jamie Hayes Neufeld for her WWW expertise that helped me write this section.

Instead, students should plan their Web search processes. Most Web browsers feature a "Search" button that gives the user access to several **search engines.** A search engine is like the Yellow Pages or telephone book. For example, Netscape's "Search" button calls up the Netscape search page, which lists eight search engines (Figure 4-2).

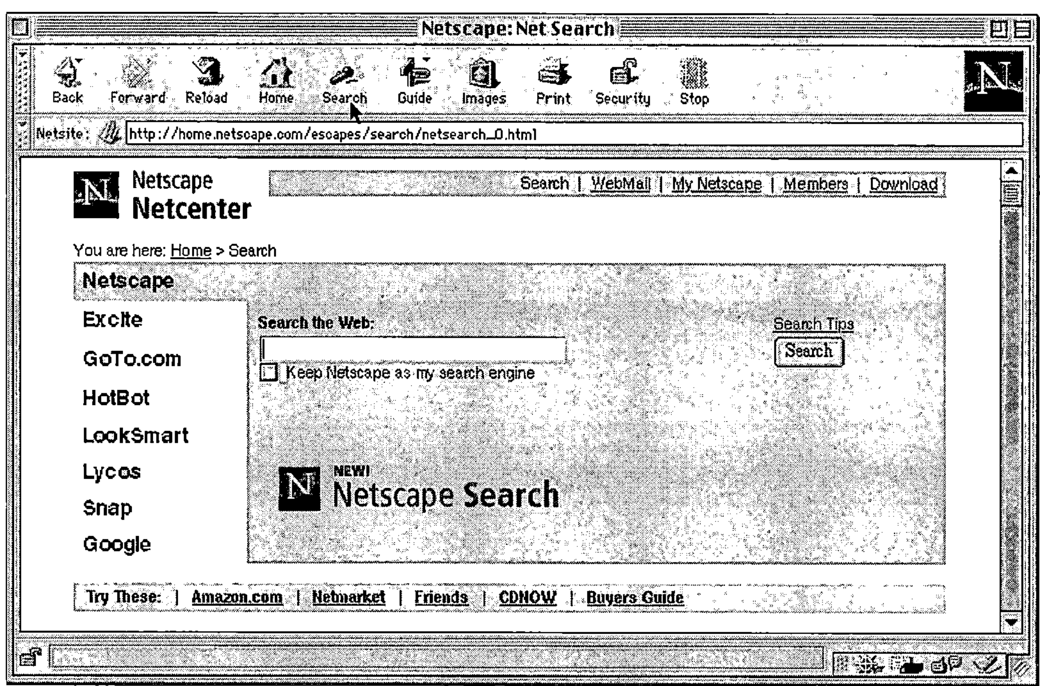

Figure 4-2 *Navigator Displaying Netscape NetCenter Search Page*

In Figure 4-2, the search engines are listed at the left of the screen; clicking on one of these search engines will access it.* Each of these search engines has a "Help" heading at the top of the page, the bottom, or both, that allows you to click and discover (a) the specific ways the engine functions, (b) how to use the engine, and (c) hints for efficient use of the engine. (Note the two "Help" headings in Figure 4-3 on the next page.)

There are two types of search engines. The first, a Web index, is like a library catalog; it indexes all Internet sites. The second is a Web directory; it organizes information into categories and subcategories. (Some search engines are both.) Examples of search engines that can be used to search efficiently and effectively for information about any topic include these:

AltaVista **http://www.altavista.com**
a powerful Web index that is most useful if you know your precise topic and can therefore take advantage of its "Advanced" search screen

Excite! **http://www.excite**
a search engine that uses a Web index keyword search strategy (preferred by some librarians for undergraduates)

Infoseek **http://www.infoseek.com**
a search engine index that is most useful for searching companies, newsgroups, Websites, or news sites

* **Note:** Web pages are updated frequently, so users who access the sites shown here may find differences in format and content between the live site and these images. However, the principles of Web use still apply.

Lycos **http://.lycos.cs.cmu.edu**
a Web index that lists only the top 20 "hits" (i.e., those materials that are most closely related to the keywords) of any search; offers refining devices similar to AltaVista

Metacrawler **http://www.metacrawler.com**
a meta-search engine that simultaneously searches numerous search engines; use for comprehensive research.

Yahoo! **http://www.yahoo.com**
a user-friendly Web directory that provides 14 basic categories to start the search, such as Arts, Business, Science, and Social Science

Another group of useful search programs is called "expert guides." These search engines are more personalized than Excite! or AltaVista. That is, they have human "specialists," people who gather information about topics and summarize that information for users. In some cases, the experts are available online to answer questions. Four of these expert guide websites are:

About	**http://www.about.com**	**Snap**	**http://www.snap.com**
Jump	**http://www.jump.com**	**When**	**http://www.when.com**

DEVELOPING KEYWORDS

When a student selects a search engine, a slot will appear on the screen that allows the student to enter keywords (also called "descriptors"), words that identify and/or describe the topic. Figure 4.3 shows an introductory AltaVista computer screen. Notice

- the general categories in the Directory beneath the title *AltaVista*; click on one of these to begin a general search.
- the Search field (the white rectangle next to the Search button) where keywords can be typed to focus the search.

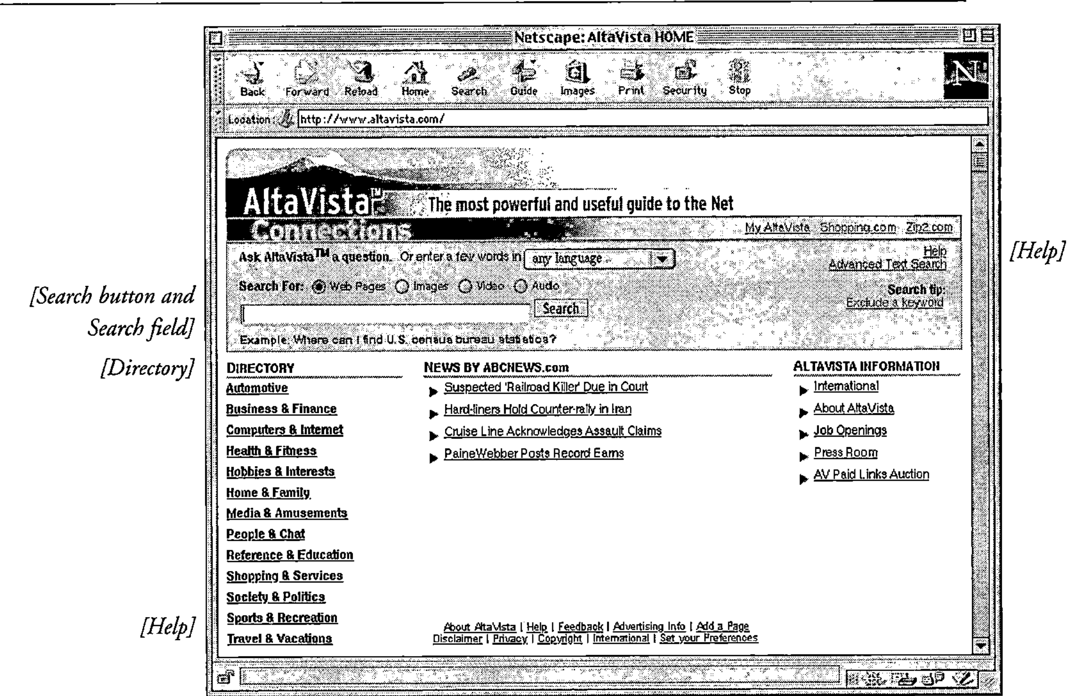

Figure 4-3 *AltaVista Search Engine*

Most students beginning research will choose three to six keywords that describe their specific topic. Effective strategies for selecting keywords include these:

- Use nouns whenever possible: *airbags children injury death*
- Put the most important words first: *Japan censorship movies films books*
- Put a plus sign ("+") before crucial words to find only sites that include every one of the crucial words: *+cost +advertisements +television +minute*
- Put a minus sign ("–") before a word to exclude sites in which that word appears: *+scent +fragrance +flowers +insects –animals +nasturtium*
- Use phrases in quotation marks instead of single words: *"Hong Kong" +"tourist shopping" +entertainment +restaurants +discos*
- Put quotation marks around the phrases: *"road rage" +causes*

Other strategies for effectively searching the WWW include these:

- Become an expert on one search engine by reading the "Help" files.
- Always recheck spelling of keywords and URLs.
- Learn to refine (i.e., narrow further) the results of a topic search.
- Be patient and flexible; search engines are not perfect.
- Understand that the WWW does not contain all knowledge.

The result of selecting careful keywords is usually a list of documents on the WWW about the topic, and the **URLs** (**U**niversal **R**esource **L**ocators, i.e., the Web addresses) of those WWW sites. Clicking on any document title will access the information. If the list is too long, adding descriptors (keywords) will further focus the search; if the list is too short, eliminate one of the keywords. Figure 4-4 shows the result of a student's search for information on the Excite! search engine about Web soap operas (daytime U.S. TV dramas). When the student clicked on the first entry in the *Directory* (Games: Online Games: Web Serials), she found URLs to Web-based soap operas.

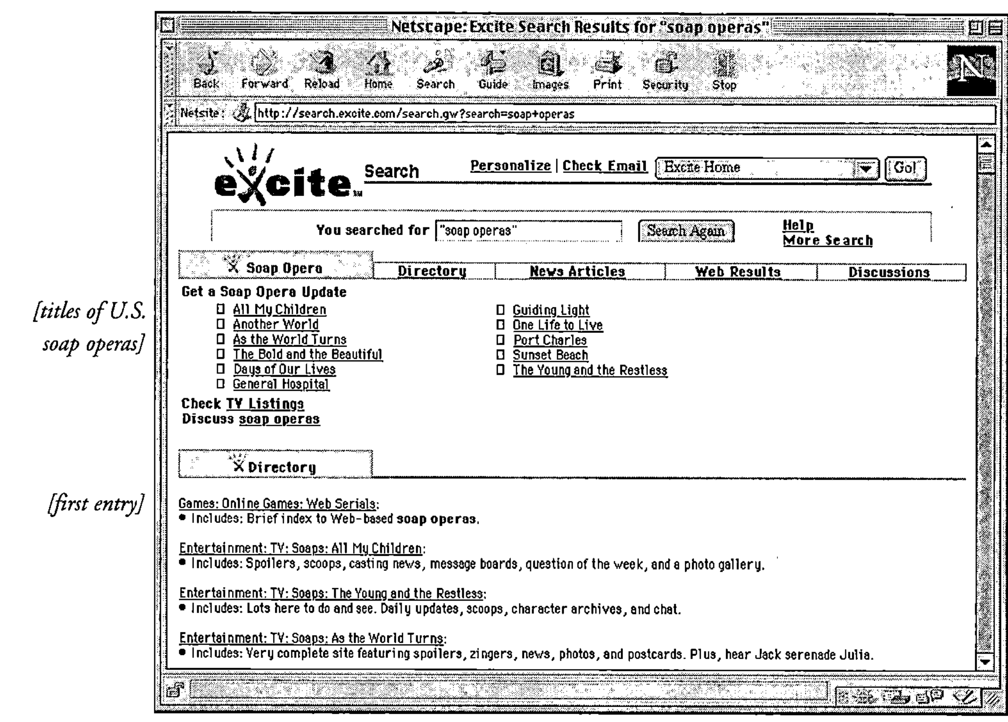

Figure 4-4 *Search Results for "Soap Operas"*

SEARCHING THE WEB WITH URLS

Students may choose to "bookmark" several WWW addresses (i.e., URLs) that are useful for academic writing, or to memorize them for easy access to those Websites from the WWW Home Page. Figure 4-5 lists four important WWW URLs.

http://www.elibrary.com
The Electronic Library offers access to articles on popular topics that writers can usually print out from the computer. If students access this site from a college or university library, there will be no cost.

http://www.w3.org.pub.DataSources.bySubject/Overview.html
The WWW Virtual Library: one of the best investigating sites on the Web; free to users.

http://www.nytimes.com
Users must first register, but then they can access the current newspaper or do a keyword search of relevant articles by then accessing **http://www.com/search/daily**

http://www.amazon.com
A virtual bookstore from which student writers with credit cards can order almost any book.

Figure 4-5 *Website Addresses (URLs)*

EXERCISE 4-C

1. With a partner or in a small group, use the strategies on page 106 for developing effective keywords for each the following topics:
   - According to birth order theory, what are the personality characteristics of first-born children?
   - Why do birds have wishbones?
   - In what ways can foot reflexology enhance health?
   - Why do cowboys wear hats?
   - How dangerous are housecats who are allowed to hunt prey outside?
2. Discuss keywords that you and your partner/group might use in an effective WWW search of your report topics.
3. With a partner, or individually, access the WWW and look at three of the following sites. Remember, WWW addresses (URLs) sometimes change, and sites sometimes disappear. If one of the URLs does not connect, choose another URL.

   http://eslcafe.com/
   http://www.longman-elt.com/dictionaries/home.html
   http://www1.bluemountain.com/
   http://deil.lang.uiuc.edu/web.pages.grammarsafari.html
   http://www.latrobe.edu.au/www/education/sl/sl.html
   http://postcards.www.media.mit.edu/Postcards
   http://www.comenius.com/idioms/
   http://www.aec.ukans.edu/LEO/holidays/holidays.html
   http://urbanlegends.miningco.com/library//weekly/aa090998.htm
   http://www.nmis.org/NewsInteractive/CNN/Newsroom
   http://www.fau.edu/rinaldi/net/elec.html
   http://www.mapsonus.com
   http://www.ohayosensei.com
   http://www.osha-slc.gov/SLTC/ergonomics/
   http://www.amazon.com
   http://www.geocities.com

http://owl.English.purdue.edu
http://eslcafe.com/slang/
http://www.usatoday.sports.com

4. Write a memo to your instructor that describes one of the sites you accessed. To review memo format, see Chapter 3, page 95.

CITING WWW MATERIAL

Chapter 3 discussed in-text citation and end-of-text citation and their appropriate forms. The reasons to use citations are (a) to give credit to the author, (b) to demonstrate to your instructor that you have researched the topic, and (c) to provide the audience with enough information to find that source. Remember that **student writers should cite a source for any information they did not know before they began their research.**

For WWW material, the in-text citation remains the same: (Last, year). For end-of-text citation, a separate reference page at the end of the paper will list complete end-of-text citations alphabetically by the author's last name. The form for WWW references is:

Last, F. (Year, Month, Day of Publication or Placement of the Materials on the WWW). *Title of document.* [Type of document described]. Retrieved [Month, Day, Year you accessed the material on the World Wide Web]: complete URL

Note: For sample citations and guidelines to using and writing citations, see Appendix A.

Writing Assignment:

Searching the WWW for the Investigating Report

Begin the research for your Investigating report on the WWW. Use one of the search engines listed above. As you locate and print relevant materials from the Web, be sure that you have complete information for your in-text and end-of-text citations (e.g., author, title, length, date, and URL).

1. In addition, take notes about your learning experiences:

   What was easy and what was difficult?
   What problem(s) did you encounter, and how did you solve the problem(s)?
   What have you learned about your Investigating topic? about the WWW?

2. Share your learning experiences with the class.

Using Nontext Materials in Academic Writing

Although most academic writing is primarily text, nontext materials are often an integral part of academic writing assignments, particularly in science, technology, and business. Some technical documents may be entirely nontext, such as the instructions for evacuating an airplane that you find in the seat pocket in front of your airline seat and the red NO SMOKING sign. Writers use nontext materials to show:

	Examples	**See page**
• how the whole relates to its parts	a pie chart	11, 122
• how something is organized	a flow chart	36, 79
• what something looks like	a photograph or drawing	41
• how something works	a diagram	58
• how things are related to each other	a graph or table	74

* Because the Internet is still relatively new, WWW reference formats continue to be modified. Visit this "APA Style" site for the most up-to-date changes: http://www.bk.psu.edu/academic/library/APAStyle.html

EXERCISE 4-D With a partner or in a small group, look at the nontext examples listed above. Discuss the way(s) in which each is an effective use of nontext materials. Which use of nontext materials do you think is most effective? Why?

SELECTING NONTEXT MATERIALS

The most important considerations in choosing and using nontext materials are audience and purpose. Writers use nontext materials to communicate ideas clearly. They select or design these materials for specific purposes: to simplify, to describe, to demonstrate.

GUIDELINES

for Using Nontext Materials

- Use visuals to emphasize and/or condense information, to clarify abstract concepts, and to depict relationships.
- The visual should be able to stand alone; it should contain everything the reader needs to interpret it correctly, including a title.
- Place the visual where it will best serve the audience (i.e., not in a clump at the end of the text, not hidden in an appendix).
- Try to fit the visual on one page.
- Never crowd a visual into a cramped space; use white space for balance.
- Introduce the visual with words just before it appears in the text.

  Table 1 depicts . . . *Table 4 displays . . .*

- Summarize, explain, and/or interpret the visual just after it appears in the text.

  Figure 4 demonstrates that . . .
  As Table 1 shows, the total cost for renovation . . .
  The photograph in Figure 3 illustrates . . .

- Keep visuals simple and focused; exclude irrelevant or excessive information.
- Number the tables and figures separately, in order of appearance.
- Locate the titles in the same place throughout. Tables are always labeled at the top; figures are usually (but not always) labeled at the bottom.

EXERCISE 4-E Look at the chart you constructed for the genetics assignment at the beginning of this chapter. How could you improve that chart for the instructor of the genetics class?

CITING NONTEXT MATERIALS

Writers who photocopy and use visuals—a chart, a table, a diagram, or another form of nontext material—must cite the source of that material immediately following the title of the visual *and* on the separate Reference page that follows the paper. The in-text citation must include the page number where the visual is located in its original source.*

The introductory and background paragraphs below illustrate effective use of nontext materials.

It's the Wave of the Future!

[Introductory statement] The wave of the future in alternative medicine has been used in the U.S. since 1913 (Hall, 1997). The technique is known as reflexology, *[Background information]* the hands-on application of pressure to points in the hands and feet. *[Thesis]* *This paper describes the use of reflexology points on the hand that can reduce stress and bring better health to many parts of the body.*

[Topic sentence] Hand reflexology has a long history, and ancient practitioners left detailed charts. These charts instruct us today by providing the exact pressure points in the hands and what body organs of the body they affect. For *[Introduction to Figure]* example, Figure __ shows the pressure points on the backs of the hands.

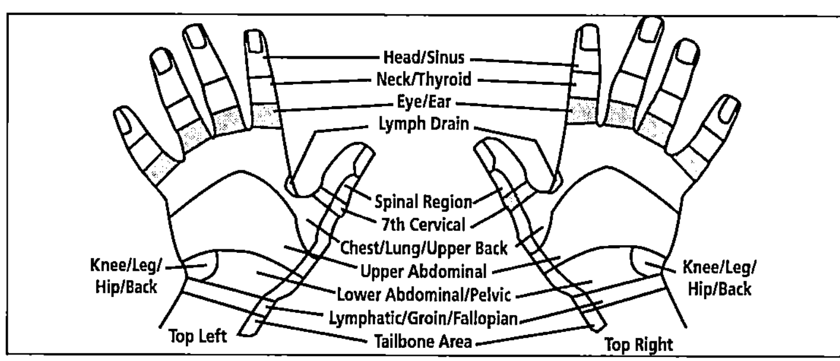

[Figure label, title, reference] Figure __ *Reflexology Points on the Backs of the Hands*
(from Rick, 1986, p. 6)

[Explanation, interpretation of the figure] Notice that the pressure points for the knee and leg, hip and back, are at the base of both hands on the outside. Other parts of the body that respond to pressure points, from the head and sinuses to the eyes and ears, are labeled.

References

[Listed alphabetically by last name] Hall, N. (1997). *Reflexology: A step-by-step guide* ("In a Nutshell" series). Monterey, CA: Element Books Limited.

Rick, S. (1986). *The reflexology workout: Hand and food massage for superhealing*. New York: Crown.

***Antwan Floyd*, U. S.**

Study the examples of nontext materials below and then do the following exercise.

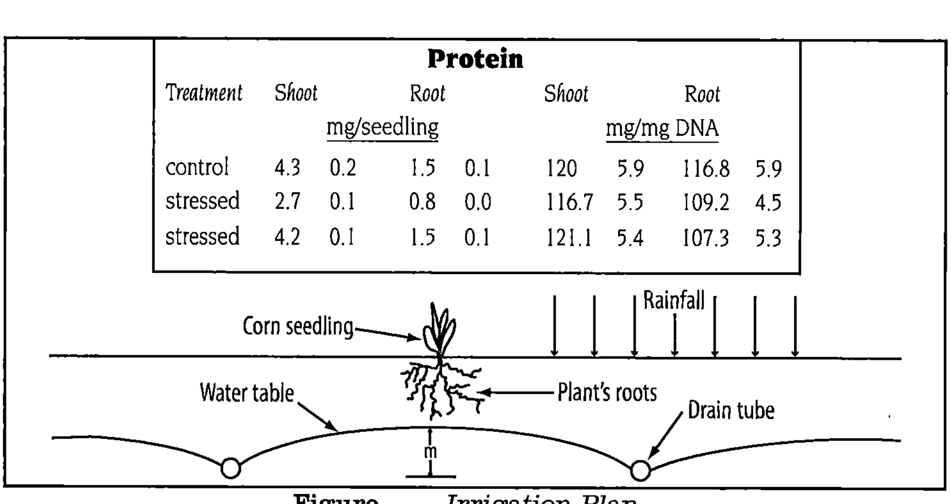

Protein

Treatment	Shoot		Root		Shoot		Root	
	mg/seedling				mg/mg DNA			
control	4.3	0.2	1.5	0.1	120	5.9	116.8	5.9
stressed	2.7	0.1	0.8	0.0	116.7	5.5	109.2	4.5
stressed	4.2	0.1	1.5	0.1	121.1	5.4	107.3	5.3

Figure __ *Irrigation Plan*

***Bianu Landu-Kalemba*, Zaire**

Table __ *Time Line for Implementation*

Date of Purchase	Learning the Scanner	Implementing the Scanner	Training Employees
	↓	↓	↓
Starting Date	Two weeks	One week	One day

***Lynne Stonemark,* U. S.**

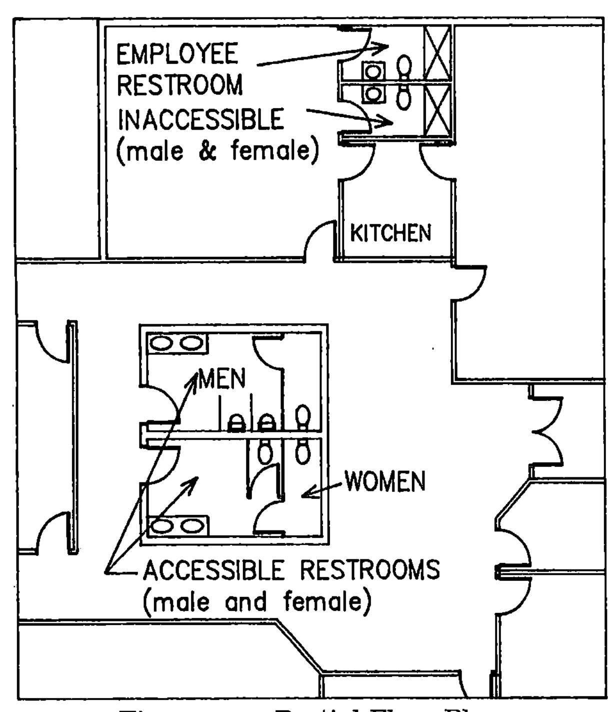

Figure __ *Partial Floor Plan:*
Existing Design of Handicap Accessible Restrooms

***Stephen Roitsch,* U. S.**

EXERCISE 4-F

1. Evaluate each of the nontext materials above according to the **Guidelines for Using Nontext Materials**.
2. For each of the nontext examples, assess the following:
   - Who is the audience?
   - What is the purpose? Suggestion: Read the title.
   - The clarity of the materials: is each comprehensible without text to explain it? What questions do you have about the materials?
   - The effectiveness of the material presented: how could the writer improve the way the nontext material "looks"?
   - The ease of identifying each of the materials: could the title be improved? How?

3. With a partner, write an introductory sentence for each of the nontext materials. Then write 1 or 2 sentences that explain and/or interpret one of the nontext materials.
4. In your opinion, which of the student samples is most effective? Why? Discuss your preference with your classmates.

EXERCISE 4-G

1. Select 3 examples of nontext materials that you might use in your Investigating essay:

   material from the WWW
   photocopy from books of journals
   your own art or graphic
   other sources

2. Be sure to note the essential information for the in-text and end-of-text citations.
3. Share your examples with a small group of classmates, and discuss the writing conventions you will use for each example.
4. With your group, use the **Guidelines for Using Nontext Materials** (p. 109) to evaluate your nontext materials and to make suggestions to help your classmates use their nontext materials.

Writing Assignment:
Beginning to Draft the Investigating Paper

Begin drafting your Investigating report. Consult the **Guidelines for Composing** (on the inside front cover of this book) as you draft your 5-paragraph report. Include the nontext materials you have chosen, and remember to write an introduction to the nontext materials and your interpretation of those materials.

Interviewing an Authority

Finding and interviewing authoritative sources about a topic can be a satisfying and beneficial experience. Authorities can be located through the campus or the city telephone directory, through friends and colleagues, and through the Internet.

PREPARING FOR THE INTERVIEW

Careful planning is the key to successful interviewing. Avoid these interview problems:

- Inadequate planning: asking spontaneous questions wastes the valuable time of the authority and often prevents the interviewer from getting essential information.
- Asking basic questions: asking questions that are easily answered in encyclopedias or field-specific dictionaries wastes the authority's time.
- Spending too long with the authority: more than 20 minutes imposes on the good will of the authority.

Prepare for an effective interview with an authority by writing thoughtfully constructed questions that are easy to understand and will result in the needed information. Then construct even more specific questions to ask after a major question. For example, after asking a question about insects and nasturtiums, *follow up* by asking "Specifically, which insects hate the smell of nasturtiums?" and/or "How can gardeners use nasturtiums to prevent those insects from destroying garden vegetables?" and/or "Are there other flower smells that those insects hate besides nasturtiums?"

GUIDELINES
for Interviews

- Consider your topic, your purpose, and your audience.
- Do initial research to answer basic questions about your topic.
- Plan your questions according to the expertise of your authority.
- Plan questions that can give you the best information in 20 minutes or less.
- Keep your questions free of your own biases or opinions (but do ask the authority for his/her opinions if they are relevant to your topic).
- Follow some of your major questions with possible follow-up questions for more specific detail.
- Immediately clarify any points you are not certain about.
- Conclude the interview by asking the authority for additional information or sources that s/he can recommend about your topic.

CONDUCTING THE INTERVIEW

Arrange a face-to-face interview, or interview the authority by telephone or by e-mail. Make an appointment for 15 to 20 minutes; if the interview will be face-to-face, ask to audiotape the interview and/or (b) to bring a friend to help take notes.

Arrive a few minutes early for a face-to-face interview, or telephone exactly on time for a telephone interview. Begin the interview with "warm-up" questions to provide background information (e.g., "How did you decide to become a botanist?" "When did you become especially interested in flowers?"). To clarify a point, ask about it immediately; people who are interviewed want the facts to be accurate.

> *Did you say that . . .?*
> *I'm sorry. I didn't quite understand. Could you repeat your answer, please?*
> *Am I correct in thinking that you agree with X about . . . ?*

Note: Arrange and conduct an **e-mail interview** similarly. Send clear, error-free questions to the authority, and write the authority again for needed clarification.

EXERCISE 4-H

Below are interview and follow-up questions asked by a student who interviewed an authority to answer the question "Why do cowboys wear cowboy hats?" Read the interview questions and the follow-up questions. Then answer the questions that follow.

Authority: Chris Jenkins, a middle-aged rancher and cowboy

- How long have you considered yourself a cowboy? Follow-up: How do you define "cowboy"?
- When did you first begin wearing a cowboy hat? Follow-up: Why?
- Do you think your purposes for wearing cowboy hats has changed over the last 25 years? Follow-up: In what ways?
- How many different styles of cowboy hats do you wear? Follow-up: How are they different from one another?
- Do you know of any other styles of cowboy hats that other cowboys wear? Follow-up: Why don't you wear those?
- Do you think you'll ever stop wearing a cowboy hat? Follow-up: Why? OR Why not?

***Garry Gottfredson,* U. S.**

1. What *basic* questions about cowboy hats did Garry *not* ask the authority?
2. How could Garry use the answers to the first two questions to show the reader that this authority is credible (i.e., believable)?
3. How did the follow-up questions help Garry collect more and better information?
4. What nontext materials could Garry include in his essay that would interest his audience?

The interview sample below was arranged by a student writing a business letter on e-mail. The authority lived in another state, and the student did not know her. Notice that the questions Melissa asked are those she could not find in other sources. That is, the expert provided valuable personal and professional information and opinions not available in books or on Websites.

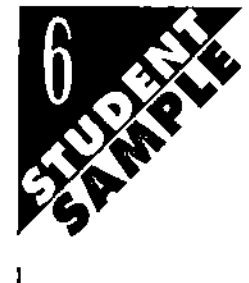

Myra S. Achorn
myra@ime.net

Dear Ms. Achorn:

I am writing you today to ask a favor. I am a freshman attending the University of Wyoming in Laramie, Wyoming. I was asked to write a paper explaining a topic, and I chose foot reflexology as my topic. My roommate, Gillian Findlay, is from Kansas City, and her mother suggested that I write you for information about that topic.

If you have time, would you please answer several questions about your profession? I have written the set of questions below. I would greatly appreciate your help and your expertise.

You can send the reply back to my e-mail: lissas@uwyo.edu, or to my mail address: Downey Hall, Room #203, University of Wyoming, Laramie, WY 87020.

Thank you,

***Melissa Stevens*, U.S.**

Questions:

1. What made you get into reflexology as a profession?
2. What have you found are the most important benefits of foot reflexology for your patients?
3. What is the most remarkable change you have seen in a patient as a result of reflexology?
4. Can you perform reflexology on yourself? Could I?
5. What kind of training did you have to become a reflexologist?
6. Do you need special certification to perform reflexology on other people in Missouri?
7. What advice would you give to others who might be interested in becoming reflexologists?

USING INTERVIEW INFORMATION

Information obtained directly from an authority can be very persuasive evidence for an audience. Writing conventions for using interview information include:

- clearly identifying the expertise of the interviewee in the text of the essay

According to X, Chairman of the Board for Nike, . . .
X, member of the Olympic Committee, . . .
Intertribal Bison Cooperative Chair X stated that . . .

- use of direct quotations from the interviewee in the text of the essay

  Professor Clark stated that "... "
  The President replied that "... "

- reference to the interview questions in an Appendix at the end of the essay

  During the interview, Yellowstone Park biologist Steve Cain said that... (See Interview Questions, Appendix A).
  When I interviewed X, she confirmed that... (see Appendix 2 for interview questions).

- referring to (or citing) the interview in the text and at the end of the text

  in-text references

  [Interview described and cited without parentheses] *in a recent interview, X, Director of the National Institutes for Health, ...*
  [Interview cited] *X stated that... (personal interview, 1999).*

  end-of-text references:

  Benjamin, D. (1998). Personal interview (May 2).
  Boyer, M. (1999). Personal Interview (March 29).

Below is a paragraph from Melissa's paper in which she uses information from her interview. Notice especially

- the reference to Melissa's interview and to the location of the interview questions ("See Appendix 1 . . .").
- the use of the direct quotations (i.e., the interviewee's exact words), which are enclosed by quotation marks.
- the use of *ellipsis:* three dots, with a space between each dot, which are used when the writer removes some words from a direct quotation.
- the use of brackets [ ] to enclose information not directly quoting the speaker.

7 STUDENT SAMPLE

[Topic sentence] *[Reference to interviewee]* *[Direct quotation, reference to Appendix]* *[In-text citation]* *[Quotation, ellipsis]* *[Bracketed added information]*

Reflexology is also successful in releasing the stress and the tension of everyday life. As reflexologist Myra Achorn points out, "When we fail to manage stress in our lives, our bodies' defense mechanism breaks down, resulting in illness and disease" (personal interview, 1997). (See Appendix 1 for Interview Questions.) Because 75% of our health problems today can be linked to stress and tension, more people are turning to reflexology as a means of relieving high stress (Carter &Weber, 1995). According to Achorn, a person "may even try self-doses of reflexology by using a cream or lotion and firmly massaging . . . the joints in each area of the foot." The result, Achorn says, is that "The pressure and massage unblock the body's natural flow of energy and improve circulation to enrich [the body's] health."

References

[Listed alphabetically by authors' last names]

Achorn, M. (1997). Personal Interview, November 17th.

Carter, M. & Weber, T. (1995). *Body reflexology: Healing at your fingertips.* Rev. Ed. Upper Saddle River, NJ: Prentice Hall.

***Melissa Stevens,* U. S.**

EXERCISE 4-I With a small group of classmates, discuss the kind of person you each need to interview for your Investigating topic (e.g., a physician, a psychologist, a physicist; a cowboy, a lawyer, a farrier, a mechanic). Use a campus or city telephone book or recommendations from others to identify at least two people who might be willing to grant you an interview.

Writing Assignment: *Developing Interview Questions for the Investigating Topic*

Develop 5 to 8 questions for an interview with an expert about your topic. Share your interview questions with a group of classmates, and offer suggestions for (a) follow-up questions and/or (b) other improvements for your classmates' interview questions. Then arrange for and complete an interview with an authority about your topic.

Coherence and Cohesion in Academic Essays

Coherence means "to stick together." An academic essay is coherent if (a) the parts of the essay are unified (i.e., they are about the same main idea) and (b) if the essay seems logical to the reader (i.e., one part "flows" into another without confusing the audience).

A well-organized essay is the basis for coherence: an essay with a carefully identified audience and purpose, a clear thesis statement, and body paragraphs that support their topic sentences. The use of these organizational writing conventions makes the essay easy to read and understand. It "sticks together" for the academic audience.

In academic writing, cohesion devices are words and phrases within a sentence, between sentences in a paragraph, and between paragraphs that unite the paragraph or essay (i.e., help it "stick together"). These words or short phrases establish relationships between parts of sentences, between sentences, between topic sentences and the thesis statements, and between paragraphs.

There are three types of cohesion techniques.

1. **The use of pronouns:** referring to a previous noun by using a pronoun makes the new sentence dependent on the previous sentence part or sentence. As a consequence, it helps to unite that paragraph.

   When **Yuko** moved from Japan to the U.S., **she** found that people were more friendly than she had anticipated.

   English is considered an international language. **It** is spoken by more than 300 million people all over the world.

2. **The repetition of keywords and phrases:** repeating keywords (or synonyms for keywords), particularly the keywords in a topic sentence, makes the paragraph seem more unified.

   Atmospheric (air) pollution of our environment has occurred for centuries, but it has become a significant health problem only within the last century. Air pollution contributes to respiratory disease and to lung cancer in particular. Other health problems directly related to air pollutants include heart disease, eye irritation, and severe allergies.

3. **The use of transitional words and phrases:** *Trans* means to move across (e.g., *trans*portation, *trans*-Atlantic). Transitional words and phrases help readers move from one sentence, paragraph, or idea to another. Transitions also help to establish the relationships between parts of the sentences and paragraphs in an essay.

USING TRANSITIONS

Academic writers usually use pronouns without considering their function as a cohesion technique, and they often repeat (or use synonyms for) keywords and phrases in their paragraphs and essays without realizing the cohesion function of repetition. However, using transitional words (sometimes called "connectors"), which is an expected writing convention in U.S. academic essays, is sometimes difficult for student writers, because

- written material in some cultures does not require the use of (or the use of so many) transitions. In U.S. academic papers, the *writer* is responsible for guiding the reader through the essay; in other cultures, the *reader* may be more responsible for "discovering" the pathway through the essay.
- many transitions in English have limited meaning (e.g., *moreover, furthermore*), and some are used differently depending on their context.

Because transitions provide valuable signals to the reader about the relationships between parts of the essay, students must learn to use them appropriately. First, transitions fulfill several grammatical functions. In the examples below, the independent clauses **[IC]** are underlined, and the dependent clauses are *italicized*.*
Notice the use of commas.

Grammatical Function

1. Introductory words
   - **At first,** we did not understand.
   - **Similarly,** Shelley's hair was curly.

   [A word or phrase, followed by a comma, that introduces an independent clause]

2. Subordinate conjunctions
   - We went ***because*** *we were excited.*
   - The party was over ***when*** *he arrived.*
   - ***Even though*** *we were late,* we were still happy.

   *[A word or phrase at the beginning of a dependent clause: notice comma use. **Note:** subordinate clauses can occur **either** before **or** after an independent clause]*

3. Coordinate conjunctions
   - Maria likes pizza, **and** José does too.
   - They write well, **but** their friend does not.

   [A word or phrase, usually preceded by a comma, that connects two independent clauses]

Hundreds of transitions are available to the academic writer. Below is a list of some of those transitions, arranged according to use and grammatical function. Notice the use of punctuation, especially commas, and of capitalization. Table 4-1 lists categories of transitions available for student writers; Student Samples that demonstrate each category are indicated in parentheses.

Note: Some uses of transitions include only introductory words. Other uses also include subordinate and coordinate conjunctions.

Table 4-1 *Transitions*

1. **Chronological transitions** signal relationship in time (see the process paragraphs in Chapter 2).

Introductory Words		**Subordinate Conjunctions**		
First**,**	Presently**,**	When . . .**,** [IC]†	*or*	[IC] when . . .
Second**,**	The next day**,**	Although . . .**,** [IC]	*or*	[IC] although . . .
Third**,**	Soon afterward	Before . . .**,** [IC]	*or*	[IC] before . . .
Next**,**	By that time**,**	During . . .**,** [IC]	*or*	[IC] during . . .
Later**,**	From then on**,**	While . . .**,** [IC]	*or*	[IC] while . . .
After that**,**	At that moment**,**	Even though . . .**,** [IC]	*or*	[IC] even though . . .
At last**,**	Within an hour	After . . .**,** [IC]	*or*	[IC] after . . .
At length**,**	Afterward**,**	Because . . .**,** [IC]	*or*	[IC] because . . .
Earlier**,**	Meanwhile**,**	Until . . .**,** [IC]	*or*	[IC] until . . .

* For a more complete discussion of clauses and sentence structures, see Chapter 9, page 290.

† [IC] = Independent Clause

2. **Spatial transitions** signal relationship in space (see the physical description paragraphs in Chapter 2).

Introductory Words

A little farther on,	Next to X,	Beyond this point,
In the next room,	Across the street,	Just to the left,
At that altitude,	At the center of the circle,	
Between those cities,	About a foot to the right,	

3. **Comparison transitions** signal similarity (see the comparison paragraphs, Chapter 2).

Introductory Words

Likewise,	Once more,	In like manner,
Similarly,	At the same time,	In much the same way,
Once again,	Compared to X,	

4. **Contrast transitions** signal a contradiction or a contrast (see the contrast paragraphs, Chapter 2).

Introductory Words

However,	Nevertheless,	Instead,
Unlike X,	Nonetheless,	On the other hand,
Conversely,	In contrast,	On the contrary,
Even so,		

Subordinate Conjunctions			**Coordinate Conjunctions**
Although . . ., [IC]	*or*	[IC] although . . .	[IC], but [IC]
Whereas . . ., [IC]	*or*	[IC] whereas . . .	[IC], yet [IC]
Even though . . ., [IC]	*or*	[IC] even though . . .	

5. **Explanatory transitions** signal explanation, an illustration, or an example (see the example paragraphs in Chapter 2).

Introductory Words

For example,	Frequently,	That is,
For instance,	Occasionally,	In order to X,
To illustrate,	Generally,	Similarly,
Specifically,	Usually,	In other words,

6. **Transitions of addition** signal additional or supplementary material (see the classification paragraphs in Chapter 2).

Introductory Words

In fact,	Moreover,	For that matter,
Naturally,	Furthermore,	As a matter of fact,
Indeed,	Of course,	
Besides that,	In addition,	

Coordinate Conjunctions
[IC], and [IC]

7. **Cause-effect transitions** signal reason or a result (see the cause-effect paragraphs, Chapter 2).

Introductory Words

Therefore,	Due to X,	Accordingly,
Thus,	Consequently,	As a consequence,
Finally,	As a result,	For this reason,

Subordinate Conjunctions			**Coordinate Conjunctions**
Because . . ., [IC]	*or*	[IC] because . . .	[IC], so [IC]
Since . . ., [IC]	*or*	[IC] since . . .	[IC], and so [IC]
			[IC], and that is why [IC]

8. **Counter-argument transitions** signal concession or compromise (see the argumentative essays in Chapter 5).

Introductory Words			**Subordinate Conjunctions**		
Of course,	*or*	However,	Although . . ., [IC]	*or*	[IC] although . . .
Certainly,		Instead,	Even though . . ., [IC]	*or*	[IC] even though . . .
After all,		Conversely,	Because . . ., [IC]	*or*	[IC] because . . .
To be sure,		In contrast,			
As noted earlier,		Nevertheless,			
On one hand,		On the other hand,			

9. **Conclusion transitions** signal summation (see the introduction and conclusion exercises, Chapter 4).

Introductory Words

To conclude,	To summarize,	To summarize,
In short,	In conclusion,	On the whole,
In brief,	Therefore,	In summary
Finally,		

EXERCISE 4-J Complete the paragraphs with the appropriate transitional words and phrases from the lists at the top of each paragraph. Use each word or phrase only once; use the capitalized words at the beginning of sentences.

Notes: Sometimes more than one transition is correct; discuss these differences with your classmates. If the transition begins with a capital letter, it goes at the beginning of the sentence.

After completing the paragraphs, answer the questions that follow.

8 STUDENT SAMPLE

[Title] ________________________________

Transitions: *Although* *In conclusion,* *, also* *, so* *In addition,* *because* *, and*

Shopping at Wal-Mart enriches my vocabulary. ________________ I don't like spending money, I like shopping ________________ it gives me a chance to practice my English. Wal-Mart is the best place to practice. It is a large store, ________________ there are many customer assistants who speak English fluently. I look for many items in many parts of the store, ________________ in each area I find a different customer assistant who is eager to help me practice my English. ________________, I am careful to read the section names; I ________________ read the information on the packages of the items I wish to buy. ________________, every time I shop at Wal-Mart, I leave the store with some new words that increase my English vocabulary.

Hamad Omar, **Saudi Arabia**

9 STUDENT SAMPLE

Why Do Birds Have Wishbones?

Transitions: *Millions of years ago,* *, but* *Today,* *; therefore,* *Unfortunately,* *, so*

Scientists who study birds (ornithologists) believe the "wishbone" (the *furcula*) developed in order to help birds fly. _______________, the furcula bone evolved by fusing the bird's two neckbones into one. _______________, ornithologists know that the muscle that surrounds the furcula stretches the V-shaped bone apart each time the wingstroke rises. Figure __ shows the wingbeat cycle of the European starling and the spreading of the furcula during the downstroke; the dashed lines (- - -) indicate the position of the furcula joint during the downstroke of the bird's wings.

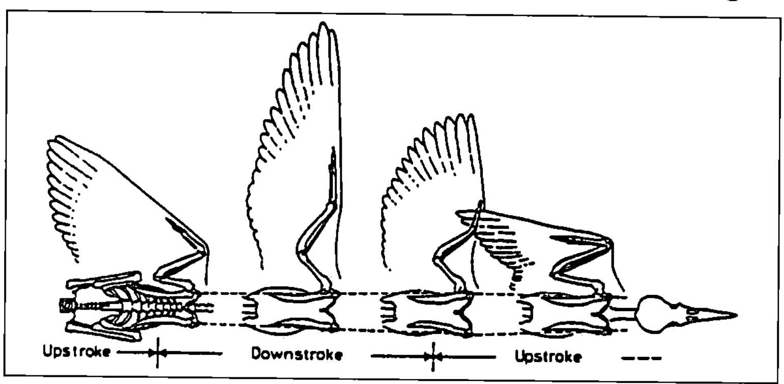

Figure __ *Flying European Starling* (Norberg, 1990, p. 207)

_______________, even today scientists do not know exactly what part the furcula plays; _______________, they continue to study the action of birds in flight. Older studies reported that the furcula stores energy during the downstroke of the wings, _______________ recent research suggests that the bone helps with the bird's breathing. Isn't it strange that so near the year 2000, we still have not solved this smallest of mysteries?

Reference

Norberg, U.M. (1990) *Vertebrate flight.* Berlin, Heidelberg: Springer-Verlag.

***Jacques Laine,* France**

_______________________________________ *[Title]*

Transitions: *, so* *Although* *For example,* *Therefore,* *Finally,*

There are three words in the Malay language that represent a person who cures diseases with traditional treatments: *bomoh, dukun,* and *pawang*. The meaning of those words depends on the status of the healer in his society. ____________, *bomoh* is a person who is in charge of a small village. He got the knowledge about healing from his ancestors, but he does not know some of the newer treatments. ____________, sometimes he cannot treat his patient. *Dukun* is a person who specializes mainly in massaging broken legs or arms. He is often a famous person, ____________ many people prefer to see him rather than pay for expensive treatment in a hospital. ____________, *pawang* is a high-ranking person in society; he is so experienced that he works for the Sultan at the palace. ____________ all of these men use a spiritual approach and nonchemical medicines to treat their patients, each is responsible for a different part of society.

***Nor Halim Hassan,* Malaysia**

1. For each paragraph above, underline the topic sentence and circle the controlling ideas.
2. Create a title for Student Samples 8 and 10.
3. Who is the audience for each student sample? Which has the most formal voice?
4. In your opinion, which paragraph is the most interesting? Why? Discuss your choice with your classmates.

Read the student samples below, and then do the exercise that follows.

Visit Me!

If you visit me in Hong Kong, you will have such fun! First, I will take you all around the city, over the pass where the monkeys sit on cement columns beside the highway (and sneak into nearby apartments to steal food!), and even to the border. Next, we'll go cruising around the city. During the day, since Hong Kong is nicknamed the "shopping paradise," I can take you to some high class boutiques or to the Standley Market where you can buy name-brand clothing very inexpensively. Hong Kong is also famous for its restaurants; we can choose American, French, or Japanese food, go to a floating restaurant for seafood, or to a hotel with a top floor restaurant that moves in a slow circle, or even a homestyle cafe. Later, you won't want to miss Hong Kong's wonderful night-life. We can go to Wan-Chi, to the discos and bars, or to the peak above the city to view Hong Kong at night. On the following days, we can visit the neighboring islands, where life is different because mostly fishermen live there, and we can hike up one of Hong Kong's tallest mountains to see the sunrise. With the busy city life and the rural country life, Hong Kong is an exciting place. So, visit me!

***Patrick Kuan,* Hong Kong**

Blue Light Specials

One way that K-Mart makes so much money is with the famous flashing blue light. Drawing shoppers like flies to garbage cans, the famous "blue light specials" unload all types of slow-moving merchandise. Whether it is sandals in a snowstorm, Halloween costumes in November, or day-old ham-and-cheese sandwiches, the blue light disposes of this merchandise, which thrifty shoppers devour like hungry dogs. Because they are caught up in the excitement and spirit of the moment, many shoppers take advantage of these specials to buy that new screwdriver they may never use or the blouse that doesn't quite fit. In addition, by purchasing the cheapest, most poorly constructed items, these shoppers assure K-Mart that they will return in a month to buy replacements. The blue-light specials are one sure way that K-Mart extracts $200 annually from every square foot of selling space in its stores.

Peter Cunningham, **U. S.**

The Cost of Television Ads

The amount of money that marketers spend to advertise their products on television depends primarily on two factors: the time the ad appears and the estimated number of people who will watch that program. For example, advertisements shown on Monday through Friday during the day cost less than those that appear in "prime-time": those hours after dinner and before bedtime (Elber, 1997). Figure __ shows the percentages of programs shown during prime-time viewing.

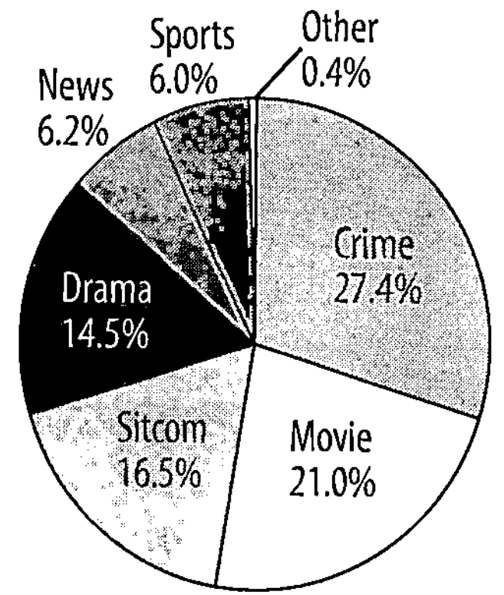

Figure ___ *Frequency of Prime-Time Program Types, 1983–1987* (Baldwin, 1989)

Prime-time ads are more expensive because the audience for the ads is larger, and it includes the people who will most likely spend money to purchase the products. In addition to the time of the ad, the popularity of the television program makes a difference in the cost. Whereas the average thirty-second ad costs $250,000, the same ad on Monday Night Football costs $400,000, and during the Super Bowl it would cost more than a million dollars. Of course, these costs do not include the costs of making the ads and paying the salary of the ad designers and marketers. No wonder products are expensive; we consumers are also paying for the advertisements!

References

Baldwin, H. (1989). *How to create effective TV commercials.* Lincolnwood, IL: NTC Business Books, Inc.

Elber, L. (1997, July 23). More wind in their sales: TV ads are competing for Emmys. *The Seattle Times*—Today's Top Stories, 1. [Newspaper article posted on the WWW]. Retrieved February 11, 1999 from the World Wide Web: http://www.seattletimes.com/extra/browse/html97/ altemmy072397.html

Myung Engle, **Korea**

EXERCISE 4-K

1. The student samples above contain many coherence techniques. With a partner or in a small group, (a) underline the transitional words and phrases, (b) circle the repeated words and phrases, and (c) put parentheses around the pronouns.
2. In Student Sample 12, discuss the ways the *second sentence* functions for the audience. Why is the second sentence necessary?
3. In Student Sample 13, identify (a) the introduction of the nontext visual and (b) the explanation and/or interpretation of that visual in the paragraph. In what ways does the material in that nontext visual help the audience?
4. In your opinion, which student sample gives the best information? Discuss your choice with your classmates.

Writing Assignment:

Revising the Report Draft for Cohesion

Incorporate the information from your interview into your report draft. Be sure to use quotation marks if you use the words of the authority, and to use in-text citations for the words and/or the ideas of that expert. Then reread the draft of your Investigating paper. Did you use any of the cohesion techniques explained above? Then do the following:

1. Underline the transitional words and phrases in each body paragraph.
2. Circle the repeated (or synonymous) keywords and phrases in each body paragraph. Did you employ this cohesion technique in successful ways for the audience? Did you give the audience enough signal words to establish the relationships between the parts of the paragraph?
3. Put parentheses around the pronouns in each body paragraph, and join the pronoun to its referent. Is the noun referent clear for each?

Revise your draft. If necessary, insert additional relevant cohesion devices to help the academic reader.

USING PARAGRAPH HOOKS

A paragraph hook* is another cohesion technique available to academic writers. Instead of linking one sentence to the next, paragraph hooks link one paragraph to the next. Paragraph hooks are based on repetition of keywords between paragraphs that help students guide their audiences: the writer repeats (or uses a synonym for) one or more keywords or phrases in one paragraph in the first sentence of the following paragraph. Writers can effectively use paragraph hooks between the introduction and the first body paragraph, between body paragraphs, and between the last body paragraph and the conclusion. The "echo" of these repeated keywords and phrases helps to "hook" the paragraphs together. Figure 4-6 depicts the use of paragraph hooks.

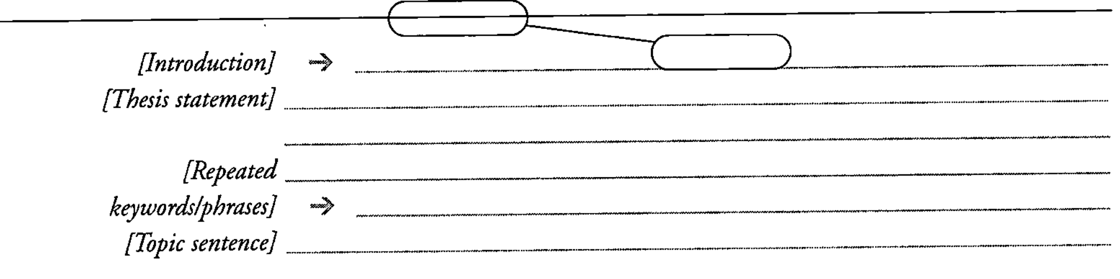

Figure 4-6 *Diagram of Paragraph Hook Use*

* From Lucile Vaughan Payne, *The Lively Art of Writing* (New York: Mentor, 1965).

Read the introduction to the essay about censorship below. Then study the different kinds of topic sentences with paragraph hooks available to the writer.

Note: Two of the topic sentences could begin background paragraphs; the last two could begin the writer's body paragraphs.

CENSORSHIP IN JAPAN

[Introduction] Nowadays in Japan, many *books* and magazines are published, and we can see a new movie in different theaters every week. Moreover, hundreds of *movies* and publications are imported from America and from European countries. Unfortunately, all artistic works, both domestic and foreign, are *censored* by the *government*. Opponents of this

[Thesis statement] government practice say that censorship should be an *individual activity*, not the duty of the *government*.

controlling ideas

Mari Kanada, Japan

Background Paragraphs

1. The **last (key)word** of Mari Kanada's first paragraph (above) can be "hooked" into the first sentence (the topic sentence) of the second paragraph and used to introduce the main idea of that paragraph.

   The constitution of the Japanese government guarantees our nation the right to freedom in artistic expression.

2. **Another keyword** (or words) in the first paragraph is hooked into the first sentence (the topic sentence) of the following paragraph:

   The Censorship Bureau is very strict in its definition of "obscene," so many works that are considered art by other countries are banned in Japan.

Body Paragraphs

3. A **keyword or phrase from the middle** of the first paragraph is hooked into the first sentence of the next paragraph; in the following example, a hook from the last sentence is used as well.

   Selection of what movies to see or what books to read is an individual adult activity in most free societies.

4. **Synonym hook:** A key idea (or ideas) in the first paragraph is referred to by using a synonym (or synonyms) in the first sentence of the second paragraph.

   In a democratic society, the people should have the right to choose what forms of entertainment they want to enjoy.

A **combination of transitions and paragraph hooks** is often the most effective means of linking paragraphs.

The fact is that the constitution of the Japanese government guarantees our nation the right to freedom in artistic expression.

Because the Censorship Bureau is very strict in its definition of "obscene," so many works that are considered art by other countries are banned in Japan.

In most free societies, however, selection of what movies to see or what books to read is an individual adult activity.

Moreover, in a democratic society, the people should have the right to choose what forms of entertainment they want to enjoy.

EXERCISE 4-L Read the paragraphs below. Circle the paragraph hooks and join them; then underline the transitions in each of the paragraphs. The first paragraph has been completed for you.

In 1889, when the British occupied Sudan, their first aim was to find land for planting cotton because many textile industries in England at that time needed cotton. After a serious study by the English agricultural experts, the Gezira area was chosen for the establishment of an agricultural project. The choice was excellent; even today, although there are now other agricultural schemes in Sudan, still the Gezira Project is the most successful.

The main reason for the success of the Gezira Project is its soil. The clay allows the construction of canals which do not require expensive concrete. In addition, the Gezira area slopes downward towards the north and west. This makes the siting of the canal system relatively easy. Furthermore, a slight ridge runs from Hag village to Masid village along the eastern edge of the project . . .

Hashim El-Hassan, **Sudan**

. . . The cross-cultural classroom was a great help to me because it was a way to extend my experience beyond the campus, and it made me share my experience and knowledge of my culture with American students.

The first time I heard about the cross-cultural classroom was when Mrs. Griswold from the International Student Office told me about the possibility of going to an American school and speaking to the students about my country. She told me that the goal of the program was to help children understand that people from foreign countries were not strange beings. I liked the idea, so I signed up with three other people. One was from India, another was from Mexico, and the third was from Sweden; I represented Saudi Arabia. We went to Washington Junior High School to speak to a seventh grade class. There were twenty-one students in the class who were about thirteen years old. The other three international students spoke first, so by the time it was my turn to present my information, I was no longer nervous.

Mohammed Al-Sayed, **Saudi Arabia**

The development of airbags for automobiles was a great step forward for highway safety. From 1989, when automakers began installing driver-side airbags, to 1997, when most new cars have airbags for both the driver and the front seat passenger, about 1,500 lives have been saved (Airbags and infants, 1996). But *there is a problem with airbags: they are killing children.*

[Thesis statement]

[Topic sentence]

In fact, for children under 10, the death rate was 34% higher than anticipated during the same period. Thirty-eight children, ages 1–9, were killed, including ten infants in rear-facing car seats, when car airbags activated.

[Long direct quotation]

> Two kinds of accidents predominate. One involves babies placed in rear-facing carriers in the front seats of cars, often dangerously close to the airbag housing. The other involves small children not belted in; they can easily be too close to an airbag when it inflates, especially since drivers often slam on the brakes just before a collision. (Norton, 1996, p. 81)

[Topic sentence]

Because airbags inflate at 200 miles per hour, small children (and very short adults) are at high risk of being hit in the head instead of the torso, and so the impact is frequently deadly.

References

Airbags and infant car safety seats. (1996, February 14). *Mayo Health.* 7 paragraphs. [Journal article posted online]. Retrieved from the World Wide Web February 13, 1998: http://www.mayohealth.org/mayo/9602/htm/airbags/htm

Norton, R. (1996, August 19). Why are airbags killing kids? *Fortune,* 81–82. [Journal article posted online]. Retrieved from the World Wide Web February 13, 1999: http://www.pathfinder.com/AAfESRAuGKtgAAQNA4/fortune/magazine/1996/960819/rea.html

***Carlos Rodriguez*, Colombia**

18 STUDENT SAMPLE

When I came to the U.S., I was aware of the lifestyle and customs of the American people, but in spite of my willingness, I have not been able to adapt to them. *Some features of the American people I don't like are their indifference to what is happening in the world, their strange behavior between couples, and their hurry to try to live as much as possible in a short time.*

Thesis sentence]

[Topic sentence]

My personal experiences have shown me that American students do not care to be informed about the world situation. Their talk is always about themselves and their city. For instance, if you ask an American student what he thinks of the political regime in Ecuador, he will only change the conversation to what he was doing over the weekend. Many of these students do not even know where foreign countries are. For example, a friend of mine met an American girl, and she asked him where he was from. He said, "Colombia," and she responded, "Oh, and how is life in Africa?"

[Direct quotation]

***Alberto Hermosillo,* Mexico**

* For a summary of revision processes, see the inside back cover of this textbook.

Writing Assignment: *Drafting the Investigating Essay*

Complete the draft of your Investigating report. Use cohesion devices and paragraph hooks to help your reader.

Revision

Re- means "again." *Re-vision* means to "look again."* The processes of revising are filled with *re-* words: *reread, reconsider, respond, reflect, rewrite, redraft.* Writers revise throughout the composing and writing process. As writers think, plan, develop ideas, and draft, they consider their audience and purpose (and revise), reread their writing (and revise), and ask themselves: *Which example is strongest? How can I engage my reader here? Have I defined this clearly?*

As writers complete their drafts, they often share their writing with "other eyes": classmates, friends, Writing Center tutors, or teachers may have valuable suggestions that will help the writer.

GUIDELINES *for Peer Response*

- Who is the audience for this draft? What are the general and specific purposes?
- Construct an essay map for your partner's draft by writing the thesis statement and the topic sentences of the essay. On the essay map, circle and join words from each topic sentence to the same ideas in the thesis statement.
- Look carefully at any nontext materials in the draft. Do they follow the **Guidelines for Nontext Materials** (p. 109)? If not, discuss the differences with your partner.
- Look carefully at the use of the words and ideas of others used by your partner in her/his draft.
  - Are the in-text citations accurate and adequate? If not, discuss the problems with your partner.
  - Are the end-of-text citations complete and accurate? If not, discuss the problems with your partner.
- What is the best part of the draft? Why? Discuss your answer with your partner.
- How can you help your partner? What suggestions can you offer that will help your partner to improve the draft? For example,
  - is more information needed in the draft? Where?
  - is a part of the draft confusing? Which part?
  - are there examples that do not seem to relate to the thesis statement and/or the topic sentence of the paragraph?
- Without looking again at your partner's draft, write three details that you remember. Show your partner these "memorable details."

EXERCISE 4-M Exchange report drafts with a partner, and complete the **Guidelines for Peer Response**.

REVISION PLANS

Of course, the most important result of readers' responses to drafts is the writer's reaction to the reader's advice. While writers should always listen carefully and consider others' feedback, it is still the responsibility of each writer to choose what suggestions to follow.

After writers complete an essay draft, and after they have asked others for feedback on their draft, they read through their draft several times, reconsidering one aspect of their drafts (e.g., organization, support, language) during each reading. Many students find that having a plan for revision helps them focus on the process.

Below are four examples of student revision plans.

I plan to expand the essay by explaining more about how women failed the first time and continued to struggle and finally managed to get equal rights with men. I will include a map with the paper to show the geographical position of Tanzania. And I will be careful to use the spell-checker on my computer so that I won't have so many errors.

***Jacqueline Mtema,* Tanzania**

I know my audience is frustrated, so I have to give a very good solution to the problem of parking. I have to include the amount of money and time to build a new parking garage. And I need to correct the verb tense errors so that I won't make my audience even more frustrated.

***Chee Hong Yeo,* Malaysia**

I chose a topic not on my authority list—computer morphing—just because I was interested in it and hadn't heard of it before. That was a mistake. Because it was so new, I had difficulty finding information about it, and because the time was short, my essay was rather pale and dull compared with my other essays. However, I am still interested in the topic, and so I have continued to look for information, and gradually I have been successful. I have found not only facts, but also nontext materials, and I have interviewed a professor in the Computer Science department. Therefore, in my revision, I will use that information to make the essay more interesting and enjoyable for my reader.

***Hongyu Zhou,* People's Republic of China (PRC)**

I will

1. reorganize some sentences (esp. the thesis and the very long sentences about autism I will break into smaller sentences).
2. add connection words to help my reader get easily from one sentence to the next sentence.
3. add some articles and correct some word forms.

***Rune Totland,* Norway**

Writing Assignment:

Revising the Investigating Report

1. Reread your Investigating report. Consider the comments of your partner.
2. Write a revision plan for your report. Then share your plan with your partner and discuss ways in which your partner might improve that plan.
3. Use the **Guidelines for Revision** on the inside back cover of this book to help revise your Investigating essay.

What Is a Norwegian *Hytte?*

[Introduction engages audience] *[Limited background information]* *[Thesis statement: intent and opinion]*

By tradition, nature, and upbringing, the Norwegian is a hunter, a fisherman, and a whaler (with skis on his feet). But in practice, the contemporary Norwegian lives, more or less, like other people in the civilized world: in a house with windows and central heating, with a television and telephone, knives and forks, and food that is boiled or fried. Although he has many comforts, his ideal is to be a son of the wilderness, independent of the European lowland civilization, with all its unnecessary luxuries. *Because the Norwegian wants to be a silent, pensive, and unfettered bird who flies his own way, he buys himself a hytte.*

[Background paragraph: definition] *[Technique of support: physical description]*

The *hytte* is a tiny house in the wilderness. It contains a bedroom or two and a combined living room with a kitchen, all very sparsely furnished, with an open fire and an earthen floor. The ideal location for the *hytte* is on a mountain top, or on a skerry all the way out by the sea, far from neighbors. But even in Norway, which has abundant mountain tops and skerries, it has become more and more difficult to find an isolated site. Often the Norwegian has to share his site with other unfettered birds. Therefore, he builds a high fence around his *hytte* that completely hides him from his neighbors, and he pretends they do not exist. He does not speak to them, and although they have been his neighbors for most of his adult life, he does not even know their names.

[Topic sentence] *[Technique of support: examples]* *[Concluding sentence]*

The Norwegian loves his *hytte* and enjoys it with his family whenever the demands of the modern age permit: summer holidays, Christmas, Easter, even weekends if the distance is not too far. He happily fetches water from a creek 250 meters away, a creek that freezes during the winter and is surrounded by bloodsucking mosquitoes during the summer. He willingly chops wood with an ax, stacks it against the walls of the *hytte*, and feels much satisfaction in using his wood for the fire. He gladly fishes in the creek and cooks his trout over the open hearth, savoring his catch. In short, he is a happy man.

[Topic sentence] *[Second sentence: narrows focus]* *[Method of development: contrast]*

However, most Norwegians have children, and as the children grow older they often hate the *hytte* because it is so boring there: no kiosks or video shops, no rock concerts or friends (there are probably potential friends on the other side of the fence, but even the children know they are not supposed to have anything to do with them). In order to keep peace in the family, eventually the hunter/gatherer Norwegian is forced to build a room with a television and a number of other modern gadgets. But because this Norwegian is, after all, a son of the wilderness, who lives a simple life in harmony with nature, he puts the electric shaver in a can of ski wax for crusted snow, conceals the telephone in a rustic bookcase (behind the Bible and a handbook on trout fishing), hides the telex in a rose-painted wooden chest with rusty iron bands, and decorates the microwave with pebbles. Figure __ demonstrates another way the Norwegian camouflages modern necessities.

[Nontext material]

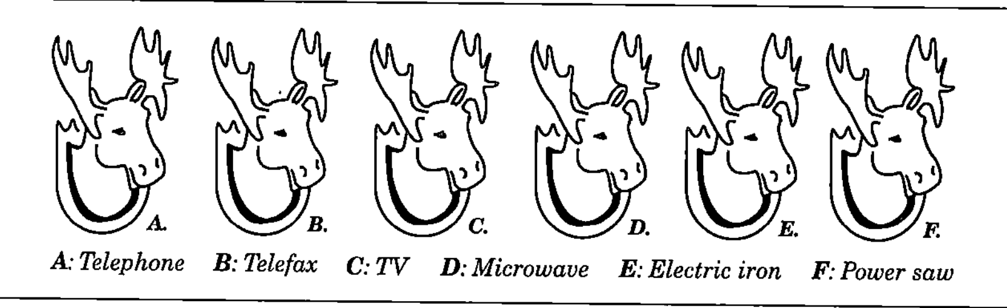

[Figure label and title]

Figure __ *Tools and Apparatus in Use at the Hytte*

[Conclusion]

Why the Norwegian feels this deep, uncivilized urge to be a child of nature is still a mystery to science. It may be due to the fact that his forefathers were simple farmers and fishermen, who lived close to the earth. But the same may also be said about the forefathers of most people. Even the ancestors of Parisians were farmers and fishermen, but the French feel no need to live on mountain tops, eat raw eggs, or speak in sentences of one syllable. There has to be an explanation. Science is working on it.

Nils Kjosnes, **Norway**

EXERCISE 4-N

1. Who is the audience for this Investigating report? How do you know?
2. What is the general purpose of the draft? (To review general purposes, see Chapter 1.)
3. In what way does the figure improve the draft? Can you suggest another piece of nontext material that Nils might have used in his draft?
4. How might Nils reorganize and plan this investigating paper for a 5-minute oral presentation to the class?

The Oral Report

Many college and university courses (in particular, but not exclusively, graduate courses) require not only a major research paper but also an oral presentation of that written material to the class. Effective oral communication of written material is therefore another important skill for students. Below are four authentic academic assignments that require both a written paper and an oral presentation of the written material.

Note: Comments to clarify the assignments are inserted in brackets [ ].

I **International Economics Research Paper And Presentation**
Write a 15–20 page paper and present it [orally] to the class. The topic must deal with some aspect of political economy. The paper should be chosen in consultation with the instructor with a rough outline submitted by the tenth week of the course. The paper should draw on the extensive literature on political economy. It should focus on policy decisions taken or under consideration in the U.S. or by other governments for dealing with specific changes to the international economic system, or on debates underway on how to reform the international monetary or trading system.

II **Wood Science Seminar Presentation**
Use your term paper to organize a 30-minute [oral] presentation for the class.

1. Greatly limit the specific area of information to be given; know more about the subject than you present. Critically evaluate and discuss the material you are presenting.
2. Provide the class with a 250-word abstract and a bibliography of at least 6 references (NO books and NO material from non-referenced sources), one full week before your [oral] presentation.

III **Contemporary Art Project: Oral Presentation**
Before you turn in your paper, you will present either a certain aspect of the paper or a shortened version of the paper to the class. You must use slides; please check with Don Turner, Slide Curator, Room 119 Fine Arts Building, as early as possible in the semester for slide projector availability. The length of the presentation will be determined by the number of students in the class; we will work this out when I schedule times for you to meet with me so that we can discuss the paper versus the [oral] presentation.

IV **Agricultural Economics: Report and Presentation**
Select a topic in consultation with the instructor and prepare a written report and an oral presentation to the class. These [oral] presentations should be 15–20 minutes in length. Use slides, handouts, etc., as teaching aids. Leave five minutes for questions and discussion by the class. The written report is due December 2. All references used in preparing the paper should be identified.

EXERCISE **4-O**

1. Each of these academic written/oral presentation assignments is incomplete; that is, the instructor will have to explain the assignments to the students. With a partner, discuss what information is missing from each assignment. What questions would you have to ask the instructor?
2. In your opinion, why do so many courses require oral presentations by students? Discuss your answer with a small group of classmates.
3. What are the characteristics of an effective oral presentation? Discuss your answer with a small group of classmates.
4. What kinds of nontext materials would be especially helpful in each of these assignments?

PREPARING FOR AN ORAL PRESENTATION

A formal oral presentation has several of the same conventions as a written presentation of material. It has (a) an audience and a purpose to consider, (b) a beginning, a middle, and an end, and (c) a main idea and specific supporting details.

Differences also exist. For example, in an oral presentation, analyzing the audience is especially important.

- The presenter must speak directly to the audience,
  - establishing a conversational tone and engaging the audience personally,
  - using appropriate eye contact and gestures to keep their interest,
  - preparing nontext materials to demonstrate his or her points.
- The audience will only be able to hear, not to read, the material presented; therefore, the speaker should
  - select a limited amount of information to include,
  - carefully predict what the audience will want/need to know, and
  - begin the presentation with clear information (e.g., writing the title on the chalkboard, handing out a copy of the outline).
- The speaking voice is as important as the grammar, word choice, and sentence structure. Therefore, the presenter must
  - practice the presentation aloud, perhaps using a tape recorder and listening to what the audience will hear,
  - try not to speak too quickly (because of anxiety), especially at the beginning of the presentation, and
  - use very clear signals and transitions (e.g., "The first point . . .," "Another reason . . .") so that the audience can follow the presentation easily.

Writing Assignment II Prepare materials from your Investigating report for a 5-minute oral report to your class. The written materials for this presentation include:

1. a two-page outline of your presentation, single-spaced *within* major sections, and double-spaced *between* major sections. Review outlining on page 21.

   Note: Use in-text citations in your outline.
2. an end-of-text reference list (see Appendix A for format).
3. nontext materials that engage your audience, such as overhead transparencies, handouts, maps, or videos.

24 STUDENT SAMPLE

Outline and Reference Page

I Introduction: aspirin is not just for a headache: it also helps to prevent heart attacks and strokes (Sutton, 1995)

[Single spaced] II Background: aspirin first identified as preventing heart attacks in 1988 when the *New England Journal of Medicine* published a five-year study (Sutton, 1995)

A. 20,000 male physicians over the age of 40 participated in the experiment
B. half of the doctors took an aspirin every day
C. the other half took a placebo
D. the group who took aspirin had 44% fewer fatal and non-fatal heart attacks, compared to the doctors who took a placebo

[Double spaced]

III. Doctors know that after having a heart attack, the chance of having a stroke increases

A. blood clots often form that can stop the blood going to the brain, causing a stroke
B. aspirin is a blood thinner; by thinning the blood, it can destroy the blood clots
C. so aspirin helps prevent strokes (Fairview Health Wise, 1998)

IV. Should you be taking aspirin? First: ask your doctor (Squires, 1997)

A. if you are over 40, and/or if you have a family history of heart disease
B. if you have already had a heart attack
C. my father takes one baby aspirin every day because of a partial blockage in his arteries (his doctor recommended it)

V. Conclusion: aspirin could save your life!

References

[End-of-text reference list]

Fairview Health Wise. (1997, July). [Online article]. Retrieved March 2, 1999 from the World Wide Web: http://www.Fairview.org/healthwise/news/aspirin.html

Squires, S. (1997, August 13). Happy 100th, aspirin. *The Washington Post,* E-1.

Sutton, J. (1995). Aspirin: The new wonder drug. *Heartline.* [Online article]. Retrieved March 2, 1999 from the World Wide Web: http://www.Heartcenter. crf. org: 8080/magazine/heartline/index.html

***Issa Asha,* Jordan**

Below is a humorous list of what not to do when you give an oral presentation:

How NOT to Give a Successful Oral Presentation

- Show that you are relaxed by pacing quickly back and forth across the stage, always looking directly in front of you.
- Be as informal as possible by
  - combing your hair as you talk,
  - dressing casually, in a loud sports shirt or teeny tank top,
  - using informal language, such as "Well, girls and boys, what's up?"
- Be memorable by making faces, using huge gestures, closing your eyes for extended periods, and staring at the ceiling during other times.
- Add "you know" at least twice in every sentence, and slip in a "fancy" word or two in every sentence as well, words such as *ineluctable* or *elegant* or *incontrovertible*, to impress your audience.
- Speak very softly so you don't waken the sleepers, and mumble so that no one can really understand you, even if they're awake.
- Use just one visual and refer to it in nearly every sentence.
- If your presentation was scheduled for 10 minutes, be sure you talk at least 30 minutes to impress your audience with your vast knowledge.

EXERCISE 4-P As you listen to your classmates' oral presentations, evaluate those presentations. Use the evaluation criteria below.

Evaluation Form: Oral Presentations	Excellent ◄			►	Poor
1. Overall organization, clarity **Comments:**	5	4	3	2	1
2. Interest and value of information **Comments:**	5	4	3	2	1
3. Usefulness and quality of handouts and/or nontext materials **Comments:**	5	4	3	2	1
4. Presentation skills **Comments:**	5	4	3	2	1
5. Overall evaluation: **Comments:**	5	4	3	2	1

Writing Assignment III Your instructor has returned several pieces of your writing, and these papers have been marked and graded. In other words, your instructor has *responded* to your writing. One reason instructors respond to their students' writing is to provide additional learning experiences for the students; another is to help students revise their writing.

1. Complete the Revision Survey (Appendix B). As you respond to that survey, consider which of your instructor's marks and/or comments helped you learn; which helped you revise; which helped you improve your writing; and which did not help you.
2. Write your instructor a memo, describing why 2 or 3 of the marks and/or comments were most helpful for you. (See p. 95 to review the memo format and to read a memo from a student to her teacher.) Give a specific example for each and describe the way(s) the mark and/or comments helped you revise.
3. Turn in your survey and your memo to your instructor.

Chapter 5

Academic Written Responses: Summary and Analysis

Simple observing takes a lot of energy because you have to concentrate on your senses: seeing, listening, smelling, touching, even smelling. Analysis is even harder. You have to observe, and then separate parts of the observation in ways that you can understand and evaluate it. I never thought writing would be this complicated.

Rima Ghaddar, Lebanon

SUMMARIZING IS AN essential academic skill. Students need to summarize instructors' lectures in their notes, material they have read, information to answer an examination question, the main ideas of articles from magazines or journals, and the results of research. An effective summary writer must be able to understand spoken and written material, distinguish between main ideas and detail, and then restate those main ideas.

In academic writing assignments, students are frequently asked to read (a journal article, a chapter in a book, a technical report), to summarize, to respond with feelings and ideas, or to analyze and/or evaluate the ideas in the written material. This chapter focuses on several types of academic assignments that ask students to use one or a combination of these skills.

These first three academic assignments require one or more of those tasks.

I **Introduction to Modern Art**

[Overall assignment] In your journal, you will write a weekly **review** [summary-analysis] of selected modern art journal articles. You will choose a current article from one of 14 journals (see the attached list) each week. Include the necessary bibliographic data and summary, but focus on your response to each article. *[Questions to answer in the assignment]* What was valuable about the article? What do you think about what you read? Is what you read contradictory to some other readings you have done? Why? How has the reading enriched your understanding (or not) of the artworks? *[Evaluation criteria]* Note: A good journal will be full of many long entries, will reflect active, regular use, and will demonstrate a good level of growth in terms of ability to think critically.

II **Adult Education**

As life-long learners, we need to possess the important skill of knowing how to find sources of information on adult education that most of us know little about. By using ERIC or the Education Index or CIJE, find an article on some facet of adult education or life-long learning of interest to you. Read it and write a 2-3 page **summary** and **critique** [response and analysis] of the article.

III **Agricultural Economics**

Four general subject areas will be addressed during this semester: (1) industrial organization, (2) product marketing, (3) international trade, and (4) marketing in developing countries. You are to **critique** [summarize and analyze] five articles not previously assigned on the reading list. Not more than two articles should be selected from one "subject area." Articles from "popular" publications are generally not acceptable. The critique should be only one page, typed single-spaced. It should contain the author, title, and source of the article including library call number (if applicable to the publication that contains the article). Give a brief **summary** of the content; critique the article by presenting your **evaluation** of the strength and weakness of the article.

EXERCISE 5-A

1. With a small group of classmates, discuss the differences between the "response" asked for in Assignment **I** and the "evaluation" asked for in Assignment **III**. Suggestion: Consider personal and impersonal language and discuss the "voice" for each paper.
2. Which of the three assignments might be the most difficult to complete? Why? Be specific.
3. In Assignment **III**, what does "popular publications" mean? In your opinion, why are articles from those publications "not generally acceptable"?
4. None of these assignments is complete. Discuss what questions you might ask the instructor in order to clarify each assignment.

Below are two paragraphs of summary-response. Each paragraph is divided nearly equally between a summary of the written material and a response in which the writers relate the material to themselves. These students were asked to select a popular magazine and to respond with one reason they might subscribe to the magazine.

[Thesis statement of opinion] *[Second sentence focuses topic]* *[Summary of* Cosmo *column]* *[Writer's personal response]* *[Personal opinion, reasons]* *[Concluding sentence]*

By reading the January 1998 issue of *Cosmopolitan* (*Cosmo*) magazine, I have discovered that this magazine is interesting because it contains columns with such titles as *sex & love, health & fitness,* and *beauty & fashion.* For example, the article on *health & fitness* offers readers "the 8 healthiest phone numbers in the United States." These 1-800 phone numbers are free for callers, and they connect readers with important institutions and associations that can provide information about diseases that affect young women such as AIDS, anorexia, and depression. Because I am 23 years old, these topics affect my life today. I am also interested in learning about how to lose weight and how to take better care of my body because I think that although appearance is not the most important thing, it does show a lot of how a person is. Therefore, the *Cosmo* articles help me increase my knowledge about body care.

***Maria Bemhaja,* Uruguay**

[Thesis statement of intent and opinion] *[Summary of photographs]* *[Personal response]* *[Personal opinion, reasons]* *[Concluding sentence]*

I am interested in subscribing to *Sports Illustrated* because of the great photographs of African-American football players in the Fall 1997 issues. For example, on the cover of the September 12, 1997, issue, two black football players, Cordell Stewart and Steve "Air" McNair, are pictured in an action shot, catching and throwing the ball respectively. In the American Football League (AFC) scouting reports, the photo of Cordell Stewart of the Pittsburgh Steelers (p. 56) also shows the muggy, hot, humid rainy day. Like many African-Americans, I tend to take an interest in black athletes, so the photographs stimulate and encourage me. And like me, most people who are interested in sports like to see photos of players in action. I can understand why *Sports Illustrated* is such a popular magazine, and I want to receive it every week.

***Adrian Hill,* U.S.**

EXERCISE 5-B

1. Circle the controlling ideas in each topic sentence in the summary-response paragraphs above.
2. Underline the cohesion devices in each paragraph: the repetition of key words and phrases, the use of pronouns, and the transitions.
3. In the margin, write which techniques of support each student writer uses: facts, examples, physical description, and/or personal experience.
4. In your opinion, which paragraph is more persuasive? Why? Be specific.

Summary Writing

An academic summary is a brief report of the main ideas in written material. The length of the summary depends on

- the *assignment*: a one-page summary, a summary paragraph, or a single sentence?
- the *length* and *complexity* of the material: a journal article or a book?
- the *audience*: what does the audience need to know?

The goal of a summary is to provide readers with a brief clear report of main ideas in written material (that readers have not read) so that

- they can decide whether or not to read all of the material,
- they understand the basic ideas about the material, and/or
- they are better prepared to continue reading (e.g., an article in a journal or a chapter in a book).

WRITING CONVENTIONS FOR A SUMMARY

Like most academic writing, a summary has a beginning, a middle, and an end. Whether the summary is 25 words or several pages in length, the writing conventions and its overall organization are the same.

1. The introduction includes

   - citation data (author, title, and other bibliographic information such as the title of the magazine or book, the publisher, etc.)
   - the single main idea (unless the title of the material is self-explanatory)

   [In italic text, words that would ordinarily be italicized appear in non-italic.]

   In the article "The Making of the Dutch Landscape," Audrey Lambert states that . . .
   "Nothing Tastes Like Roadkill," an article in Sports Illustrated *by Robert H. Boyle, . . .*
   According to author Matt Bai in his article "A Report from the Front in the War on Predators" (Newsweek, *May, 1997), . . .*
   Liu Zongren, author of the memoir Two Years in the Melting Pot *(China Books, 1988), presented . . .*

2. The body of the summary presents the main ideas in the material, which writers can find by

   - locating the thesis statement and topic sentences in the material, and using them to help plan the summary.
   - using the headings and the sub-headings in the article. For example, if a student were summarizing this chapter, she or he might list the *headings* (Summary Writing, Analysis, Writing Analyses of Written Material, etc.) and use them to plan the summary. If the summary assignment required some detail, she or he might also list the *subheadings* (Writing Conventions of the Summary, Evaluation of the Summary, Writing a Short Analytic Report, etc.).*

3. The conclusion parallels the conclusion of the author, in brief form:

   Thallmeyer concluded with a recommendation to . . .
   As a result of the research, Stokes believed that . . .

---

* In this textbook, headings and subheadings appear in the left margin, with headings in larger letters and important words capitalized, and subheadings in smaller all-capital letters. On this page, "Summary Writing" is a major heading, and "Writing Conventions for a Summary" is a subheading.

In addition to these writing conventions, summaries require use of some specific vocabulary and punctuation.

Verbs: Use appropriate reporting verbs in your summary (see other reporting verbs in Chapter 9, pp. 286–287). Notice that summaries usually are written in the past tense.

> *Koyama* ***described*** *the necessity of. . . . He* ***distinguished*** *between . . .*
> *The results of Boyle's research* ***indicated*** *that . . .*
> *The third section of the article* ***included*** *a history of . . .*
> *In the conclusion of the report, Valerio* ***predicted*** *that . . .*

Sentence structure: Use sentence-combining techniques to eliminate unnecessary or repetitive words and to join ideas.*

Vocabulary: It will be necessary to use some of the author's terms and the words that precisely describe the ideas in the written material, but for alternative vocabulary, try to use some synonyms.

Cohesion: Use transitions to help the reader with direction and to identify relationships between parts of the summary (See Chapter 4).

Punctuation: Journal article titles are put in quotation marks with all the major words capitalized ("Title of the Journal Article"), and the titles of books and journals are *italicized* with all the major words capitalized (*Title of the Book*).

Citation: Instructors usually expect summaries to contain the full end-of-text reference for the material being summarized. (See Appendix A for information about APA citation style.)

Below is an introductory paragraph for a book review essay. The paragraph that follows this introduction will contain a more complete summary of the book.

[Introduction of article] *[Bibliographic information]* *[Main ideas of book]* *[Summary of reviewer's opinion]* *[Thesis statement of opinion]*

Born to Rebel: Birth Order, Family Dynamics, and Creative Lives (New York: Pantheon Books, 1996), a book by Frank Sulloway, has resulted in great controversy among educators and researchers. Sulloway contends that competition between "firstborns" and "latterborns" for their parents' attention has created a predictable pattern of sibling rivalry, with firstborns striving to maintain the *status quo* upheld by their parents, and rebellious latterborns who try to overthrow the *status quo.* In my opinion, despite Sulloway's long years of research, his results are unscientific, illogical and too subjective to be of use. *Sulloway's conclusion, that birth order is at least partly responsible for a child's personality, is no more relevant and valid than astrology.*

Reference

Sulloway, F. (1996). *Born to rebel: Birth order, family dynamics, and creative lives.* New York: Pantheon Books.

***Sarah State,* U.S.**

* For information on and practice with sentence combining, see Chapter 9.

CHARACTERISTICS OF A SUCCESSFUL SUMMARY

The qualities of an effective summary are:

1. **Objectivity**: Only the author's ideas should be included in the summary. The opinions and judgments of the summary writer (such as whether the article was "good" or the book was "boring") belong in the analysis or the response to the summarized material.
2. **Completeness**: Depending on the assignment, the summary should contain every main idea in the article. Stating only the first main idea, or only one main idea with details to support it, will give the reader an incomplete idea of what the article was about.
3. **Balance**: The summary writer must give equal attention to each main idea, but must stress the ideas that the author stressed. For example, if the author wrote 70% of a journal article about one main idea and devoted 30% to two other ideas, the summary should reflect that ratio.

GUIDELINES *for Summary Writing*

- Read the material quickly, looking for main ideas.
- Read it again carefully, absorbing the information as you identify and mark the main ideas: the thesis statement, the topic sentences, and/or the headings and subheadings.
- Write the main ideas on a separate sheet of paper. Use quotation marks (" . . . ") in your notes if you use three or more of the author's exact words in sequence.
- Cover the author's written material and study your notes. Then check the written material to be certain you have all of the main ideas.
- Consider the audience for and the purpose of your summary.
- Select the major ideas and arrange those ideas in the same order as the author organized them.
- Introduce the summary with a sentence that includes the title, the author, and relevant bibliographic information.
- In the body of the summary, include the main ideas, arranged to achieve objectivity, balance, and completeness. Remind your reader that you are summarizing by using the author's name (or a pronoun or a synonym) and/or the title of the material (or a pronoun or a synonym) to introduce the main ideas.
- To conclude the summary, study the conclusion of the written material and briefly present the recommendation(s), the solution(s), the result(s), or the prediction(s) of the author.

Writing Assignment 1

Not all summaries are about academic material. We also summarize in our everyday lives.

1. Using the **Guidelines for Summary Writing,** write a summary of one television program or one film you have seen recently (not a news program)
   - in approximately 25 words; then,
   - in 25–50 words; then
   - in approximately 100 words.
2. With a small group of classmates, discuss the differences among the three summaries you wrote. Which was the easiest to write? Which was the most difficult? Why?

EVALUATION OF THE SUMMARY

Because summary writing is such a valuable academic skill, practice, evaluation, revision, and additional practice in summaries are essential for students. Use this **checklist** to evaluate summaries: Does the summary

Summary Checklist

- introduce the written material appropriately and completely?
- include all the important (main) ideas of the original material?
- report the information accurately?
- omit unnecessary words and phrases?
- omit most or some details (depending on the assignment)?
- read smoothly through the use of sentence combining and the use of transitions *(also, thus, therefore, however,* etc.)?
- provide the audience with a clear idea about the content of the material?
- have completeness, objectivity, and balance?

Writing Assignment II Read the 441-word article below. As you reread the article, cover the article after each paragraph, and list the main idea(s) of that paragraph on a separate sheet of paper. When you have finished reading the article, re-check each paragraph with your notes, making certain that you have listed the main ideas. Then, using the **Guidelines for Summary Writing,** write a 50–60 word summary of the article.

Body-Image Blues

[Introduction] In the U.S. today, body image—how we look at ourselves, and whether or not we like what we see—depends on a number of factors: our relationships with others; what mood we're in when we look in the mirror; how much cultural pressures mean to us; and how much we are influenced by the media. Unfortunately, many Americans, and most American women, are dissatisfied with their body image, particularly with their *[Thesis statement]* weight, and they are even less accepting of their physical characteristics than they were twelve years ago.

[Background paragraph] The editors of *Psychology Today* published the results of a February 1997 survey of 4,500 readers (86% women and 14% men) and compared them with a similar survey in 1985. David Garner, director of the Toledo Center for Eating Disorders, stated the purpose of the survey: "We *[Direct quotation]* wanted to try and understand the growing gulf between actual and preferred shapes" (p. 123). The survey showed that more than a third of all survey responders said they were dissatisfied with their bodies; only 40% of the women were "somewhat" satisfied. Evidently media models such as Cindy Crawford and Sharon Stone have had a terrible effect on *[Techniques of support: facts, examples]* the ways women see themselves; more than 60% of the women surveyed were dissatisfied with their weight and thus disapproved of their bodies. In fact, when the survey asked, "How many years of your life would you trade to achieve your weight goals?," the results were unsettling. Fifteen percent of women and 11% of men said they would give up more than five years of their lives; 24% of women and 17% of men were willing to give up more than three years!

[Topic sentence] Another factor that influenced body image was the way in which others viewed the survey respondents. If, for example, their childhood and adolescent friends, or, later, their mates, didn't think they looked great,

[Topic sentence] they were likely to feel devastated. Those feelings often lasted for years, even decades, no matter how the respondent actually looked today.

While no solution to this problem of body image is forthcoming, respondents to the survey were asked to share their experiences in improving their body images. Among their suggestions:

[Technique of support: examples]

- developing criteria for self-esteem that go beyond appearance
- engaging in behavior that makes you feel good about yourself
- controlling what you can, and forgetting about what you can't

[Conclusion] The editors of *Psychology Today* also recommended sources to further investigate the problems of body image, including the following Websites:

The Melpomene Institute Body Image Page: http://www.melpomene.org/bodimg.htm
Body Image: http://www.health-net.com/image.htm
gURL: http://www.gurl.com/

Reference

[Reference to journal article]

Garner, D. (February, 1997). The 1997 Body Image Survey: An in-depth look at how we see ourselves. *Psychology Today, 132,* 98–105.

***Andrea Schmidt,* U.S.**

EXERCISE 5-C

1. Exchange summaries with a partner and read your partner's summary. Use the **Summary Checklist** on p. 140 to evaluate the summary.
2. Discuss your evaluation with your partner.
3. Consider your partner's comments about your summary. How might you revise your summary to improve it?
4. Revise your summary and turn it in to your teacher.

EXERCISE 5-D Reread Student Sample 4 on page 140. With a small group of classmates, discuss the ideas in "Body-Image Blues" and respond to those ideas.

- How do you feel about the main idea of the article?
- Have you discovered similar attitudes in your own life?
- Do you agree with what the author identifies as the reasons for the obsession with body weight in the U.S.? Can you think of other possible reasons?
- What solution(s) might you suggest for this problem?

Writing Assignment III

1. Read (or reread) one of the sample student essays in this book. (See the list of student essays at the end of the Table of Contents.) Using the **Guidelines for Summary Writing** (p. 139), write a summary of the essay for an audience who has not read it (a) in a single sentence and (b) in a summary of 80–100 words.
2. Exchange summaries with a partner. Use the **Summary Checklist** on page 140 to evaluate the summary to help your partner make revisions.
4. Work with your partner to revise your summaries.

Analysis

Many academic classes require analysis: students might analyze the organs of a frog in biology class, the constituents of a rock in geology, the behavior of a young child in a human development class, or the nutritional value of a fast-food meal. To *analyze* means:

- to observe something carefully
- to separate that "thing" into separate parts
- to investigate the parts
- to study the relationships of the parts to the whole
- to discover how you think and/or feel about it
- to support your ideas and opinions.

Students may also be asked to analyze a problem and investigate a solution to the problem; by examining the cause(s) and/or effect(s) of the problem and by evaluating possible alternatives, students can make recommendations about a solution. For example, a student might notice that the university bus service ends at 5:30 each weekday evening, yet classes are offered until after 9 P.M. The problems of having no transportation to an evening class and the possible dangers of walking alone after dark to the campus need to be solved. The student might analyze the problem by (a) observing the problem, (b) interviewing the campus director of transportation about the history of the problem, (c) surveying students to determine the severity of the problem, and (d) investigating possible solutions. Then the student might recommend a solution and support that recommendation with facts and examples.

Below are three examples of authentic analytic assignments. Explanations of vocabulary are given in brackets [ ]. Read each assignment and complete the exercise that follows.

[Analysis task]
[Organization of task <u>underlined</u>]
[Questions to be answered]

I **Contemporary Art Survey**
For each visiting lecturer, write a 2-page critical **review** [analysis] of the presentation. Consider the <u>content</u>, its <u>importance</u> to you, and what you have <u>learned</u> from it. How has each helped (or not helped) your understanding of class material? How does each relate (or not relate) to the readings in your textbooks? Each paper will be formally written; its purpose is to analyze the value of the presentation.

II **Introduction to Film**
For each film we view and analyze in class, select another film by the same director and view it outside of class. Then write a 2 or 3 page **review** [analysis] of that film, using the criteria we have discussed in class.

III **Organization Design and Change**
Team Case Report, Phase 2: Analysis
Analyze the chosen corporation for your case study in terms of the theories and concepts covered in this course: show how the company illustrates certain models, analyzing whether observed company relationships are consistent with ideas and relationships from the textbook, and why you think so. Describe the external environment; include examples and tangible details. Include pictures or drawings. The important thing is to show you understand the course material well enough to apply the concepts to a real organization. You must include concepts from three text chapters; you may select whichever chapters you wish.

[Nontext materials required]
[Audience expectations]

EXERCISE 5-E

1. With a partner or in a small group, decide which is the easiest assignment. Which is the most difficult? Why?
2. Which assignment asks for a response as well as an analysis? How do you know?
3. Each assignment relates the analysis to class material. Discuss the ways in which this relationship will influence the students' papers.
4. None of these assignments is complete. What questions might you ask the instructor in order to write a successful paper for each assignment?

WRITING A SHORT ANALYTIC REPORT

One form of academic analysis is the short report (usually two to four double-spaced pages). The Investigating paper assigned in Chapter 4 was a short analytic report: an explaining essay that uses data (i.e., facts and statistics) and examples, but usually not personal experience, to support the analysis.

Another analytic assignment, for students in a marketing class, might investigate ways in which advertisers make decisions about placing advertisements in popular magazines. The student writers will discover that hundreds of magazines are published in English every year, from *House Beautiful* to *Seventeen*, from *Popular Mechanics* to *Muscle*, from *Byte* to *World War II*. Each magazine is published for a "target audience," that is, a segment of the U.S. population who will be most likely to purchase (or subscribe to) the magazine. Whether to advertise a product in the magazine depends on the target audience of that magazine.

As the students gather information about target audiences, they may create charts that categorize types of popular magazines (e.g., magazines that focus on sports, news, hobbies) and types of advertisements (e.g., those that appeal to young, poor, well-educated people; those that appeal to older, richer, less educated people; those that appeal to middle-aged men whose major interests are cars and sports; those that appeal to younger women whose major interests are fashion and beauty). As they analyze those data, the students may be able to form a hypo*thesis* (i.e., to state a *thesis*) about the relationship between marketing decisions and target audiences.

The *purpose* of the short report is to draw conclusions and/or to make recommendations from analyzed data. Its overall *organization* is similar to that of the explaining essay. Figure 5-1 outlines this organization.

Introduction
- introduces the reason for writing the report
- ends with a **thesis statement of intent and/or opinion** such as
  - *This essay investigates . . . and recommends . . .*
  - *The results of the analysis demonstrate that . . .*

Background paragraph does one or more of the following:
- gives a history or description of the problem or topic
- describes procedures for data collection
- uses non-text materials (e.g., charts, tables, figures)

Body paragraphs: each
- presents point(s) for analysis in the topic sentence
- relates parts of the analysis to the whole
- supports analysis with facts, statistics, examples, and description

Conclusion
- brief summary of analysis
- recommendation and/or solution

Figure 5-1 *Overall Organization of a Short Analytic Report*

This short analytic report analyzes the target audience for a magazine.

TEEN Readers

[Reason for the report] *[Thesis statement of opinion]*

In order to identify the target market for a product, I selected and analyzed a popular magazine called *TEEN*. I found that, from its fluorescent pink and purple cover to its short gossipy articles, *TEEN* magazine is a brightly colored, photograph-filled, eye-catching publication whose target audience is young girls, aged 10 to 14.

[Background paragraph] *[Process of data collection]*

To analyze *TEEN*, I investigated the overall impact of the magazine by studying the cover and the Table of Contents of several issues. In addition, I read the articles in the magazine and examined the advertisements.

[Topic sentence] *[Support: facts, examples, description]*

The article titles on the cover of the August 1998 issue of *TEEN* were typical of the language and focus of the magazine, which clearly appealed to the junior high school set: "Back to School Blitz!" "Boyfriend Betrayal!" "Guys Get Real!" The cover girl appeared to be about thirteen years old but actually was 19-year old Katie Holmes, a television actress on a "steamy" primetime "high school show." Photographs of young women abounded inside the magazine. However, all of the models are 5 to 10 years older than the target audience, and all have the clear skin and sophisticated look that the young readers evidently seek.

[Topic sentence] *[Support: facts, examples, description]*

The articles in *TEEN* follow a pattern: short sentences, short paragraphs, and easy vocabulary, all surrounded by color and visual effects. None was more than a page in length, and many were single paragraphs. For example, in the one-page cover story (p. 58) "The Diva of Dawson's," Katie Holmes discussed her new movie, *Disturbing Behavior*, a horror film, and her "adorable costar," James Marsden. The other articles in the magazine used informal language ("She read for 'The Ice Storm' and was hired on the spot!"), and were so full of graphics that it was difficult to distinguish the advertisements from the articles. This was clearly an editorial decision: for instance, a half-page beauty column about nail polish was immediately followed by an ad for the same product.

[Topic sentence] *[Support: facts, examples, description]*

The Table of Contents demonstrated that the focus of this magazine is two-fold: how to look better, and how to get boys to like you. For example, monthly column titles included "The Hottest Look for Eyes," "Pout Pencils," "Banishing Bothersome Bumps" (i.e., pimples), "Just Right Jeans," and "Hoods Are Hot!" Articles dealing with boys included "Dangerous Dates" and "Guy Likes, Guy Gripes." These were accompanied by photographs of handsome young men (again, 5 to 10 years older than the preteen readers of the magazine), sophisticated, muscular, and dressed in expensive casual clothes. Celebrity gossip stories made up the rest of the "information" in *TEEN*, about such trendy topics as who "heartthrob" Leonardo DiCaprio was presently dating and what actor Matt Damon was doing with his life.

[Conclusion: summary, recommendation]

The results of my analysis show that if a company's products include (a) beauty products, (b) clothes for young women, and/or (c) "health" products that are involved with weight loss or clear skin, *TEEN* is a perfect vehicle for print advertising. However, the ads must be appropriately designed for the audience: colorful, splashy, and bold, with engaging photographs and graphics.

***Geralyn Johnson*, U.S.**

EXERCISE 5-F

1. With a group of classmates, discuss the process of analysis for this report. What was observed? separated? investigated? Suggestion: Look at the topic sentences.
2. How does the writer think and/or feel about this magazine? That is, in your opinion, how objective or subjective is the analysis?
3. What specific products might be successfully advertised in *TEEN* magazine? Give reasons for your choices.
4. Contrast the differences between the academic language of Geralyn's analysis and her examples of less formal language from the magazine. Use the list about differences between written and spoken language on p. 5 to help your discussion.

Writing Assignment IV

1. With a partner, summarize Geralyn's analytic report in 25 to 50 words.
2. Share your summary with another pair of partners; use the **Summary Checklist** on p. 140 to analyze the summary.
3. Discuss the other pair's summary with them. Listen to their analysis of your summary.
4. With your partner, revise your summary.

Writing Assignment V

Write a 2 or 3 page report (double spaced) that analyzes the target audience of a popular magazine. Use specific examples and details from the magazine to support your analysis.

To prepare for your analysis, study (a) the cover of the magazine, (b) the Table of Contents, and (c) the advertisements in the magazine. Based on your investigation, identify and describe the audience for the magazine.

Directions:

1. Use three-column note-taking like the example below to gather information (see Chapter 2 to review this form of pre-writing).

Facts	Feelings	Appeals to
Cover		
• Brad Pitt (actor)	• handsome, looks friendly	• young women, 15–25
• magazine name	• exciting, eye-catching	• young women interested in current beauty topics
• article titles: bright colors	• want to buy the magazine	
Table of Contents		
• articles about beauty, school, and date clothes	• suggestions will make readers prettier	• high school and college women
Advertisements		
• beauty products, clothing, solving dating problems	• good ideas to make readers more popular	• middle-class women with some money

2. Identify the target audience in terms of gender and interests; approximate age, economic status, social status, amount of education, and perhaps in terms of hobbies or religious/political beliefs, depending on your chosen magazine.
3. Using the data you have collected, analyze the target audience: What people would buy this magazine? Why?

Note: You might also interview one or more persons who enjoy the magazine, asking those readers why they think the magazine is appealing.

4. Use the overall organizational format (Figure 5-1 on p. 143) and Student Sample 5 to draft your short report.
5. Use examples and specific detail from the cover, the Table of Contents, and the advertisements in the magazine to support your ideas.

EXERCISE 5-G

1. Exchange the draft of your short report with a partner.
2. As you read your partner's analysis, consult the overall organization in Figure 5-1. Does his/her analysis follow those writing conventions?
3. Discuss your answers with your partner.
4. Listen to your partner's comments about your report.

Writing Assignment: *Revising the Analytic Report*

Reread your short report. Use (a) the **Guidelines for Revision** (on the inside back cover of this book) and (b) your discussion with your partner to plan the revision of your report. Write a 50–75 word revision plan (to review revision plans, see p. 126).

Writing Analyses of Written Material

Usually, as you read an article (or book or report), you will respond to the material by forming general positive or negative feelings or opinions about the ideas in the material. Analysis* requires more detail:

- Why do you agree (or disagree) with the author?
- What support do you have for your opinion?
- How do you evaluate the author's idea(s)?
- What support do you have for your evaluation?

When you analyze the ideas from written material, try to follow these guidelines.

GUIDELINES *for Analysis of Ideas from Written Material*

- Read the material carefully and reread it, marking the points (i.e., the ideas) you choose to discuss and/or evaluate.
- Take notes about your agreement/disagreement, about your evaluative comments, or about your ideas or questions concerning the selected points in the written material.
- Use one or more of the Collecting Strategies in Chapter 2 to gather support for your opinions, your evaluative comments, or your ideas (i.e., your analysis).
- Identify facts, examples, physical description, and/or personal experience suitable to support your opinions or ideas about points in the written material.
- Decide on an overall thesis statement that agrees or disagrees (or perhaps both) with the main point(s) of the written material.
- Use the overall organization for the Explaining essay (p. 66) to draft your analysis.

Writing Assignment VI

In recent years, a major political controversy has focused on the growing number of handguns in the U.S. On the one hand, the millions of members of the powerful National Rifle Association oppose government legislation of gun ownership. On the other hand, a number of people in the U.S. think that owning handguns should be made illegal.

* Analy*ses* is the plural of analy*sis*.

The two letters to the editor of a newspaper below represent opposite viewpoints. Select the letter with which you *disagree*. Write a memo to the author of that letter, **analyzing** the issue, and stating and supporting your opinion.

Note: Because you are writing this memo to one of the original letter writers, you do not need to summarize the letter, only to refer to it: "In response to your recent letter, ..." For this memo:

- Follow the memo format. (To review memo format, see p. 95).
- Use facts and examples to support your opinion from your knowledge and personal experience and from the letter you agree with.
- Use appropriate citations for the material you use from the letter you agree with.

According to Howard Mohr, Vice President of the National Sportsman's Association, ". . . ."

Review the writing conventions for using and citing direct quotations on page 190 and in Appendix A.

Dear Editor:

There are four reasons why the U.S. government must not outlaw handguns in this country. First, banning handguns is a violation of the rights of fifty million honest, law-abiding citizens. The U.S. Constitution gives all Americans "the right to bear arms," so any restriction of private ownership of guns is unconstitutional.

Second, an armed citizenry is the only defense against crime and against the takeover of the U.S. by a foreign country. Furthermore, the right of self-defense is a fundamental one in this democratic country. If I know how to use a gun and feel I need one, no one should have the authority to deny me that right.

Third, don't confuse the owning of handguns with crime. Most of my law-abiding friends own handguns and use them for hunting, target practice, and self-defense. Instead of seizing our property, strengthen the criminal justice system so that criminals who use handguns in crimes are severely punished. Convict criminals—not guns.

Fourth, banning handguns would not work. If handguns were illegal, guns would still be owned despite the law; the

Dear Editor:

Handguns must be banned on a national level in order to reduce the rising crime rate in the U.S., a rate that is directly proportional to the number of available handguns. Today in the U.S., there are 50 million handguns; a handgun is sold every 13 seconds, adding 2 million handguns each year. By the year 2010, there will be 100 million handguns in the U.S.—will we be safer?

Probably not. The statistics involving murder with handguns in the U.S. are remarkable. During the Vietnam war, for example, more Americans were murdered with handguns in the U.S. than were killed in Vietnam. Recently, the city of Los Angeles reported 32 murders with handguns in a single week. During a single year, more than a dozen children were killed in four states by classmates who opened fire in their schools. Today, handguns are responsible for half the nation's murders. The fact is that people with handguns are far more likely to kill people than those armed with any other weapon.

Making handguns illegal will not affect hunting rifles and shotguns. But such a law will eliminate the small, easily concealed "Saturday night specials" used so often by robbers or muggers.

people who bought them would be then real criminals, and the profits would go to organized crime. Those of us who obeyed the law would therefore be defenseless; we would be at the mercy of the armed muggers and thieves. Nobody in his right mind would turn in his gun and thereby become a willing victim.

Don't abuse our liberty and put our country in jeopardy by outlawing handguns. Handguns are an American culture symbol that cannot be eliminated. Remember: guns don't kill people. People kill people.

Harlan Mohr, Vice-President
National Sportsman's Association
Austin, Texas

These handguns simply prompt and perpetuate violence in society.

We live in a "gun culture," left over, perhaps, from our history of frontier justice, but the result of this culture has been that the the U.S. statistically has more homicides than anywhere else in the world. The U.S. government needs to reverse the trend by banning the sale, import, and manufacture of handguns and by passing tougher restrictions to keep handguns out of circulation.

Nelson T. Shield III, President
Handgun Control, Inc.
Washington, D.C.

EXERCISE 5-H Exchange analysis memos with a partner. Read your partner's memo.

1. Has your partner used the correct memo format? If not, suggest one change that might help him/her revise the form of the memo.
2. Does your partner support ideas and opinions adequately with facts, examples, personal experience, and/or physical description? Suggest one change that might strengthen the support in your partner's memo.
3. Did your partner use appropriate citation (and/or direct quotation) forms in the text of the memo? Suggest one change that might help him/her to revise the citation(s) or quotation(s) in his/her revision.
4. What do you think is the greatest strength of your partner's memo? Communicate that opinion to your partner.

Revising and Editing Essay Drafts

"Re-visioning" (looking again) and revising an essay draft is usually a time-consuming and often a frustrating process. From the prewriting process to revising, writers are often too involved in their writing to "see with other eyes," the eyes of their audience. Consequently, knowing whether or not to add an example, to use different or additional detail, or to reorganize a paragraph may be difficult decisions.

Several opportunities for "other eyes" can help writers. First, most U.S. colleges and universities have a writing laboratory or a learning center that offers tutoring to enrolled students. Discovering this resource and learning to use it provides students with a support system for any academic writing assignments. In addition, students can ask native English-speaking friends to read and comment on their writing.

"Editing" a draft of a paper means to reread the paper and focus on the language of the paper, looking for language errors: spelling, verb tense agreement, punctuation problems, and the like. Editing a paper before turning in the final draft can be a difficult process because writers can be too involved with their writing to see language errors. To detect language errors in their writing, students can:

- read the draft aloud, and listen to the words and sentences,
- read the essay backwards (i.e., read each sentence, beginning to end, but start with the last sentence in the essay),
- ask a native English speaker to read the paper, looking just for language errors, and then discuss those errors.*

Of course, the writer is responsible for the final paper. Therefore, she or he needs to evaluate any suggestions received. It is possible, for instance, that classmates will have inadequate information about the topic, or about the language in the essay, to provide accurate and/or relevant information. However, seeing the topic from "another pair of eyes" may open the writer's mind to ideas that she or he might not have had. Therefore, after considering the comments of classmates, the writer will choose the revisions for his or her essay.

The student writers below have shared their drafts with "other eyes," asked specific questions about their own writing, and received advice that helped them revise their essay drafts.

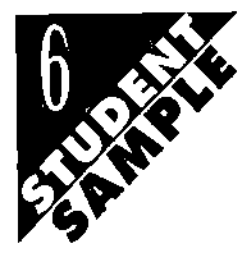

At the beginning of the class, I was reluctant to talk with my U.S. friends about my drafts. However, after my first successful experience, I understood that they could help me. For example, last week when I asked my friends to look for mistakes in my memo, Daniel showed me that I had not used quotation marks correctly, and he taught me the right way. Also, Steve showed me two words I had spelled wrong, and he helped me correct those words. Steve also showed me where to change the prepositions I had used incorrectly. Therefore, when I revised my memo, I was able to feel more confident.

***Khalid Alseleem,* Saudi Arabia**

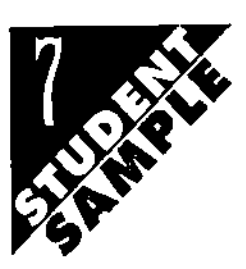

I knew that I needed more detail in my explaining essay about my learning styles, but I didn't know which details. Because I am not afraid to ask questions, I asked the Writing Center tutor for help. She asked me questions about my examples, and when I answered them, she was interested in my details. Therefore, it was not too difficult to revise my essay. My tutor was really helpful. She saved me from the endless rough drafts that are so frustrating because her questions made me think in a different way about my audience. When we spoke together, we found the solutions to my problem.

***Vielka Garibaldi,* Panama**

---

* Of course, the native English speaker should not *make* the editing changes; the writer must do that. However, for language problems such as article and preposition use, which are often difficult for ESL writers, using native speakers of English to identify errors and suggest (not write) corrections can be an efficient and effective learning experience.

When my peer response group discussed Michel's problem-solution essay about farmers' fight against insect pests in Senegal, he said he disliked his conclusion because he thought it was too short and too brief. Although we didn't have knowledge about his topic, we suggested that he might give a prediction or a recommendation. Then Michel gave us some examples of each, and we saw how much he knew about his topic.

***Sandra Harris,* Indonesia**

My roommate didn't know very much about my arguing topic (whaling in Norway), but it was interesting to hear her views about the topic. Even though her suggestions for support of my argument weren't so useful for me, listening to her ideas contributed to my knowledge about my audience and showed me the information that I needed to add in my background paragraph.

***Anne Lene Ejeldavlie,* Norway**

EXERCISE 5-I

1. Select another human resource outside of your class and discuss your memo with that resource (e.g., a Writing Center tutor, a native English speaker, a friend).
2. Reread your memo and consider that person's suggestions.
3. Consider also your peer's suggestions (from Exercise 5-D above).
4. Revise your memo, and then read it again to edit for language errors.
3. Turn your memo in to your instructor.

Writing Academic Summary-Analysis Assignments

Summary-analysis assignments are often called *reviews*: a *book review* (sometimes called a *critique*) asks students to read the material, **summarize** the written material, and **analyze** a part or all of the material. Because academic assignments label summary-analysis assignments in different ways, students must learn to interpret such assignments. Below are three authentic academic assignments that focus on or include summary-response/analysis writing. Explanations of some terms are included in brackets [ ].

I **Introduction to Political Science**

[Assigned task] Write a five-page **review** of a book concerning elections in America. *[Organization of task]* About two-thirds of the review should **summarize** the contents of the book. The concluding third should relate the book to [i.e., use your own ideas to show how the book relates to] some of the themes about American elections that we have discussed in this class. The book should be approved by the instructor. The review is due March 13th.

II **Graduate Seminar: Erosion and Sedimentation**
Semester Project Paper
Write a report, 10–40 pages in length, about one of the issues in erosion and/or sedimentation listed below. Your report will include a full historical and current description of the issue, a recent **literature review** [i.e., summarize and analyze several articles about the issue], and a description of the methods you would use to confront the issue.

III **Microcomputers for Educators**
Critique Assignment
Summarize and **evaluate** two articles related to the use of the microcomputer in your field of study. In 1-2 word-processed pages, explain how the idea(s) presented in the article can (or can not) be applied to your knowledge of the microcomputer and/or to your field of study. Each critique will be evaluated on format, grammar, content, spelling, and time liness of submission.

[Evaluation criteria]

EXERCISE 5-J With a partner, discuss ways to complete each of the above academic assignments successfully. Describe

1. what the general and specific purposes of each assignment might be for the student writer.
2. what the writer must summarize.
3. whether a response or an analysis (or both) is expected.
4. what additional questions students might ask the instructor about each assignment.

DIFFERENCES BETWEEN SUMMARY-ANALYSIS ESSAYS AND OTHER ACADEMIC ESSAYS

Because the summary-analysis essay differs somewhat in its content from other academic assignments, the overall form for the essay also differs slightly. For example, the introduction begins with the author, the title, and the bibliographic data of the written material. Another difference in the introduction is that instead of following the introductory sentence with limited background material about the topic, the next one or two sentences in the introduction summarize either (a) *all* of the main ideas of the written material or (b) just the main ideas of the written material that the analysis will focus on.

Note: The first time the author is cited, his/her full name is used. Thereafter, the student writer refers to the author(s) in one of the following shorter ways:

- title + last name: *Dr. Christenson, Ms. Mohr, Drs. Wyrick and Le Court*
- last name only: *Christenson, Mohr, Christenson and Mohr*
- the author(s): *"According to the author, . . ."*

The organization of the body paragraphs also differs from the typical Explaining essay. First, if the audience has not read the material, and/or if the assignment indicates that the summary should be a substantial part of the essay, a background paragraph will begin with a reference to the article and/or the author. Then it will contain a more complete summary of the written material. In contrast, if the audience has already read the material, or if the assignment specifies that the summary should be brief, the background paragraph is omitted. Instead, the introduction is expanded slightly with one or two additional sentences of summary to remind the reader about the material. Then, at the beginning of each body paragraph, the point to be discussed in that paragraph is summarized briefly.

Next, because the reader must be able to distinguish between the ideas in the written material and the student writer's ideas and opinions, the body paragraphs begin with a reference to the author and/or to the title of the written material, followed by a description of one point made by the author.

X believes that *According to X,* *The article suggests that*

Only then, beginning with a transition (such as *Nevertheless, However, In my opinion)* does the topic sentence of agreement or disagreement occur, following by sentences of support for the writer's ideas and opinions.

The conclusion of the summary-analysis essay also begins with a reference to the author and/or the title of the written material. It continues with a brief summary of the conclusion, and it may also contain a recommendation that is directly related to the original written material. Figure 5-2 depicts the overall organization for a summary-analysis essay.

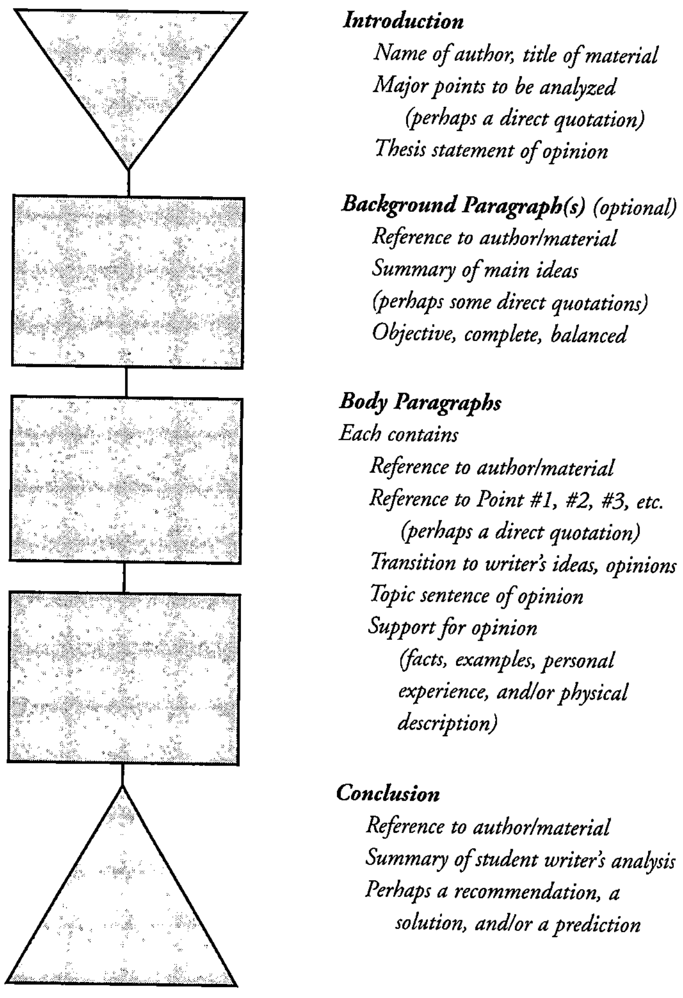

Introduction
Name of author, title of material
Major points to be analyzed
(perhaps a direct quotation)
Thesis statement of opinion
Background Paragraph(s) (optional)
Reference to author/material
Summary of main ideas
(perhaps some direct quotations)
Objective, complete, balanced
Body Paragraphs
Each contains
Reference to author/material
Reference to Point #1, #2, #3, etc.
(perhaps a direct quotation)
Transition to writer's ideas, opinions
Topic sentence of opinion
Support for opinion
(facts, examples, personal
experience, and/or physical
description)
Conclusion
Reference to author/material
Summary of student writer's analysis
Perhaps a recommendation, a
solution, and/or a prediction

Figure 5-2 *Form for the Summary-Analysis Essay*

Below is a student's summary-analysis essay. The assignment was an in-class essay, and the summary is written for an audience who has already read the article; therefore, the summary is brief. Read the essay and then do the exercise that follows.

Analysis of "Addictions in America"

[Introduces author, title] [Summarizes main ideas of article] Dudley Erskine Devlin's essay "Addictions in America" makes three main points. First, Devlin demonstrates that many in the U.S. have problems with substance abuse; they are addicted to tobacco, alcohol, and drugs. He believes that there are only two possible solutions to the problem of addiction: complete deregulation or "zero tolerance." While I [Thesis statement] agree that some Americans have addiction problems, *I disagree with Devlin's proposed solutions.*

[Reference to author's idea] Devlin's first proposal is to deregulate; that is, he suggests removing the warning labels from cigarettes, abolishing the drinking age, and legal- [Transition, topic sentence] izing such drugs as cocaine and heroin. However, I believe that Devlin's understanding of deregulation is flawed and that his solution would be a disaster. First, cigarettes and alcohol are already "legal" for *adults* in the U.S. Making cigarettes and alcohol available to young children goes against common sense; with so much research proving that cigarettes cause disease and death, we have the responsibility to protect the inno- [Support: facts, description] cents in our country. Furthermore, if crack were legalized, more people would be tempted to try it. Unfortunately, recent research has demonstrated that a single experience with cocaine gives a person a seventy to eighty percent chance of becoming addicted. We should be at least as careful with cocaine and heroin as we are with antibiotics, yet we would never allow the sale of an antibiotic that had a 70 to 80% chance of maiming or killing an unsuspecting person.

[Reference to author's idea] The other solution brought up by Devlin is "zero tolerance." That is, Devlin suggests that we make newer, harsher laws that make even a single use of cigarettes, alcohol, or addictive drugs punishable by stiff fines and [Transition, topic sentence] long prison terms. In my opinion, this is a naive solution. The amount of time and money it would take to monitor everyone in the U.S. for use of [Support: facts, example] these substances would be enormous; such a plan would turn the country into a police state, with George Orwell's "Big Brother" peering over every shoulder. And it wouldn't work: when alcohol was illegal in the U.S., more liquor was consumed than in the decade following its deregulation.

[Reference to author] Instead of Devlin's ideas of deregulation or "zero tolerance," I think that the answer is education. We have already seen the attitude towards cigarette smoking grow less and less tolerant as more people learn about [Solution] the dangers of smoking. If, for instance, the U.S. spent the money we now spend to control the influx of illegal drugs into this country on the education that begins with very young children, we could curb the desire for young Americans to experiment with drugs.

***Juli Pederson,* U.S.**

EXERCISE 5-K

1. With a partner, answer the questions on the **checklist** (p. 140) about Juli's summary.
2. In the two body paragraphs, put the transitional words and phrases in parentheses.
3. Circle and join the paragraph hook(s) between the last body paragraph and the conclusion.
4. What improvements would you and your partner suggest to the author?

STUDENT SAMPLES: ACADEMIC SUMMARY-ANALYSIS ASSIGNMENT

Undergraduate summary-analysis assignments that involve both reading and writing usually ask students to evaluate an article from a magazine or a book. Below is an article that served as the written material for analysis in a first-year university placement examination. The article is followed by examples of student analyses of the article.

Directions: Read the following passage. In an organized and detailed essay, **summarize** its main ideas and then **explain** why [i.e., *analyze* why] you agree or disagree with what the article says. Support your agreement/disagreement with specific examples from your experience or outside reading and/or with an **analysis** of the essay's argument.

Family Values in America

Dudley Erskine Devlin

[Background] In recent months, the political debate about family values in America has taken center-stage. "Lesser" problems like crime, the economy, oil spills, foreign wars, and global warming have faded into the background, and the babble of voices haranguing us about "family values" has increased in frequency and volume. The social critics offer two very different solutions. One group of family reformers says that we should return to the days of the traditional family. Another group believes that it's too late to restore the old nuclear family structure; instead we need to fix our culture so everyone in the community helps raise the children, including aunts and uncles, grandparents, shop owners, and television producers. In this essay, I explain both positions and then offer my own argument, which is *[Thesis statement]* that moral values really have nothing to do with family structures. We just need to back off and give kids some space.

Here are some examples and statistics that the social critics cite to illustrate the seriousness of the family values problem:

- In America, more than half of all marriages end in divorce, and more than one-third of all children are born to single mothers.
- In a recent poll, 81% of Americans thought that TV's effect on children caused a decline in family values. As if to illustrate, a five-year old in New York recently watched an episode of a television program, and then, imitating what he saw on TV, set his own house afire, resulting in the death of his two year-old sister.
- In California recently, a six year-old boy and twin eight year-olds broke into a house to steal a tricycle. In the process, the burglary turned violent, and these children assaulted and maimed an infant child.

These examples, the social critics argue, prove that there is a clear connection between the breakup of the traditional family structure and the rampant increase in materialistic, self-centered, violent child and adolescent behavior. Many of these critics think that the decline of the nuclear family—those families with a father who works and a mother who stays at home with her 2.5 children—has created a generation of children and teenagers that thinks nothing of cheating, stealing, or hurting other people to get what they want. Family values, they believe, have disappeared. These critics believe that we can trace the problem of the decline to a fragmented family structure: single parents raising children, "blended" families with children from multiple marriages, families where one parent is dating, and families with workaholic or absentee parents who provide material possessions but little guidance.

The solution to these problems, according to these social reformers, is a return to the nuclear family. They exhort men to assume responsibility for their relationships and to take their rightful place as the patriarch of the family. Conservative religious speakers such as Jerry Falwell argue that feminists have destroyed family structures and traditional moral values by leaving their role as mother to work outside the home and by having children out of wedlock.

The second group of reformers favors a communal or "whole village" approach. These people argue that family structures have already changed, in part for some very good reasons. First, women and children need to be able to leave abusive and hostile relationships. Columnist Barbara Ehrenreich speaks for this group when she says that "domestic violence sends as many women to emergency rooms as any other form of illness, injury or assault." Second, women—and men—need to have more freedom to balance child care with career demands. Since family structures have already changed, we need to think about a larger, cultural solution. This group argues that children should be raised by many people in a community: grandparents, babysitters, shopkeepers, teachers, little league coaches, and friends, as well as television programs such as "Sesame Street" and "Touched by an Angel." These reformers believe that we need cultural reform that focuses on forces outside the traditional family that can teach children "family" values.

This second group of reformers, however, faces a daunting task. They, too, want U.S. culture to move back to the horse and buggy days, when children treated teachers and other community members with respect. Today, however, if a teacher scolds a student, the student may pull a knife—or at least initiate legal action. If an older driver chides a teenager who just cut him off, the teen could shoot him. Today, children watch 2,000 hours of TV every year and see over 6,000 acts of violence a year. Think of the work—not to mention the censorship problems—required just to reform the media, possibly by using warning labels, perhaps by installing a V-chip, or even by turning off the worst of the violent television programs.

My own belief is that social critics have wildly exaggerated the problem. First, there is, in fact, no demonstrable relationship between a person's family structure and their moral values. Some bad kids come from good homes; some good kids come from bad homes. The family structure itself does not insure good values. Second, we have to realize that this new generation is different; we must have faith that kids will grow up fine. They just need a little time and space to adapt to the world without the meddling of a bunch of social reformers. Sure, there are a few kids who are out of control, but does that mean we have to go out and start preaching at everyone to fix their families? And does that mean we should start censoring television programs? Focusing on rebuilding an older culture will not work. Time changes, and we must "go with the flow."

Basically, both of these reform groups need to take a deep breath and calm down. After all, children simply go through stages as they grow up. We know that by the time they become adults, most of them turn out fine. I think we just need to relax a bit. Just give kids some space!

Below are several paragraphs that first-year students wrote in response to the article. **Note:** Each paragraph was written by a different student.

11 STUDENT SAMPLE

Introduction #1

[Introduces article and author] [Summary of the author's main ideas] [Thesis statement of disagreement]

In his article, "Family Values in America," Dudley Erskine responds to the question, "What is the solution to declining moral values in today's society?" Devlin provides two answers, the first being a return to a time when the traditional family was the norm, and the second an adjustment to our culture that would involve the entire community—including television programs—in the raising of children. Devlin then adds his own solution: "Give kids some space!" I disagree with Devlin's assertion; instead, I believe a middle ground can be found where respect for people and communities is taught from an early age by a child's family (nuclear or otherwise) and is reinforced by a child's environment.

12 STUDENT SAMPLE

Introduction #2

[Introduces article and author] [Brief summary of author's main ideas] [Thesis statement of agreement and disagreement]

In Dudley Erskine Devlin's essay on family values, he presents the reader with two differing opinions on causes for the decline of values and morals in America's families. Some social critics argue, he says, that America should turn back to the traditional nuclear family with a mother, a father, and 2.5 kids. Others desire to have entire communities raising and educating children in the "correct" conservative manner. Indeed, both ideas are conservative; both want America back in the good old days. Mr. Devlin takes a more liberal stance: as times change, he says, we should just "go with the flow" and let kids be kids. I personally take a more moderate opinion. Although I believe in letting children explore their environment and test its boundaries, as Devlin suggests, equally important is giving children a solid foundation—one that does not reek of daily violence outside their home and inside their televisions.

13 STUDENT SAMPLE

SUMMARY

Background Paragraph #1

[Reference to the author and the article] [Brief summary of article] [Direct quotation] [Direct quotation]

Devlin's article points out that the social reformers have noticed a definite connection between the decline in family values and the decline in traditional family structures. The results have been an increase of adolescent violence and unacceptable behavior. These reformers believe that action must be taken to return our society to the days when the father provided a sturdy, solid and moral foundation for the family and the mother stayed "at home with her 2.5 children." Another group of social reformers believe that the time has passed for the nuclear family, but that instead, the entire community should participate actively in raising all the children in what Hillary Clinton's book called "the whole village" approach. The author disagreed completely with both these groups of reformers; he states that there is "no demonstrable relationship between a person's family structure and their moral values." He recommends that children should be left alone to do what they want, and then they will grow into fine adults.

Background Paragraph #2

[Reference to author and article] [Summary of article] [Direct quotation] [Direct quotations]

Devlin begins his essay with facts and examples of divorce rates, negligent one-parent families, and murderous children. Turning to solutions proposed by groups to deal with the decline of values, he demonstrates that those who wish to return to the 1950s traditional family are just dreaming because "focusing on rebuilding an older culture will not work." Similarly, those who believe in "the whole village approach" will also find that solution impossible because times have changed: if a teacher scolds a student, the student may pull a gun and shoot that teacher. Devlin then professes that the issue is blown out of proportion, that if we give kids "a little time and space to adapt to the world," they will "grow up fine."

Body Paragraph #1

[Reference to author] [Reference to author's point] [Topic sentence] [Student writer's support: facts, examples] [Conclusion]

The example Devlin chose of the five year-old who imitated a television program and set his house ablaze is a fine illustration of the impressionability of young kids as well as their inability to separate fact from fiction, or right from wrong. I agree with the social reformers: children learn from imitation, and therefore they need good models to imitate. Research has shown that children of racist families often adopt their family's racist ideas, and children who survive an abusive childhood learn not how to love but how to hate, and they will carry these lessons into their own abusive relationships. In America, where single parenting is the norm and divorce is more popular than marriage, it is no surprise that what kids today need is not more freedom, but more stability.

Body Paragraph #2

[Reference to author/point] [Brief summary] [Topic sentence] [Student writer's support: analysis of Devlin's argument] [Conclusion]

Devlin states that critics on the right claim that the nuclear family was the deciding factor in shaping the behavior of the current generation, and that, with its disintegration, values like self-responsibility, respect for others, and respect for authority have been lost. Devlin is wrong in his assessment that a single style of child-rearing is responsible for the loss. Values can be communicated by any family structure, so long as care-takers are devoted and conscientious. Whether those caretakers are grandparents, foster parents, gay partners, or spread over half a dozen relations is immaterial, so long as they contribute time and attention. Inattentive parenting, parents who themselves lack the time for attention or the values to communicate: these should be the central issues in Devlin's argument, not the structure of the family.

Body Paragraph #3

[Reference to author/point] *[Student writer's opinion]* *[Support: facts, example]* *[Conclusion]*

Devlin's argument that the aggressive and violent behavior he describes in his opening paragraphs is just a phase and that these kids will "grow up fine" <u>is lunacy</u>. If we allowed society to observe a serial rapist as one who is just letting off steam, then our nation's fragile values would indeed collapse under the strain. Research has suggested that many violent criminals possess a genetic predisposition towards violent acts. Some scientific experiments are beginning to confirm this idea. For example, studies show that very young children who are consistently cruel to animals often grow into violent adults. Of course, if these children are genetically predisposed toward violence, we should not discriminate against them, but society must focus on the control of these children.

18 STUDENT SAMPLE

Body Paragraph #4

[Reference to author/point] *[Topic sentence]* *[Student writer's support: facts, examples, description]* *[Direct quotation]*

Devlin admits that "Time changes," and that we should "go with the flow," but <u>he seems to forget</u> a stronger argument that I would use to <u>support his idea</u> of "relaxing": that history often repeats itself. There have been many times in U.S. history when parents were worried about their unruly children. In fact, in the 1920s, many parents felt that their children were unmanageable and running wild. Many young adults turned to smoking and drinking and to the new dances. Elders were shocked and feared the future. The 1960s was also a time of turmoil and self-exploration for young people; they experimented with sex and drugs, and their parents wailed about the decline in moral values. Mr. Devlin is, therefore, <u>correct;</u> as generations change, experiences change. Sometimes it is necessary to "go with the flow" and see what happens.

19 STUDENT SAMPLE

Conclusion #1

[Reference to author] *[Brief summary]* *[Recommendation]*

Neither Mr. Devlin nor I want the horse and buggy "good old days" back in America. Change is essential and inevitable in time. But, unlike Mr. Devlin's opinion, I believe it is necessary for some control to be added to America. We should not raise another generation of children with the sounds of gunfire singing them to sleep. People need to learn tolerance so that children will feel safe and secure.

Conclusion #2

[Transition, reference to author] In conclusion, while I disagree with Devlin, I support the social critics of our family structures today. A return to the nuclear family is, I realize, *[Brief summary]* impossible; a single-parent family is much healthier for a child than an abusive or alcoholic one. Kids are easily influenced, though, and need to be *[Direct quotation]* surrounded by examples of respect and love. "More space," which Devlin recommends, means more freedom, and to kids, freedom is power. But for the very young, power hurts, power destroys, power corrupts, and as the *[Solution]* six year-old from California showed, power kills. Mr. Devlin, kids don't need space. Kids need stability, respect, love. I say that teachers, parents, *[Recommendation]* and everyone else should get as close as they can to their kids.

EXERCISE 5-L

1. With a small group of classmates, look at the writing conventions in Figure 5.2 (p. 152) and decide whether or not the paragraphs above follow those conventions.
2. In your opinion, which of the introductions and which of the background paragraphs is the most effective? Give reasons to support your opinion.
3. Which of the body paragraphs and which of the conclusions is the most effective? Discuss your opinions with a small group of classmates; support your opinions with specific evidence.
4. What other facts or examples from your own experience could you add to the body paragraphs that analyze and respond to Dudley Erskine Devlin's article?
5. With your classmates, offer specific suggestions to the writers of two of the sample paragraphs that would help those writers improve their paragraphs through revision.

Writing Assignment VII

1. Read the following essay (Student Sample 21). Then, using Figure 5-2, plan a 500–700 word summary-analysis essay. Use one or more of the prewriting strategies in Chapter 2 to gather supporting materials for your response.
2. Select an audience for this essay: your classmates? a person who has not read the essay? Analyze that audience, using the **Guidelines for Audience Analysis** (pp. 72–73), and then state both the general and the specific purpose(s) you have for your summary-analysis essay.
3. Use the **Guidelines for Composing** (on the inside front cover of this book) as you draft your essay.

SHOULD A WOMAN WORK OUTSIDE THE HOME?

In recent years, it has been observed that in those societies where women work outside their homes in the company of men, there exist many serious social problems. Many studies have been conducted worldwide concerning the advantages and disadvantages of having women working outside their homes. The basis for each study was the following question: Is it helpful or harmful to women and to their society to have women work outside their homes?

Some people consider that the work of a woman outside the home gives her equal rights with men, social independence, and financial freedom. Perhaps each of these results seems to be true on the surface, but this point of view is actually very narrow and superficial. It certainly does not take into consideration the serious social problems which are a direct result of women in the work fields who constantly compete with, come in contact with, and keep company with men. Consider just the religious view: all the heavenly books are quite clear about woman's place in the world. The Bible and the Koran particularly state that women should stay at home and do the housework.

The basic fact is that women are not like men; both are different naturally in physical stature and emotional capabilities. God provided each with certain talents and features which help him or her in life. For example, there are certain jobs which are suitable for each sex simply because of physical abilities and limitations. Men can do work which needs great physical strength and endurance: bricklaying, working with heavy machinery, or other kinds of construction work. For women, these jobs are impossible because of their limited physical strength. On the other hand, there are some jobs most suitable for women: nursing, raising children, and housework. Women can do these jobs more efficiently because they are naturally fit for such work; they have patience and emotional endurance to do small tasks again and again without getting bored. Emotionally, men are better equipped to make strong decisions and to deal with problems that arise from making serious decisions about serious and critical problems. Women, on the contrary, are much better suited for the patience and kindness involved in raising children, and the children develop better as a result of the mother's kindness and understanding.

Moreover, God made man to take care of woman; in fact, God made woman from a part of man and gave man the woman to keep him company. Therefore, it is the duty of the man to provide a secure shelter for the woman, and he must also provide for her financially. He does his duty by working in the outside world, thereby giving her the opportunity to stay home and be both physically and financially secure. Woman, on the other hand, has as her duty to take care of the man—and his children—within the home. She does this by cooking, cleaning, and keeping the household at its best. This partnership between men and women is based on God's law and has survived for hundreds, perhaps thousands, of years.

However, today, as we see in the societies where the women go to work, there are many problems which may in the end destroy society as we know it. First, many people, especially men, do not find jobs because women have taken those jobs. Therefore, the men, with decreased job chances, and unemployment, are pushed to commit crimes. Children also take the wrong way because they have the feeling that their fathers and mothers ignore them; their parents push them off on the baby-sitters, and these parents have no time to direct and look after their children. The fathers do not even know what their children do during the day since their mothers are also absent from the home, and so the fathers cannot discipline the children. This breaking apart of the family is the cause of the high rate of divorce; as the women become financially independent, they flee the responsibilities of being wives and mothers.

Not only do the crime rate and the divorce rate in such countries rise; the morals of such a society are lowered or completely lost. As women desert their natural jobs as keepers of virtue and teachers of culture, they too are assailed by the temptations of the world. For instance, in the past, when women stayed at home, it was rare that a woman committed a serious crime such as robbery or murder, but today it is not so unusual. As women become more and more a part of the men's world, their association with men results in immoral acts, the consequence being that many more women are becoming illegitimately pregnant. And at the present time, abortion for unmarried women is a common occurrence; sometimes it is even considered legal in these societies. This last example gives sufficient proof about the utter degradation and loss of morals in a society where women work outside their homes and bring themselves in contact with men.

In brief, having women work outside the home is morally wrong from a religious point of view. It is also a form of social injustice, for the consequences of having women in the work force cause great social problems. Finally, the long-term effects of allowing women to work outside their homes will be a change in the character of women, which will eventually destroy societies and indeed whole nations.

***Mohammed Akode Osman,* Sudan**

EXERCISE 5-M

1. Exchange summary-response drafts with a partner. As you read your partner's draft,
   A. use the **Summary Checklist** on page 140 to determine to effectiveness of the summary in the introduction of the essay.
   B. use Figure 5.2 (p. 152) to evaluate the use of appropriate writing conventions in your partner's draft.
   C. write two questions that will help your partner improve the writing conventions in her/his draft.
2. Ask your partner about his/her audience and try to "become" that audience. Does the essay fulfill the expectations of that audience? Why or why not? Discuss your answer with your partner. Be specific.
3. In two of the body paragraphs of the draft, underline the cohesion devices (repetition of key words and phrases, use of pronouns, and use of transitions).
4. What do you think is the greatest strength of your partner's draft? Tell your partner why.

Writing Assignment:
Revision

1. Reread your draft and consider your partner's suggestions for revision and editing. Then write a revision plan for your summary-analysis essay.
2. Use the **Guidelines for Revision** on the inside back cover of this book to revise your essay.
3. Reread your draft, editing for language errors.
4. Rewrite your essay.
5. Turn in your essay and your revision plan to your instructor.

Writing Assignment VIII Write a memo to your instructor in which you discuss your experience of writing the summary-analysis essay. (Review memo format on p. 95.) List what was easy and difficult; what problems you encountered and how you solved them; and what you learned from the experience.

Writing Assignment IX Read an article from a major news magazine (*Time, Newsweek, U.S. News and World Report*) or read an editorial in a newspaper. Use Figure 5-2 (p. 152) to write a two-page (approximately 500 words) summary-response to that article, using the processes and strategies explained in this chapter. Remember: because your audience (i.e., your instructor) has not read the article, you must summarize more completely in a background paragraph that follows the introduction.

1. Use the **Guidelines for Composing** (on the inside front cover of this book) as you draft your essay. Remember to include a reference page with the bibliographic data for your chosen article.
2. Exchange your draft with a partner. Use the **Summary Checklist** on page 140 to determine to effectiveness of (a) the main idea summary in the introduction of the essay and (b) the more complete summary in the background paragraph.
3. Use Figure 5.2 (p. 152) to evaluate the use of appropriate writing conventions in your partner's draft.
4. Discuss with your partner your suggestions for improvement of his/her draft. Listen to his/her comments about your draft.
5. Use the **Guidelines for Revision** on the inside back cover of this book to revise your essay.
6. As you edit your essay, consult a native English speaker to help you find and correct language errors.

Written Summaries and Analyses of Academic Research

Most graduate students (and many undergraduate students who are studying in their majors fields) are asked to

- *review the results of a research article* that has been published in a journal in their major fields
- prepare an *annotated bibliography* about a class-related topic
- write a *literature review* about a single research topic

In such assignments, the summary may make up most of the essay, with only brief comments from the student writer about the "usefulness" of the results or about future research that needs to be done. In some cases, the assignment may require only a summary.

Below are two academic assignments for summary and/or analysis of academic research. Read the assignments and then do the exercise that follows.

I Fisheries and Wildlife (Undergraduate Course)
Prepare an **annotated bibliography** with a minimum of 10 references for one of the selected wild animal species (or a group of species, like bats) and for one disease (or group of diseases, like intestinal parasites) from the Central Rockies Region (Arizona, Colorado, Idaho, Montana, New Mexico, Utah, and Wyoming). The species and disease must be approved ahead of time to avoid duplication.
The **summary** or **abstract** for each reference should be short (4–6 lines) and should include the disease and the species studied, the locations and dates, and should emphasize the sample size, results, and conclusions, but not necessarily techniques.
Provide a subject index for each reference, with the common and scientific names of the species and diseases and location (see attached example).

II Erosion and Sedimentation (Graduate Seminar)
Write a recent **literature review** on one of the following topics. The review will be 5–8 double-spaced pages, and no source should be older than two years.

Soil Erosion Control Methods
Sheet Erosion
Control of Reservoir Sedimentation
Mud Flow and Debris Flow
Sediment Measurement Techniques—Reservoir Deposits

EXERCISE 5-N

1. Which of the assignments above do you think will be easier to complete? Why? Discuss your answers with a partner or a small group.
2. Which assignment requires an analysis as well as a summary? How do you know?
3. Neither of these assignments is complete, and the language in each is sometimes confusing. With a partner or a small group, decide which questions you should ask the instructor in order to write a successful paper.
4. In Example **I**, how will inclusion of an example by the instructor help the students?

WRITING THE SUMMARY-ANALYSIS OF A RESEARCH REPORT

This type of assignment resembles the written summary-analysis assignments discussed earlier in the chapter, but only a small proportion of the paper may contain analysis. Indeed, the paper may not even have a thesis statement of *opinion* in the introduction. Instead, it may have a thesis statement of the writer's *intent* to review the article(s) (see Student Sample 23 below).

Gathering information for the summary of a research report can be a simple process because most research articles published in journals begin with an **abstract**: a summary of the written material that follows the title and author(s) of the article. Below is an example of an abstract from a research report.

[Title] *A Survey of Meteorological Disasters in the Taiwan Area*

Abstract

[Introduction] Natural disasters caused by severe weather associated with tropical cyclones, Mei-Yu frontal systems, cold waves, and significant droughts, which occurred in the past twenty-two years over the Taiwan area, were *[Body]* investigated. It was found that tropical cyclones and the attendant torrential rains and high winds were the most serious meteorological hazards during the period 1971-1992, in which 96 deaths and 317 injuries resulted, and 3864 houses were destroyed. The damage for crop loss was estimated at an average of two billion NT dollars annually. Disasters *[Conclusion]* caused by other disastrous weather phenomena were also surveyed and are reported in this paper.

Shinn-Liang Shieh **and** ***Cheng-Kai Chen,*** **Republic of China (ROC)**

By reading the abstract, writers can discover the main ideas in the article. Then, by reading the headings and subheadings in the article, the writer can locate the more important details.

The summary of the research article will follow the order of the article: usually one or more paragraphs that provide the background and focus of the research; one or more paragraphs that describe the methods (i.e., processes) and/or materials used in the research; and one or more paragraphs that summarize the most important results of the research as well as the discussion of those results. Figure 5-3 depicts the basic form for a summary–analysis of a research report. Notice that it is similar to the form for other summary–analysis assignments.

Introduction

- provides appropriate bibliographic information (title, author, journal, issue, inclusive page numbers)
- a brief summary of the problem area studied
- a thesis statement of intent such as
  This essay reviews . . . and comments on . . . .

Body paragraph(s) include

- a statement of the question(s) the author attempted to answer
- a summary of methods and materials used
- *[Major findings, conclusions]* a summary of data and results
- a summary of discussion

Conclusion (Analysis)

- *[Analysis]* comments on the value (i.e., practical significance) of the study
- comments on additional research needed or link to research you are planning

Figure 5-3 *Organization of an Analysis of a Research Report*

Depending on the assignment, the analysis of a research report can identify any problems in the research design or in the discussion of results; evaluate the applicability or practicality of the research; and/or suggest future research that will build on the current article.

Below is an example of a research report summary-analysis.

Review of Research Report

[Thesis statement] *Several studies have documented that different cultures produce different attitudes toward breastfeeding.*

[Introduction: type of research] In a large-scale survey and interview qualitative research project, J. M. Pascoe and A. Berger (1985) compared high school girls' attitudes *[Bibliographic data]* in Israel and the United States. In "Attitudes of High School Girls in Israel and the United States toward Breastfeeding," the researchers *[Summary of results]* found that Israeli girls had much more positive attitudes toward breastfeeding than American girls, and a higher proportion of Israeli girls reported that they planned to breastfeed their children. In statistical analysis of the data, the researchers found that the Israeli girls were significantly higher in their belief that their mothers had more positive views toward breastfeeding than did American girls' mothers. The study *[Analysis: link to student's research]* adds support to other studies I am using in my research that native women of other countries may have more positive attitudes toward breastfeeding than American women.

<u>Reference</u>

Pascoe, J. M. & Berger, A. (1985). Attitudes of high school girls in Israel and the United States toward breastfeeding. *Journal of Adolescent Health Care, 6,* 28–30.

JinQiu (Jenny) Yang, **People's Republic of China (PRC)**

WRITING AN ANNOTATED BIBLIOGRAPHY

An annotated bibliography is a list of several citations of articles; following each citation is a brief note (annotation) that summarizes the article. In an annotated bibliography, the writer identifies, locates, reads, and writes a brief summary (and sometimes a short comment, depending on the assignment) about *each* of a group of research articles about a single topic. Below is a sample of a single annotation.*

Note: The writing conventions for an annotated bibliography require the writer to begin with a formal citation of the source.

Annotated Bibliography Entry

[Bibliographic entry]

Picart, S. & Genies, E. (1996). "Electrochemical study of 2,5-dimercapto- 1,3,4,-thiadiazole in acetonitrile," *Journal of Electro-analytic Chemistry, 408,* 53–60.

[Summary/Abstract of research article]

In this research the electrochemical behavior of DMCT and its derivatives were studied on platinum by potential sweep voltammetry in acetonitrile. Reactions and redox potentials of the dithiol, thiolate, dithiolate and dimer forms of DMCT were characterized. The reaction mechanism and kinetics of the disulphide-thiolate redox couple were investigated. The results demonstrated that the reaction is chemically reversible but kinetically slow at ambient temperature, which is common to many organodisulphide compounds; oxidation of thiolate occurs via the formation of thiyl radical which dimerizes in disulphide. For the dithiolate, oxidation proceeds in two steps: the dithiolate of the dimer is first formed and is further oxidized to give oligomers. This reaction, in the same manner as for oxidation of the thiolate form, is chemically reversible but kinetically hindered.

[Analysis: comment on research results]

NOTE: although this report adds support to previous research, the pKa of 2.1 in the water may be anomalous; additional research needs to be done.

***Eiichi Shoji*, Japan**

WRITING THE LITERATURE REVIEW

Another type of research analysis assignment is the literature review. In a term paper or thesis, the literature review takes the annotated bibliography assignment one step further: writers summarize results of several (or even many) studies in one area of research, briefly commenting on the similarities and differences as well as evaluating the value of the results for the research work they are doing. But instead of just listing each research report separately (as in the annotated bibliography), the writer *synthesizes* the information by categorizing the reports and summarizing and analyzing by category. The writer groups the studies he or she is synthesizing according to a principle: from the earliest to the most recent research, or from reports that agree with the hypothesis to reports that disagree, or from reports of large-scale research to reports of smaller-scale research, etc.

For this type of research-based assignment, the paper will consist mostly of summary. Whether or not the writer comments on (i.e., analyzes) the reports depends on the assignment. Below is an example of a paragraph from the literature review of a doctoral thesis.

* For consistency, in these examples I have changed the field-specific citation formats to APA.

Paragraphs from a Thesis Literature Review

[Introduction: historically organized] [Summary] [Synthesis of development of research technique] [Multiple authors] [Current theory] [NO analysis]

Serological reactions were posed by de Barjac and Bonnefoi (1962) for B. thuringiensis classification as to their subspecies according to antigenic reactions of the flagellar protein (H-antigen) possessed by the young motile cells of this species. Heimpel (1967) concluded that H-antigens proved to have very reproducible biochemical characteristics.

This technique was later discussed in detail by de Barjac (1981). She described the preparation of H-antigen suspension and H-antisera, as well as agglutination and cross-saturation techniques. Another technique for H-serotyping of B. thuringiensis (BT) isolates was proposed by Ohba and Aizawa (1978) and was extensively described by Padua et al. (1980).* Most researchers used flagellar typing as a major tool for classifying subspecies of BT, although biochemical characteristics have been retained as part of the classification process. Dulmage and Aizawa (1982) reported that electrophoretic patterns of esterases produced by vegetative cells of BT could also be used to distinguish subspecies of this organism. Recent information reported that there are 35 subspecies of BT, based on H-serotyping, enterase patterns, and biochemical profiles (Crickmore et al., 1995).

References

[Article from published proceedings of conference presentation; multiple authors] [Author publishing alone listed before the same author publishing with others] [Foreign language journal article] [Chapter in an edited book] [Journal article] [References listed alphabetically by author's last name]

Crickmore, N., Zeigler, J., Feitselson, E., Schnepf, B., Lambert, D., Lereclus, C., Burk, G., & Dean, D. H. (1995). Revision of the nomenclature for *Bacillus thuringiensis* cry genes. In *Program and abstracts of the 28th annual meeting of the Society for Invertebrate Pathology,* Bethesda, Maryland p. 14.

de Barjac, H. (1981). Identification of H-serotypes of *Bacillus thuringiensis.* In K. Burges (Ed.), *Microbial Control of Pests and Plant Diseases,* pp. 35–43. New York: Academic Press.

de Barjac, H. & Bonnefoi, J. (1962). Essai de classification biochemique et serologique de 24 souches de Bacillus de type *B. thuringiensis. Entomophaga, 3,* 223–229.

Dulmage, H. T. & Aizawa, K. (1982). Distribution of *Bacillus thuringiensis* in nature. In E. Kurstak (Ed.), *Microbial and Viral Pesticides,* pp. 224–238. New York: Marcel Dekker.

Heimpel, A. M. (1967). A taxonomic key proposed for the species of the crystaliferous bacteria, *Journal of Invertebrate Pathology, 12,* 152–170.

Ohba, M. & K. Aizawa. (1978). Serological identification of *Bacillus thuringiensis* and related bacteria in Japan. *Journal of Invertebrate Pathology, 32,* 303–409.

* When a source is written by multiple authors, the in-text citation lists the first author + "et al.," which is a Latin abbreviation for "and others." The end-of-text reference must contain the names of all authors.

Padua, L. E., Ohba, M. & Aizawa, K. (1980). The isolates of *Bacillus thuringiensis* serotype 10 with a high preferential toxicity to mosquito larvae. *Journal of Invertebrate Pathology, 36,* 180–186.

***Walid Maaty,* Egypt**

EXERCISE 5-O

1. With a partner or a small group of classmates, discuss the writing conventions for Student Samples 22–25 above. Although you may not be able to understand every term, you can describe the ways each writer followed appropriate conventions.
2. In Sample 22, what will the next paragraph be about? How do you know?
3. In Sample 25, which journal seems to be most helpful for the student writer? Suggestion: look at the reference list.
4. In the references for Sample 25, the de Barjac and Bonnefoi article has a French title. What does that tell you about the student writer?
5. Which of these types of research report summary-analysis will you probably use in your major field? Discuss your answer with your classmates.

RATIO OF SUMMARY TO ANALYSIS IN ACADEMIC ASSIGNMENTS

As you have learned in this chapter, the percentage of summary and analysis in an academic assignment depends on the 3 **As**: **A**ssignment (purpose), **A**udience, and **A**vailable material. For example, assignments that ask for a "brief summary" and/or a "thorough analysis" demand a somewhat different essay than an assignment that calls for "a complete summary with a brief opinion in the conclusion." Moreover, an audience that has not read the material usually needs a more complete summary.

Note: Even if your instructor has read the written material, the assignment may ask for a full summary so that you can demonstrate your ability to communicate the main ideas and your understanding of that material. Figure 5-4 depicts approximate ratios of summary to analysis in academic assignments.

Situation	Summary	Analysis	Example
Audience has not read the material and needs an extended summary	40%–50%	50%–60% (use a background paragraph)	**Figure 5.2,** p. 152
Audience has read the material and expects a detailed analysis	20%–30%	70%–80% (no background paragraph)	**Figure 5.2,** p. 152
Research article review; extended summary, limited analysis	70%–80%	20%–30%	**Figure 5.3,** p. 164

Figure 5-4 *Ratio of Summary to Analysis in Academic Assignments*

Remember: When in doubt about the ratio of summary to analysis in an assignment, ask necessary questions about the instructor's expectations for the summary-analysis assignment. For example,

- How brief or how detailed should the summary be?
- Is *only* a summary required? (A research report, for example, might require an extensive summary of several articles, and nothing more.)
- Is a response required? If so, should you
  – write about your own feelings and/or ideas?
  – relate the written material to your own experience?
  – use personal experience to support your feelings/ideas?

- Is an analysis required? If so, should you
  - form opinions or comment on the ideas or results of the material?
  - support your opinions or ideas with facts, examples, and/or description?
- Should you respond and/or analyze
  - parts of the material that you select or
  - all the main ideas in the written material?

DISCIPLINE-SPECIFIC CITATION FORMATS

In this textbook, you have been using the APA style for in-text and end-of-text citations. However, many academic fields have unique citation formats, and in some disciplines there are several possible citation styles. The major style formats are usually described in a book-length manual. Students can find these style manuals in the reference section of the college or university library, or they can purchase the style manual used in their major field. Some of these are:

American Psychological Association Publication Manual (APA)
American Chemical Society Style Guide (ACS)
American Society of Agronomy Publications Handbook
American Geophysical Union Style Guide (AGU)
American Medical Association Manual of Style
Council of Biology Editors Style Manual (CBE)
Gregg Reference Manual (for business writing)
Chicago Manual of Style

Access to a style manual for your major field can make the citation in research writing easier. Other ways to learn about the appropriate citation format for your major field are to:

- ask a major professor or advisor about the acceptable style format; many academic departments have their own graduate student manuals that contain basic information about citation style(s),
- ask a reference librarian for assistance,
- look in the prestigious journals in your major field for examples to imitate, or look at a recent master's or doctoral thesis in your major field for examples to imitate.
- find excerpts from the appropriate style manual on the World Wide Web.

EXERCISE 5-P Locate information about the appropriate citation style for your major field by (a) asking a professor or a reference librarian, (b) photocopying in-text and end-of-text citations from 2 or 3 prestigious journals in your field, (c) looking at a recent master's or doctoral thesis in your field, or (d) finding examples of the citation style on the WWW. Give examples of the following about your major field's citation format.

1. The name of your field's citation style: ______________________
2. Sample in-text citation: ______________________
3. Is there a difference between citations for material used in your own words and citations used for direct quotations? If YES, what is/are the difference(s)?

   ____

4. Placement of in-text citations: ______________________
   - in parentheses, immediately following the material ______________
   - in small type, in parentheses, raised above the line ______________
   - no parentheses, numbers raised above the line ______________
   - Other (specify) ______________________

5. Title of end-of-text citation page (e.g., References, Bibliography): ____________
6. How are the end-of-text citations organized? ____________________
   - alphabetically by author's last name ____________________
   - alphabetically by title ____________________
   - chronologically, as they occurred in the article ____________________
   - Other (specify) ____________________
7. Write a sample end-of-text citation. ____________________
8. Did you discover more than one citation format available in your major field? If so, describe the differences. ____________________

____

Writing Assignment X This is a scientific/technical assignment. Select and analyze a recent research report (one published within the last two years) in one of your major field's journals, or in a journal about a field in which you are interested. Your audience for this assignment is an instructor in your major field. Your specific purposes for this assignment are to

- learn about a current area of research
- summarize the experimental methods and approaches used
- summarize the results and discussion of the study
- comment on the practical significance of the study
- comment *briefly* on the usefulness of the work for other researchers (or for you).

Note: You may write a single paragraph of summary, or you may choose to write several paragraphs to summarize the article. However, your analysis should be 1 or 2 sentences only.

Directions:

1. Use the information about overall organization in Figure 5-3.
2. Use the *Abstract* in the journal and the headings and subheadings in the article to help write the summary.
3. Use the form on page 164 to help draft your summary-analysis paragraph(s).
4. Use your field-specific citation style for the in-text and end-of-text references.

EXERCISE 5-Q

1. In a small group, compare and contrast your field-specific citation styles. What are the similarities and the differences among the several citation formats you are discussing?
2. Describe the research report you are summarizing and analyzing to your group. Remember that if your classmates do not have enough technical knowledge to understand the research, you must choose your words carefully.
3. Discuss with your group any problems you are having with this scientific/technical assignment. Are your problems different from other group members' problems? What solutions can you suggest for the problems being discussed?

Writing Assignment XI Write a memo to your instructor that describes (a) the help you gave and (b) the help you received from your peer response groups as you wrote your summary-analysis assignments in this chapter. Use, for example, the group discussions you participated in from Writing Assignments I, III, IV, and X, and Exercises 5-C, 5-D, and 5-H. Be specific: use the names of the classmates who offered you suggestions, and whom you offered suggestions. Suggestion: Review Student Samples 6 and 7 on page 149.

Chapter 6

Persuading an Audience:

The Arguing Essay

Struggling with the different essays in this course, I have begun to understand more in depth the American way of writing. For example, while I have appreciated the freedom to express our opinions in both writing and speaking, I have been most pleased to learn how to support my opinions and to persuade others in the American way. In addition, analyzing writing topics from other courses has given me feelings of confidence and independence. I am even beginning to enjoy writing!

Mebrat Gesese, Ethiopia

PERSUASION IS an activity we practice every day: convincing a younger brother to share a toy, persuading an instructor to postpone the due date of a paper, convincing a friend to go to the movies. Written persuasion is sometimes more difficult because the reader does not see the writer's facial expressions, hear his or her voice, or experience his or her presence. For this reason, writing persuasive essays demands careful planning, analysis of the audience, and sufficient evidence.

EXERCISE 6-A Read the persuasive paragraph below. Notice that the student writer has identified—and writes directly to—his audience (classmates who are tired of the winter climate) and that he has clearly stated the purpose of the paragraph (to persuade the readers to come to his country). What supporting techniques does this writer use to persuade his classmates?

Come to Vietnam!

During a long harsh winter in Iowa, wouldn't you like to get away from the snow and go to the beach? If you have the time, I know the place. I am talking about the best stretches of white sand beach in the whole of Southeast Asia. I know you have excellent beaches in the U.S., but the beaches near my home are more beautiful than Fort Lauderdale and Malibu combined. Just picture this: white hot sand, so white that you need to wear sunglasses to guard against the glare, and so hot that your bare feet will jump. The temperature is always in the nineties, but the cool breeze from the sea will keep you comfortable. I know you would love to learn to surf, and that you hate crowded beaches. This beach gets the best waves in the world for surfing. You will be amazed at how tall the waves get! Best of all, you will be the only person surfing because the Vietnamese don't surf. Of course, there will be just a few beautiful girls to watch you, and they will be excited with your achievements. One last thing: it is cheap to come to my country, and while you are there you will stay with my family, so you will have no expenses. Just imagine yourself, surfing along the endless beach under the hot sun, and come to Vietnam!

***Binh Tran,* Vietnam**

Persuasion in Academic Writing

Most academic writing assignments are tests. Consequently, for most students, the purpose for these assignments is to persuade the instructor that they (a) understand the material being taught, (b) can apply the information to issues or situations outside the class discussion, (c) are capable of integrating classroom material with sources investigated outside the classroom, and/or (d) can present material using appropriate writing conventions.

In addition to persuading the instructor about the students' competence, academic writing assignments often ask students to persuade the audience that an idea or an opinion is **valid**: that whether or not the readers agree with the writers, they believe that the ideas or opinions have been supported. Although personal experience can be used to support ideas and opinions in academic writing, other forms of support are often expected by the U.S. academic audience: facts and examples from survey results; interviews with authorities; results of experimental research; and material from books, journal articles, field-specific encyclopedias, and dictionaries.

ARGUMENT

Persuasion is the goal of both oral and written argument. The objective of oral argument is to succeed in persuading the opponent that an idea or opinion is valid. In academic writing assignments, argument is often a part of a larger assignment: the writer may be asked to (a) *summarize* an article about an issue, give an opinion about an issue, and support that opinion (i.e., *persuade*), (b) *investigate* an idea, *analyze* that idea, and provide *persuasive* evidence that supports the analysis, or (c) *explain* a problem, *describe* solution(s) to a problem, select a solution, and demonstrate why that solution is best (i.e., *persuade*).

AUDIENCE ANALYSIS

Because persuasion is directly related to the listener or reader, audience analysis is particularly important in argument. In addition to identifying the basic characteristics of the readers (e.g., knowledge of and interest in the topic, educational background, socio-economic status), academic writers must also analyze the readers'

attitude toward the topic,
possible attitude toward the writer,
possible objections to the writer's opinion, and
reaction to the intended purpose of the arguing paper.

ORAL ARGUMENTS

When we argue orally, the issue usually has two sides. That is, the controversy has two opposing answers, often *Yes* or *No*.

Should we go to Vietnam for our vacation? (*Yes* or *No*)
Should I take biochemistry next semester? (*Yes* or *No*)
Is fast food less nutritious than food cooked at home? (*Yes* or *No*)
Should U.S. universities offer more scholarship assistance to international students? (*Yes* or *No*)

Of course, oral arguments can have several sides, and sometimes several people in a group will argue for several different opinions.

What is the most challenging team sport? (*X* or *Y* or *Z* or . . .)
How should non-major college/university courses be graded? (*X* or *Y* or *Z* or . . .)
Which solution to ozone depletion is best? (*X* or *Y* or *Z* or . . .)

Because face-to-face arguments have the advantage of the physical presence of the participants, persuasive techniques are strengthened by facial expressions, loudness of voice, body language (advancing menacingly, putting an arm around the opponent's shoulders), and gestures.

In formal oral arguments, called debates, two persons or groups present opposite sides of the argument as strongly and as intellectually as they can. They use supporting evidence (facts, examples, description, personal experience) as well as some of the physical strategies listed above. They defend their side of the argument, and they try to **refute** (i.e., weaken, discredit, or destroy) the arguments of those on the other side of the debate. The winner of the debate is the person or group who most successfully presents and defends one side of the argument while refuting the opposing argument. Here are two typical debate topics and arguments for and against each.

Should the TOEFL be required for every student entering college or the university whose first language is not English? (*Yes* or *No*)

Yes, because
- Students must be language-proficient.
- There has to be a standard.
- It helps students study.

No, because
- It doesn't measure real proficiency.
- It's an inauthentic examination.
- It harms students.

Should police have the legal authority to stop and search a person and his/her automobile without "probable cause"? (*Yes* or *No*)

Yes, because
- It protects all citizens.
- If you're obeying the law, you don't have any worry.
- It helps catch criminals.
- It gives police the power they need.

No, because
- It violates civil rights.
- It instills fear of the police in the non-criminal population.
- It inconveniences and embarrasses non-criminals.
- It gives police too much power.

WRITTEN ARGUMENTS

In written arguments, as in formal debates, the topic usually has two sides, the *pro* (*Yes: for* the issue) and the *con* (*No: against* the issue). The *con* issues of the argument are called the "counter-arguments." Because writers of arguments do not meet their audience face-to-face, they must use strong supporting evidence for their arguments. Furthermore, they must expect that at least some of their readers will hold the opposing view; therefore, like the debater, they must summarize and then attempt to **refute** (i.e., weaken, discredit, or destroy) the arguments of the opposition.

Some written arguments have more than two sides, particularly if the issue is a problem with several possible solutions:

Which car should I purchase? (*A* or *B* or *C* or . . .)
Which method of weed removal is most cost-effective? (*A* or *B* or *C* or . . .)

However, this chapter focuses only on the *Yes* or *No* questions. For example, instead of discussing the multiple choices for the questions above, we can narrow and restate the questions into *Yes* or *No* questions:

Is the Saturn the best car for me to purchase? (*Yes* or *No*)
Should the National Park Service use natural pesticides for weed removal? (*Yes* or *No*)

Below are three academic assignments that require students to develop and support ideas and opinions; comments in brackets [ ] clarify the assignments.

I **Introduction to Management**

[Citations required]

Write a 5-page, **fully referenced** paper that discusses [and **supports**] **your opinion** about the ideal management performance review [from several possible models].

II **Introduction to Political Science**

[At least 8 citations required]

Do you support the decision to deploy women for military service? Why or why not? Write an 8–10 page **research** paper (minimum sources: 8) that presents and **supports your opinion** on this issue.

III **Environmental Issues**

In an 8-10 page paper, **analyze** one of the environmental issues below. Use the following components of issue analysis: summarizing

[Organization of task]

the problem or issue; describing the differing beliefs (those ideas concerning the issue, whether true or false), values (the guides that reflect the relative importance of the beliefs), and/or solutions (the various strategies used to resolve the issue) that exist; **your position** about the solution of the problem or issue; **evidence** that supports the value of your position. Suggested issues:

- Should current federal and private proposals for protecting the nation's waterfowl population be improved?
- Should oil and gas development be permitted in the Arctic National Wildlife Refuge?
- Are toxicity standards for solid waste storage and disposal appropriate?
- Should the National Park Service continue its "let burn" policy when natural fires occur within park boundaries?
- Are natural pest management techniques in agriculture as effective and efficient as petrochemical methods?

EXERCISE **6-B**

1. For each of the assignments above, students are required to *explain* as well as to *argue*. What will students explain in each essay?
2. For Assignment **III**, arguing is only one of several objectives. In addition to explaining, what else will students do to fulfill the assignment?
3. With a partner or in a small group, analyze the academic assignments above.

   How will you organize each of the papers?
   What kinds of resources might you use for evidence in each?
   How might you use non-text materials in each of the papers?

4. For Assignment **II**, divide the class in half; assign one side of the argument to each side. Each group should (a) list the major arguments for both sides of the argument and (b) discuss the possible evidence for each side of the argument.
5. Exchange lists of arguments. Evaluate the strength of the other group's arguments: which side of the argument is the most persuasive?

Selecting an Argumentative Topic

Whether the student writer is fulfilling an assignment given by an instructor or choosing a topic, an arguable topic must be controversial. It must have at least two sides, and the audience for the paper must contain some readers who will agree and some who will disagree with the writer's opinion. If, for instance, the topic concerns whether or not the earth is flat, no argument is possible. To test a topic, state that topic as a *should* question and see whether the answers to that question could be either *Yes* or *No*.

Should first-year students be required to live in the dormitories? (*Yes* or *No*)
Should physical education classes be required for college/university graduation? (*Yes* or *No*)
Should undergraduate U.S. students study abroad for at least one year? (*Yes* or *No*)

Note: Because it is often stronger to argue the *pro* side of an issue, try to structure the *should* question so that the answer to your side of the issue is *Yes*. For example, if the answer to the question "Should first-year students be required to live in the dormitories?" is *No*, restate the question as "Should first-year students be allowed to live off-campus?" (for which the answer is now *Yes*).

EXERCISE 6-C

1. Consult the authority list you wrote in Chapter 1. Add topics to the list that you know about, that you are interested in, and that you would like to know more about.
2. Which of the topics on your authority list has a "piece of the pie" that is controversial? Select 2 or 3 of those controversies and write *should* questions about each of them.
3. Discuss your *should* questions from **#2** in a small group. Discover which of the topics also interests your classmates.
4. With your classmates, discuss the topics below that have been used by other college/university students in this course. Which interests you most? Why?

   Should the Olympics allow professionals to compete?
   Should my college/university be smoke-free?
   Should students be asked to evaluate their teachers?
   Should pornography on the Internet be censored?
   Should motorcyclists be required to wear helmets in the U.S.?
   Should students work for one year between secondary school and college?

Writing Assignment I

Select one of the *should* controversies that you discussed with your classmates in Exercise 6-C, or choose another *should* controversy. Write a 4–6 page paper in which you persuade your audience that your opinion about the controversy is valid.

The audience for this paper is **hostile**. That is, your reader is mean, unpleasant, and argumentative; he doesn't like you, and he doesn't agree with your opinion. In fact, he will never be persuaded that you are correct. At most, he will grudgingly agree that you have an opinion worth considering. Your purpose is to persuade this hostile audience that your opinion has merit and that your evidence is worthwhile.

Writing Assignment:
Collecting Information

1. Use 2 or 3 Collecting Strategies to gather information that you know about your topic (to review Collecting Strategies, see Chapter 2).
2. Make a list of questions about your topic for which you need to find answers. At the end of each question, write one way you might find the answer (such as an interview or a journal article).
3. Use the **Guidelines for Composing** (on the inside front cover of this textbook) to begin drafting your essay.

Writing Assignment:
Audience Analysis

Analyze the audience for your Arguing essay, using the following categories:

- readers' knowledge of and interest in the topic
- educational background and socio-economic status of the audience
- your relationship to the audience: expert to novice? classmate to classmate? more experienced to less experienced? student to instructor?
- audience's attitude toward your topic: passionately interested? hostile? ignorant but willing to learn? mildly interested? professionally interested? bored?
- audience's possible objections to your opinion
- readers' reaction(s) to the intended purpose of your arguing paper

Planning the Arguing Essay

The audience expects the student writer to know—and to present—both sides of the argument. Making a *pro-con* chart (such as Figure 6-1) that answers the *should* question helps students gather the arguments on both sides of the issue.

Question: *Should acupuncture become an accepted part of mainstream medicine?*

Pro *(Yes, because . . .)*

A history of thousands of years of use demonstrates that it heals some medical problems.

It is a completely non-harmful, non-toxic process.

Acupuncturists are highly trained medical professionals who must pass rigorous examinations.

Con *(No, because . . .)*

There is no acceptable empirical research that conclusively demonstrates healing.

The theory is unscientific.

There is no quality control in the U.S., so there is a danger to patients.

Figure 6-1 *Pro-Con Chart*

The goal for the Arguing essay assignment in this chapter should be three or four strong arguments for the *pro* side of the controversy. As students enter the *pro* (*Yes, because* . . .) arguments on their *pro-con* chart, they should evaluate each *pro* argument with the overall organization and the hostile audience in mind.

- Prioritize each *pro* argument: which is the strongest? the weakest?
- Is each *pro* argument easily supportable with facts and examples that will persuade the audience?
- Is one of the *pro* arguments a small part of a larger argument? If so, include it in the larger argument.
- For each argument, what interesting, new, and/or valuable information can the writer provide for the hostile audience?
- Is one of the *pro* arguments weaker, one that might not be persuasive for the hostile audience?
- Is the *pro* argument a fact that is accepted by both sides of the controversy? If so, use it only in the introduction or the background paragraph.

For the *con* (*No, because*. . .) side (the counter-arguments) of the issue, consider:

- Is each of the counter-arguments (opposing arguments) a major point that a hostile audience would recognize?
- Are any of the counter-arguments parallel to the *pro* arguments? For instance, does the *pro* argument say that *X* is less expensive, and the *con* argument say that *X* is more expensive? If so, list these parallel arguments next to each other.
- Can each of the counter-arguments be refuted (weakened, discredited, or destroyed)?

The Thesis Statement in Argumentation

Use an *although-because* sentence from the *pro-con* sheet to state your topic. This sentence will (a) incorporate the major arguments on both sides of the argument, (b) demonstrate that the controversy exists, and (c) provide a basic plan for the essay. In fact, a shorter form of the *although-because* sentence can become a thesis statement. Here is an example of a complete *although-because* statement, followed by a shortened form that could become the thesis statement for the Arguing essay.

Complete *Although-Because* Statement

[Counter-arguments]

Although the powerful American Medical Association has so far refused to recognize the usefulness of alternative medical techniques such as acupuncture because U.S. physicians believe that no scientific theory or empirical research support the claims of healing, and that the lack of quality control in the U.S. can easily result in harm to patients, *acupuncture should become an accepted part of the mainstream medical profession* **because** (a) it has a history of thousands of years of use that demonstrates its success in healing some medical problems, (b) it is a completely non-harmful, non-toxic process, and (c) it is done by highly trained medical personnel who must pass rigorous examinations.

[Student writer's thesis statement of opinion]

[Pro arguments]

Shortened *Although-Because* Statement

Although the powerful American Medical Association has so far refused to recognize the usefulness of alternative medical techniques such as acupuncture, *I believe that acupuncture should become an accepted part of the mainstream medical profession* **because** thousands of years of practice by highly trained personnel has demonstrated its success in healing some medical problems.

[Student writer's thesis statement of opinion]

Note: An even shorter thesis statement that does not include all of the major points in the *pro-con* chart can be used as the thesis statement:

Shortened Thesis Statement of Opinion and Intent

Acupuncture has proved its effectiveness over hundreds of years; it should therefore be an accepted part of the mainstream medical profession.

Writing Assignment:
Drafting the Thesis Statement

1. Make a *pro-con* chart for your Arguing topic; then write an *although-because* statement. Share your chart and your *although-because* statement with a partner or a small group of classmates. Offer additional arguments to your partner or classmates for their *pro-con* charts, and offer suggestions for refuting the counter-arguments.
2. Write a shortened form of your *although-because* statement as the thesis statement for your Arguing essay, or construct another, even shorter, thesis statement. Share your thesis statement with your classmates, perhaps by writing it on the chalkboard.
3. Offer suggestions for improving your classmates' thesis statements.

"VOICE" IN THE ARGUING ESSAY

In an oral argument, your actual voice is often as important as your body language, your facial expressions, and your gestures. Your voice can sound positive or negative; it can be soft or loud, deep or high, angry or reasonable. While winning the argument is important in North American culture, winning by physical or verbal intimidation—as the idiom "winning at any cost" states—is not usually culturally appropriate. For instance, in formal debates, using a reasonable voice in the presentation of material and the refutation of counter-arguments is usually more effective than shouting or verbally attacking the opposition.

Written "voice" can also be positive or negative, angry or reasonable (see p. 6 to review "voice" in writing). For example, Student Sample 1 in this chapter is written with a conversational voice. Binh Tran addresses his classmates directly, using personal pronouns (*you* and *I*), informal language (*jump* and *cheap*), and personal experience. In contrast, an engineer describing a computer model may use formal, technical language that communicates reasonably, efficiently, and effectively. The counter-argument about acupuncture (above) uses a formal, academic voice, with scientific words, complex sentences, and an objective approach: this is the written voice often used in the presentation of written material.

Organizing the Arguing Essay

As students draft the Arguing essay, they will make several decisions about organization and presentation. They will create a clear title and decide whether or not the Arguing essay needs a background paragraph. They will consider the opposing arguments and how best to refute them, and they will select an overall organizational plan.

THE TITLE FOR THE ARGUING ESSAY

Because the *should* question is focused directly on the Arguing topic, it might be used as the title for the paper, or it might be incorporated into the title. Here are some examples.

Should the Use of Marijuana Be Legalized for Medical Use?
Women in the Military: A Good Decision?
Should Oil and Gas Development Be Permitted in the Arctic National Wildlife Refuge?
Natural Pest Management Techniques: An Alternative to Petrochemicals
MANAGEMENT PERFORMANCE REVIEWS: WHICH IS BEST?
Should Medical Research about Human Cloning Be Legalized?

THE OPTIONAL BACKGROUND PARAGRAPH

Like other academic writing, an Arguing essay may contain a background paragraph—usually the first body paragraph after the introduction—that gives the audience necessary information for a complete understanding of the essay that follows (see Chapter 3, p. 73 to review background paragraphs). If the issue is familiar to your audience (such as whether first-year students should be required to live in the dormitories), a background paragraph may be unnecessary. But for most academic assignments, a background paragraph helps the reader.

In an Arguing essay, the background paragraph should be as objective as possible: its function is not to persuade, but to inform.

2 STUDENT SAMPLE

BACKGROUND PARAGRAPH

Should Students Be Required to Purchase a Meal Plan?

[Topic sentence] *[Definition]* *[Introduction to figure]*

Every student who lives in the dormitories has to select a Board Plan offered by the Residence Halls and Food Service Office. "Board," as defined in the U.S. idiom "room and board," means the meals a person in dormitory pays for. At the university, different dormitories have different food plans, as depicted in Figure __.

White, McIntyre, Downey, or Orr Hall Meal Plans
- "Unlimited" access/week (i.e., can attend every meal)
- 15 accesses/week (5 breakfasts required)
- 12 accesses/week (5 breakfasts required)

Hill Hall
- "Unlimited" access/week (i.e., can attend every meal)
- 15 accesses/week (5 breakfasts required)
- Any 9 accesses/week
- Any 7 accesses/week

Crane Hall
- "Unlimited" accesses/week (i.e., can attend every meal)
- 15 accesses/week (5 breakfasts required)
- 12 accesses/week (5 breakfasts required)
- Any 9 accesses/week
- Any 7 accesses/week
- Any 5 accesses/week
- Any 5 lunches/week
- Any 3 accesses/week
- No Board Plan

Figure __ *Board (Meal) Plans*

[Explanation of Figure]

As Figure __ demonstrates, different dormitories have different meal plans; some have many more alternatives than others. In fact, one dormitory, Crane Hall, even has a "no meal" option for its residents.

***Yasser Irfan,* Pakistan**

Writing Assignment: *The Background Paragraph*

Draft a background paragraph for your Arguing essay. Include at least two in-text citations for research in the paragraph (see Appendix A for a review of APA citation).

REFUTING THE COUNTER-ARGUMENT(S)

Intelligent readers expect an academic arguing paper to present counter-arguments—the opposing issues in the argument. If the writer does not demonstrate an awareness of the counter-arguments, readers might think that the writer has not explored the issue thoroughly (i.e., the writer is lazy), that the writer is not aware of the writing conventions of academic argument (i.e., that the writer is not informed), or that the writer is deliberately presenting only one side of the argument and is trying to avoid the counter-arguments (i.e., that the writer is trying to trick the reader).

Consequently, writers must anticipate the opposition and must attempt to refute the opposing arguments. They may introduce the counter-argument(s) with an appropriate transition, such as

Opponents of this position argue that . . .
Another argument against X is that . . .
Critics of this position point out that . . .
It may be objected that . . .
Several questions come to mind: . . .
At this point, one may wonder . . .
Certain objections must, of course, be considered:

After stating each opposing viewpoint, student writers must refute that counter-argument. They should indicate the beginning of the refutation by using an appropriate transition, such as *However, In contrast, Although, Even though, Despite,* or *In spite of.* Here is a possible counter-argument refutation for the acupuncture argument described above.

[Counter-argument]
[Contrast transition]
[Student writer's topic sentence of refutation]
[Support for topic sentence]

Many medical doctors refuse to recognize acupuncture because they believe that the theory behind the practice is non-scientific. However, the answer to this viewpoint lies in the definition of "unscientific." In the U.S., its meaning requires a large number of published empirical studies of thousands of patients, with statistical results and control groups, before the medical community will accept the practice (or the cancer drug, or the development of nutrition classes in medical school) as valid. In many other countries in the world, a "scientific theory" is one that has stood the test of time: if a medication or a practice has been used for hundreds or thousands of years, and has proved successful for thousands of patients, can the medication or the practice be "unscientific"? For acupuncture, the answer is even more clear: can a practice that "does no harm" (the first rule for medical doctors) and provides relief from many medical problems be considered unproved and therefore not be used by mainstream medical personnel?

As students approach each counter-argument, there are three ways to weaken or disprove it:

1. Correct the facts of the counter-argument: they are **incorrect.**

   The argument that solar energy is not efficient when compared to fossil fuels is **no longer correct**. Indeed, recent research has demonstrated that for geographic areas that receive at least 300 days of sun a year, newly developed solar energy systems are as efficient, and sometimes more efficient, than gas or oil heating (Harding & Becker, 1998).

2. Show that the counter-argument is not directly related to the issue: it is **irrelevant.**

   Despite the fact that Truscott's report cites a dozen studies that "prove" that correcting grammar errors in ESL student writing is ineffective, every study cited focuses on native English speakers; therefore, while the studies may be valid, they **do not relate** directly to ESL students.

3. Show that although the counter-argument is true and relevant, it is not enough to overcome your *pro* arguments: it is **insufficient**.

   Although North American food is fast and quite easy to fix, sitting down to a dinner that tastes like cardboard and is not much more nutritious makes eating a task rather than a pleasure.

Of the three refutation approaches, the compromising third solution, insufficiency, is most widely used. That is, the writer accepts the fact that counter-arguments exist, but provides evidence that the strength of those opposing arguments is inadequate, that the arguments on the other side of the issue are stronger.

EXERCISE 6-D Below are three examples of counter-arguments and the topic sentences that follow them. Identify the counter-argument refutation approaches (i.e., **incorrect**, **irrelevant**, or **insufficient**) and suggest ways you could provide evidence for the writer's opinion.

Note: Some refutations may use more than one approach.

COUNTER-ARGUMENT

Hospitalized Children: Can Visits from Dogs Make a Difference?

One argument against using dogs as therapists is that they may frighten rather than cheer the children. In contrast, recent research (e.g., Blackman, 1996; Davis, 1988; Hume, 1996) demonstrates that well-trained dogs stimulate socialization, fulfill children's needs for intimacy, and even increase the survival rate for severely ill children.

References

Blackman, D. (1996, August 2). What is animal-assisted therapy? [Online article]. Retrieved March 3, 1998 from the World Wide Web: http://dog&play.com/therapy.htm

Davis, J. H. (1998, February). Implication of the human-animal companion bond in the community. *Home Healthcare, 31,* 32–35.

Hume, L. (1996, August). Profile of an appropriate therapy dog. [Online article]. Retrieved March 3, 1998 from the World Wide Web: http://rehabnet.com/aft/aft2/html

Pablo Etcheverry, **Argentina**

COUNTER-ARGUMENT

Some people object to eating raw fish, saying that it is unhealthy, "disgusting," and even dangerous. **Although** some raw fish can be all of these things, if the fish is selected carefully and prepared properly, fresh fish (*sashimi*) tastes sweet and melts in your mouth. It is very healthy and **not at all dangerous.**

Kazue Suzuki, **Japan**

COUNTER-ARGUMENT

Executives in automobile manufacturing state that airbags are safe when the person is wearing a seatbelt and the airbag is deployed properly. **Even though** that statement may be true for a man of average height and weight, it is untrue for women of small stature and for young children because the airbag, exploding at 200 miles per hour, hits these shorter humans full in the face, often killing them (Norton, 1996).

Reference

Norton, R. (1996).Why airbags are killing kids. *Fortune, 9,* 60–62.

Ivan Hernandez, **Venezuela**

USING ROGERIAN ARGUMENT

Written argument requires that the writer select a "voice" carefully. Traditional argument strategies can be directly confrontational, waging a war against the opposition and trying to "win at any cost." However, most effective academic argumentative writing uses a reasonable "voice" and often uses a moderate, less confrontational approach. In the latter, the writer tries

- to reach out to the readers, even those whose beliefs differ, by immediately finding similarities with them,
- to persuade the reader by explaining both sides of the issue rather than by simply refuting opposition argument,
- to negotiate with the audience rather than fighting against them, and
- to reduce the differences between the hostile audience and the writer by offering compromise rather than insisting on an opposing recommendation or solution.

Culturally, this approach, based on psychologist Carl Rogers's writings and thus called "Rogerian argument," is effective because it focuses on communication rather than on winning. The more sensitive or controversial the issue, the more a Rogerian argument strategy may be necessary. That is, the more strongly readers feel about a position, the more they will feel personally attacked when that position is refuted, the more they will react defensively, and the less they will be open to accepting new ideas. But readers who believe that the writer recognizes their viewpoints and is sensitive to their beliefs are more likely to consider a different point of view. Strategies useful in effective Rogerian argument include:

- avoiding a war-like confrontational stance by establishing "common ground," by indicating that the writer shares the reader's beliefs, values and concerns,
- presenting the writer's character (i.e., personality) as understanding and empathetic,
- accurately stating (not overstating) the *pro* side of the issue
- presenting the opposing views of the issue fairly, and
- directing the argument toward a compromise or a flexible solution.

Of course, counter-arguments must still be refuted. Therefore, academic written argument most often uses a combination of traditional and Rogerian argument. But because the audience will include readers who both agree and disagree with the writer's opinion, using a reasonable voice and exploring a compromise solution are essential.

Below are four counter-argument paragraphs. Each is preceded by (a) the title of the arguing essay and (b) the thesis statement of that essay. Read the paragraphs and then do the exercise that follows.

Note: The organizational plan (*A, B,* or *C*) for the Arguing essay is included in the annotations and explained in the next section starting on page 184.

Grading Freshman Composition

[Thesis statement] *From my point of view, the freshman composition class should be a pass/fail course rather than an A–F graded course.*

[Plan A] *[Counter-argument]* *[Topic sentence]* *[Traditional refutation; confrontational voice;* ***incorrect]*** *[Conclusion]*

The core requirements for the university include passing freshman composition with a "C or higher." However, the grade you get in this class has nothing to do with your English abilities or your writing skills. Instead, you are forced to read about writing, to write reference lists, to write about personal experience, and to take tests about the words that English teachers use to talk about writing. Foreign students who want to learn to speak and write English better do not get this opportunity in this class. For example, there is no work on grammar and no exercises to help our speaking abilities. Moreover, the class has nothing to do with students' major fields. We do not learn to write engineering papers or laboratory reports, and even the bibliography exercises are not right for my field, engineering. Therefore, if it is impossible to change the rules for graduation and not even include this class, at least it should be a pass/fail class.

Ivar Noer, **Norway**

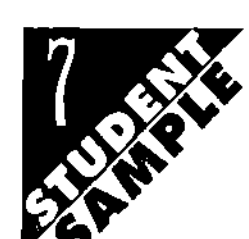

The Green Revolution

[Thesis statement] *Although the Green Revolution contributed to resolving the famine in Third World countries, its achievement has been limited by its negative effects.*

[Plan C] *[Counter-argument #1]* *[Topic sentence]*

In Africa, the introduction of Green Revolution technology, in particular the initial capital to buy fertilizer and pesticides that was provided by the Agency for International Development (AID), was very successful. However, in subsequent years, farmers could not pay their debts. The social and economic effects were disastrous: some farmers lost their land;

[Traditional refutation; reasonable voice; ***insufficient****]* others had to return to their traditional subsistence farming, which resulted in poorer quality and nutrients. Moreover, agricultural pests that traditional farming practices had overcome for a thousand years returned with a vengeance (Oldfield, 1989). Therefore, the difference between short-term gain and long-term loss is evident.

Reference

Oldfield, D. (1989). *The green revolution: Technology and society.* New York: Harcourt Brace.

Marcelo Salgado, **Argentina**

Should Graduate Students Teach Undergraduates?

[Shortened although-because *thesis]* *Although most international graduate students have strong background knowledge in their major fields, most do not have the experience or the knowledge to be successful university teachers.*

[Plan B] *[Counter-arguments]* *[Information from interview]* *[Traditional refutation;* ***incorrect****]* *[Topic sentence]* *[Rogerian compromise]*

According to Professor Patricia Byrd, Director of the International Teaching Assistant (ITA) Training Program, most international graduate students can become excellent teachers of undergraduates if they are first required to complete the ITA program. During this semester-long intensive course, the students learn about U.S. educational systems, the complexities of academic classrooms, and the expectations of U.S. students, as well as working on presentation skills such as pronunciation, lesson planning, and asking and answering questions. <u>Unfortunately</u>, the results of my survey of 25 native English speaking undergraduate students demonstrates that a majority of those undergraduates (86%) believe that international graduate students are not effective teachers, even if they have completed the ITA training program. <u>However</u>, it is possible that, as Dr. Byrd also explained, if the U.S. undergraduates were also educated about the value of ITAs, and if those undergraduates were given appropriate cultural information and coping skills, many of them might change their minds about ITAs.

Bo Ruan, **People's Republic of China (PRC)**

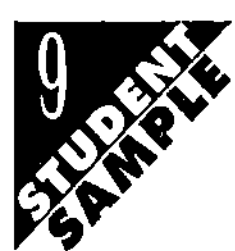

<u>Birth Control in China</u>

[Shortened although-because *thesis]* *Although many Chinese couples would prefer to have more than one child, birth control is not only an important and strategic step for developing China, but also it is profitable for Chinese women and Chinese children.*

[Plan B] *[Rogerian approach: shared beliefs]* *[Traditional refutation;* ***incorrect****]*

It is true that we Chinese love children very much, and we would choose to have more than one child. Some people even say that the government limit of one child per family infringes on human rights. But what are human rights? They must be based on the benefit for the whole of human kind, not based on the benefit for one family. At present, China is a poor country, and the living standard is so low, that the most basic human

[Conclusion] rights are the rights to live without fear of hunger or disease, and to raise a child into a better standard of living. For this reason, many couples in China are advocating for the government rule of one child per family.

***Ru Chien,* People's Republic of China (PRC)**

EXERCISE 6-E

1. With a partner or in a small group, discuss the Rogerian approaches used in the counter-argument refutations above. How does each author reach out to the audience?
2. In Student Sample 7, the writer compromises with the audience. Discuss why you think this is or isn't a persuasive approach.
3. What effect does the use of authoritative quotes, references, and survey information have on the persuasive quality of the counter-argument paragraphs?
4. Which paragraph do you think is the most persuasive? Why?
5. Look at the counter-arguments in Exercise 6-D. In what ways can you make the refutations of those arguments more Rogerian?

Writing Assignment:
Refuting the Counter-argument(s)

1. Use your *pro-con* chart to identify 2 or 3 major counter-arguments about your Arguing topic. Then list ways of refuting each of those arguments.
2. Do you already have the necessary evidence (facts, examples, experiences, or description) to refute each counter-argument? If not, list resources that you will need for that refutation.
3. Share your counter-arguments and refutation resources with a partner or a small group of classmates. Discuss the refutation techniques and resources of your partner or classmates, and offer information to help.
4. What Rogerian approaches might you use to refute the counter-arguments? Discuss these approaches with your group. Be specific.
5. Write a rough draft of your counter-arguments for your Arguing paper.

Overall Organizational Structures for the Arguing Essay

Organizing your arguments in order of importance and strength is essential for effective communication and persuasion, and the placement and refutation of counter-arguments are often determined by (a) the audience and (b) the available material. For some Arguing essays, you might choose to cite and refute the counter-arguments late in the essay; in others, confronting the counter-arguments immediately might be more successful.

Arguing essays have many of the same writing conventions as Explaining essays. That is, these essays begin with typical introductions and end with typical conclusions; they also have the option of a background paragraph. There are three possible overall structures for argumentative essays: Plans **A**, **B**, and **C**. Below are outlines for each plan. Each includes a student example of prewriting, an outline, and an essay map. (Examples of refutation of counter-arguments for each of the organizational plans were demonstrated in Student Samples 6–9 above.)

PLAN A

The first plan, outlined in Figure 6-2, begins with the weakest *pro* argument and builds to the strongest *pro* argument, then confronts the counter-arguments in a final paragraph just before the conclusion. If the *pro-con* chart demonstrates that (a) there are just one or two major counter-arguments and that (b) these counter-arguments do not parallel the *pro* arguments, Plan A is the best choice.

Organizational Plan A

I Introduction + thesis statement of intent and opinion
II Background paragraph (optional)
III Pro argument #1 (weakest argument that supports your opinion)
IV Pro argument #2 (stronger argument that supports your opinion)
V Pro argument #3 (strongest argument that supports your opinion)
VI Con argument(s) and refutation of the counter-argument(s)
VII Conclusion (summary + recommendation, solution, prediction)

Figure 6-2 *Overall Organization for Arguing Essay: Plan A*

PLAN A

Question: *Should we focus on the development of solar energy systems?*

Pro *(Yes, because . . .)*
- The source (the sun) is free.
- The source is inexhaustible and plentiful.
- The systems are safe, non-polluting.
- The systems need only simple technology.

Con *(No, because . . .)*
- The systems are costly to build.
- The systems are inefficient compared to fossil fuels.

Audience: classmates
Purpose: to educate and persuade the audience about the coming importance of solar energy
Techniques of support: facts, examples, physical description
Argumentative thesis statement of intent and opinion (*although-because*):
***Although** solar energy systems are initially costly and have been inefficient, we need to continue to develop solar energy* **because** *the source is free, inexhaustible, safe, and needs only simple technology.*

OUTLINE (**Plan A**)

I Introduction: explanation of energy problem
II Background paragraph: about sources of energy
III Pro #1: resource of the sun is free, plentiful, inexhaustible
IV Pro #2: resource of the sun is safe and nonpolluting
V Pro #3: systems are built with simple technology (use of non-text material)
[Counter-arguments] VI Counter-argument paragraph about cost and efficiency
A. short- vs. long-term costs and efficiency
*[Refutation: **Insufficient**]* B. initial investment high, but eventually much less expensive
C. research will continue to increase efficiency
VII Conclusion: brief summary plus the solution to the energy problems (i.e., solar energy) and a recommendation to pursue research in solar energy technology

Ragab Moheisen, **Egypt**

PLAN B

Plan B, outlined in Figure 6-3, follows the optional background paragraph with the counter-argument paragraph, then continues with two to four *pro* argument paragraphs. If the *pro-con* chart demonstrates that the counter-arguments (a) are not parallel to the *pro* arguments, and that (b) the arguments are limited to one or two opposing viewpoints, but that (c) these arguments are very important and need to be confronted immediately, Plan B should be the writer's choice of overall organization.

Organizational Plan B

I Introduction + thesis statement of intent and opinion
II Background paragraph (optional)
III *Con* argument(s) and refutation of the counter-argument(s)
IV *Pro* argument #1 (weakest argument that supports your opinion)
V *Pro* argument #2 (stronger argument that supports your opinion)
VI *Pro* argument #3 (strongest argument that supports your opinion)
VII Conclusion (summary + recommendation, solution, and/or prediction)

Figure 6-3 *Overall Organization for Arguing Essay: Plan B*

PLAN B

Question: *Should the city expand and change its public transportation services?*

Pro *(Yes, because . . .)*

- There are only 4 short routes with one bus for each route.
- The current bus schedules are inadequate:
  - Buses run only from 6 A.M. to 6 P.M.
  - Buses run only once an hour.
  - Schedules are often not followed.
- We need more buses to serve the students better.

Con *(No, because . . .)*

- The buses on current routes are never full.
- Buses are free for university students.

Audience: Director of Public Transportation
Purpose: to change and expand the current bus system
Techniques of support: facts, examples, personal experiences

Argumentative thesis statement of intent and opinion (*although-because*):
***Although** this city has a bus system and the bus fare for students is free, this city needs to expand and change its public transportation system **because** that will better serve the students.*

OUTLINE (**Plan B**)

I Introduction: statement of the controversy + thesis statement

[Counter-arguments] II Counter-argument paragraph (cost and use issues):

*[Refutation: **irrelevant, insufficient**]*

A. no reason to think that expanded service will charge students a fee
B. even if students pay a small fare, the expanded service will make the fare worth it
C. more students will ride the buses if they run more often and on time, especially with additional publicity about the changes

III Pro argument #1: limited service makes it difficult to go anywhere (results of student survey)

IV Pro argument #2: limited and often inaccurate time schedule poses many problems for students, especially those with night classes (university has a responsibility to extend bus service in the evening)

V Conclusion: recommendation of a solution to the problem and a prediction (what will happen if the improvements are not made)

***Angela Henao,* Mexico**

PLAN C

Plan C, outlined in Figure 6-4 below, differs from the first two plans; its organization more closely follows the summary-analysis organization explained in Chapter 5. Following an optional background paragraph, the writer begins each body paragraph with a statement of a counter-argument. Then a contrasting transition (e.g., *however, in contrast, although*) introduces the topic sentence for the paragraph. The rest of the paragraph contains the evidence that supports the topic sentence. If the *pro-con* chart demonstrates that the counter-arguments parallel the *pro* arguments, Plan C should be the choice of overall organization.

Note: In Student Sample 12 below, the "extra" *pro* arguments are included in the refutation of parallel arguments; they are bracketed [ ].

Organizational Plan C

I Introduction + thesis statement of intent and opinion
II Background paragraph (optional)
III Counter-argument (C-A) #1 + *Pro* argument #1 to refute it
IV Counter-argument (C-A) #2 + *Pro* argument #2 to refute it
V Counter-argument (C-A) #3 + *Pro* argument #3 to refute it
VI Counter-argument (C-A) #4 + *Pro* argument #4 to refute it
VII Conclusion (summary + recommendation, solution, and/or prediction)

Figure 6-4 *Overall Organization for Arguing Essay: Plan C*

PLAN C

Question: *Is selective harvesting beneficial for forests?*

[Parallel pro *&* con *arguments]*

Pro *(Yes, because . . .)*
- Harvesting trees is healthy for the environment
  1. increases productivity
  2. reforestation solves problems
  3. appropriate management allows total forest land to remain stable
  4. forests are renewable

["Extra" pro *arguments*

- [Timber is indispensable material for modern life.]
- [Timber industry provides jobs.]

Con *(No, because . . .)*
- Cutting trees is harmful to the forest:
  1. destroys natural resources
  2. forests destroyed, land ugly
  3. causes erosion and landslides
  4. need to preserve forests naturally

Audience: educated public
Purpose: to explain the controversy and to persuade the audience that harvesting trees can be environmentally sound
Techniques of support: facts, examples

Argumentative thesis statement of intent and opinion (*although-because*):
Although *preservationists believe that cutting trees harms the environment by destroying valuable natural resources, conservationists and forest managers believe that selective harvesting is actually good for forests and for people* ***because*** *it increases productivity and provides jobs and timber.*

OUTLINE (**Plan C**)

I Introduction: basic controversy explained + thesis statement

II Background paragraph: define "selective harvesting" and "appropriate management"; give history of the problem ("healthy harvesting" vs. "destruction" of the forests)

[C-A:1 + refutation: incorrect] III Counter-argument #1 + *Pro:* forests destroyed (not with good management; reforestation makes forests renewable)

[C-A: 2 + refutation: insufficient] IV Counter-argument #2 + *Pro:* causes erosion and landslides (knowledgeable forest management harvests carefully; selective cutting prevents problems)

["extra" pro arguments] [C-A: 3 + refutation: insufficient] V Counter-argument #3 + *Pro:* destroys natural resources [timber an indispensable material for modern life]; [forest industry provides jobs]

[C-A: 4 + refutation: incorrect] VI Counter-argument #4 + *Pro:* harmful to the environment (good management actually helpful to the forest; increases productivity)

VII Conclusion: compromise with recommendations: there should be limitations and standards for harvesting trees; must have appropriate forest management so that everyone benefits

***Shinsuke Yamazaki,* Japan**

Note: If some of the counter-arguments parallel the *pro* arguments, but some do not, the writer may need to follow Plan C and add a counter-argument paragraph just before the conclusion. However, persuading the reading audience with a "mixed" plan is often difficult to manage successfully.

WRITING AN ESSAY MAP

For an Arguing essay to be persuasive to its audience, careful organization is crucial. Writing an essay map can demonstrate the strengths and the possible weaknesses of an organizational plan. Below are two essay maps for Arguing essays.

13 STUDENT SAMPLE

ESSAY MAP

[Plan A] My audience: the Director of the Animal Health Program in Paraguay. This is a central institution in charge of performing investigations and making recommendations to farmers about the best ways to control certain diseases.

My purpose: to persuade the Director that artificial insemination for disease control is effective and less expensive than the traditional methods.

Introduction: I explain the general situation that now exists and tell what the paper will discuss.

Background paragraph: I mention the vaccine's effect on cattle and the duration of immunity. I think the Director knows about the problems that surround the vaccine, but I remind him by emphasizing that the farmers now have to vaccinate twice a year, and that sometimes animals do not respond to the vaccine.

Body paragraph: (*Pro* argument) I introduce my basic argument for artificial insemination as an alternate way of eliminating the disease. My preference for artificial insemination becomes clear.

Body paragraph: (*Pro* argument) I demonstrate the differences between vaccination and artificial insemination. I lead to the conclusion that artificial insemination is less work and, in the long term, more lasting.

Body paragraph: (Counter-arguments) Opponents say that artificial insemination takes more work, more training of farmers, and more money. I demonstrate by the use of a chart and by citing the newest research studies that artificial insemination is only more expensive at the beginning. After the farmers are trained, within a short period of time, it will be cost-effective and will take less work.

Conclusion: I summarize the problems with vaccination, and I state that artificial insemination can eliminate the disease in a short time. I stress again that artificial insemination is economically feasible in the long term, and I recommend that its use be investigated further.

***Cesar Prieto,* Paraguay**

ESSAY MAP

[Plan B] I Thesis statement: *Computer literacy courses should be required for graduation from the university.*

II Background paragraph: The numbers of computers sold and the percentage of computer-literate people have risen remarkably in the past ten years.

III Counter-argument paragraph: Of course, some students are still afraid of computers, and some believe that their lack of knowledge about computers will give them a bad grade in a required class. However, fear of computers can be overcome with education, and a required computer literacy class can be offered for a pass-fail grade.

IV Pro-argument #1: Computer literacy can help students in their university classes.

V Pro-argument #2: Knowledge of computers is essential in the working world.

VI Pro-argument #3: Learning about computers helps students in the real world.

VII Conclusion

***Elfego Orozco,* Guatemala**

Writing Assignment:

The Essay Map

1. Review essay maps in Chapter 3, page 81.
2. Use one of the forms in that chapter, or the form of Student Sample 14 above, to write an essay map for your Arguing essay. As you prepare your essay map, choose one of the organizational plans (Plan A, Plan B, or Plan C).
3. Share your essay map and your *pro-con* chart with a partner.
   A. At the end of the essay map, identify the organizational plan used by your partner. Does the plan reflect the *pro-con* chart?
   B. Write two questions in the margins that will help your partner improve his/her essay map.
   C. Discuss with your partner the questions you wrote.

What Kinds of Evidence, and How Much?

Evidence that supports opinion is so vital in an Arguing essay that without adequate support, the essay will not convince the reader. Therefore, the question of the amount and the kinds of evidence must be asked. The answer to that question depends on the 3 **As**: **A**ssignment (purpose), **A**udience, and **A**vailable material.

Of the three, audience is the most important in decisions about kinds and amount of evidence. If, for example, the readers are friends and relatives who will accept opinions because they like and trust the writer, no proof is necessary, and it will not be necessary to include the opposing views of the argument. If the readers are people who agree with the *pro* argument, the writer will not need much evidence. Of course, when only one side of the argument is presented, the essay is an Explaining (not an Arguing) essay (i.e., Why the answer to the question is *yes*), or you are writing **propaganda**: influencing the audience by presenting only the best ideas on one side of the argument.

For an academic audience, some of whom do not know the writer, and some of whom might not agree with the *pro* argument, the amount and kind of evidence depends on the point being supported. Therefore, because the audience is not entirely known, the strength and the validity of evidence must be more, rather than less, substantial. It will take less evidence, however, to support an argument about a smaller and more local topic (such as the benefits of an evening shuttle bus) than a larger, more national or international topic (e.g., whether there should be a universal ban on nuclear weapons). A general rule is that *if a writer is not certain whether she or he has provided sufficient evidence, probably that writer needs to find additional support.*

Kinds of evidence that are available to writers include the writer's own knowledge; information from interviews and survey results; material from books, articles, newspapers, maps, videotapes, dictionaries, field-specific encyclopedias, computer databases such as *ERIC*; and the vast amount of information available on the World Wide Web (WWW).*

PARAPHRASING OR QUOTING SOURCES

Information from books, journals, and other library resources may be used as direct quotations or may be paraphrased.

Direct Quotations

1. Direct use of a source means using the author's words and ideas in an exact word-for-word transcription of a passage.

*[It-text citation in parentheses **before** final period]*

> "Supporting the parents may be a local group; beyond the local group may be a national organization such as the John Birch Society" (Burress, 1989, p. 31).

2. If one or more words is omitted from an exact quotation, an ellipsis replaces them: three dots, each separated by a space.

[Quotation marks used at beginning and end of quote]

> "Ultimately . . . the censors will win as the books fall into disuse" (Hoffman, 1998, p. 157).

3. If one or more words is added by the writer as an editorial comment to a direct quotation, it is indicated by brackets [ ].

[Page number of quotation required]

> "The chill factor has extended to the present and future ordering of new books [by public school librarians]. The way is paved for continued infringements on academic freedom, not only for librarians, but for teachers and students as well" (Andersen, 1996, p. 376).

* For introductory information about the WWW, see Chapter 4.

Paraphrase

1. Indirect use of a source usually involves a paraphrase or a summary of an author's ideas. Whereas a summary is a brief statement of the main ideas, a paraphrase is a retelling of the some or all of the author's ideas in the writer's own words.

   Original Text

   Thailand's economy remains sound. GNP growth nearly reached 10% last year and should continue to be strong because of the many major projects in the pipeline. Although the balance-of-payment outlook for the next few years is clouded, the development of natural gas should begin to diminish Thailand's dependence on imported energy by 2001.

   Paraphrase

   [It-text citation required; page number not required]

   According to van Agmael (1996), the future of Thailand's economy seems healthy. If the GNP continues to grow at about 10% per year, many important projects already planned can be implemented. In addition, Thailand's natural gas development will reduce her need to depend on foreign energy.

2. To cite paraphrased material that consists of more than one sentence, do not cite each sentence individually. Instead, refer to the source in the first sentence, either generally or specifically.

General:	**Specific:**
Recent research . . .	According to [author's name], . . .
A study of [topic] . . .	[Author's name] reported that . . .

3. Use cohesion devices (pronouns, repetition of key words, and transitions) to link the next two or three sentences to the first.

   Research has shown that sea water intrusion—the migration of salt water into fresh water aquifers—is due to the overdraft of the fresh water. If there is fresh water replenishment, the sea water is pushed back. *Therefore*, increasing fresh water aquifer supplies in areas of risk can provide a solution.

4. Finally, cite the source, usually at the end of the last sentence of the paraphrase.

   In fact, an additional 1500 gallons of fresh water in a million gallons of sea water mitigates sea water intrusion (Freeze, 1997).

Read the arguing essay below. The lines in each body paragraph have been added to indicate where evidence for the student writer's opinions should be written.

15 STUDENT SAMPLE

Grades in Non-Major Courses in U.S. Colleges and Universities

[Sentence engages readers] In Norway, university students, even undergraduates, focus all of their studies on their major field courses. For example, engineering students take all of their courses, every term, in the school of engineering. *[Limited background information]* However, every undergraduate student at the University of Wyoming is required to take many courses that have little or no relevance to their field of study. In addition to being a waste of time and money, these courses are required to be graded with letter grades (A, B, C, D, or F), and those grades are added to the Grade Point Average (GPA) of every student. *[Shortened thesis statement of intent and opinion]* *Although students graduate from the university with a broader education as a result of these courses, I believe that the courses should be graded pass/fail, and that the grades for these courses should not become part of the students' GPAs.*

[Topic sentence] *[Background paragraph: definition, history]* *[Direct quotation, in-text citation]* *[Examples]* *[Interview information]*

Historically, state and federal laws in the U.S. require that all public (i.e., "land-grant"] universities require that students receive a broad education that includes a percentage of courses not in their chosen major fields. That is, in order to graduate, all students must "successfully complete, with a grade of C or higher" up to half of their courses in non-major fields (University Bulletin, 1998, p. 23). The courses include Political Science, English composition, mathematics, psychology, art or music. The grades for these courses are added to students' overall grade point average (GPA). According to Graduate Dean Donald Warders, the requirement for these "liberal arts" courses is part of the mandate of land-grant universities and cannot be changed without an act of Congress. However, Dean Warders states that no law mandates the type of grading used in the courses.

[Topic sentence] *[Second sentence focuses paragraph]* *[Support needed: facts, examples]* *[Concluding sentence]*

The most important reason for non-major classes being graded only pass/fail is to respect the student's choice of a field of study. When someone chooses a major, then the university should do its utmost to accommodate the wish, and to allow the student to take as many courses as possible in that field. ______________________________

____

____

After all, with the tuition being so high, the university should consider student opinion and student needs in this matter.

[Topic sentence] *[Second sentence narrows topic]* *[Evidence needed: examples, description]* *[Concluding sentence]*

Another aspect of the required grades for non-major courses is the effect on the GPA, which is printed on the graduation certificate. The GPA is very important because graduate schools and potential employers look at it when evaluating an application. ______________________________

____

____

Therefore, non-relevant (i.e. non-major) grades should not be part of the GPA.

[Topic sentence] *[Proof needed: personal experience, facts, examples]* *[Concluding sentence]*

The worst part of giving grades for these many non-major courses is that students do not have enough time to concentrate on their major-field courses because they have to spend so much time on the irrelevant courses.

____

____

____

If, on the other hand, the courses were offered for a pass/fail grade that did not appear as part of the GPA, at least the students could prioritize their study time for their major-field classes.

[Topic sentence] *[Support needed: examples, experiences, description]* *[Concluding sentence]*

Finally, these courses are especially irrelevant, and unfair, for international students because they will be of little use when the students return to their homes. ______________________________

____

____

Because international students have come to the U.S. to obtain the best possible education in their major fields, having to take these non-major courses causes resentment and frustration.

[Counter-argument *[Interview information, in-text citation]*

University administrators who oppose pass/fail grades for non-major courses state that students should graduate from the university with broad academic knowledge, not the "specialist" education that is reserved for graduate study in the U.S. (Warders, 1998). In addition, they believe that if students had the option of choosing pass/fail grades for non-major courses, the students would not work hard in those courses; consequently, they would not obtain the breadth of education needed for graduation.

[Topic sentence] [Traditional refutation: ***insufficient***] While both of these arguments may be true, we must remember that students are responsible individuals who must be allowed to make their own choices. These choices may not include whether or not they take courses not in their majors, but students should be able to decide about the type of grade they receive in non-major courses. [Survey information, reference to Appendix] In a recent survey of university students (See Appendix), 85% of the respondents stated that their major field classes were more important than the required "liberal arts" courses. Furthermore, [Survey results] 57% of those students responded that they believed that such courses should not even be required. One U.S. sophomore wrote, "It's such a drag. It shouldn't be necessary to work so hard to get good grades in those non-major courses." Another student, a junior electrical engineering major from Malaysia, wrote that "The courses in Political Science and English, which are not my majors, are skills I'll develop anyway while living in the U.S." Fully 90% of the students surveyed, regardless of age, class, gender, major field, or country of origin, answered that if the courses had to be required, the pass/fail grading system was preferable.

[Conclusion transition] In conclusion, while I understand that the non-major course requirements must continue, I believe that the grading system for those courses [Summary] should be changed. My survey demonstrated that most undergraduate students at the university agree with me. Therefore, I believe that the [Recommendation] university administrators should consider student opinions concerning the required non-major courses and the grading system at the university.

References

Onarheim, T., Jr. (1998). Survey of Undergraduate Students.

Warders, D. (1998). Personal interview, April 13.

Appendix __: Survey of 112 Undergraduate Students

Directions: I am writing a paper for my English composition class and have chosen as my topic the non-major courses required of all undergraduates for graduation. Please take a few minutes to complete this survey so that I can use your opinion in my paper. Return the completed survey to me as soon as possible, either handing it to me or putting it in campus mail: the address is already on the survey—you just need to fold the survey in three parts and staple it so that the address shows.

Class: F S J Sr Major Field: ________________

Country of Origin: ________________ Age: _____ Gender: M F

		Yes	No
1.	Are you in favor of the option of a pass/fail grading system for non-major required courses?		
2.	Would you work less if you were only given a pass/fail grade in non-major courses?		
3.	Do you think that your major-field courses are more important than the required non-major courses?		
4.	Do you believe that non-major courses should not be required?		

Comments: ________________________________

Thank you for your time!

Tolleif Onarheim Jr., **Norway**

EXERCISE 6-F

1. Circle the controlling ideas in the thesis statement and the topic sentences in Student Sample 15.
2. Underline the cohesion devices in the body paragraphs of the essay.
3. Make a *pro-con* chart for Tolleif's essay. Are there other major arguments you can add?
4. With a small group of classmates, discuss the types of evidence (e.g., facts, examples, experience, description) that could be used in each body paragraph in Tolleif's essay. Then give specific examples from your own experience and knowledge that could be used.
5. In what ways did the background paragraph help Tolleif's essay? Do you have any questions you would ask the writer about information in that paragraph?
6. Which organizational plan did Tolleif use? Why? Would you suggest another plan? Why or why not?
7. How did the use of the interview and the survey strengthen Tolleif's persuasion?
8. What nontext materials would strengthen Tolleif's essay? Be specific.

Writing Assignment:

Drafting the Argument Essay

1. Write a rough draft of your Arguing essay. Include the counter-arguments and your refutation.
2. Exchange essays with a partner.
3. Try to become a hostile audience as you read your partner's essay. Does the essay contain enough evidence? Is the evidence persuasive? Suggest ways in which your partner might strengthen the evidence, and listen to your partner's suggestions about your essay.
4. As you read your partner's draft, use the **Guidelines for Peer Response** (p. 127) to help your partner. Then discuss your questions and comments with your partner.

Logical Fallacies

In argumentative essays, rational thought is a strong persuader. If the essay is based on emotions or feelings, or if the thought is flawed (and therefore not reasonable), the argument is weakened. A logical fallacy* (*fallacy* is related to "false") is a statement or opinion that is irrational. Below is a list of logical errors (i.e., fallacies) commonly made by students in argumentative essays, with suggestions for specific solutions. Of course, using good evidence along with these solutions is the best way to persuade an audience.

Note: Comments made in brackets [ ] clarify the terms and examples.

Types of Logical Fallacies

Hasty Generalization *[hasty means "too quickly"]* Jumping to conclusions.

All required university courses are boring.
(All) Science fiction books are not worth the time it takes to read them.

Solutions: Avoid very general words like *everybody, all,* and *never,* which are impossible to prove. Instead, qualify statements with words such as *almost all, most, in some cases,* and *usually.*

Stereotype A hasty generalization applied to people.

(All) Happy families make happy children.
All English teachers have green eyes.
(All) Women psychologists can't be trusted.

Solution: Qualify and specify your statements with words such as *many, sometimes, only rarely,* and *often.*

* The terms that identify these logical fallacies are used by logicians to describe the fallacies.

Oversimplification *[too simple]* Too few choices, sometimes limited to *either/or*

> What's wrong with this country? Just *one* thing. There are 11.5 million women who started but never finished high school.
>
> "Love it or leave it" [a bumper sticker that means "*Either* love this country *or* leave it."]

Solutions: Qualify your statements. For example, "One thing that is wrong with this country is . . ." or "Two ways to confront this problem are to love it or leave it."

Post Hoc Ergo Propter Hoc *[Latin phrase]* Literally means "After this, therefore because of this" Or, *X* happened before *Y*; therefore, *X* caused *Y*.

> He got straight As because he smoked a cigarette before every class.
>
> The rooster crowed. The sun rose. Therefore, the rooster made the sun rise.

Solution: Make sure that *time* is not the only link between cause and effect.

Red Herring *[a herring is a small fish]* A statement that has no direct relevance to the topic, often inserted deliberately to distract the reader.

> Crime, communism, and delinquency are on the rise. Therefore we had better abolish the federal income tax.
>
> High taxes on cigarettes will force teenage smokers to become criminals.

Solution: Be precise. If there is a relationship between ideas A and B, and the relationship is not obvious, explain that relationship to the reader.

False Authority Arguing that a person who is competent in one field will necessarily be competent in another.

> James Johnson is an outstanding congressman. Therefore, he would be an excellent preacher/teacher/president/garbage collector.
>
> Since Dr. Kissinger taught at Harvard, his ideas about foreign policy must be correct.

Solution: Be certain that your sources are authorities in your topic area, and evaluate the credibility of the sources you use.

False Statistics Using numbers and statistics that do not prove what the writer says they prove. False statistics confuse the reader and prove nothing.

> Super-Slim Artificial Yogurt will help you lose weight because it has only 50 calories per ounce. [How many calories is that? How will that help you lose weight?]
>
> 90% of the body's activities are controlled by minerals!
>
> Easiest part-time millionaireship income! $10,700+ daily possible!

Solution: Numbers and statistics can be used as persuasive evidence, as in the following examples, if the information is accurate and relevant.

> Measles is a highly contagious viral disease still seen worldwide, with about 31 million cases a year. Almost 1 million children died in 1997 of complications, including pneumonia. Measles can be prevented by vaccine, but more than 95% of people need to be vaccinated in order to halt the spread.
>
> The Poudre School District receives $112.3 million in annual tax dollars. Of that, slightly more than half goes to teacher salaries ($58.6 million), while non-classified and classified staff salaries (e.g., bus drivers and office workers) make up an additional 20% of the budget.

But the use of numbers and statistics for the purpose of lying to or fooling the reader is fallacious. To ensure that numbers and statistics are relevant and accurate, ask yourself specific questions:

What is the source?
How accurately are they applied?
Why were they gathered? How are they being used?
Are they recent or dated? Are they too limited to be generalized?
Are they the result of thorough study or mere speculation?

Vice and Virtue Words [vice *means negative, and* virtue *means positive]* Using words that have more than just a dictionary meaning. In addition, these words have positive or negative meanings associated with them.*

Do you want your sons and daughters to fall victim to the nuclear conspiracy? Or die at the hands of this menace?
The first choice of discriminating travelers is Holiday Inn, a prestige hotel for those who expect the best.
This book is a great read for any patriotic citizen fed up with today's sleazy, vacuous media.

Solution: Vice and virtue words can used to raise good and bad feelings in your readers; that is, they can be used to persuade. But be sure to have logical support.

GUIDELINES
for Logical Analysis

- Remember never to say *always* and *never* (and *all, none, everyone, no one,* and *nobody*). Reasonable thinking should be reflected in reasonable language. All-inclusive statements can rarely be supported, so specify and qualify.
- Even if you are sure that one thing is the cause (or the effect) of another, it may not be the only cause (or the only effect). Be careful not to oversimplify.
- Suspicious words such as *undoubtedly* and *obviously* are often followed by hasty generalizations and oversimplifications. Do not use them.
- As you write, continuously consider your persuasive purpose and your audience. Any opinion you have must be qualified and specified, and must be supported completely with facts, examples, personal experience, and/or physical description.

EXERCISE 6-G Identify the logical fallacies in the following sentences. Some sentences may contain more than one logical fallacy. Remember that each sentence has been taken out of context, so it is possible that some of them would not be fallacious if they were considered within the whole context. Therefore, if you can create an adequate context, you may be able to prove that some of these sentences *could* be logical.

1. Working conditions could be improved if women workers did not take so much time off for sick leave.
2. She couldn't sleep last night, so she failed the quiz this morning.
3. The United States, in formulating and applying its future foreign policy, must choose between a return to strict isolationism and total global commitment.
4. People in developing countries cannot govern themselves.
5. Everyone who works for General Motors is rich: the median salary is $50,000 a year.
6. The law is a good one because Senator Kennedy introduced it, and he is a good and honest man.

* For more about associative meanings of words, see page 43.

7. Of course Hawaii is the healthiest spot in the world. Life expectancy there for men is 80.1 years, as compared with 68.2 years for men on the mainland.
8. The airport is obviously unsafe. There have been three crashes there in as many years.
9. America is a land of easy-spending millionaires, sexy blondes, fabulous Park Avenue apartments, and easy morals. How do I know? Monsieur, I see your American movies!
10. Ban aerosol sprays or we'll all die of skin cancer!

Writing Assignment:

Revising the Argument Essay

1. Using the **Guidelines for Revision** (on the inside back cover of this textbook) and your partner's comments, reread and begin to revise your Arguing essay.
2. Reread your revision to check for logical fallacies. In particular, check the **Guidelines for Logical Analysis** on page 196.
3. Edit your essay for language errors.
4. Complete the revision of your essay.
5. Read three Arguing essays written by your classmates. Take notes about each essay. Which did you prefer? Why? Be prepared to state "I liked X's argumentative essay about Y because . . ."

EXERCISE 6-H Analyze the following passage in terms of logical fallacies. Do not merely agree or disagree with the statements, but analyze line-by-line the reasoning processes involved. Do not substitute your ideas for Devlin's. Rather, analyze his argument objectively and logically. Use the **Guidelines for Logical Analysis** (p. 196) and the questions that follow the passage to begin your analysis.

> Seven months ago I was in South Vietnam under the auspices of the National Association for the Advancement of Underdeveloped Countries (NAAUC). Before arriving in South Vietnam, I had studied at length the causes of the political upheaval of impoverished countries and had concluded that the Buddhists were responsible for the situation in Vietnam because they refused to adjust their policies to the changing political forces.
>
> Thus, when I arrived in South Vietnam and saw a Buddhist monk engulfed in flames, my opinion was confirmed: the Buddhists want to rule South Vietnam just as the United States tried, before the First World War, to maintain their political and economic isolationism while secretly trying to control the British government of Lloyd George. Therefore, the single question that must be asked is, "Should the U.S. forces in Vietnam eliminate the Buddhist faction in order to effect national unity?" The answer is obvious: everything else has failed; this is the only recourse.
>
> Although this may seem a startling conclusion, the facts show that only after the Buddhists began to publicly burn themselves did the government of President Ky begin to crumble. Indeed, should the United States continue to subvert the ideals and principles of the South Vietnamese when the Buddhists are the source of the difficulty? Since Christianity teaches us that suicide is against the laws of God, we can see the Buddhists' political actions are without any moral justification.
>
> Therefore, the U.S. policy-makers should embark on a new course of action: minimize the efforts against the Viet Cong and devote their main force to a correction of this poisonous thorn in the side of the American lamb, a thorn which is dispersing and submerging the democratic way of life!
>
> Dudley Erskine Devlin
> *Journal of Political Inequality* (JPI)
> December 4, 1970, pp.181–182

Questions to begin your analysis:

1. What do you know about the credibility of the writer? What about the historical context for this passage? What more do you need to know?
2. Should you be suspicious about finding the conclusion in the introduction?
3. What is the Buddhist belief about suicide?
4. Look carefully at the vice and virtue words in the conclusion. How are they used to persuade the reader?

Credibility of Authors and Student Writers

Any argument, oral or written, is strengthened if the speaker/writer has the respect of the listener/reader. The more authoritative the sources are about the topic—including interviews with experts, materials from books and the World Wide Web—the more the reader will believe them.

To strengthen and support the ideas and opinions in their Arguing essays, student writers can identify the professional background expertise of the sources they use.

Recent research by certified financial planner Suze Orman . . .
Michio Takeuchi, a financial advisor on the Tokyo Stock Exchange, . . .
Director of the Canadian Guidance and Counseling Foundation David Riggar . . .
Kevin Allison, who won the Nobel Prize for Biochemistry in 1992, . . .
In his current best-seller, The Workings of the Mind, *MIT professor of linguistics Stephen Pinker . . .*

One way that academic authors who publish their work demonstrate credibility is by biodata.*

Example of Academic Biodata

________________ is Associate Professor of English at California State University, Sacramento, where she is TESOL Program Coordinator. Her co-authored teacher-resource book on teaching ESL writing was published in 1998. She has presented many papers at national and international conferences and is currently engaged in further research on various aspects of responding to student writing.

Usually, student writers cannot claim expertise in the academic papers they write. However, if they write about topics about which they are experts, and/or they use personal experience to support an idea or opinion, student writers can demonstrate their own credibility. In the student samples below, for example, the writers show their qualifications by referring to personal experience.

Introduction: Problem-Solving Essay

Security for women on college/university campuses, especially at night, is often a problem. That is certainly the case at my university. I live on an all-girls' floor in Braiden Hall, and my friends and I are frightened to walk alone after dark. We are concerned about the lack of

[Personal experience]

* *Bio* means "life"; *data* means "information." Usually the biodata about an author of a journal article is located at the bottom of the first page or at the end of the article.

security lights on the campus, so when we have night classes, we usually form a small group to meet a student who has a night class and walk with her back to the residence hall. Although the campus police assure us that the campus is safe, I feel uneasy about my safety. Therefore, I decided to research this question by surveying women who live on and off the campus, and to investigate the security measures taken on other campuses.

Renuka Gunawardena, **India**

Background Paragraph: Evaluating Essay

[Personal expertise] For the past five years I have worked as a ski instructor at the Winter Park ski area, teaching beginners how to navigate the "bunny slopes." Most of my students have rented skis that are inappropriate for beginners, and so they have greater trouble learning the basics of the sport. In contrast, students who have bought skis designed for beginners, and who use those skis regularly, learn faster and enjoy the sport more. Interviews with fellow ski instructors, as well as my own experience, led me to evaluate three types of skis for the novice skier, using the criteria of affordability, durability, and overall quality.

Kiff Forbush, **U. S.**

Writing Assignment II This is an exercise in creative writing. To strengthen your Arguing essay, show your audience that you are an authority about your topic. Write 30-50 words of "creative biodata" that describe how important, how well-known, and/or how well-educated you are about the topic. This biodata can appear at the end of your completed Arguing essay. Truth is not a part of these biodata, but of course, biodata used for academic writing *must* be factual.

Note: Although biodata are usually written by the author, writing convention requires that they be stated in the third person, as though someone else were writing the material. Therefore, in this assignment, use your full name and the title you create for yourself, then just your last name in successive sentences. Use the appropriate pronoun (not *I*, but rather *she* or *he*). Use Student Samples 18–19 as examples.

Biodata

After receiving his doctorate from Florida Citrus University (FCU), Jason Klimpke has spent twenty years working to improve orange juice. Klimpke has consulted with the governments of several countries to set up the infrastructure for their orange growing industry. In 1998 he received the highest award for nutrition research at the International Citrus Convention.

Jason Klimpke, **U.S.**

Zak Zwerin is a doctor of veterinary medicine who directs the National Animal Health Program in Washington, D.C. His publications include several books and many articles about brucellosis. He has recently been named to the Presidential Commission on buffalo herds in Yellowstone National Park.

***Zak Zwerin,* U.S.**

Student Samples

Arguing Essays

Marriage in Russia: More Choices Needed

[Engages audience] Marriage is a very strong and respected institution in Russia, but because of cultural changes in the past decade, society's view of marriage *[Limited background information]* now seems especially inflexible and inhumane. The foundation of this inflexibility is Russian popular opinion that still rejects the idea of couples living together before they marry; instead, only official marriages are acknowledged. However, there are many reasons why more and more *[Shortened although-because thesis]* people choose the non-traditional way of living together prior to marriage, despite the societal pressures.

[Plan B] *[Background paragraph]* The traditional view of marriage in Russia is not based on religious beliefs, as it is in many other countries; it is not based, for example, on whether or not marriage is a sacrament ordained by God, on the idea that *[Summary of counter-arguments: marriage stabilizes (a) legally, (b) ethically]* sexual relations are immoral outside of marriage, or on the belief that sexual relations should be only for the procreation of children. Instead, this conservative view is based on the idea that official marriages stabilize society by making partners ethically and legally responsible for each other.

[Refutation of counter-arguments] In terms of ethics, younger Russians believe that a piece of paper with the government seal cannot make people more responsible and stable than they already are (Landsberg, 1997). If the couple is in love and cherish each *[Traditional refutations: (a)* ***incorrect,*** *(b)* ***insufficient****]* other with patience and respect, it is not necessary for them to be officially married. In contrast, if a couple has a poor relationship, official marriage will not improve it and, of course, will not keep partners together. However, it is unfortunately true that marriage makes partners legally dependent on *[Techniques of support: examples, facts]* one another. That is, after people get married, they are no longer treated by society like individuals. For example, one partner cannot legally make official decisions without the permission of his or her spouse. Indeed, if one partner needs to go on a business trip, he or she cannot do it without the *[Old, outdated evidence]* official agreement of the spouse (Geiger, 1967). While this legal constriction may have been necessary in the old political system, it is out-of-date in the *[Identification of reliable source]* Russia of the new millennium. According to the major Russian news source, ITAR-TASS, the younger generation today are not willing to be so dependent; it makes them feel insecure and nervous (1997). In many cases, the *[Paraphrase, in-text citations]* resentment caused by these dependency laws often affects the couple's relationship. This fact is demonstrated by the rising divorce rate in Russia since the fall of the Soviet Union (ITAR-TASS, 1997).

[Topic sentence, pro argument #1] Living together before marriage has one obvious advantage: the couple gets to know each other better so that they can reach a wise and mature decision about marriage. If the partners marry too quickly, they enter into marriage without a full understanding of each other's habits and personalities. For example, two of my Moscow University classmates decided to live together after graduation because they were in love, but their parents, who were expressing the popular opinion about marriage in Russia, pressured them to get officially married. While dating, they had seen only the good sides of each other, but after marriage they found that they were not at all compatible. For instance, Igor found that Tatyana was a very neat person who "had no imagination"; Tatyana began to describe Igor as an "immature disorganized boy." As they discovered the negative sides of each other's personalities, they became more and more unhappy, and finally, after just one year of disillusion, they got divorced.

[Transitions]
[Method of development: cause-effect]
[Techniques of support: personal experience, example]

[Topic sentence opinion, pro argument #2] Another reason that couples should live together before marriage is that the population in Russia includes people from many different cultures and even religions. While dating, young people do not usually seriously discuss all aspects of their traditions because they are so fascinated by each other that nothing seems to be an obstacle in their relations. However, some time after marriage, the couple discovers that the national customs of the partners are different, even contradictory, and if they do not compromise, their marriage will most likely be unsuccessful. For example, my mother was a young modern Russian woman who was going to have a career as well as a family, but my father belonged to the Armenian culture that expected a woman to be a housewife and a servant for her husband. Before their marriage, my father did not show his demand for a traditional wife, so my mother did not expect the changes in their relationship after the marriage. Neither was ready to make a concession, and their marriage failed. If they had lived together prior to the official ceremony, they would have discovered each other's cultural peculiarities and then had the chance to make an informed decision about their futures.

[Cohesion device: repetition of key words]
[Method of development: cause-effect]
[Techniques of support: personal experience, example]

[Topic sentence, paragraph hooks, pro argument #3] Perhaps the most important reason why our society should accept the idea of living together before marriage is the imperfect divorce laws in Russia. Despite all the recent changes, contemporary Russian society still has the old divorce regulations initiated during the Communist years. Strict divorce laws originally had been enacted in the 1930s, but in 1944 even more obstacles were placed before couples seeking to end their marriage (Riasentsev, 1967). Applying for a divorce became even more expensive, and couples seeking divorce had to go before a people's tribunal, where attempts were made to reconcile the couples. If reconciliation failed, couples were sent to superior court, where their cases were heard and the divorce was granted or denied (Von Frank, 1979). The same laws exist today; if a couple is going to get a divorce, the partners have to be ready to spend a lot of time, money, and energy. Now, according to an article in the *Los Angeles Times*, the cost for a divorce in Russia is about 450,000 rubles, equal to the average monthly salary in Russia (Landsberg, 1997). Although a couple seeking divorce does not have to go before the people's tribunal, they still face a confrontational divorce hearing, in which each must show to the jury how bad their marriage has been. Because the divorce will not be granted unless the stories persuade the jury, the partners usually present the worst of each other's personalities, and they blame each other. It is therefore not a surprise that it is rare in

[Paraphrase, in-text citation]
[Methods of development: process, cause-effect]
[Identification of reliable source]
[Techniques of support: facts, examples]

[Paraphrase, in-text citation, multiple authors] Russia when people remain friends after the divorce (Nadelson & Polonsky, 1984). Furthermore, according to popular opinion in Russia, the divorced person is either mentally unstable or dishonorable. It is therefore difficult for anyone who is divorced to get a good job offer or a job promotion, and if that person decides to marry again, public opinion will discourage the new relationship (Rheinstein, 1972). [Concluding sentence]

[Conclusion] [Concluding techniques: summary, recommendation] In the new atmosphere of freedom and individual choice in Russia, I think that if people have the right to be married and to have a family, they also need the right to choose whether or not they live together before marriage. In fact, I believe that partners should have the right to choose what relationship they prefer, including whether or not they marry officially at all. The old rules imposed by Communist society should not apply to the new society that has evolved today.

References

[References listed alphabetically by last name of author]

Geiger, H. K. (1967). *The family in Soviet Russia.* Cambridge, MA: Harvard University Press.

ITAR-TASS. (May 15, 1997). Institution of family to exist in Russia always.

[Newspaper article] Landsberg, M. (July 6, 1997). Fall of Communism fails to alter "no fuss, no muss" divorces in Russia. *Los Angeles Times,* 19A.

[Book reference] Nadelson, C. C. & Polonsky, D. C. (1984). *Marriage and divorce: A contemporary perspective.* New York: Guilford.

Rheinstein, M. (1972). *Marriage, stability, divorce, and the law.* Chicago: University of Chicago Press.

[Non-English book reference] Riasentsev, V. A. (1967). *Semeinoe Provo.* Moscow: Iuridicheskaia Literature.

Von Frank, A. A. (1979). *Family policy in the USSR since 1944.* Palo Alto, CA: R & E Research Associates.

***Maragarita Vaiman,* Russia**

21 STUDENT SAMPLE

The Necessity of Korean Foreign Language Education for Korean-American Children

[Introduction: audience engagement, limited background information] Many Korean permanent residents in the U.S. face a serious problem: children who do not speak their native language. While these immigrants feel relieved from their hard lives, the speed of their English proficiency is slow like a turtle's pace; in contrast, that of their children is as fast as a rabbit. At the same time, the necessity of Korean language education becomes controversial. Some parents do not want their children to learn Korean; they want their children only to learn English. In my opinion, Korean language education not only promotes the development of children but also brings domestic peace, which is a common aim of immigrant homes; furthermore, Korean language education helps children understand the culture of their ancestors. [Shortened although-because thesis; controlling ideas circled] [Plan C]

[Counter-argument #1]
[Topic sentence]
*[Rogerian refutation: ("we"); **incorrect**]*
[Method of development: comparison-contrast]
[Techniques of support: facts, example]

Some parents insist that they need not teach the Korean language to their children. Their opinion is that if children learn two languages at same time, they will have low language ability because they will divide that ability. <u>However</u>, *we* have nothing to worry about on that point. According to educational research, children who learn two (or more) languages at the same time can improve their thinking faculties and their creative abilities (Omaggio Hadley, 1993). For example, in Canada, children who spoke only English learned their school subjects in French in elementary school. The results were that these children not only could speak French proficiently after two or three years, but also had increased creative power, more sophisticated thinking faculties, and greater adaptability and intellectuality than other children who spoke only one language (Baker, 1996). Therefore, children who learn both Korean and English may be better, not worse, students.

[Paragraph hooks]
[Counter-argument #2]
[Topic sentence]
[Transitions]
*[Rogerian refutation: **insufficient**]*
[Methods of development: comparison-contrast, cause-effect]
[Concluding sentence]

Other parents refuse to teach Korean ~~to~~ their children because the children are unwilling to study and learn. <u>Consequently</u>, family problems occur when the parents insist that their children learn Korean. <u>In contrast</u>, <u>however</u>, Korean language education can be positively related to domestic peace. <u>First</u>, children tend to adapt themselves to American culture and to learn the English language quickly and easily, <u>but</u> their parents often have difficulty expressing their thoughts in English freely. If the parents cannot understand English well, <u>and</u> the children cannot understand Korean, a generation gap occurs. This gap can become wider and wider each day, <u>and</u> <u>finally</u> it will bring about family troubles. If the communication between parents and their children is poor because of the language, children will surely live in a world different from their parents. To prevent their children being lost from ~~them,~~ parents should insist on teaching the Korean language to ~~their~~ children.

[Paragraph hooks]
[Counter-argument #3]
[Topic sentence]
*[Traditional refutation: **incorrect**]*
[Identification of reliable source, in-text citation]
[Concluding sentence]

The strongest argument against teaching children Korean is that many Korean immigrant parents think that their children should become Americans as quickly as possible. Therefore, they refuse to interfere with the assimilation process by teaching the children the language and culture of Korea. *This is a serious mistake.* Koreans are a minority in the U.S., so keeping in touch with their culture and ancestors is especially necessary in order to keep their pride and security. While assimilation of the new culture is good, keeping the old culture is just as important. According to researchers Sandra Schecter and Robert Bayley (1997), someday the children will ask themselves where they came from; they will have a need to know about their culture. To understand that culture, they must learn their native tongue because the language is an important element that forms spiritual values and racial consciousness.

[Concluding <u>transition</u>]
[Techniques: summary, recommendation]

<u>In conclusion</u>, Korean language education is desirable for the children themselves as well as for their parents. What is most important is that the language is not only a means of communication, but also a link to the mind and the soul of the culture. Therefore, Korean language education in immigrant homes is important. It should be required.

<u>References</u>

[References listed alphabetically by last name of author]

Baker, C. (1996). *Foundations of bilingual education and bilingualism* (2nd ed.). Clevedon, England: Multilingual Matters.

Omaggio Hadley, A. (1993). *Teaching language in context* (2nd ed.). Boston: Heinle & Heinle.

[Recent journal article] Schecter, S. R. & Bayley, R. (1997). Language socialization practices and cultural identity: Case studies of Mexican-descent families in California and Texas. *TESOL Quarterly 31*, 3, 513–541.

***Sung Sik Pak,* Korea**

EXERCISE 6-I

1. Circle the controlling ideas in the thesis statement and the topic sentences in Student Sample 20.
2. Without looking again at the essays, make a list of the specific details that you remember; share your details with your classmates
3. Make a *pro-con* chart for each essay. Has the writer included the most important arguments on both sides of the issue?
4. With a partner or a small group of classmates, evaluate both essays. Use the **Guidelines for Peer Response** (p. 127) to begin your evaluation. In addition,
   A. describe the credibility of each writer
   B. use the **Guidelines for Logical Analysis** (p. 196) to check Student Sample 21 for logical fallacies
   C. discuss whether each writer has successfully refuted the counter-arguments.
5. What nontext materials might each writer use to clarify and support the points, and/or to further engage the audience?
6. Which essay did you find most persuasive? Why? Discuss your opinion with your classmates.

Writing Assignment III Write a memo to your instructor, describing what you learned about academic writing as you drafted and revised your Arguing essay. In addition, explain what was easy and what was difficult about writing the essay, what problems you encountered and how you solved them. (Review memos on p. 95.)

Chapter 7

Evaluating in Academic Writing: The Problem-Solution Essay

My most painful lesson in writing the problem-solution essay was that I didn't get started soon enough. Then the person I wanted to interview was out of town and didn't return my e-mail or phone calls. The most important book I needed had been checked out, and I had to wait to read it, and the best journal for my topic wasn't available in my college library, so I had to order it through interlibrary loan. By the time I finally had gathered enough information to write my paper, the deadline for the paper had already passed.

Lars Raastad, **Norway**

IN PREVIOUS CHAPTERS you have practiced and developed your academic writing skills, including analysis of assignments and expectations of the instructor; collection strategies; overall essay organization; the use of supporting detail and methods of development; the writing conventions for Explaining, Summary-Analysis, and Argument essays; the use of cohesion devices; and the appropriate use of sources.

In this chapter, you will practice and extend your knowledge about academic writing and research by focusing on (a) evaluation processes used in academic writing, (b) writing conventions for the Problem-Solution paper, and (c) evaluation of source materials.

Evaluating

We e*valu*ate (i.e., judge the *valu*e of something) every day, often unconsciously: "What a *horrible* movie!" "I had such a *great* vacation!" "She is a *wonderful* person." We make positive or negative judgments about the world around us, and we are constantly exposed to the opinions and judgments of others.

Each of these judgments is like the tip of an iceberg; beneath each judgment lies the standards on which the judgments rest. These standards are called "criteria."* For example, the criteria for a successful vacation for one person might be warm weather, isolated beaches, and opportunities to meet fun-loving people; for another, the standards for a successful vacation may include going on museum tours, eating at expensive restaurants, attending the theater, and staying at a five-star hotel. Thus, while many criteria for evaluation may exist, selection of the most relevant and important criteria for an evaluation is often an individual matter.

EXERCISE 7-A

1. With a small group of classmates, choose one topic from each of the two categories (*buying, selecting*) to evaluate. Choose an *audience* and a *purpose* for each evaluation.

   - buying: a car an airline ticket shampoo
   - selecting: a major an apartment a dentist

2. Develop 3–5 criteria for each of your selections.
3. Share your audience, purpose, and criteria for the evaluation with your classmates.

EVALUATION PROCESSES

Formal (i.e., deliberate) evaluation has several steps. First, the selection of criteria depends on the *purpose* of the evaluation and the *audience* for that evaluation. For instance, a student deciding which courses to take might investigate such criteria as the time for each course, the teacher, and the required books. Generally, the purposes of conscious, deliberate evaluation are to

- examine two or more options
- demonstrate the strength of one of the options
- select an option for oneself or recommend your chosen option to others.

Comparing and contrasting are fundamental methods of development in evaluation.† For example, writers might analyze the similarities and/or differences between two newspapers for their coverage of international news; they may evaluate several brands of athletic shoes for tennis, or three major-field courses they may take, by comparing and contrasting the tennis shoes or the courses. They might compare and

---

* "Criter*ion*" is the singular of "criter*ia*."

† To review comparison and contrast, see Chapter 2, pages 51–54.

contrast the advantages and disadvantages of two or more alternatives: the selection of a graduate school, the solution(s) to a problem, the choice of a commercial product (e.g., a computer, a camera, an Internet provider). The purpose for such a comparison and/or contrast is to determine, for a specific audience, which is the "best" newspaper, camera, or graduate school for that audience.

Thoughtful evaluation requires not only knowledge about the purpose and the audience but also some expertise about the topic. For example, the criteria used to evaluate products usually emphasize usefulness, practicality, convenience, and cost because those criteria represent the reasons consumers choose the product. The criteria developed by a student to evaluate which course to take will be based on that student's judgments about what she expects and needs. In each case, developing criteria is based on the writer's investigation of and consequent increase in knowledge about the topic.

EXERCISE 7-B Below are two lists of criteria for restaurants, one developed by college/university students and one by the parents of those students. The criteria are listed in order of decreasing importance for each audience. Compare and contrast the criteria on the two lists. Then discuss the ways in which the audience and purpose for each list differ.

College/University Student List	Parent List
• cost	• quality of the food
• take-out capability	• atmosphere
• amount of food per serving	• type of food
• type of food	• cost
• distance from the campus	• cleanliness

Below are three academic assignments that require evaluation.

I **Food Science and Nutrition** (Essay Examination)
Evaluate the risk-benefit ratio of food additives.

II **Marketing** (Paper)
Write a short paper (3 pages maximum) that identifies a real, current example of product positioning. Determine the probable approach(es) to the positioning and target market, and gather evidence to support your determination. Supporting materials should be attached and appropriately labeled. *Evaluate* the organization's strategy. Does their approach seem reasonable? Why or why not? Are there changes you would recommend to the company?

III **Introduction to Political Science** (Essay Test)
Evaluate how a candidate's stand on drug legalization might affect his/her chances during the year 2000 elections. Explain the broader implications of this issue on elections and the political sphere in America.

EXERCISE 7-C

1. With a partner or a small group of classmates, analyze the audience (using the **Guidelines for Audience Analysis**, p. 72) and discuss the general and the specific purposes for each of the evaluative academic assignments above.
2. Discuss and then develop evaluative criteria for two of the academic assignments.
3. Discuss ways in which you could find and use sources to support your evaluation for the criteria for each of the two topics. Be specific.
4. Each of the assignments is incomplete. Decide what questions you might ask the instructor about each topic.

EVALUATING IN ACADEMIC WRITING

Evaluating is part of academic problem-solving. Writers evaluate the attitude of the audience toward the problem and the solution in order to persuade that audience. They develop evaluative criteria in order to compare and/or contrast alternative solutions to the problem, and they use the evaluated information to recommend the best solution.

Evaluation is part of analysis: to take apart, study, describe, and evaluate. In academic writing, students are often asked to evaluate (to make judgments about) a book or article, a course or teacher, a laboratory experiment or a computer model, a business plan or case study. Writers of academic evaluations must be able to

- explain and describe the reason (i.e., the purpose) for the evaluation,
- develop appropriate criteria on which to base the evaluation,
- state clear positive or negative judgments for each criterion, and
- provide adequate evidence that supports each of those judgments.

Because evaluation usually has a persuasive purpose, audience analysis is crucial. The evaluator needs to know not only the demographics of the audience (i.e., age, education, interests, socio-economic status) but also the readers' knowledge and experience with the topic, their attitude toward the topic (and perhaps toward the evaluator!), and their potential reactions to the evaluation.

EXERCISE 7-D

1. With a partner, look at the criteria for the Evaluation of Oral Presentations (p. 133). Add two criteria to the form. Then, with another set of partners, discuss why you added those criteria.
2. Read the criteria given in the **Guidelines for Peer Response** (p. 127). Eliminate one criterion. Then, with another set of partners, discuss why you chose that criterion to eliminate.
3. Study the Criteria for Evaluation of the learning styles essay on page 93. What criteria would you and your partner add? Why?

Below are five student evaluations about the peer response work in a composition class. Read the paragraphs and then do the exercise that follows.

Last week we were talking in our peer group about our first essay. After I described my topic, the food we eat at our New Year's celebration, Nawal told me gently that she was not so interested in that topic. Ismail was kind of interested, but he didn't know what questions to ask to help me. Fortunately, Victor was able to ask questions about my ideas, and he suggested that I talk with my friends from Cambodia so that I could give more detail about the special foods. Then he said he would love to read about that detail. After that, Ismail thought of some helpful ideas, so I think at least two people will be interested in my essay.

***Vinh Hong,* Cambodia**

The peer response groups in class gave me an opportunity to talk to my classmates in a concerned environment. For example, I really did not know the strategies to follow to write a good investigating paper, so I asked my peers. Ioan and Jacques made me appreciate my topic, and they asked questions that helped me organize the steps to follow.

Aldrin Banguebe, **Gabon**

Even though I think the peer response work in class is always too short, I believe that we benefit from the experience. For example, when we were writing the evaluating essay, Dharma explained that he wanted to evaluate a restaurant. Our group tried to help him develop criteria; I told him what I expected from a waiter and from the food when I go to a restaurant. I think that together, Edgardo, Muchlish and I helped Dharma define his topic.

Nabeel Burhan, **Iraq**

My peer response group experiences have not been positive. I think the personal opinions of my classmates about my papers is not important, and I don't use their personal points of view when I revise. When they point out mistakes, I don't really believe them. Besides, I can manage to write my papers by myself; I don't need their "help."

Maki Suzuki**, Japan**

I was having trouble with the hostile audience aspect of my arguing essay. My draft ranted and raved about my frustration with the audience without dealing with the audience effectively. Luckily for me, I brought the draft to class, and I really appreciated the feedback I received from my classmates. Zhou made me realize the problem with my voice in the essay, and Meg helped in persuading me to treat the audience as real people I might know. Their honest opinions and support helped me see how to revise my draft.

Kokyeang Chin, **Malaysia**

EXERCISE 7-E

1. With a partner, list the criteria used by the students to write their evaluations.
2. Which criteria do you agree with? Why? Which criterion do you think is most important? Why?
3. What criteria might you add to this list? Why?
4. List 5 criteria that you and your partner would use to evaluate small group work in this course.

The Problem-Solution Essay

Problem-solving is also part of our everyday lives. How can we get better grades? How can we get along better with a roommate? How can we successfully complete a biology experiment? Moreover, problem-solving assignments are frequently part of academic course work. As writers confront problems and seek solutions—how to solve an insect problem for an agricultural crop, for example, or how to persuade a college/university administrator to keep the campus library open longer in the evenings—they demonstrate many of the writing and research skills students have practiced in this course.

The overall organization of Problem-Solution papers is similar to the basic Explaining essay (see p. 67), but they differ somewhat in content and in purpose (i.e., focus). Specifically, Problem-Solution papers usually contain (a) a background paragraph that demonstrates the problem, (b) one or more paragraphs of evaluation of alternative solutions (called a "feasibility study"), (c) a persuasive proposal—of one or more paragraphs—for one solution, and (d) one or more paragraphs describing the implementation of that solution. The outline in Figure 7-1 shows the overall organization of the Problem-Solution essay, as well as the writing conventions and research skills needed to fulfill the expectations of the academic audience.

Note: Not all Problem-Solving essay assignments require all of the elements below; some academic assignments emphasize two or three of the elements and ignore others.

[Engages audience; thesis statement]	**I**	**Introduction**
[Describing, examples, observing, definition; use of external resources]	**II**	**Background paragraph demonstrating that a problem exists**
[Investigating, explaining; using comparison, contrast, process, cause(s) and effect(s)] *[Designing interviews, surveys; using books, articles, the WWW]* *[Using Rogerian argument, counter-argument techniques, non-text materials]* *[Process, classification, reasons; analysis]*	**III–VII**	**Body paragraphs** • explore several solutions to the problem • develop and evaluate a feasibility analysis of those solutions • present sources to use as evidence • propose one solution to the problem • persuade the audience that one solution should be adopted • present an implementation plan for the proposed solution
[Summary, recommendation]	**VII**	**Conclusion**

Figure 7-1 *Overall Organization of a Problem-Solution Essay*

Below are two authentic academic problem-solving assignments. Notice that neither of the assignments is clearly identified as "Problem-Solution." Therefore, identification of the problem and solution has been inserted in brackets [ ]. Notice also that evaluation is required in each of the assignments.

I **Environmental Health Report**

Choose a current **problem** in environmental health and write 4–8 pages of text, exclusive of title page, bibliography, and figures or tables. Use at least four good references, including books, journal articles, government publications, or other acceptable published materials.

Prepare your paper according to the following general format:

A. Introduction: A clear statement of the problem, who is affected, its magnitude (the number of people affected and the seriousness of the effect) [**evaluation**].

B. Detailing of the "science" of the problem: Describe the agent (chemical, biological, or physical), how it affects health, and how man interacts with it.

C. **Control** of [**solution** to] the **Problem**: Discuss any applicable local, state, or federal laws; who is responsible for taking care of the problem, if anyone; what they can do, or what they are doing.

[Student writer's opinion, persuasion]

D. Future needs: In your opinion, what should we do in the future to **eliminate** [**solve**] this problem?

II **Agronomy Seminar Paper**

The paper should design a pest management scheme at two management levels (high input and low input) for a cropping system of your choice in an ecological zone of your choice. Target **pests** [**problem**] should include an insect, a disease, a grass weed, and a broadleaf weed. The following should be included in your paper:

- description of the region and the environment
- literature review (cite several references)
- economic **analysis** [**evaluation**] of each **control option** [**solution**]
- **evaluate** expected impacts of the project.

EXERCISE 7-F

1. Each of these academic writing assignments is incomplete. That is, instructors in the courses will have to discuss the assignments with their students because not all of the directions have been written. With a partner, discuss what information is missing from each of the assignments. What questions would you need to ask the instructor?
2. For one of the assignments, plan a survey. Whom would you and your partner (or classmates) survey? What information would you seek? How might you use that information?
3. What kinds of nontext materials would be especially helpful in each of these assignments? Why?

Writing Assignment I

Write a 3–4 page Problem-Solution essay (750–1000 words) in which you investigate possible solutions to a local problem by

- explaining that a problem exists
- analyzing [evaluating] alternative solutions
- proposing a feasible solution
- suggesting an implementation plan
- persuading your audience that your solution is viable.

Your audience for this essay is a person who has the authority or the position to consider the necessary changes you will recommend to solve the problem. You will interview this person about the problem and later send him or her a copy of your Problem-Solution paper.

Your purpose for this paper is to persuade the appropriate person to act: to do, fix, change, improve, subsidize, ban, reorganize, or make legal (or illegal) something about the problem you explain.

Preparing to Write the Problem-Solution Essay

Although students could write Problem-Solution essays about national or international problems (such as global warming, breast cancer, or adolescent violence), writing about local problems that students know about personally can make the writing process more satisfying. The student writer can identify a problem and a person who can help to solve that problem, then interview that person and address the paper to that person.

Furthermore, some students who have described local problems and recommended possible solutions have been responsible for actually solving those problems. A student from Malaysia, Chee Hong Yeo, wrote about the fact that international students were charged twice as much for student health insurance at a university as were U.S. students; the result was that the cost of health insurance for international students decreased. In another case, Yehan Wijesena, a student from Sri Lanka, noticed that the lack of STOP signs in a residential area next to the college campus had caused an unusual number of car accidents; his recommendation resulted in the installation of several STOP signs that made the area safer.

EXERCISE 7-G With a small group of classmates, discuss 2 or 3 local problems you have identified. Which problem interests your classmates? What experiences have your classmates had with each problem? What solutions do your classmates suggest for each of the problems?

Writing Assignment: *Collecting Information*

After you select a local problem, begin to gather information about that problem, using at least two Collecting Strategies (see Chapter 2). Summarize what you already know about the problem and note what you need to know. Decide where you can locate information, and identify the person (or persons) you should interview.

AUDIENCE ANALYSIS

Because a successful Problem-Solution paper must persuade the audience, careful audience analysis is essential. Below are student samples of audience analysis.

Problem: The business *Shear Class Beauty Salon* is unprofitable.

Audience: Owners: Laura Almendares and Gerry Sanchez

- attitude toward the problem: concerned; know it exists; eager to solve it
- probable objections: cost
- probable reaction(s) to the paper: gratitude

***Michele Nottage,* U.S.**

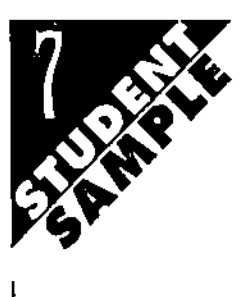

Problem: The meat served in the dormitory is always covered with strange sauces that taste terrible.

Audience: John Leonard, Director of Food Services

- attitude toward problem: skeptical (does not believe it is a serious problem that affects many students)
- probable objection(s) to solution: cost, inconvenience of the change
- probable reaction(s) to the paper: interest (I hope)

***G. W. Choi,* Korea**

Writing Assignment: *Audience Analysis*

After you select your topic, select 2 or 3 potential interviewees whom you might contact (i.e., people who have the authority and/or position to make the change you will recommend). Using the **Guidelines for Audience Analysis** (p. 72), list the characteristics of these potential interviewees. Then share your list with a partner.

DEMONSTRATING THAT THE PROBLEM EXISTS

The Background Paragraph

Selecting a problem to be solved requires more homework than any other academic assignment topic. Not only must the writer select and thoroughly analyze the audience, but she or he must evaluate the topic to make certain that it *is* a problem and that it can be solved. Otherwise the writing task can be both frustrating and embarrassing, as three students who were not careful in their preparation discovered.

One student decided that she would write about the problem of campus safety and would recommend solving the problem by (a) installing telephone call boxes on the campus and (b) asking the campus security officers to give safety talks in the dormitories. During her interview with the Director of Security, she discovered that the call boxes were already in place and that the safety talks had been given regularly for several years.

Another student decided to investigate the problem of aging, deteriorating library books. Fortunately, a kind reference librarian demonstrated that the problem did not exist.

Another student chose the topic of making guns illegal. However, as he began to research his topic, he discovered that although a solution was possible, the Constitution of the United States mandates the right of the citizenry to bear arms. Therefore, although the problem was local, the solution—an amendment to the Constitution—was national and all but impossible to achieve.

Some effective ways to discover whether or not a problem exists are to

- informally ask other people on the campus (starting with your classmates) whether or not they are aware of the problem
- design a survey to ask about the existence of the problem formally
- ask students at other colleges or universities, through the Internet, whether or not the problem exists on their campuses
- search library resources and/or the World Wide Web for information about the problem.

Remember that, in the Problem-Solution paper, the background paragraph describes the problem and its severity, using research to demonstrate the existence of the problem.

Writing Assignment:
Describing the Problem (The Background Paragraph)

Write a background paragraph, using specific detail, that describes the problem you have selected. Use information from your knowledge and experiences and from the experiences of others to demonstrate the severity of the problem. Use additional information you have collected from other sources to support your ideas. Cite your in-text sources, and start your end-of-text reference page. (See Appendix A for APA style format.)

USING HEADINGS

For longer and/or more complex academic writing assignments—and, in some fields of study, for all written assignments—student writers can choose to use headings to introduce each major part of the essay, and perhaps subheadings to label subtopics within the major headings. Scientific and technical papers almost always depend on headings and subheadings to remind readers of the progress of the paper. Typically, these headings include *Introduction, Literature Review, Methods and Materials, Results, Discussion,* and *Conclusion.* Textbooks also use headings and subheadings to help the audience; headings on this page, for example, include the most important, most general heading ("Using Sources in Academic Research") and a more specific subheading ("Using Headings"). (An example of an even more specific subheading can be found on page 217: "Writing Conventions for the Content of a Survey.")

For academic essays in the humanities and social sciences, ask the instructor about the appropriateness of using headings. For the Problem-Solution essay in this chapter, headings are appropriate. The headings could include *Background, Analysis of Solutions, Implementation Plan,* and *Conclusion.* For examples of headings in a Problem-Solution paper, see Student Sample 24, page 236.

Using Sources in Academic Research

Individual background knowledge, as well as personal observation and experience, can be engaging and strong evidence to raise the consciousness of readers. For example, Naoko Otsuki wrote about the problem of returning to her country after she completed her academic work in the U.S. In the background paragraph below, she presented her observations of the disadvantages of the Japanese respect for harmony.

8 STUDENT SAMPLE

[Thesis statement of opinion]

Harmony is prized in most facets of life in Japan, but I believe the ways that harmony is practiced, especially in the educational system and in the workplace, are not beneficial to Japanese society.

Background Paragraph: Demonstrates that a Problem Exists

[Topic sentence] *[Techniques of support: personal experience, examples]*

When I returned to Japan after living five years abroad, I was startled to find the hindrances to my freedom of expression at school as a result of the concept of harmony. First, all students are required to wear uniforms to school; while most Japanese students accept this regulation, I could not understand why we needed to wear this attire. Instead of promoting harmony, I felt that it repressed my individuality. Second, it is no exaggeration to say that Japanese students never state their opinions in class, nor do they take a definite stand; even if the professor addresses a question directly to them, Japanese students attempt to

[Methods of development: definition, comparison and contrast]

conceal their opinions. I realized that "harmony" does not describe these practices. As a musical term, "harmony" is a combination of successive sounds of *various* pitches that make a chord. In other words, harmony can only be created when individuals, each having their own opinions and each valued for having those opinions, come together. Otherwise, harmony is a form of repression.

***Naoko Otsuki*, Japan**

Notice that following her description of her personal experiences and observations, Naoko uses a fact (a definition), comparison, and contrast to strengthen her description of how deeply the concept of harmony exists in the Japanese school system (i.e., how serious the problem is).

USING INTERVIEW INFORMATION IN RESEARCH

For many academic writing assignments, the information that results from interviewing one or more authorities provides valuable information to use as evidence in the paper. (Review the purposes and uses of interviewing in Chapter 4, pages 112–113.) For the Problem-Solution essay, interviewing a local authority can provide such information as the history of a problem and of solutions that have been tried previously. Further, it can establish a bond between the student writer and the authority that may be helpful in persuading the authority.

Writing Assignment:
Preparing for the Interview

1. Select an appropriate interviewee for your Problem-Solution paper and locate contact information for that person.
2. Use the **Guidelines for Interviews** on page 113 to prepare for the interview. Such questions (and follow-up questions, given here in brackets) should include:
   - What is your opinion of the severity of this problem?
   - What can you tell me about the history of this problem? [How long has it existed?]
   - Have actions been taken to solve the problem? [What are they? What were the results of those actions?]
   - In your opinion, what is the best solution to this problem? [What are the problems concerning that solution?]
3. Share information about your interviewee and your interview questions with a small group of classmates. Offer suggestions to your classmates about possible interview questions and follow-up questions.
4. Using your experience with your classmates' interview questions and the criteria in the **Guidelines for Interviews**, *evaluate* and revise your interview questions.

Writing Assignment:
The Interview

1. Arrange and conduct the interview.
2. After the interview, re-*evaluate* the attitudes of your interviewee toward the problem and the solution, and adjust your essay plan as necessary.
3. *Evaluate* the information from your interview. What can you use as evidence? Are there interesting direct quotations?
4. Review the ways to use and cite interview information (see Appendix A).

DESIGNING AND ADMINISTERING A SURVEY FOR RESEARCH INFORMATION

Surveys* are written documents that ask a group of people, called "respondents," to answer questions or respond to statements. The goal of survey designers is to collect information about a topic from people who are typical of those involved in the topic.

The group of people surveyed are called a "representative sample" (i.e., respondents who *represent* a typical group). For example, for research about a medical problem that occurs in hospital patients, a "representative sample" of hospital patients with that problem would be surveyed. To evaluate the top brands of orange juice, the survey would be given to orange juice drinkers.

Valid—that is, authoritative, effective, strong—is an important word in survey research. At least 15–20 responses are needed to provide adequate (valid) data for a Problem-Solving essay. Because some people will not complete and/or return a written survey, at least 20–25 surveys should be distributed.

GUIDELINES

for Survey Design

1. **Identify** the "representative **sample**" (the group of people) you will survey; e.g.,
   - college/university students on one floor of a dormitory
   - undergraduate international students
   - cybersnoopers
   - students who drive and drink
   - students in 3 of your classes
   - members in a student organization
2. Carefully **examine** the type of information you are interested in. If, for example, you are investigating jet lag, your questions or statements could include these:

   1. How seriously do you suffer from jet lag? <u>*Some*</u> <u>*A lot*</u> <u>*Terribly*</u>
   2. Which of the following techniques do you use? (Circle one)

      A. Stay awake until it's time for bed in the new location
      B. Take a nap when I arrive
      C. Eat a diet low in carbohydrates before I leave
      D. Other (list): ______________________________

3. **Keep it short and simple** (the **KISS** rule). Do not make a survey too difficult or too long. Usually a survey should be a single page.
4. Develop a **simple scale**. Do not ask for lengthy written answers. Instead, give a choice of possible answers:

   Circle *or* X *or* check (✔) one
   Always *Usually* *Sometimes* *Rarely* *Never*

   SA A NS D SD
   [SA=Strongly Agree; A=Agree; NS=Not Sure; D=Disagree; SD=Strongly Disagree]

   5 4 3 2 1
   [5 = Excellent; 4 = Very Good; 3 = Good; 2 = Needs Improvement; 1 = Poor]

5. Confine each **statement** or **question** to **one idea** only.

   Do you like peanut butter? *Yes* *No*
   Do you like chicken salad? *Yes* *No*
   Do you like ice cream? *Yes* *No*

   NOT Do you like peanut butter, chicken salad, or ice cream? *Yes* *No*

6. **Arrange** the survey on the page so that it is clear, uncrowded, and appealing.

---

* To review the differences between interviews and surveys, see page 102.

7. Give **respondents opportunities** to **comment** (in their own words) (a) after the options you have chosen and (b) at the end of the survey because
   - some respondents may choose an option you have not considered.
   - some respondents may prefer to comment in their own words.
   - respondent comments are strong, credible support when quoted directly.
8. Make **returning** the survey **easy** by providing clear information and materials, such as enclosing a self-addressed stamped envelope, instructing the respondent to return the survey directly to you (e.g., in a class you are both taking, at the main desk of the dormitory where you both live), or by offering to pick it up.
9. Ask several people to complete the draft of the survey and to **report any** problems or **suggestions** for revisions.

Developing a survey is not difficult, but unless the designer considers both purpose and audience carefully, the information collected will not be useful. Moreover, because the written survey is usually given to people who will complete it and return it later, the respondents cannot ask about survey items that confuse them. Therefore, the questions and statements on the survey must be clearly and carefully written.

Writing Conventions for the Content of a Survey

- a descriptive title
- an introduction describing the reasons for the survey
- clear directions about completing the survey
- demographic data (i.e., requested information about the respondent, but NOT his/her name)
- the questions or statements to be completed by the respondent
- a space for written comments at the end of the survey
- information about how to return the survey to the designer
- an expression of appreciation for the time spent by the respondent

Complete the student-designed surveys below. Then do the exercise that follows.

[Title] **Baby Clothes' Colors in Different Cultures**

[Introduction: reason for the survey] Hello! We are taking a first-year composition course, and our assignment is to survey international students at the university about the colors used in their country for babies. Will you please help us by completing the questions below? It will take just two minutes, and your *[Directions]* time will help us get a good grade!

[Demographic data] Your country ______________________

Your class (Circle one) Fresh Soph Junior Senior Grad Student

Your major field of study ______________________

1. What color(s) do very young babies in your culture wear?
   boys ____________ girls ____________
2. What color(s) do babies in your culture wear for celebrations (such as baptisms, welcoming parties, etc.)?
   boys ____________ girls ____________
3. What color(s) are not usually worn by babies in your culture?
   boys ____________ girls ____________
4. Why? ______________________

[Comments] Other comments: ______________________

[How to return the survey] Please return to Sophie in the attached envelope. Just drop the envelope in campus mail.

[Appreciation] THANK YOU!! THANK YOU!! THANK YOU!!

Sophie Gros, **France**
Yi Wu, **People's Republic of China (PRC)**

Survey: Extending Coe Library's Hours

This survey was designed to get your opinion about whether or not the library should stay open later more hours. Coe Library is now open from 7:45 A.M. to 11:00 P.M. from Monday to Thursday 7:45 A.M. to 7:30 P.M. on Friday 11:00 A.M. to 11:00 P.M. on Sunday.

I will use the opinions gathered in this survey to write a paper for my composition class, and I will send a copy of the results to the Director of the library.

Your name ______________________ Major ____________
Class: F S J Sr Grad Other (Circle one) Age ____________

1. How many nights a week do you stay in Coe Library until it closes?
   7 ___ 4–6 ___ 1–3 ___ Never ___ (check one)
2. Are you usually finished using the library when you leave?
   Yes ___ No ___
3. If the library was kept open longer on Mondays through Thursdays, what time do you think it should close?
   12:00 A.M. ___ 1:00 A.M. ___ 2:00 A.M. ___ Never ___
4. If the library was kept open longer on Fridays through Sundays, what time do you think it should close?
   Friday: 9:00 P.M. ___ 10:00 P.M. ___ Other __________
   Saturday: 9:00 P.M. ___ 10:00 P.M. ___ Other __________
   Sunday: 12:00 A.M. ___ 1:00 A.M. ___ Other __________
5. How many nights a week do you go to Coe Library immediately when it opens?
   7 ___ 4–6 ___ 1–3 ___ Never ___
6. If the library opened at a later time Mondays through Fridays, what time would you prefer?
   8:30 A.M. ___ 9:00 A.M. ___ Always open ___ Other ______
7. If the library opened at a different time on Saturdays and Sundays, what time would you prefer?
   8:30 A.M. ___ 9:00 A.M. ___ Always open ___ Other ______

Other comments: ____

____

Thank you very much for you time and consideration!

Hang (Allen) Du, **People's Republic of China (PRC)**

SURVEY: DUI

Hello! I'm doing an essay about driving under the influence of alcohol, which requires a survey about the topic. If you are willing to help me by answering these questions, I will be most thankful.

This survey is anonymous, so please answer honestly!

If you have questions, please e-mail me: erland@uwyo.edu

Class ______________ <u>Gender:</u> Male Female (circle one) Age ______
Minimum age for legal drinking in your country ______
Country ______________ Do you drink alcohol? ______
If **no**, please begin answering the numbered questions below.

- If **yes**, how often? 1 or 2 times per week ______ more ______ (Check one)
- If yes, do you drive after you have been drinking? ______
- If yes, have you ever been issued a ticket for DUI (driving under the influence of alcohol)? ______

<u>Directions</u>: For each of the questions below, please circle either **Y** (Yes) or **N** (No).

1. Do you know people who regularly drive when they are influenced by alcohol? Y N
2. Have you been a passenger in a vehicle in which the driver had been drinking? Y N
3. Do you think people who have been drinking should decide for themselves if they are capable of driving or not? Y N
4. Are people generally capable of driving after having 5 beers? Y N
5. When you go out with a group that drinks, do you appoint a designated driver? Y N
6. Do you think the laws against drinking and driving are too strict? Y N
7. Do you think the police enforce the drinking and driving law too strictly? Y N
8. Do you think the punishment for driving under the influence is too heavy? Y N

Other comments: ____

____

Erland Skogoy Hval, **Norway**

EXERCISE 7-H

1. With a partner or in a small group, discuss your results from the three surveys above.
2. Identify the audience(s) and the purpose(s) of each survey. How do you know?
3. Evaluate the student surveys in terms of the **Guidelines for Survey Design** (p. 216). Make a list of ways in which each of the surveys could be improved, and share your suggestions with the rest of the class.
4. Discuss the ways in which each survey designer could use the information from the survey as evidence in an essay assignment. Be specific!

Tabulating Survey Data

The more carefully the survey has been designed, the easier it is to collect, report, and interpret the data. Usually the writer tabulates the results and translates those results into percentages and/or averages because numbers are easily understood, and averages and percentages are stronger than individual results. For example, Table 7.1 depicts the tally (i.e., the count) and the results of Erland Hval's survey about driving under the influence (Student Sample 11, p. 219).

Table __ *Results of Hval's Survey*

Question	Yes		No	
	Number	*Percent*	*Number*	*Percent*
1	18	81%	2	19%
2	10	50%	10	50%
3	3	8%	17	85%
4	10	50%	10	50%
5	5	25%	15	75%
6	7	35%	13	65%
7	10	50%	10	50%
8	7	35%	13	65%

Total Number of Students Surveyed: 26
Total Number of Responses Received: 20

Writing Assignment:
Developing the Survey

Using the **Guidelines for Survey Design** (p. 216), develop a survey about your topic for a representative sample of respondents. Make 3–5 copies of your survey draft.

EXERCISE 7-I

1. Explain to a small group of classmates the audience for and the purpose of your survey.
2. Share your survey draft with your group and ask them to complete your survey.
3. As you read your classmates' draft surveys, ask questions about confusing parts, and suggest ways to improve their surveys.
4. Use the criteria listed in **Guidelines for Survey Design** and the suggestions of your classmates to evaluate and revise your own survey.
5. Administer your survey to a group of representative respondents.

REPORTING SURVEY RESULTS

Writers use survey results to support their ideas and opinions. Therefore, it is necessary to (a) introduce the use of the survey in the background paragraph of the essay, (b) include a copy of the survey in an Appendix at the end of the essay, (c) present the results in the essay, and (d) cite the survey in the text. There are several ways to report survey results.

- Refer to the survey and state whether its results agree or disagree with previous research.

  Results of a survey of 15 university students who were first-born children supported the previous research (see Appendix A for the survey).

- In the background paragraph, describe and refer the reader to the survey in the Appendix (on a separate page, at the end of the essay).

In addition, a survey (Gros and Wu, 1998) of twenty international students at the University of Wyoming was used to determine the clothing colors of babies in different cultures (see Appendix 3 for the survey).

- Describe the survey briefly and give the general results of the survey to support an idea in a body paragraph.

The survey (Ford, 1997) asked 15 undergraduates to identify their personality characteristics. More than 75% of the respondents indicated that they fit the profile of first-borns, and more than 60% characterized themselves as independent achievers who were conscious of time and were well-organized. Table __ gives the average percentages for the group.

- Introduce results, report them in a table, and interpret them for the audience.

The results of the survey confirmed my belief that a great majority of typical university students wanted to learn more about the culture of Sweden; 83% chose culture as one of their top three choices. Table __ depicts the top five other choices students made and the percentage for each.

Table __ *Students' Choices for Topics in an Ethnic Study Class About Sweden*

History	Holidays	Economy	Industry	Traditions
41%	34%	34%	34%	21%

Direct quotations from survey respondents can also be powerful evidence. If the survey provides respondents with a "Comments" space, those comments can be used as direct quotations in the essay. Although survey respondents will not provide their names, the writer can use demographic data (personal information about the respondents that will not identify the individual). Notice the use of such data in this student sample.

Since more than a third of the students responding to the survey were business majors, it is not surprising that so many students wanted to learn about industry and the economy. As student number 18, a twenty-year-old male, answered question number 3, "Going on my interests listed in the previous question and my accounting major, I would be interested in how business works in Sweden."

[Demographic data]
[Direct quotation from student comment]

***Ann Wallskog,* Sweden**

Writing Assignment:
Using Survey Results

1. Collect the completed surveys and tabulate the results.
2. Evaluate the results of your survey. What can you use as evidence? Are there interesting direct quotations from the "Comments" section?
3. Review the ways to use and cite interview information (p. 113) and the examples of in-text survey citations in the Student Samples above.

Evaluating Sources

Information sources can be valid and strong or unreliable and weak. Therefore, the **GIGO** statement—**G**arbage **I**n, **G**arbage **O**ut—applies. If the material is poorly planned, badly presented, biased, or incomplete, the evidence will be weak and ineffective. In contrast, the better designed the survey, the more carefully selected the material from books and journals, the more likely it is that the results will be valid (i.e., believable, persuasive). Student writers who use source materials should therefore evaluate the materials by analyzing the following information about the author(s) of those materials.

GUIDELINES
for Evaluating Sources

- Evaluate the **credibility** (i.e., reliability, trustworthiness) of the human source (the interviewee, the researcher, the author) by
  - reading his/her biodata
  - examining his/her background and/or expertise based on external criteria:
    - > the person's current work and previous work (e.g., Michael Jordan about basketball, or the Pope about Catholic religious beliefs)
    - > published work by that person
    - > the recommendations of others
  - analyzing his/her potential for bias (e.g., the president of the National Rifle Association on gun control, or a spokesperson for the tobacco industry on the risk of cancer from smoking).
- Evaluate the **accuracy** of the content by
  - examining the preparation (i.e., methods) of the materials used in an article
  - determining the age of the materials; usually the more recent, the more reliable
  - studying the strength of the results (e.g., how large was the sample for a survey? how much research has the interviewee done? how many examples of the observations made by the interviewee/author?)
  - noting other materials used to substantiate the primary resources: in-text citations, a bibliography, other publications by the human source(s).
- Evaluate the **relevance** of the materials by
  - analyzing how the material relates exactly to the narrowed topic of the essay
  - examining how the material supports the ideas and/or opinions
  - determining the level and "voice" of the material (e.g., too technical? too superficial?).

EXERCISE 7-J

1. Read or reread the following student essays in this textbook.
   - Chapter 3, page 94 — Student Sample 21, by Matt Mickleson
   - Chapter 6, page 200 — Student Sample 20, by Margarita Vaiman
   - Chapter 7, page 236 — Student Sample 25, by M. Lorena Magnotta
2. Take notes on the human source(s) used in each essay. Include the interviewees.
3. Evaluate the strength and the validity of the source(s) in each essay. In your opinion, which source(s) are most persuasive and credible? Why?
4. Share your choice(s) with a small group of classmates. Be prepared to support your choice(s).

Writing Conventions for the Problem-Solution Essay

The writing conventions for the Problem-Solution essay are important because the organization is somewhat complex. It is therefore necessary to be particularly careful about following only one of the four or more possible organizational patterns. Choice of the pattern depends on the 3As: Assignment (purpose), Audience, and Available Material. For this Problem-Solving paper, the writer will use the **Alternative Pattern** (see below). For future academic assignments, another of the patterns may be selected.

The number of body paragraphs also depends on the 3As. One assignment may ask for three to five alternatives, while another may require that only one solution be presented. One instructor may assign an implementation plan that includes extensive research and time lines that will occupy several paragraphs; another instructor might not require any implementation plan as part of the paper. Students must analyze the assignment and the audience expectations as they plan their Problem-Solution papers.

Below are three authentic academic assignments. Clarifying information is bracketed. In Assignment **I**, notice that the directions require only "the best solution"; in Assignments **II** and **III**, multiple alternatives must be evaluated; and none of these assignments requires an implementation plan.

I **Introduction to Sociology**
Volunteerism has been a vital part of American society. However, recent societal changes such as (a) the longer work week and (b) a great majority of women entering the workforce have caused volunteer levels to decrease [**problem**]. Write an 8 to 10 page **analysis** [**evaluation**] that describes (a) the history of volunteerism in America, (b) the contemporary view of volunteerism, and (c) the best **solution** to the **problem** of decreasing volunteerism in our society.

II **Water Resources Planning Project**
Select a water resources project from your experience or from the literature. Analyze the project and in your own words briefly describe the planning phases as defined by the American Society of Civil Engineers presented in the lecture on January 27. For example, define the goals, the **problem**, and **analyze** [**evaluate**] some **alternatives** [**solutions**], impacts, decisions, etc. Specifically describe any unique characteristic of the problem that significantly impacted the planning process, for example, specific constraints regarding politics, financing, the environment, etc.

III **Introduction to Education**
In recent decades, America has fallen behind other first-world countries in educating its youth. Write a 10-page paper, using at least three sources (including at least two periodicals), that discusses the **problems** in America's public school system today. In this paper

- give background information that **evaluates** the situation: when did the U.S. lose its edge? Could this have been preventable?
- research different educational reforms and reform theories. Would these work in real schools? [**evaluation**] Have they already been tried? Did they work in part or as a whole?
- compare our system with that of two other countries. What do these countries do differently? What similarities are there?
- offer **solutions** for the U.S. education system. Would you combine existing reforms or implement a totally new idea?

EXERCISE 7-K

1. With a partner or in a small group, select two of the academic assignments above. Define and discuss each problem. Then identify specific solutions for each.
2. For each of the two academic assignments you and your partner (or classmates) chose, plan an interview. First, decide the kind of person who might be an authority about the topic. Then write 6 to 8 questions you might ask the authority in the interview.
3. Discuss and develop evaluative criteria for each of the two assignments you chose.
4. What kind(s) of nontext materials would be especially helpful in each of the two assignments? Be specific.

Note: Feasibility analysis is discussed on pages 228–230.

Each conventional problem-solving pattern is outlined below; each is followed by an essay map (i.e., the topic sentences for each body paragraph) in that pattern.

Simple Problem-Solving Pattern

I Introduction

II The problem: identify and demonstrate its existence

III The solution(s)

IV Answering possible objections and problems caused by the solution

V Conclusion: recommendation and call to action

Figure 7-2 *Overall Organization: Simple Problem-Solving Pattern*

13 STUDENT SAMPLE

[Thesis statement] I *Due to inadequate training of English teachers, high school students in Hong Kong are weak on oral English.*

[Demonstration: problem exists] II Even though in all Anglo-Chinese schools in Hong Kong, English textbooks are used, most high school students are not competent in spoken English, and the use of "Chinglish" is widespread.

[Solution] III Better training for English teachers must be mandated by the university teacher-preparation programs.

[Answering objections] IV Some of the recommendations for improved teacher-preparation will certainly be expensive; however, by increasing tuition and using further government subsidies, this problem can be overcome.

[Conclusion: prediction, call to action] V It is clear that if the problem is not solved in the near future, Hong Kong may lose its important role as the great financial center of the world, the bridge between East and West.

Winnie Chan, **Hong Kong**

Alternative Problem-Solving Pattern

I Introduction

II The problem: identify and demonstrate its existence (background paragraph)

III Evaluation of alternative solution 1; why it is not feasible + evidence

IV Evaluation of alternative solution 2; why it is not feasible + evidence

V Evaluation of alternative solution 3; why it is feasible + evidence and answering possible objections

VI Implementation plan; evidence

VII Conclusion: summary, call to action

Figure 7-3 *Overall Organization: Alternative Problem-Solving Pattern*

[Thesis statement of opinion, intent]	I	*Because I found my 30-minute appointment in the Writing Center insufficient, I decided to investigate the severity of the problem for other students; in this paper, I propose a solution.*
[Demonstration: problem exists]	II	According to the 1998 Writing Center Spring Semester Survey, I am not the only student who believes that Writing Center appointments for tutorial help should be longer.
[Solution 1 + evaluation; not feasible]	III	One solution is to extend the 30-minute appointment to 45 minutes. However, Dr. Jane Nelson, Director of the Writing Center, opposes this solution because the extended time would not allow the Writing Center to serve as many clients.
[Solution 2 + evaluation; not feasible]	IV	Another solution might be more use of the electronic online tutoring from the Writing Center. However, a majority of students who responded to my survey indicated that they preferred to have their tutoring face-to-face.
[Solution 3 + evaluation; feasible; paragraph will answer objections]	V	The best solution is a sequenced approach: a client works 30 minutes with a Writing Center tutor, then 30 minutes by himself/herself, then another 30 minutes with a Writing Center tutor.
[Implementation + evidence]	VI	Based on the survey results of both the Writing Center Survey and my survey, I recommend that the Writing Center initiate a pilot program next semester to test the sequenced approach.
[Conclusion: summary, call to action]	VII	In conclusion, because the Writing Center exists as a service to the students, and because many students are interested in experimenting with the sequenced approach, the pilot project is an appropriate solution.

***Zeenat Chowdhury,* Pakistan**

Step-by-Step Problem-Solving Pattern

I Introduction
II The problem: identify and demonstrate its existence (background paragraph)
III Recommended solution and reasons why the solution is necessary and feasible
IV Plan for implementation: Step 1
V Plan for implementation: Step 2
VI Plan for implementation: Step 3
VII Conclusion: call to action

Figure 7-4 *Overall Organization: Step-by-Step Problem-Solving Pattern*

15 STUDENT SAMPLE

[Thesis statement]	I	*Women sports reporters are held in low repute.*
[Demonstration: problem exists]	II	Historically, women who chose to be sports reporters have been denigrated and discriminated against.
[Recommended solution + feasibility]	III	Women must be encouraged and supported to become sports reporters.
[Implementation: Step 1]	IV	First, parents and teachers should encourage young girls to get involved in playing sports.
[Implementation: Step 2]	V	Next, university schools of broadcasting and journalism must be positive about admitting women who want to study to become sports reporters.
[Implementation: Step 3]	VI	Finally, male sports players must be educated to accept women sports reporters.
[Conclusion: summary, call to action]	VII	In conclusion, education and encouragement are the keys to women's success as sports reporters.

Barbara Kassler, **Germany**

Point-by-Point Problem-Solving Pattern

I Introduction
II The overall problem: identify and demonstrate its existence
III One part of the problem, its solution, evidence to support the solution, and refutation of possible objections
IV Second part of the problem, its solution, evidence to support the solution, and refutation of possible objections
V Third part of the problem, its solution, evidence to support the solution, and refutation of possible objections
VI Conclusion: implementation, call to action

Figure 7-5 *Overall Organization: Point-by-Point Pattern*

[Thesis statement of intent]	I	*In this paper, I identify three major problems with the current student health insurance policy and recommend that the university negotiate with another insurance company.*
[Demonstration: problem exists]	II	Student health insurance is compulsory for all international students at the university; however, students have so many problems with the coverage in the current policy that some students give up entirely and pay for private doctors as well.
[One part of the problem, solution; answering objections]	III	First, although we pay a great amount for health insurance, the policy does not cover all health problems, and many services require an additional fee. (Solution to follow.)
[Second part of the problem, solution, answering objections]	IV	Next, the Student Health Center is open only during business hours during the weekdays; during other hours and on the weekends, we must either pay for private care or wait until the Health Center opens.(Solution to follow.)
[Third part of the problem, solution; answering objections]	V	Finally, the insurance policy for international students is different from the policy other university students have; it is more expensive, and it covers fewer health care expenses. (Solution to follow.)
[Conclusion: implementation, call to action]	VI	In conclusion, university officials should work with international students to advocate for a better and fairer health insurance policy.

Somrux Raksasap, **Thailand**

EXERCISE 7-L

1. With a small group of classmates, study the Student Samples for each of the overall organizational patterns for Problem-Solution papers above. Which topic interests you most? Why? Be specific.
2. Which essay map seems most persuasive to you? Why? Discuss your choice with your classmates.
3. Select two of the essay maps and discuss what other solutions might be possible.
4. For one of the essay maps, write a second sentence for two of the body paragraphs. In what ways will the second sentences help the readers?
5. In your opinion, how formal will the language be in each of the Problem-Solution essays? Write the numbers of Student Samples 13 to 16 where you think they belong on the "Formal—Informal" scale below. Then discuss your decisions with your classmates.

more formal ◄——————————————► less formal

Writing Assignment:

Organizing the Problem-Solution Essay

1. As you continue to gather information about your Problem-Solving topic, consider where that information will be presented in your essay.
2. Draft an essay map for your essay, using the Alternative Problem-Solving Pattern.
3. Share your essay map with a partner and discuss possible revisions.
4. Consider your partner's comments, reread your essay map, and revise it as necessary.

Feasibility Analysis of Alternative Solutions

One of the goals of a Problem-Solving paper is to evaluate a number of solutions and to recommend the best of them. Because most problems will inspire a variety of possible solutions, do not quickly select the most obvious solution. Instead, consider several solutions; compare and contrast the advantages and disadvantages of each; decide which is the most "feasible" (i.e., possible). Strategies to discover the possible solutions to a problem include (a) studying the history of the problem, (b) listing the cause(s) of the problem, and (c) using "what if?" to brainstorm solutions.

Evaluating each solution begins with developing criteria. While some criteria will depend on the specific topic, all solutions must be evaluated by at least the following:

- **Feasibility:** Will the solution actually solve the problem?
- **Logical Considerations:** Cost-effectiveness, practicality, ethicality, legality
- **Consequences** of the solution: What additional short-term and long-term problems might the solution cause?

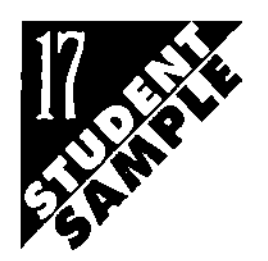

Problem: The university daycare center does not enroll children under three years of age, so many married students cannot use the facility.

[Causes of the problem] Causes:

- Infants and young children require more care.
- They require more specialized care.
- It would cost too much money.

[Possible solutions] Solutions:

1. Change the policy of the center to admit infants and children under the age of three.
2. Develop another facility for infants and very young children.

Solution #1: The daycare center should admit infants and children under three years old.

- Feasibility: This would solve the problem.
- Cost-effectiveness: It would be very costly for the center and for the parents.
- Practicality: Questionable—may be too many problems, too much money.
- Ethicality: It is ethical because the university has a duty to serve all its students.
- Potential short-term problems: The need for more space and special equipment; additional staff and higher tuition (i.e., persuade parents to pay); care standards may change; younger children are more likely to become ill.
- Potential long-term problems: A drop in enrollment due to cost (and loss of income for the center); possible parental unhappiness.

***Olga Jacoby,* Poland**

In the Problem-Solving paper, writers may (a) describe their evaluations in paragraph form or (b) use a combination of sentences and charts or logs to demonstrate the results. The following feasibility evaluation uses a three-column log to lay out its evidence in the evaluation of Solution #1.

Problem: University buildings that are not handicapped-accessible*

Solutions:

1. Do not schedule classes in any building that is not handicapped-accessible.
2. Require services in non-accessible buildings to make their services available on the ground floor of the building.
3. Make every building handicapped-accessible.

Criteria	Judgment	Evidence
Cost-effectiveness	positive	no cost at present
Practicality	negative	loss of classrooms in non-access buildings
Ethicality	problematic	university mission is to serve all students
Legality	problematic	federal law requires all public buildings to be handicapped-accessible by 2001
Short-term problems	negative	loss of classrooms (34% of classrooms not accessible; only 1.4% of students disabled)
Long-term	negative	failure to comply with federal law by 2001 will result in law suit
Public perception	negative	the public expects more from the university

Elizabeth Aguilera, **Colombia**

Writing Assignment:
Evaluating Feasibility

Make a three-column log like the one above that evaluates the solutions you have selected. For your three-column log, list the criteria, your judgment, and the evidence for *each* of your solutions.

Note: Continue to gather necessary support for your evaluation.

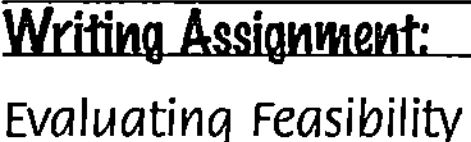

WRITING FEASIBILITY ANALYSIS PARAGRAPHS

Most Problem-Solution assignments require analysis of more than one solution to the problem. By presenting and then discarding one or more solutions, writers demonstrate that they have carefully considered the most important, most relevant options before they make their recommendations.

In general, a paragraph that evaluates a solution is based on the criteria developed by the writer. Like most paragraphs, the analysis begins with a topic sentence. The evaluation (a) states the criteria, (b) judges according to those criteria, and (c) supports the judgment with facts, examples, physical description, and/or personal experience. In a Problem-Solution paper, the solution that is recommended by the writer is usually discussed last, with the implementation paragraph following (if such a paragraph is part of the assignment).

* Handicapped access means that people with disabilities such as paralysis can get into and around in the buildings—by using, for instance, ramps and elevators instead of stairs.

Student Samples 19–21 analyze solutions. The title of the Problem-Solution essay, and the thesis statement for each, appears at the beginning of each example.

SOLUTION NOT RECOMMENDED

Evening Shuttle Services

[Thesis statement of intent and opinion] *Because the university offers many evening classes, the fact that there is no public transportation service available to students is a serious problem.*

[Solution #1] One solution is to provide car-pooling. The university could set up a volunteer program that would pick students up in front of the library every *[Analysis: advantages]* half hour between 6 P.M. and 10:30 P.M. The clear advantage of this solution is its cost-effectiveness; the university would provide neither cars nor drivers. *[Disadvantages: support from survey results, experience, facts]* However, upon closer investigation, this solution is not feasible. First, my survey results showed that a single car would not be sufficient for the numbers of students who need transportation. Even four cars would not fulfill that need, and with the addition of each car, the process of scheduling volunteers becomes more and more complex. Next, the recruiting of volunteers would almost certainly grow more difficult with time, and as with most volunteer efforts, the reliability of even a well-run program would be problematic. *[Support from interview information]* Finally, according to Corrine Sheaffer, Manager of Fleet Operations, the legal problems with insurance would prohibit the university from participating in such a program. Therefore, this solution is not possible.

***Naoko Shoji,* Japan**

SOLUTION NOT RECOMMENDED

Preventing *Brucellosis* Transmission

[Thesis statement of intent] *Instead of killing the bison infected with* brucellosis *in Yellowstone National Park, there are several options to solving the problem of* brucellosis *in the herd being transmitted to cattle in the area.*

[Solution #1] The most obvious solution to the possibility of the transmission of *brucellosis* from the bison to cattle from the ranches that surround Yellowstone is to keep the bison and cattle separate. According to the *[Analysis: evidence from book, in-text citation]* *Jackson Hole Guide*, the bison herd, which shares grazing areas with cattle in Grand Teton National Park, is already kept separate in many areas by fences (Sheraton, 1999). Moreover, Yellowstone Park biologist Steve Cain stated that while federal officials have never guaranteed that bison and cattle will be kept separated, Park Service personnel try to keep the animals *[Direct quotation from book]* apart: "We know the areas that the bison habitually use, so it is not all that difficult to identify potential contact points. We are lucky with the Jackson herd because they frequent areas that are away from the cattle allotments" *[Disadvantages: not feasible]* (cited in Shelton, 1999). Ranchers, however, believe that whenever a bison crosses into cattle-grazing areas, because of a trampled fence or because a fence does not exist in all areas, the possibility of transmission occurs. Since it is impossible to guarantee that all fences are in fully operable condition at all moments, and since the entire park cannot be fenced, some wandering occurs. Consequently, this solution is not 100% effective.

***Lidao Bao,* People's Republic of China (PRC)**

SOLUTION RECOMMENDED

Preventing Fish Kill in Acid-Rain Influenced Lakes

[Thesis statement of intent] *This essay discusses the best known ways to prevent fish kills, both theoretically and from my practical experience.*

[Solution #3] The newest method to treat acid-influenced lakes is a short-term chemical treatment that involves neutralizing water with calcium products. *[Evidence from journal article, in-text citation]* In Norway we have government-supported calcium supply projects that add calcium by helicopter and trucks (Jakt & Fiske, 1991). However, the largest amount of work is done on small lakes by private citizens. I have worked with and watched one project in Norway for several years. Last year, for example, my father and I brought about 4000 pounds of *[Support: personal experience, knowledge]* shell-sand to our area with a snowmobile. The shell sand is crushed by the force of the water and gives off calcium; it is one of the most efficient ways to increase the pH value rapidly. In fact, we found that the fish had returned the following spring. By delivering the high calcium content sand to the highest of the mountain lakes, we ensured that the calcium *[Disadvantages + advantages]* would spread to all the lower lakes in the area before going to a stream and down to the sea. Although the practice of adding calcium to the lakes is time-consuming, my father and I enjoy the time together and benefit when we return to the lakes to fish the following summer. Last summer, my grandfather, my father, and I caught 110 fish! My grandfather said, *[Direct quotation]* "This is unbelievable—just like forty years ago!"

Reference

Jakt, A. L. and Fiske, N. F. (1991). Liming acid ponds in Norway. *Hunting and Fishing*, 1, 28.

Frank Eikeland, **Norway**

EXERCISE 7-M

1. With a small group of classmates, list the criteria used to evaluate the solution in each of the three feasibility paragraphs above.
2. What kinds of nontext materials might each of the authors use to strengthen and clarify their feasibility analyses? Be specific.
3. In your opinion, which of the paragraphs is the most persuasive for its intended audience? Why? Discuss your answer with your classmates.
4. Discuss the advantages and disadvantages of the solutions you have selected for your Problem-Solution paper. Offer your peers suggestions for their feasibility analyses.

Writing Assignment:
Writing the Feasibility Paragraphs

1. Continue to gather evidence and information about the problem and the solution(s) in your paper as you draft 2 to 4 feasibility paragraphs for the solutions you selected. Have you decided to use headings in your Problem-Solution essay?
2. Use the criteria in the **Guidelines for Evaluating Sources** (p. 222) to evaluate the strength and validity of your feasibility analyses.
3. Exchange paragraphs with a partner, and try to become the audience for your partner's feasibility paragraphs. Then discuss the strength(s) of his or her analyses; offer specific suggestions or ask questions that will help your partner write more persuasively for his or her audience .
5. Reread your feasibility analyses. Consider your partner's comments and revise your feasibility paragraphs.

Implementation of the Recommended Solution

In addition to selecting the best solution to a problem, writers must demonstrate how the solution will be put into practice. In general, undergraduates may be able to suggest an implementation plan without specific budgets enumerating equipment, new personnel, and dissemination costs. In longer, more complex assignments, however, writers might spend ten to twenty pages describing an implementation plan.

Two typical ways to present an implementation plan are a chart of key steps and a time line. A time line can depict the training of employees on a new computer. A chart might list the key steps or the sequence in a proposed implementation plan. Student Samples 22 and 23 demonstrate implementation plans.

Problem: The police in ______________ harass university students.

Solutions: see Table __ below

Table __ *Implementation Plan: Police Harassment*

[Chart]

Recommendations:	*Cost*	*Proposed time line*
Policy change: police officers to get out of their cars, meet the public	none	immediately, ongoing
Inservice education: public relations how to treat students with respect how to smile and interact more	$1000/year (interaction specialist)	fiscal year 2000–2001, other years thereafter as necessary
Hiring more mature police officers: less likely to overreact	$5200/year (added salary)	begin in fiscal year 2000, ongoing
Increased initial job training: police in other countries receive twice as much training	$12,500/year (2 officers, 6 more months)	begin in fiscal year 2002, ongoing

***Jon Boeckman,* Norway**

Problem: The business *Shear Class Beauty Salon* is unprofitable.

Solutions: evaluation of tanning bed operation, customer service survey, more focused advertising, construction of a business plan

[Time line]

Short-term implementation plan (within 3 months)

- sell tanning bed
- administer and evaluate a customer survey
- education of owners concerning a business plan

Long-term implementation plan (within 12 months)

- formulation of a business plan
- initiation of promotion and advertising
- purchase of site insurance

***Michele Nottage,* U.S.**

EXERCISE 7-N

1. Write the evaluation of Solution #1 in Student Sample 17 (p. 228) in paragraph form; state both the problem and Solution #1 in your topic sentence.
2. Choose one of the implementation plans (either Student Sample 22 or 23) and write a paragraph that describes the plan.
3. In your opinion, who are the audiences and what are the purposes for Student Samples 19–23 (above)? Share your opinions with your classmates.
4. Which of the four topics—in Student Samples 19–23—is the easiest to solve? the most difficult? Why? Discuss your answers with your classmates.

PERSUADING THE AUDIENCE

Some of the most important persuasion techniques in a Problem-Solving essay are (a) using an appropriate, reasonable voice (review on pp. 6 and 177), (b) providing adequate evidence, and (c) choosing a Rogerian approach for the presentation of a recommended solution (review on p. 181). Using Rogerian techniques such as establishing writer credibility, describing shared beliefs and concerns with the audience, and being willing to compromise, will strengthen the persuasive quality of the Problem-Solution paper.

EXERCISE 7-O

1. For Student Samples 17 and 18, discuss the persuasion techniques that the writers have used (e.g., voice, Rogerian approaches, evidence), and give specific examples to support your opinions.
2. In what ways might the writers of each implementation plan in Student Samples 19–23 more effectively demonstrate their shared beliefs and concerns with their audiences? Be specific.
3. For each of the four topics, how formal will the language be? Write the number of each Student Sample—19, 20, 21, 22, and 23—where you think they belong on the Formal—Informal scale below. Then discuss your decisions with your classmates.

   more formal ◄——————————————► less formal

4. Discuss the implementation plan for your Problem-Solution topic with a small group of classmates. Help your classmates by making suggestions and asking questions about the persuasiveness and feasibility of their implementation plans.

Writing Assignment: *Implementation Plan*

Review the Rogerian approach (p. 181). Draft an implementation paragraph that presents your plan in ways that will persuade your audience. Remember to state both the problem and your recommended solution in your topic sentence.

EXERCISE 7-P

1. Share your implementation plan with a partner, and try to become his or her audience as you read the implementation plan. Discuss ideas that you think will help make your partner's plan more persuasive, and listen to your partner's suggestions for your plan.
2. Consider your partner's comments as you reread and revise your persuasive implementation paragraph. Then consider using a visual (e.g., a chart, a diagram, an illustration) to strengthen the persuasiveness of your paragraph.

Writing Assignment: *Drafting the Problem-Solution Essay*

Continue to evaluate the sources and the materials you are using to support your ideas as you integrate the Feasibility Analysis paragraphs and the Implementation Plan into your Problem-Solution paper. Use **Guidelines for Composing** (inside front cover of this book) to complete the draft of your Problem-Solution essay.

EXERCISE 7-Q

1. Exchange essay drafts with a partner.
2. As you read your partner's draft, use the **Guidelines for Peer Response** (p. 127) to help your partner. Then discuss your questions and comments with your partner.

Writing Assignment:

Revising and Editing the Problem-Solution Essay

1. Reread your Problem-Solution essay. Considering your partner's comments and the **Guidelines for Revision** (on the inside back cover of this textbook), revise your Problem-Solution essay. Remember to
   - integrate the interview and/or survey results into your draft.
   - include the nontext materials, with your introduction to the nontext materials and your interpretation of those materials, as you write.
2. Reread your essay, editing for language and sentence structure errors.

Sending the Problem-Solution Essay

Because this Problem-Solution essay has an authentic audience (the person interviewed who has the position or authority to make the change), a copy of the paper will be sent to that reader with a cover letter (i.e., a letter that will be the first page, the "cover," for the essay).

To review writing conventions for the business letter, see page 4. In the student sample below, notice the writing conventions for a cover letter.

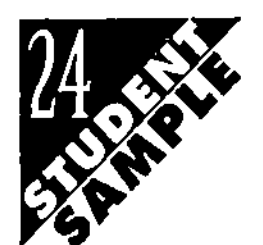

Cover Letter for the Problem-Solution Essay

[Return address]
McWhinney Hall
Room 262
University of Wyoming
Laramie, WY 82071

[Date] April 22, 1999

[Address of reader] Mr. Dennis Dreher
International Student Advisor
University of Wyoming
Laramie, WY 82071

[Introduction] Dear Mr. Dreher:

[No indentation] *[Single space]* You may remember our conversation about three weeks ago, when we discussed the problem of international students working on campus during the school year. I appreciated your time and your expertise, and I used the information you gave me when I researched the problem. As I promised, I am sending you a copy of the paper I turned in to my instructor in my first-year English composition class.

[Double-spaced between paragraphs] In this paper, I report the results of a survey of 46 UW students, and I summarize the information I found on the World Wide Web from several other universities concerning their solutions to the problem of inadequate jobs for international students. I also examine several potential solutions,

and I recommend that the International Student Office become actively involved in advocating that directors of various on-campus units strongly consider international students for jobs in those units. I also offer suggestions for the implementation of this recommendation.

[Request for reply] I hope you will consider my recommendation and the suggestions included in this paper. Will you please write me about your reactions to the paper? My campus address is Room 262 McWhinney Hall. Thank you again for your interest in my topic and for all your assistance.

[Close] Sincerely,

[Hand-written signature] Edgardo Cerqueira

[Typed name] Edgardo Cerqueira

Argentina

Figure 7-6 shows the writing conventions for addressing the envelope.

[Name and address of sender]

Edgardo Cerqueira
262 McWhinney Hall
University of Wyoming
Laramie, WY 82071

STAMP

[Name and address of receiver]

Mr. Dennis Dreher
International Student Advisor
University of Wyoming
Laramie, WY 82071

Figure 7-6 *Sample Envelope*

Writing Assignment II After your instructor has returned your essay, revise the essay so that the authority to whom you are sending the essay will not be distracted or irritated by errors. Then write a cover letter for your essay.

EXERCISE 7-R

1. Exchange the draft of your cover letter with a partner. Read and discuss each others' drafts. Then revise and edit your cover letter.
2. Attach the letter to your revised Problem-Solution essay.
3. Use a business envelope (4½" x 9½") or a larger manila envelope, depending on the size of your paper. Address the envelope and mail or deliver the envelope to your audience.

A SMOKING SOLUTION

[Introduction engages reader]

Landu Kalemba is a student at the University of Wyoming (UW), and he, like many other students, smokes. Since he has lived in the dorms, he has had to find a place where he can smoke. He is just one of the many students gathered outside any of the residence halls smoking together; often they are huddled together against the cold winds of Laramie. The university provides students with a room, a bed, and a meal plan, but many students also need a place to smoke where they can avoid the harsh weather conditions. Although smoking is legal for people over 18 years of age, student smokers who live in the dorms are as surprised as I was to discover that smokers tend to have fewer rights than other citizens. *The university has a responsibility to offer students who smoke a safe, convenient place to smoke.*

[Thesis statement]

[Heading]

Background

"Nowadays, smoking is something that may not be completely accepted in our society, and against it, a culture and atmosphere in which smoking is widely seen as a socially unacceptable and unhealthy habit, have been created" (National Center on Addiction, 1996). However, according to the results of the survey I conducted, 8% of students at UW smoke (Figure 1).

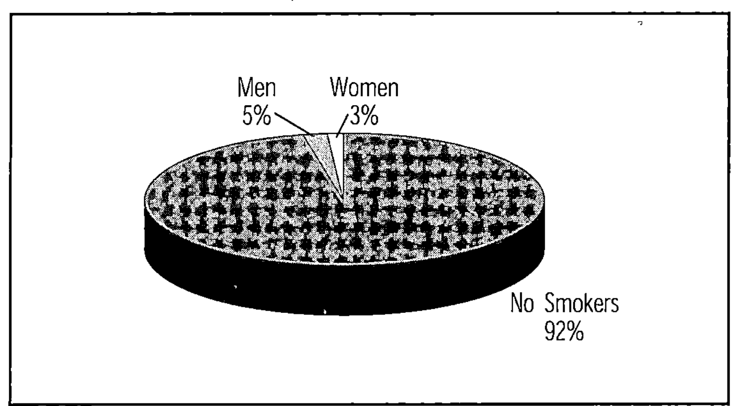

Figure 1 *Percentage of Student Smokers and Non-Smokers at UW*

At UW, and at many other schools in the U.S., there are strict smoking limitations (American Lung Association, 1997; Kansas State University, 1994). A smoking ban in the UW dormitories was supported by an all-student vote in 1992 and was then approved by University Regulation 180 which prohibits "the use of smoking devices in public places and in places of employment at the University of Wyoming, except in designated smoking areas" (Regulation 180, 1993). Furthermore, like many colleges and universities in the U.S., the UW Code of Conduct for Residence Halls and Food Services states that "smoking is prohibited in all residence halls and dining areas" (p. 15). Figure 2 illustrates the areas in which smoking is prohibited.

[Page number for direct quotation

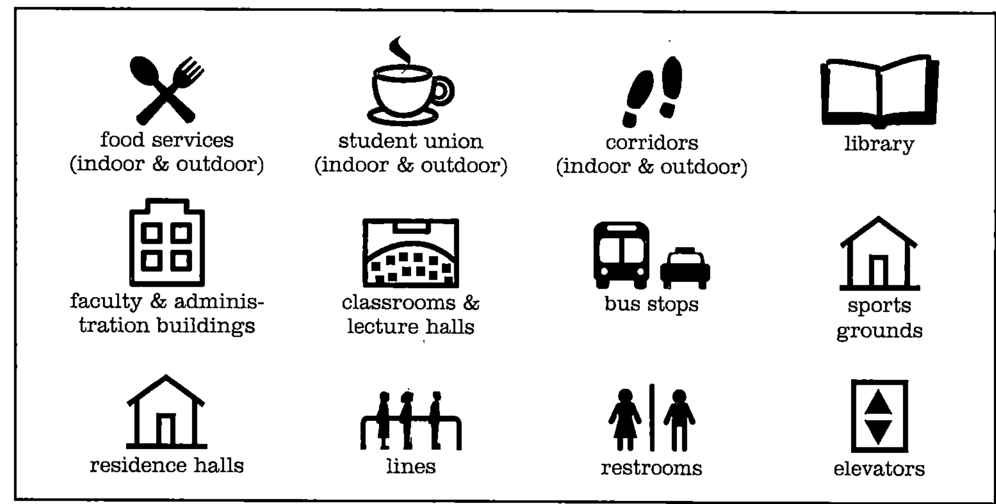

Figure 2 *Non-Smoking Areas (adapted from Chia-Zhi, 1996)*

[Interpretation of Figure 2] Although Regulation 180 implies that there are areas designated for smoking, there are no indoor places where students can smoke; even the Student Union is non-smoking. As a consequence, smokers have rights given by the Regulation that are not being respected at UW. That is a problem. Clearly, something must be done to improve this condition. After studying the problem, interviewing the Director of Residence Halls (see *[References to Appendices]* Appendix A for the interview questions), and conducting a survey of fifty UW students who smoke (see Appendix B for the survey), I believe that *[Statement of possible solutions]* there are three alternatives which UW authorities should consider: provide a special floor in one of the residence halls especially for smokers; designate a smoking lounge on the top floor of several (or all) dormitories; or allow smokers to smoke on the balconies that exist in Downey Hall or Orr Hall. For each of these alternatives, smokers could be offered the first choice of living in the selected resident hall.

[Feasibility analysis] <u>Analysis of Alternative Solutions</u>

The first possible solution is the designation of a special "smoking floor" in one of the dormitories. The floor would be the top floor because smoke rises; designating the top floor would mean that non-smokers—on the lower floors—would not suffer the effects of second-hand smoke. As one *[Direct quotation from survey comment]* of the students on the survey commented, "I don't think non-smokers should have their lives put in danger from second-hand smoke." The greatest advantage of this solution is that smokers would not have to face *[Advantages]* the cold winters in Wyoming just to have a cigarette. Also, since all students on the floor would be smokers, nobody would be offended by the smoke. Non-smokers would not have to smell the smoke, and smokers would not have to listen to non-smokers complain and cough, as they now do as they leave the dormitory and encounter the crowd of smokers. The greatest *[Disadvantages]* disadvantage, according to Mike Olsen, Director of Residence Halls, would be the cost of renovating the top floor of the dormitory with an "appropriate *[Direct quotation from interview]* venting system" that would allow the smoke to be vented to the outside of the dormitory. Another disadvantage, Olsen stated, is that the number of smokers changes from year to year; perhaps one year not enough smokers would sign up to live on the floor, and the next year too many smokers might want to live on the floor. The university would either lose money or have several angry smokers to placate. Finally, despite the venting system, [Paragraph hooks] the smell of smoke would undoubtedly remain on the floor, so that incoming students, even though they are smokers, might not want to live there.

A second alternative is to designate a smoking lounge on the top floor of several (or every) residence hall. This would solve the problem of having to smoke in blizzards and rainstorms although it is not as convenient for the smokers, especially those who live on other floors. The single rooms on the far ends of the top floors could be used as lounges. Of course, these rooms will also need to have carefully designed ventilation systems. In this way, smokers and non-smokers could live in harmony without discrimination and without danger to the non-smokers (Allen, 1997). The greatest disadvantage is the cost of (a) joining two single rooms at the end of a hall and (b) installing the ventilation system. Moreover, according to Olsen, the loss of two single rooms in a dormitory is costly for the university.

[Topic sentence] Of all the suggested solutions, the most cost-effective would be to allow smoking on the balconies of Downy or Orr Hall. Mr. Olsen supports this alternative because it is the most feasible. First, students rarely use these balconies during much of the year when the weather is cold; second, simply designating the balconies as smoking areas would cost nothing. Moreover, non-smokers could easily avoid the balconies; thus they would be spared second-hand smoke. However, the students surveyed do not think this alternative solves the problem. Only 25% of the smokers surveyed think that the balconies would be a good place to smoke because they still risk pneumonia: that is, the balconies are open to the weather and are only minimally more convenient than areas outside the doors of the dormitory.

[Introduction to Figure] Figure 3 depicts the results of survey responses to the alternatives.

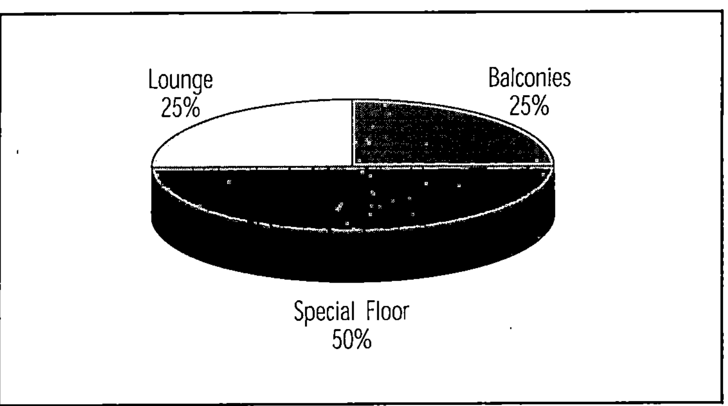

Figure 3 *Survey Responses to Smoking Solutions*

[Interpretation of Figure 3] Half of the student smokers surveyed favor the special smoking floor while, similar to the responses for the balcony solution, 25% selected the smoking lounge solution. As one of the respondents wrote, "Regardless of how the university administration feels about students smoking, they should make every effort to provide adequate areas for those students."

Figure 4 summarizes the advantages and disadvantages of the three alternatives.

Current	Cost	Advantages	Disadvantages
students smoke just outside main doors of the dormitory	on-going clean-up: $1000 a year	• safety for non-smokers: *various* – inside: *excellent* – outside: *poor*	• inconvenient for smokers • cold for smokers • ongoing mess and clean-up
Alternatives	**Cost**	**Advantages**	**Disadvantages**
#1 renovating the top floor of the dorm	ventilation system: $750,000	• convenience for smokers: *excellent* • safety for non-smokers: *excellent*	• implementation: – 18 months – loss of rooms/rent • possible non-occupancy by smokers
#2 renovating two dorm rooms on one floor of the dorm	ventilation system: $260,000	• convenience for smokers: *very good* • safety for non-smokers: *very good*	• implementation: 7 months • permanent loss of two dorm rooms
#3: permission to smoke on the balconies	equipment, ongoing clean-up, $1000	• convenience for smokers: *fair* • safety for non-smokers: *very good*	• not perfect • smokers not happy

Figure 4 *Summary of Alternative Solutions*

Recommendation and Implementation

While I agree with the surveyed students that a designated dormitory floor would be most convenient, and I understand that the solution to permit students to smoke on the balconies is the most feasible, I think the best solution is to have a smoking lounge on one (or more) floors of several (or all) the dormitories. A lounge would provide a place to smoke without having to go outside, and students would not have to smoke in their rooms, thus not ruining the rooms.

[Conclusion] Even though the university has to invest money in the project, this solution is best because it has the advantages of the other alternatives without major disadvantages. Therefore, I recommend that the university seriously consider implementing this solution. In the meantime, I suggest *[Recommendations]* that the university immediately change the rule to allow smoking on the balconies of Downey and Orr Halls as an interim solution to the problem. By being responsive to the UW students who smoke, the university in essence will be respecting the rights of both smokers and nonsmokers.

References

[Double spaced]

Allen, J. (1997, October 17). Passive smoking actively hurts students. *Oregon Daily Emerald.* [Newspaper article posted on the World Wide Web]. Retrieved April 14, 1998 from the World Wide Web: http://www.uoregon.edu/ode/archive/v99/1/971017/opin.html

American Lung Association. (1997). *American Lung Association Survey finds that smoke-free colleges permit smoking.* [Online article]. Retrieved April 14, 1998 from the World Wide Web: http://www.lunususa.org/noframes/global/news/association/college.html

Chia-Zhi, T. (1996, September 30). *Creating a smoke-free campus.* [Online article] Retrieved April 14, 1998 from the World Wide Web: http://www.nusunix2.nus.sg/nuss.sg/nussu/smokefree

Kansas State University (1994, July 14). Guidelines for smoking in campus buildings. *Department of Environmental Health and Safety.* [Report posted on the World Wide Web]. Retrieved April 14, 1998 from the World Wide Web: http://www.ksu.edu/psafe/envhealth/smoking.html

The National Center on Addiction and Substance Abuse at Columbia University. (1996). *The smoke-free campus: Introduction.* [Online article]. Retrieved April 14, 1998 from the World Wide Web: http://www.casacolumbia.org/pubs/aug93/sfc-int.htm

University of Wyoming. (1993). *University regulation 180,* Revision 1.

University of Wyoming. (1998). Smoking. *Code of conduct for residence halls and food service: Terms and conditions of the 1998-1999 residence halls and food service contract.*

***Maria Lorena Magnotta,* Argentina**

EXERCISE 7-S

1. With a partner or in a small group, write a 50–75 word summary of "A Smoking Solution." Exchange summaries with another pair or small group. Use the Evaluation of Summaries (p. 140) to discuss that summary. Then discuss ways to improve the summary with the writers of the summary.
2. With your partner or small group, decide which problem-solving organizational pattern Lorena used in her essay and label each of the sections of the essay.
3. List and then evaluate the sources used by Lorena in the essay. Use the **Guidelines for Evaluating Sources** (p. 222) for your discussion.
4. Study the World Wide Web sources used in this essay. What different types of sources did Lorena find? How do you know?
5. In your opinion, did Lorena select the most feasible solution? Discuss your opinion with your classmates; be prepared to support your opinion.

Chapter 8

Using and Evaluating Library Sources: The Academic Paper

Learning to use the library was the best part of this course for me. I started early in the semester by using the WWW and getting used to the online catalogs, and that experience helped me do homework in my other classes, too. When I finally learned how to find books and magazine articles, I felt confident, and I am carrying that confidence with me to my future university classes.

Sahil Halim, Bangladesh

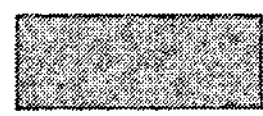

THE FINAL PAPER in this course is typical of the research paper frequently assigned in college and university classes as a term paper or a semester project. The research paper assignment is designed to give students opportunities to

- demonstrate knowledge they have acquired through the textbook and lectures,
- investigate a topic outside of class, usually through library sources,
- analyze and synthesize the materials,
- present the information according to the expected writing conventions, and
- perhaps present the information orally to the class (see p. 131 for a discussion of oral presentations of written material).

Often, the research paper assignment will include several parts, each of which is similar to one of the previous papers written in this course. That is, while most research paper assignments require explaining (*what? how? why?*), many also ask for other objectives such as problem-solving, analyzing, and arguing. In the sample assignments below, notice the multiple purposes of each assignment.

I **Water Resources Semester Project**
Select a water resources project from your experience or from the literature. **Analyze** the project and in your own words briefly **describe** the planning phases as defined by the American Society of Civil Engineers (presented in the lecture January 27). For example, **define** the goals, the problem, some alternatives, impacts, decisions, etc. Specifically **describe** any unique characteristics of the problem that significantly impacted the planning process, for example, specific constraints regarding politics, financing, the environment, etc. Student presentations of the projects to the class will be 30 minutes in length.

[Analyzing] *[Explaining* what*]* *[Defining]* *[Oral presentation]*

II **Environmental Health Research Paper** [Undergraduate]
Write a formal report of 8–10 pages about an environmental health problem, excluding title and bibliography pages, figures and tables. Minimum requirements include eight recent research sources: books, journal articles, government publications. Prepare according to this format:

- clear **statement of the problem** (who is affected, how many, seriousness of effects)
- detail of the "science" of the problem: **describe** the agent (chemical, biological, or physical), how it affects health, and how man interacts with it
- **control of the problem:** applicable local, state, or federal laws; who is responsible (if anyone), what they can do, or what they are doing
- **your opinion** about what we should do in the future to eliminate the problem.

A five-minute presentation of your topic to the class is required before you turn in your paper.

[Explaining] *[Explaining* what, how, why*]* *[Problem-solving]* *[Evaluating]* *[Oral presentation]*

Below are three more authentic assignments for the traditional research paper. Read them and do the exercise that follows.

I **Human Resources Management**
Write a 5–7 page (double-spaced) research paper that will give you a strong exposure to the field of Human Resources Management. You should research both the academic and the practitioner's literature on the topic and give me an up-to-the-second report on what is being said and done in the area. Use APA citation form. You should be an

"expert" on the topic when you are finished, and your expertise should show in the paper. Good academic form is, of course, one of the expectations. A list of topics will be made available in class and will be assigned to specific individuals. The research paper will account for one quarter (25%) of your course grade.

II **Environmental Project Design**

The term paper should be written as what USAID terms a PPD (preproject document), which is used to justify the need to create and implement a project. The paper should design a pest management scheme at two management levels (high input and low input) for a cropping system of your choice in the ecological zone of your choice. Target pests should include an insect, a disease, a grass weed, and a broadleaf weed. You will present your project to the class orally during the final two weeks of class.

The following should be included in your paper:

- description of the region and the environment
- description of the cropping system
- description of each pest
- literature review (cite several pertinent references for each above)
- description and economic analysis of each control option
- description and justification of the two management schemes
- plan for implementing the two schemes from preplanting through harvest
- expected impacts of the project

III **Biochemical Engineering**

Write a term paper addressing in as much detail as possible a specific topic in biochemcial engineering. The topic chosen must not be in the same area in which you are doing or have done research work, and must be of current interest to the biotechnology field. The paper must be written as if it were to be published in a refereed journal (*Biotechnology and Bioengineering* is suggested as a guideline for paper preparation).

The maximum length for the paper is 10 single-spaced typewritten pages, not including tables and figures. Term papers will be graded according to the following: detailed outline 20%, oral presentation 20%, final manuscript 60%.

Following is a list of suggested topics, although each student is encouraged to develop his/her own option:

- Tissue culture
- Production of chemicals from lignocellulosic residues
- Enzyme immobilization
- Thermodynamics of biological growth
- Bioconversion of hemicellulose hydrolyzates

EXERCISE 8-A

1. In Assignment **I,** what does the instructor mean by "good academic form"? How will the writer fulfill this part of the assignment?
2. For Assignment **III**, discuss the meaning of "refereed journal." What will the writer do to fulfill this part of the assignment?
3. None of these term paper assignments is complete. Discuss the questions you would ask the instructor in order to prepare a successful research paper for each of the assignments.

4. With a small group of classmates, write a list of *Guidelines for Analyzing Writing Assignments* that will help other students. Use the experiences you have had during this course. Share your guidelines with your classmates.

Writing Assignment I Select a topic from your major field, or a topic from your authority list, or a topic from another field of interest. Write a research paper of approximately 2,000 words: about 10 pages, not including references, nontext materials, appendices, or front material, such as the cover sheet and the Table of Contents.

- Use a minimum of 8 sources (a maximum of 15 sources), some of which are books, some of which are journals/magazines, and some of which are from the WWW.

  Note: At least 3 of your sources must come from sources published during the last three years.
- Identify and analyze your audience, including not only such characteristics as knowledge of and interest in the topic, educational background, and socio-economic status, but also the attitude of the audience toward the topic and their reactions to the purpose of the paper.
- Use necessary pre-writing and group discussion techniques to (a) focus the purpose(s) of the research paper, (b) discover what you need to know about your topic, and (c) identify how to find that information.
- Include three of the essay forms you have studied in this course: analyzing, remembering, investigating, explaining (*what, how, why*), evaluating, problem-solving, and/or arguing.
- Include a background paragraph or section.
- You may decide whether to use
  - headings and subheadings and/or
  - your major field citation style instead of APA style.
- Locate or design 2–4 nontext visuals and include them in your research paper.
- Design and use either an interview or a survey in your research paper.

Preparing to Write

Although the length of a research assignment may seem to demand a very large subject, narrowing the subject to a topic is essential for clear, detailed writing. Below are two examples of topics that were too broad and therefore needed narrowing:

I

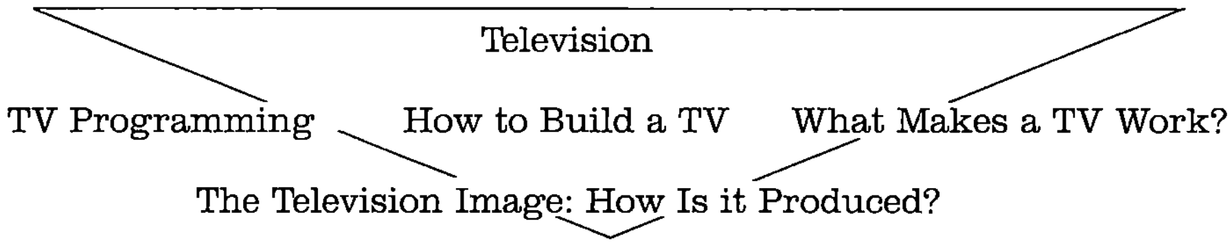

Television

TV Programming How to Build a TV What Makes a TV Work?

The Television Image: How Is it Produced?

***Alfredo Chorro,* El Salvador**

II

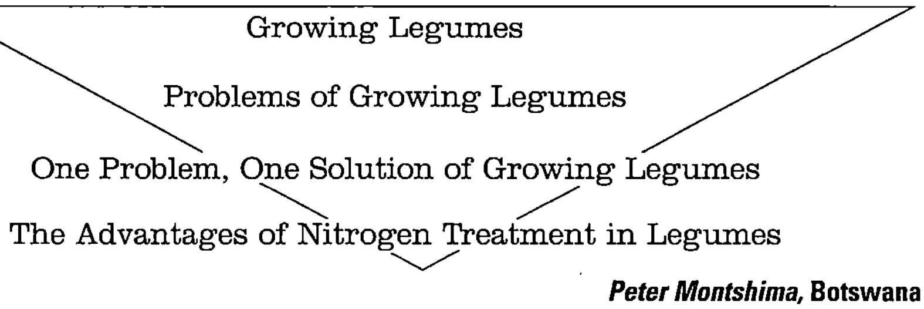

Growing Legumes

Problems of Growing Legumes

One Problem, One Solution of Growing Legumes

The Advantages of Nitrogen Treatment in Legumes

***Peter Montshima,* Botswana**

Following is a list of topics that students have used to write successful research papers. These students included graduate students, who often wrote about topics in their major fields; undergraduate students, who usually selected topics of interest; and high school students, who chose topics they knew about but wanted to know more about. Listed at the end of each topic are essay forms that were used in the paper; notice that Explaining is part of every research paper.

	Topic	Essay forms
Graduate Student Topics	Aeroflotation to Remove Grease and Oils from Water: Advantages and Disadvantages	*[explaining* what, how, why; *analyzing; problem-solving]*
	Input and Output of the Tigris River: Control and Distribution of Water	*[explaining* what, how, why; *problem-solving; persuading]*
	Classroom Activities that Increase Creativity in the Preschool Child	*[explaining* how, what, why; *analyzing]*
	The Radiation Process Used to Mutate Barley	*[explaining* what, why, how; *summarizing; analyzing]*
	The Pronunciation Problems of Japanese Speakers of English	*[explaining* what, how, why; *problem-solution]*
	The Effects of Vestibular Stimulation on Autistic Children	*[explaining* what, how, why; *summarizing; remembering; problem-solving]*
Undergraduate Topics	The Process of Diamond Cutting	*[explaining* how; *analyzing]*
	Analysis of a Bookstore's Inventory Control System	*[explaining* what, why; *problem-solving]*
	Women in Islam	*[explaining* why; *arguing]*
	The Feasibility of Buying a Paint Chip Repair Business	*[explaining* what, why; *arguing]*
	Censorship in Junior High School Libraries	*[explaining* what, how, why; *problem-solving; arguing]*
	Problems of Undergraduate Foreign Students in the United States	*[explaining* what, why; *analyzing; problem-solving]*
High School Topics	Injuries in Hockey: Can They Be Prevented?	*[explaining* what, how, why; *analyzing; remembering; arguing]*
	Animals and Poisonous Plants: How Do the Animals Know?	*[explaining* how, why; *investigating]*
	How to Adapt an Engine for the Best Racing	*[explaining* how, why; *arguing]*
	UFOs: Fact or Fiction?	*[explaining* what; *arguing]*
	Carbon Monoxide and Health	*[explaining* what, why; *arguing]*

DEVELOPING A TIME LINE FOR THE RESEARCH PAPER

Many students make the error of not planning ahead for their first research papers, which are usually assigned during the first month of the course, but the paper is not due until the end of the course. Students who wait until the week before the paper is due will find that (a) many other students have checked out materials, (b) the library—the online catalog, the World Wide Web (WWW), the other resources—are crowded, and (c) the librarians are very busy. A time line can make the processes of research writing more successful.

To construct a time line, the writer works backward from the due date of the paper and includes such activities as reflecting and pre-writing, collecting sources, designing and completing the survey or the interview, evaluating source materials, drafting, assistance from peers or the campus writing center, and revision. The student writer tries to think of the potential problems involved in researching and writing, and considers his or her schedule of other classes, examinations, other major papers, and time-consuming assignments. Figure 8-1 depicts a typical time line for a semester project.

	Task	By This Date
[Pre-writing]	Select topic and reflect	February 4
	Pre-write and write questions	February 10
[Collect materials]	Library work: begin (+ narrow topic)	February 12
	Drafting paper: begin (organize, take notes)	February 15
	Library work: continued (locate sources)	February 22
[Draft]	Design and arrange for my interview	February 26
	[study for and take mid-term exams]	
	Take draft to Writing Center (help solve my problems)	March 10
	Library work + WWW complete (citations complete)	March 20
[Feedback]	Complete interview and put information in my draft	April 2
	Complete first draft of paper	April 8
	"Other eyes": group in class + Writing Center	April 13
[Revise]	Revise and edit draft	April 22-23
	Final visit to WC + final revision and editing	April 26
	[study for biochem exam]	
	Paper Due! [biochem exam]	April 28

Figure 8-1 *Time Line for an Academic Research Paper*

STUDENT SUGGESTIONS FOR RESEARCH

Because researching and writing a longer paper requires additional planning, students have found that five suggestions make the task easier:

- Learn all you can about the library first.
- Be patient. Plan to work for long periods of time in the library.
- Be flexible about your topic. Let the materials you find modify the topic.
- Try to think like a librarian as you search for materials.
- Whenever you have a problem, ask a reference librarian for help.

EXERCISE 8-B

1. With a small group of classmates, write a tentative schedule (i.e., a time line) for your research paper. Share your time line with the rest of the class.
2. Discuss 2–4 of the research topics listed on page 245 that interest you. Why do you think the students chose those topics? What problems might they encounter?
3. Discuss potential topics and audiences for your research paper with your group. Offer suggestions to other group members that will help them make decisions about their research topics and audiences.
4. As you discuss topics, take notes about possible general and specific purposes for your research paper. Do you want to inform, entertain, and/or persuade your audience? Are you interested in explaining (*what? how? why?*), arguing about an issue, solving a problem?

PRE-WRITING

The student notes below demonstrate a combination of pre-writing strategies about what the student writers know and questions that they need to answer (in capital letters) in their library research.

Construction Productivity Improvement

[Keywords] • keywords for searching: "construction productivity" "task management" "productivity engineering"

[Focus] • systematic approach for performing tasks in

EXPLANATION NEEDED! — the quickest way, the most economical way; the goals are to ?????? GET!

• objections to applying the techniques of productivity engineering
  - facilities vary for each project GET STATISTICS!
  - product is different every time
  - work force is not permanent
  - operations are not repetitive LOOK FOR MORE!

EXAMPLES NEEDED— but similarities between construction and manufacturing are far greater than the differences

[Locate information]

FIND:	NEED MORE INFORMATION ABOUT:
• Roundtable Reports	• major areas of task management
• Statistics from top 400 companies	• construction productivity improvement
• Tables & examples of productivity factors	• hierarchical models
• Examples of successful communication	

Kamalian Shaat, United Arab Emirates

SUBJECT:	Mountaineering Equipment	KEYWORDS:
TOPIC:	The Best Footwear for Summer Mountaineering	hiking + shoes
AUDIENCE:	Beginning Mountaineers	mountaineering + equipment
PURPOSE:	To recommend what footwear is best	mountaineering + footwear + shoes

QUESTIONS:

Why is it important to choose good footwear?

[About content] What kind of footwear is the best for mountaineering in the summer?

How can one choose the best footwear for himself or herself?

Who to survey?

[About the library] How to find information in books, magazines, and the Web?

When is best to evaluate that information?

[About writing conventions] How to find/design nontext materials?

How to complete the references?

Yoko Fukada, Japan

SHOULD ROBOTS BE ELIMINATED IN
THE INDUSTRIALIZATION PROCESS IN INDONESIA?

	I. INTRODUCTION: background of industrial conditions		Keywords:
	background of employment and		robots + industry
	population conditions		robots + Asia
			unemployment +
	PRO (+)	CON (-)	"social problems"
[Strongest arguments]	— high productivity	— unemployment	
	— does not increase problems	— social problems	
	(no striking for wages)	— work monotonous	
		— expensive	
	GET STATISTICS	FIND EXAMPLES	Are there other
			counter-arguments?
	II. Explain that robots work monotonously but	REFUTE	
	expensively		
[Strong argument]	III. Creates unemployment	FIND	
[Stronger argument]	IV. Does not create new jobs (unemployment)	MORE	
[Strongest argument]	V. Results in social problems	INFO	
[Recommendation? prediction?]	VI. Conclusion		

Joni Swastanto, **Indonesia**

Identifying Necessary Library Sources

Asking questions about a topic can lead students to relevant library research strategies.

1. **Questions that require a single, factual answer:** Look in the general reference materials such as general and field-specific encyclopedias, specialized dictionaries, and almanacs.
   - *What is the boiling point of carbon dioxide?*
   - *What is nihilism?*
   - *Who built the Statue of Liberty?*
2. **Questions concerning a process:** Look in a book or a textbook about the topic. Locate these materials with a subject search on the online catalog.
   - *What are the advantages of the Krebs cycle?*
   - *How is sugar refined?*
   - *When is role playing used effectively?*
3. **Questions that need a broader discussion and current information:** Look in books about the subject, and in current journals/magazines. Use the online catalog to locate the (a) books and (b) indexing databases of magazines and journals in the appropriate field.
   - *Are there alternative fuels for internal combustion engines?*
   - *What are the psychological effects of noise?*
   - *What is the role of chromium in human nutrition?*

STRATEGIES FOR TAKING NOTES FROM LIBRARY RESEARCH MATERIALS

One of the most effective strategies for student researchers is to design a research plan. The first consideration is how to record and organize information.

- on 3" x 5" cards?
- in a spiral or 3-ring notebook?
- highlighting photocopied material?
- in a file on a computer database?

Below are examples of student strategies for extracting and organizing information for the research paper. Patricia kept hers on notecards; Julio kept his in a notebook.

Vegetation as an Environmental Element in the City

[Call number]	HT153	Fran P. Hosken	[Author]
[Title]	H65	NY: Macmillan	[Publisher]
	THE LANGUAGE OF CITIES	1991	[Date]
	• The purpose of the city is to increase the choices for		[Notes]
	personal satisfaction—the choices "for work and jobs,		[Quotation]
	health and recreation, education and culture," and to		
	fulfill our personal goals. (p. 21)		[Page of quote]
	• Soon 75% of our population will live in urban areas. (p. 4)		

[Call number]	HT151	Thomas R. Detwiler &	[Authors]
[Title]	D46	Martin Mories	
	URBANIZATION AND ENVIRONMENT	Ann Arbor, MI, 1996	[Place of publication, year]
		Univ of Michigan Press	[Publisher]
	• Environment (definition): "is an aggregate of external		
	conditions that influence the life of an individual or		
	population, specifically the life of man; environment		
	ultimately determines the quality and survival of life."		
	(p. 66)		[Page of quote]

***Patricia Alvarenga Flores,* El Salvador**

5 STUDENT SAMPLE

RURAL DEVELOPMENT IN PERU

[Student's number of source]

4. Cotler, J. (1992). The mechanics of internal domination and local change in Peru. *In Peruvian nationalism, a capitalist revolution,* Ed. D. Chapman, pp. 106–17. New Brunswick, NJ: Transaction Books.

[Notes]

- internal colonialism (dual societies)
- *mestizo* vs. Indian (explanation: lack of self-esteem)

- urban bias (p. 77)

[Statistics] 1940: urban population, 25%

[Pages] 1961: urban population, 42% (pp. 123–127)

[Citation: APA style] 5. Fitzgerald, E.V.R. (1996). *The state and economic development: Peru since 1968.* London: Cambridge University Press.

[Facts]
- Peruvian economy: (p. 98)
  modern sector
  export production

[Details] large-scale industry and finance
2/3 income generated
1/3 employment

[Examples] traditional sector (p. 99)
containing the mass of peasants (producing for the domestic food market), artisans, small trades, service workers
generates 2/3 unemployment
accounts for 1/3 net income

6. Alberti, Giorgio. (1991). *Basic needs in the context of social change: The case of Peru.* Paris: Organization for Economic Cooperation and Development.

[Quotation]
- Inca period: "one of the most highly developed civilizations dating prior to the Spanish conquest" (p. 34)
- colonial heritage: hacienda institution (p. 35)
- dual society in terms of economic system

***Julio Alegria,* Peru**

STRATEGIES FOR DRAFTING THE ACADEMIC RESEARCH PAPER

Many students have found that their drafting processes must change when they are writing a long paper. Some useful strategies are to

- begin to draft the paper wherever the best material exists (the introduction? the background paragraph? another body paragraph?)
- draft the paper in small sections, as though writing several short essays
- "weave" the library material into the paragraphs
- use in-text citations during the writing so they are not forgotten
- when using an in-text citation, add the end-of-text citation to the Reference page immediately.

As they draft and do research for material, students take notes under the major headings selected for the paper. The example below shows a general outline of a research paper, with sources and notes beneath each heading.

<u>Disabled Student Accommodations on the University Campus</u>

I Introduction

II Background Paragraph
"All college campuses receiving federal funds were required, by 1980, to be made accessible to persons with disabilities" (Velleman, 1990, p. 48)

III – VIII Body of Essay (6 paragraphs)

"Mobility is of primary importance to everyone because it means freedom. . . . People with physical disabilities often are unable to use conventional transportation and consequently remain homebound" (Wiener et al., 1995, p. 125).

"The new one-story apartments were designed to make disabled people's mode of life more comfortable" (personal interview, Augusta Gold).

The bathroom has special rails around the walls and above the bathtub. Similar to the kitchen sink, the bathroom sink and the bathtub each has a one-spigot faucet (Taylor et al., 1997).

Students show disrespect to people with disabilities when they park in spaces designated for the disabled (results from survey).

IV Conclusion
All premises contain an accessible route into and through the building (Blotzer, 1995).

References

Blotzer, A. & Richards, R. (1995). *Sometimes you just want to feel like a human being.* Baltimore, MD: Paul H. Brookes Publishing.

Gold, A. (1998). Personal Interview, March 29th.

Taylor, S. J., Biklen, D., & Knoll, J. (1997). *Community integration for people with severe disabilities.* New York: Teachers College Press.

Vaiman, V.(1998). Disabled Student Survey.

Velleman, R. A. (1990). *Meeting the needs of people with disabilities.* Phoenix, AZ: Oryx Press.

Wiener, J.M., Clauser, S. B., & Kennell, D. L. (1995). *Persons with disabilities.* Washington, DC: The Brookings Institution.

***Vladimir Vaiman,* Russia**

Writing Conventions for the Academic Research Paper

While research assignments are generally longer than other papers, the overall form of the paper remains the same: the introduction, the body, and the conclusion. However, the introduction and conclusion may be longer; the background paragraph may extend to two paragraphs; there will be more body paragraphs; and the body paragraphs may be somewhat longer and contain more support.

Here is the order of the final draft for a research paper. Each of these bulleted (•) sections begins on a new page. (See the end of this chapter for student samples of each of these research paper sections.)

- Title page
- Table of Contents or Outline
- Abstract *[Summary]*
- Body of the paper
    - Introduction paragraph(s)
    - Background paragraph(s)
    - Body paragraphs
    - Conclusion paragraph(s)
- Reference List
- (Appendices)

Figure 8-2 *Order of the Academic Research Paper*

PLAGIARISM

Using sources in a research paper (a) gives credit to the author, (b) demonstrates that the writer has done research, and (c) gives more authority to the ideas in the paper. Writers must cite a source for any information that they did not know before beginning the research.

Students who do not cite their sources often suffer embarrassment because academic readers feel very strongly—negatively—about students who use the ideas and words of other authors without citing sources. Plagiarism—the use of ideas and/or words of others without citation—is unethical and illegal in the U.S. In colleges and universities, students can fail a class or even be dismissed from the school for plagiarism.

There are several levels of plagiarism:

- **Word-for-word copying:** The writer copies exactly what is in the original text.

Comments: The writer must enclose the text in quotation marks, identify the source in the text, and give the complete reference at the end of the paper to prevent a charge of plagiarism. Yet a research paper cannot simply be a list of direct quotations. A reader might then justifiably feel that the writer's personal contribution to the paper was insignificant.

- **The "patch job":** The writer takes phrases from the original text and "stitches" them together with his or her own linking words (such as *the, and,* and *however*) so that the major part of each sentence is not the writer's words or ideas.

Comments: This is not considered plagiarism if the writer uses quotation marks around any phrase of more than three consecutive words taken directly from an author, then gives the in-text citation that includes the page number(s) from which the direct quotation has come. However, a research paper that has more direct quotations than the student's words is usually considered weak writing.

- **The paraphrase:** The writer substitutes his or her own words for the author's words, but uses the author's ideas without citing the author.

Comment: Any ideas that belong to another author must be cited immediately following the ideas. In addition, a paragraph-long paraphrase about one author's ideas does not fulfill the task of research, which is to integrate and synthesize the ideas of more than one author with the ideas of the student writer.

To avoid plagiarism:

- Take careful notes from research material.
- Use quotation marks in notes to indicate use of the author's words.
- Write the complete in-text and end-of-text citation for each set of notes.*
- Integrate the ideas of more than one author in paragraphs of the paper.

Note: It is not appropriate for a writer to use and/or cite an article that he or she has not read. Just using the abstract, for example, and not locating the article itself, is dangerous and unethical.

Native English speakers have nearly as many problems with citations as ESL writers. One teacher reported, for example, that a first-year composition student turned in an essay draft without adequate citation. She warned the student that the paper would receive an "F" if he did not revise his original sources and cite the materials. When the teacher read the final draft, she found the citation "SIK" several times. Thinking that SIK was perhaps a website or an acronym, she turned to the Reference page and found:

---

* For examples of APA style formats and sample references, see Appendix A.

SIK. This is **Stuff I Know.** I put this on ideas that should be cited but I cannot remember where I learned this information.

The student received an "F" on the paper, of course.

Preparing to Use the Library

Research papers require some library research. Therefore, students must be proficient at identifying, locating, and evaluating the books, journal articles, maps, field-specific encyclopedias and dictionaries, and other materials that are located in the college or university library.

The amount of material published each year in the United States is staggering: the Library of Congress, which receives a notice or copy of every book published in the U.S., contains more than sixty million books and adds more than three million each year. Even a moderately small university library will contain a million books. Because of the sheer bulk of the material, a successful student researcher must know how to look for appropriate materials. A researcher who does not practice library search strategies may grow old (without results) in the library!

GOING TO THE LIBRARY

The student researcher's first visit to the academic library should be informational.

At the General Information Desk, ask

- how to check out (that is, borrow) library materials.
- for a printed list of basic information: open hours, book check-out rules, overdue fines, computer printer "credit-cards," etc.
- about library tours: if and when they are given, how to join one, or if there is a self-guided tour (usually by audiotape) that can be done alone.
- for a "library locator" list that will tell where materials are located in the library.
- whether there is additional printed information about the library, such as handouts that explain the online catalog system, a brochure that lists available databases, computer printouts about search strategies, etc.

Locate and become familiar with

- the computers that contain the online library catalog that allows researchers to locate all library materials, both in that library and in other academic libraries, and to access to the World Wide Web.
- the reference desk, where an experienced Reference Librarian will answer research questions.
- the general reference section, where researchers will find many general and field-specific encyclopedias and dictionaries.
- the periodical display shelves, where recent issues of magazines are kept.
- the reserve desk, where instructors put printed materials for the use of students in their classes.
- other places of interest:
  - the microtext area (microfilms and microfiche)
  - the government documents area
  - the foreign newspaper area
  - the interlibrary loan department
  - the photocopy machines.

Next, students begin to learn as much as possible about the language used by librarians. Figure 8-3 gives basic definitions of some library terms.

call number	The identification number for each piece of material in the library. The call number is essential to finding anything. R43 K867 — **R** = Medicine (locator letter); **K** = First initial of author's last name **Note:** The first letter in a call number (**R** in the call number above) indicates where the material in the library is located (check the library locator or ask a librarian).
the stacks	The shelves where books are stored according to their LC system classification.
journals	Academic magazines (i.e. periodicals).
"to recall"	For a book (or other library material) that has been checked out of the library, the student can request that the material be "recalled." The library will contact the borrower and demand that the book be returned. The student will then be notified and can pick up the book at the circulation desk.
interlibrary loan	A service offered by the library to obtain materials "on loan" from other libraries.
government documents	Reports, papers, and other printed of information published by the U.S. government, state, and local government agencies. To find these sources, students need to ask a librarian for assistance.
microfilm, microfiche	Documents (e.g., newspapers, some magazines) that are stored on a roll of film or a sheet of film. The library supplies special film equipment to read these materials.

Figure 8-3 *Library Terms*

THE LIBRARY OF CONGRESS SYSTEM

The Library of Congress (LC) system is the cataloging system used by most academic libraries in the U.S. The Library of Congress assigns an identification call number to every piece of library material. A student who learns how to use the LC system in his or her college/university library will be able to use most academic libraries in a similar way. Some of the subject categories, and three examples of subcategories, for the LC system are listed in Figure 8-4.

A General Works
B Philosophy, Psychology, and Religion
C General History
D Old World History
E U.S. History
G Geography
H Social Sciences — Sub-Headings: HF Commerce; HG Finance
J Political Science
K Law
L Education
N Fine Arts
P Language and Literature
Q Science — Sub-Headings: QB Astronomy; QE Geology; QC Physics; QK Botany; QD Chemistry; QR Bacteriology
R Medicine
S Agriculture and Forestry
T Technology — Sub-Headings: TA Engineering; TJ Mechanical Engineering
U Military Science
Z Bibliography

Figure 8-4 *Library of Congress (LC) Subject System Categories*

Understanding how materials are categorized in a library also helps student researchers locate those materials.

- All books with similar call numbers are shelved *alphabetically*. That is, call numbers beginning with **A** are shelved before those beginning with **B**; QA is shelved before QB.
- All books with similar call numbers are shelved *numerically*. A75 is shelved before A342, and QA170 is shelved before QA789.
- Books with call numbers that begin with the same first letter are shelved in the same area. For example, call numbers for Technology books begin with T, and all **T**s are shelved in one part of the library. Books that begin with **R** are about Medicine and are shelved together in a different part of the library.

EXERCISE **8-C**

1. Ask a reference librarian to help you locate a subject-specific encyclopedia or dictionary in your major field. Look up a topic or a term and read about it.
   A. Write the call number for the reference book.
   B. Where are books with that call number located in the library? Write the bibliographic citation for the book in APA Style.
2. Locate some material stored on either microfilm or microfiche and view that material on the appropriate machine. Share your experiences with your classmates.
3. Locate the library's newspaper area. Are there newspapers from other countries?

UNDERSTANDING PERIODICALS

Periodicals are materials that are published periodically (i.e., weekly, monthly). *Magazines* are popular periodicals, those written for the general public (e.g., *Newsweek, People, Sports Illustrated*). *Journals* are periodicals published for academic, specialized audiences (e.g., *Chemical and Engineering News, Journal of Family Psychology, Speech*). Each published magazine/journal is called an *issue*.

There are literally hundreds of thousands of periodicals published in English—150,000 in the sciences alone. Although most academic libraries have only a small fraction of those periodicals, searching for information in them can be more complicated than locating and using information from a book. Fortunately, like all library materials, magazines/journals are organized by **call number**, according to their content. Current (i.e., recently published) issues of magazines/journals are "displayed" on shelves in a special place or room in the library. Slightly older issues (6 months to 1 year old) are usually stacked just below the newest issue. Therefore, researchers looking for a recent article will not locate that article in the stacks.

Older issues of the periodicals are stored in the stacks, according to their call number. First, though, a specific number of issues are *bound* into hardback "books" that contain the annual (or quarterly, or semi-annual) issues of the periodical, arranged chronologically. Each of these hardback books is called a *volume* (abbreviated *Vol.* or *V.*) of the journal and has a volume number as well as the call number of the periodical. For example, a popular weekly newsmagazine like *Time* may have four bound volumes for each year. Each volume contains three months (12 issues) of the magazine: January–March, April–June, July–September, and October–December. A monthly journal such as *Science* will have a single bound volume that includes all twelve monthly issues (issues 1–12, January–December).

EXERCISE **8-D**

1. Go to the display shelves of current periodicals. Walk up and down the aisles. Write the titles of several magazines that you find (a) interesting, and/or (b) surprising, and/or (c) related to your major field.

2. Are the periodicals organized alphabetically by title? by call number? Write the call numbers for five periodicals.
3. Select one periodical that might be helpful for your research paper. Use the call number to find older, bound volumes in the stacks. Look at the Table of Contents of one issue from the most recent bound volume. Write a complete end-of-text citation in APA style for one of the articles.

LIBRARY ETIQUETTE

Always Be Courteous

Part of the job of a reference librarian is to help students with their research. Nevertheless, there are appropriate and inappropriate questions and behaviors that student researchers should know before using the expertise of reference librarians. Students will find that everyone who works in the library will be much more willing to help if the students are patient and polite, and if they say "please" and "thank you."

Next, students should not expect a reference librarian to do their work for them. In most academic libraries, an "open stack" policy prevails; students locate and check out material themselves. In addition, most librarians have neither the time nor the desire to do students' research. These four questions from students offended librarians because they showed that the students had not taken responsibility for their work.

1. I have to write a 10-page research paper about an environmental health issue. What should I do?
2. My research paper is due tomorrow, and the book I want is checked out. Can you get me another copy today?
3. Where do I get some stuff about skydiving?
4. Can you get me some materials about a pest management scheme on the World Wide Web? And can I pick it up after my next class?

In contrast, these four questions are appropriate because they demonstrate that the students have been working but have encountered a research problem.

1. I've looked on the computer catalog to find information about my topic, and I found a good magazine article. I copied down the call number of the magazine, but I don't know how to find the magazine. What's my next step?
2. I'm writing a paper about *X*, and I've looked on the Web for information. Unfortunately, 600 sources are listed. Could you please help me find better keywords?
3. The topic assigned in my Water Resources class requires that I use several technical reports. I've never used tech reports before. Will you please show me how?
4. I've already found some books that are helpful for my term paper, but I think some current newspaper articles might be good sources. How do I go about finding a few articles?

Note: Librarians are the best resources in the library. Use their expertise early and often in your research processes.

Other guidelines for library etiquette include:

- Be quiet and polite.
- Obey the rules (e.g., no food or drink, time limitations for computer use).
- NEVER replace materials in the library. Leave them somewhere (such as on a table or beside the photocopy machine) so that a library employee can reshelve them. This keeps materials from being accidentally misplaced.

Using the Online Catalog

In past decades, students began their research by consulting a card catalog in which each of the library's materials was listed. Today, most college/university libraries have the card catalog information on computers. The introduction of computer searching has simplified the process of library research and dramatically cut the time and frustration levels of student researchers.

The online catalog *indexes* (arranges alphabetically by subject, title, and author) and *cross-references* (i.e., links library resources to related information under other headings or terms).

The online catalog provides quick access not only to books but also to magazine articles, so the student's job is initially much faster and easier. There are many different online systems, so each student must practice the instructions on the computer screen to become an efficient researcher. While the online catalog can be accessed from any computer that has the necessary memory and software, it is preferable to begin working *at the library* where a reference librarian is available to answer questions and to give advice.

Figure 8-5 gives definitions for some commonly used online vocabulary.

author/title search	A search for sources on the online computer that begins with the researcher typing in an author or a title.
database	Any body of information collected and arranged for easy access through a computer. Some databases are very broad (that is, the library's database of *all* materials). Some databases are much more specialized (such as the Zoological Record).
index	A systematically arranged list of sources (books, journal articles) that gives enough information for each item to be found. Online indexes are called "databases."
keyword search	A search for sources on the computer that begins with the researcher typing in descriptors (key words) that may be subjects, concepts, ideas, and/or dates.
menu	A computer screen where the user is offered a number of options from which to choose (such as subject, author, or title).

Figure 8-5 *Online Catalog Terms*

Note: Many libraries are part of a consortium of several libraries in the region. The online catalogs provide information about materials in all of the consortium libraries. If materials are available in another consortium library, the reference librarian can provide information about how to order those materials. If a library does not belong to such a consortium, students may still order materials from other college/university libraries through *interlibrary loan.*

Online Search Strategies for Library Research

In the same way that students develop keywords ("descriptors") to search the World Wide Web, students beginning their research papers start with a "keyword" (or "Word" or "Subject") search. That is, for their online search, they will identify keywords or phrases that describe their topics. Often the most successful keyword searches are the result of combining two or more keywords or phrases because a combination of keywords narrows and focuses the search.* For instance, a student who investigates the control of destructive agricultural pests could begin her search with *pests.*

* For more specific information about developing and using keywords, see pages 105–106.

However, she may focus her search by supplementing the word *pests* with the phrase "*agricultural control,*" thus narrowing the number of sources to be found. (See examples of keywords in the Student Sample 2 on page 247 and in the examples below.)

Below are four titles for research topics, with specific and more general descriptors.

7 STUDENT SAMPLE

[Title] RELEVANT ELEMENTS IN PLAYGROUND DESIGN

Keywords:
playgrounds
"outdoor playgrounds"
"playground equipment"
playground design
children play parks
"outdoor recreation" children
children "physical development"

Aurora Valls de Novoa, **Venezuela**

8 STUDENT SAMPLE

[Title] SATELLITE USES IN INTERCONTINENTAL COMMUNICATION

Keywords:
satellites microwaves
satellites communication
satellites telecommunications

Sami Lazghab, **Tunisia**

9 STUDENT SAMPLE

[Title] ELEMENTARY SCHOOL TEACHING METHODS IN IRAN

Keywords:
Iran "elementary schools"
Iran "primary schools"
Iran teaching teachers
Iran "teaching methods"

More General Keyword: Iran education

Mahvash Hojjati, **Iran**

[Title] THE RADIATION PROCESS USED TO MUTATE BARLEY

Keywords: barley irradiation barley mutation "mutated barley"

More General Keywords:
vegetables irradiation
agriculture irradiation

Sylvia Estrada, **Nicaragua**

EXERCISE 8-E

1. With a partner, select keywords for your topics. Discuss ways to focus your library search by refining your keyword list: use nouns, list the most important word first.
2. Discuss your keywords with another pair of partners, offering suggestions to focus their library search.
3. Revise your original list of keywords.

SEARCHING THE ONLINE CATALOG

Figure 8-6 shows a computer screen for a keyword search. The student researcher, whose topic was an examination of the biological control of agricultural insect pests, typed in the keywords and phrases "*insect pests*", *agriculture*, and "*biological control*." Notice the list of library materials directly related to the student's keyword search.

You searched: [SUBJECT ▼] ["insect pests" agriculture "biological control"] [Search]

SUBJECTS (1-5 of 5)		Year
Biological control by natural enemies:	SB933.3 D43	1991
Biological control with egg parasitoids:	SB933.3 B557	1994
The ecology of agricultural pests:	SB975 E28	1996
Fungi in biological control systems:	SB975 F86	1998
Natural enemies DOCUMENTS	AG1.2 B21	1998
3 additional entries		
Biological control and integrated crop protection	SB950.2 B56	1992
Biological control	SB975 B536	1995
Biological control DOCUMENTS	A1.68 R244	1989

Figure 8-6 *Computer Screen for Keyword Search*

Notice that the list in Figure 8-6 contains six books; the call number for each begins with SB. Two of the sources are government documents; their call numbers, which begin with A, indicate that they will be located in another part of the library. **Note:** For many research topics, materials that have been recently published are often more helpful for the student researcher and more persuasive for the audience. In general, student writers should select the most recent sources and then work backward in time as they choose sources.

Next, the student clicked on the first source; another computer screen appeared, filled with more specific information about that source. Figure 8-7 shows the expanded information screen.

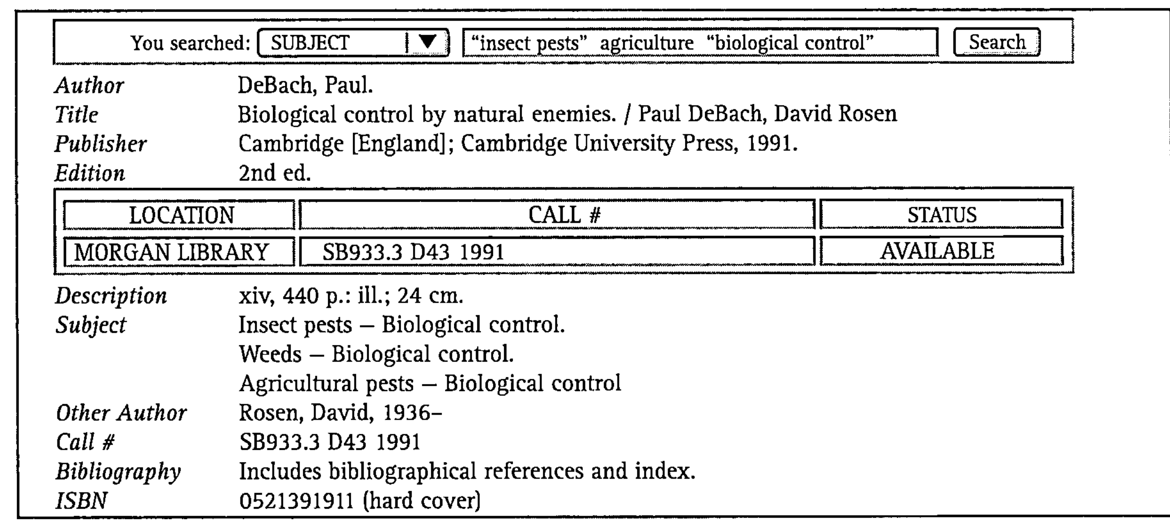

You searched: [SUBJECT ▼] ["insect pests" agriculture "biological control"] [Search]

Author DeBach, Paul.
Title Biological control by natural enemies. / Paul DeBach, David Rosen
Publisher Cambridge [England]; Cambridge University Press, 1991.
Edition 2nd ed.

LOCATION	CALL #	STATUS
MORGAN LIBRARY	SB933.3 D43 1991	AVAILABLE

Description xiv, 440 p.: ill.; 24 cm.
Subject Insect pests – Biological control.
Weeds – Biological control.
Agricultural pests – Biological control
Other Author Rosen, David, 1936–
Call # SB933.3 D43 1991
Bibliography Includes bibliographical references and index.
ISBN 0521391911 (hard cover)

Figure 8-7 *Expanded Information about One Source*

Notice that Figure 8.7 gives the student adequate information to locate the book, a limited description about the contents of the book, and an indication that the book is "Available," that is, it has not been checked out of the library. The student can now locate the book (in the **SB** section of the library) and, if it proves helpful, check it out.

EXERCISE 8-F

1. Search your library's online catalog system by using your keywords to find information about 4–8 **books** about your topic. If necessary, ask for help from a reference librarian.
2. Print any screens that may be helpful for your research.
3. Based on your keyword search, do you need to modify or revise your topic?
4. Share your online catalog experiences with a small group of classmates.

USING PRINTED INDEXES TO IDENTIFY MAGAZINE/JOURNAL ARTICLES

Periodicals (also called magazines or journals) are the most widespread source used by researchers because they contain specific articles on specific topics rather than the more general information usually contained in books, and they usually contain more recent information about topics than do books.

One way to identify magazine/journal articles is by using the printed indexes in the library. These indexes are lists of articles, arranged alphabetically (usually by subject), that have been published in a number of journals. The most widely used index is *The Reader's Guide to Periodical Literature.* It indexes (i.e., lists) articles from more than 100 popular magazines (such as *Time, Popular Science, House and Garden,* and *Popular Mechanics*). If students learn to use the *Reader's Guide,* they will know how to use many of the more specialized indexes in the library: *Applied Science and Technology Index, Biological and Agricultural Index, Business Periodicals Index,* and *Social Sciences Index.*

The format of these indexes uses headings, subheadings, and cross-references indicated by *see* and *see also.* Figure 8-8 shows the format of a printed index and an example of that format.

Format:

Heading

Subheading

Last, First. Title of the article. Title of the journal. Volume, issue, page number(s). Date of publication.

Example:

Drought

Africa

Beltrando, G. & Camberlin, P. Interannual variability of rainfall in the eastern Horn of Africa and indicators of atmospheric circulation. *International journal of climatology,* 13, 5, p. 533–546, July/August 1993. 9 fig, 23 ref.

See Africa–History

Figure 8-8 *Format and Example of a Printed Index Entry*

Notice that the article about drought in Africa in Figure 8-8 has 9 figures and 23 references, and that the student researcher should *See* another heading and subheading for a related topic: "Africa–History."

Many printed indexes are more specialized; some have abstracts (summaries of each article) as well as bibliographic information. Below is a brief list of a few of those indexes.

Abstract of Tropical Agriculture	*Forestry Abstracts*
Electrical Engineering Abstracts	*Computer Abstracts*
International Political Science Abstracts	*Environmental Abstracts*
Nutrition Abstracts and Reviews	*Humanities Index*
Selected Water Resources Abstracts	*Index Medicus*
Psychological Abstracts	*Chemical Abstracts*

IDENTIFYING MAGAZINE/JOURNAL DATABASES ONLINE

Most printed indexes are now also online; they are called "databases." Because the computer can search several indexes simultaneously, online searching is an even more efficient way to identify journal articles. In Figure 8-9 below, notice that

- the list of subjects on the left allows the student researcher to search the online databases by general subject.
- the search has been narrowed from *Business* databases to *Business: International* databases by clicking *Business: International* in the left column.

Online Databases

Search Comments

Databases by Subject

Agriculture:
Botany, Horticulture, Plant Science
Arts & Humanities:
Apparel Design & Production, English, Foreign Languages, Interior Design, Journalism, Literature, Music, Philosophy, Religion, Speech Communication, Textiles
Biography
Business:
Accounting, Computer Information Systems (CIS), Management, Finance, Marketing, . . . more.
Business: International
Earth Sciences:
Atmospheric Science, Ecology, Environment, Geology
Education
Engineering & Construction
Ethnicity, Race, Gender & Sexuality

Business: International

Asia-Pacific
Asia-Pacific Business Journals (full text)
Asia-Pacific Directory
Bridge World Markets News (full text)
Canadian Business & Current Affairs (full text)
Real Estate Canadian Business Directory
Delphes European Business
Extel International News Cards
Hoppenstedt Directory of German Companies
IAC Globalbase
International Business Directory

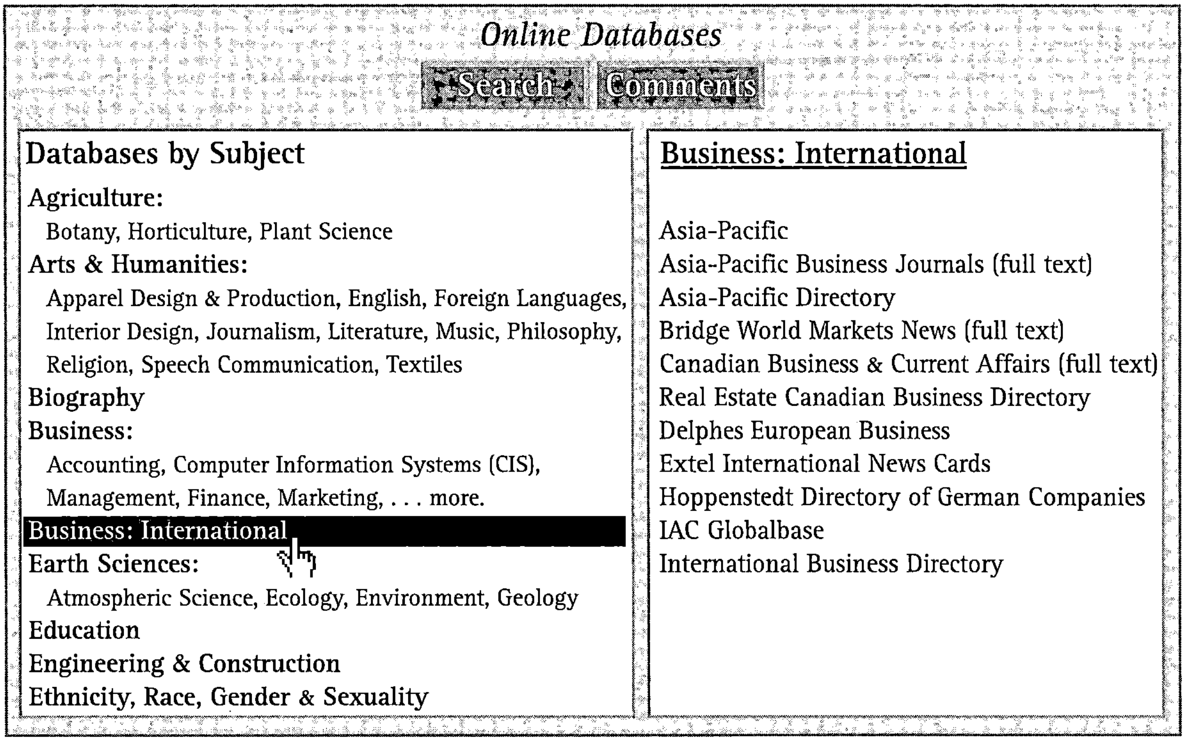

Figure 8-9 *Online List of Subject and Discipline-Specific Databases*

In Figure 8-9, notice that the subject list and the online database list are alphabetically arranged by heading/title. The student researcher clicked on Business: International in the left column; the next step will be to click on one of the relevant databases in the right column.

Figure 8-10 shows the first references of a successful online search on the AGRICOLA (agricultural) database for journal articles. For keywords, the student typed *Sudan "nitrogen fertilizer."* The journal articles in Figure 8-10 are presented in order of their "relevancy rank"; that is, the first article contains all the keywords the student typed in (1000). The next article is only half as "relevant" (500).

Subject Area: Agricultural Sciences
Database: AGRICOLA

From 1993 To current

Author [ ]
Title [ ]
Any Field [Sudan "nitrogen fertilizer"]

Show [26 ▼] [Citations ▼] [10 ▼] at a time.

These records were found in the database:

AGRICOLA 1993–current

Record: 1 of 4 / Relevancy Rank: 1000 View Full Record
TI: Non-acid-forming mixed fertilizers in Sudan. I. Their effect on certain chemical and biological changes in the soil-fertile zone and on plant growth.
AU: Taylor, JR Jr; Pierre, WH
SO: Journal of the American Society of Agronomy. August 1995. v. 87(8), p. 623–641

Record: 2 of 4 / Relevancy Rank: 500 View Full Record
TI: Effect of nitrogen fertilizer rate on nitrate content of hybrid sudangrass hays.
AU: Selk, GE; Wagner, DG; Strickland, GL; Hawkins, SE; Janloo, S
SO: Research report P / Nov 1998. (P-933) p. 148–152

Record: 3 of 4 / Relevancy Rank: 499 View Full Record
TI: Influence in Sudan of placement of ammoniated and non-ammoniated supernitrogens on efficacy of the phosphate.
AU: Ross, WH; Whittaker, CW; Adams, JR; Rader, LF Jr
SO: Journal of the American Society of Agronomy. Feb 1996. v. 88(2) p. 125–135.

Record: 4 of 4 / Relevancy Rank: 490 View Full Record
TI: Returns from research in economies with policy distortions; hybrid sorghum in Sudan.
AU: Ahmed, MM; Masters, WA; Sanders, JH
SO: Agricultural economics: the journal of the International Association of Agricultural Economists. Aug 1995. v. 67 (2) p. 183–192

Figure 8-10 *Reference Page from an Online Database Search*

The student can now click to "View Full Record" for each of the articles: more information about the article will appear, usually including an abstract that the student can print.

Another student was interested in the ways plants are used as medicine, particularly for the prevention of disease. The student researcher typed in the keywords *"transgenic plants" "disease prevention."* The online *Applied Science and Technology* database provided several journal articles. The student wanted more information—to "View Full Record." Figure 8-11 shows the abstract and additional information for one of the articles.

[Database = Applied Science and Technology Abstracts | Search = sh: (plants and medicine) | Results = 2 records Record = 2

Libraries with Item | Get/Display Item | E-Mail Records

Next Rec | Prev Rec

Ownership: Check the catalogs in your library.

AUTHOR:
TITLE: Grow your own edible vaccine.
SOURCE: Chemistry and Industry no8 (Apr. 17 '95) p. 288
STANDARD NO: 0009-3068
DATE: 1995
PLACE: United Kingdom
RECORD TYPE: art
CONTENTS: feature article
ABSTRACT: U.S. researchers have moved toward the goal of inexpensive and easy-to-handle vaccines with the discovery that transgenic plants can produce a hepatitis B virus protein that provokes the same immune response in mice as commercially available vaccines. A team from the Roswell Park Cancer Institute in Buffalo and Texas A&M University has reported that the plant-produced antigen keeps its "prompts" for stimulating B- and T-cell lymphocytes when it is expressed in transgenic tobacco.
SUBJECT: Hepatitis, Infectious -Vaccines
Transgenic plants
Genetic engineering - Medicine

Figure 8-11 *Complete Online Record for One Journal Article*

Notice that the "Full View" of the article gives the researcher adequate information to locate the article, an abstract (i.e., a summary) of the article, and additional keywords that the student can search. In addition, the student can click on the "Get / Display Item" to read the **full text of the article online**.

EXERCISE 8-G

1. Search your college/university's online database system by using your keywords to find information about 4–8 recent **magazine/journal articles** about your topic. If necessary, ask for help from a reference librarian.
2. Print any screens that may be helpful for your research.
3. Based on your database search, do you need to modify or revise your topic?
4. Share your online database experiences with a small group of classmates.

Locating Library Sources

Essential information for locating sources includes the correct, complete call number, the correct, essential bibliographic data (author and title, plus volume, issue, and page numbers for periodical articles), and the library locator.

LOCATING BOOKS IN THE STACKS

Use the call numbers of relevant books and the library locator (to find the place in the stacks where the books are shelved). Several call numbers may have the same initial letters (such as **HL**, for business). If that is the case, look at other books (a) that are shelved in the same areas and (b) that may be useful.

After you locate a book,* do NOT read it. Instead, look in its index and/or the Table of Contents. If the keywords for your topic are not listed, do not spend further time with the book. If keywords are listed, note the page number(s) and look briefly at those pages. Then, if the information looks helpful, do one or more of the following: check out the book to work with later; copy the essential bibliographic data; make photocopies of the title page and the back of the title page (for the bibliographic data); photocopy the pages relevant to the research; take notes about the material. Remember: do NOT replace the book on the library shelves; put it on a table or in a re-shelving area.

EXERCISE 8-H

1. Use the call number and the library locator sheet to *locate* 4–8 books about your topic. Do most of the books have the same initial letter(s) in the call number? Are most of the books located in one area of the library?
2. Write the bibliographic data for one book you located in "your place" in the library that is not on your online list but that (a) you found in the same shelving area and (b) you think might be helpful for your research topic.
3. Did you find any useful nontext materials in the books you located? If so, write an in-text and end-of-text citation for each.
4. Share your location experiences with your classmates:

   What was easy and what was difficult?
   What was surprising?
   What problems did you encounter, and how did you solve them?
   What did you learn from the experiences?

LOCATING PERIODICALS [MAGAZINES, JOURNALS]

Some online databases provide complete texts of articles in some periodicals, as in Figure 8-11 above. If that is the case, the student can retrieve the article and (a) read it on the computer screen and (b) print it. More often, student researchers will have to locate magazine/journal articles in the library after they have identified them online. First, the student must determine whether or not the library has the journal. If the journal is not available, the student should seek assistance from a reference librarian to identify a library that has the journal, and then retrieve a copy of the article.†

If the article is available in the library, locate the periodical by its call number. Look on the display shelves for current issues, or beneath the display shelf for issues from the last six months to a year. If the article is more than a year old, locate the bound volumes of the periodical through the call number, identify the correct volume, find the correct issue inside that volume, and locate the page numbers of the article in that issue.

Briefly look at each magazine/journal article. If the information looks helpful, be certain to gather all the necessary bibliographic data: author, title, date of publication, volume, issue, and inclusive page numbers. Photocopy the article.

EXERCISE 8-I

1. Locate 4–8 magazine/journal articles about your research paper topic. Photocopy any article that will be helpful.
2. What problems did you encounter as you searched for the articles? How did you solve them? Share your location experiences with your classmates.
3. Now that you have had these experiences, what advice about searching for magazine articles would you give to a novice student researcher? Discuss your suggestions with your classmates. Be specific.

---

* If a book (or a periodical article) is not available in the college/university library, ask the reference librarian for assistance in ordering the book from (a) another consortium library or (b) interlibrary loan.

† Depending on the policies of the library, retrieving articles and other materials from other libraries may include a fee. Ask a reference librarian.

Writing Assignment 11 Write a progress report, in memo format, to your instructor concerning your research paper. First, review memos on p. pp. 95–96. Then examine Student Sample 11 for the content conventions of the progress report.

11 STUDENT SAMPLE

PROGRESS REPORT

April 3, 1999

TO: (Instructor's Name)

FROM: Nanna Meyer *Nana Meyer*

RE: Progress Report: Semester Project

[Introduction: reason for the memo] For my term project, "Case Study: Nutrition and Weight Control Analysis," I have collected four sources, and I have written 674 words of my rough draft. I am keeping the schedule I planned for this research, and I believe I am making satisfactory progress.

[Work summarized] *[Problems and solutions, in detail]* During the six hours I spent in the library, I had three problems. First, my initial topic (nutrition and weight control) was too broad, and my keyword search resulted in over 300 sources. I narrowed my topic to a case study of nutrition and weight loss and exercise; I am analyzing the progress of a 23 year-old college female. Second, two of my major sources were checked out, but I recalled them, and both have proved very helpful for my paper. Third, I found the same material in three sources, so I didn't know how to cite that material. I asked the tutor at the Writing Center, and she suggested that I cite the source that I wouldn't otherwise be able to use in my paper; I thought that was a good idea, and I did it.

[Survey completed] I have completed the requirement for primary source material in my paper by designing and administering a survey to 25 university undergraduate women concerning weight problems and weight control. I have included the results of that survey in the background paragraph of my paper to demonstrate that the problem of weight and dieting exists on the university campus.

[Report of work remaining and of time line] *[Assurance that the work will be completed]* My time line requires that I finish the rough draft of my paper before April 15th. I will meet that deadline. At the same time, I will continue searching for the newest journal articles about my topic and checking the WWW for additional nontext materials. As I finish gathering the data for my report, I will conduct a final interview with the subject of my research and then develop recommendations for my report. Then I will complete the final draft of my paper, two days before the due date. I will therefore have time to read the paper again before I turn it in.

***Nanna Meyer,* Switzerland**

EXERCISE 8-J

1. Read 3 or 4 progress reports written by your classmates. Which did you prefer? Be prepared to say: "I liked X's progress report about Y because . . ."
2. What did you learn about research time lines and organizational strategies from your classmates' memos?

3. Below are other problems mentioned by students in their progress reports. Discuss these problems with a small group of classmates, and offer solutions to each problem.

   A. When I entered my topic on the computer, I didn't get any sources.
   B. The library didn't have the journals I needed.
   C. Sometimes I found the right place in the stacks, but the book wasn't there.
   D. Most of the library material in my paper comes from one book.
   E. I can only find material for my topic in old books and encyclopedias.
   F. I have some good examples from something I read, but I can't remember the reference.
   G. The person I was going to interview hasn't returned my calls.

Identifying and Locating Sources on the Web

The WWW* has been described as a virtual library with constantly expanding resources. Indeed, anyone can place material on the Web; anyone can design and maintain a website. The major advantage of this freedom is that we have unlimited access to nearly unlimited resources: the Web is available 24 hours a day; news sources can update information immediately; and materials are generally free. Figure 8-12 defines some WWW terms.

browser	A software program, such as Netscape Navigator or Microsoft Internet Explorer, that helps users access the WWW.
search engine	An online service that enables WWW users to find relevant sites.
URL	Universal Resource Locator: a WWW address.
bookmark	A customized menu option on one's browser created to enable the user to return quickly to a specific URL.
homepage	The first page of any website.
hyperlink [hotlink, link]	Highlighted words, icons, or graphics that, when clicked on, take user to a related URL.
cobweb	A website that has not been updated; a dead website.

Figure 8-12 *WWW Terms*

Almost certainly student researchers will consult the WWW about their research topics, using keywords to search for information, and bookmarking files for future reference.

DISADVANTAGES OF WWW RESOURCES

There are several disadvantages to the open access and sheer bulk of information on the Web. Student researchers must be aware of those problems and the strategies they can employ to solve those problems.

- Even the most sophisticated search engines cannot keep up with the proliferation of WWW sites. Although these can help users locate more than 500,000 sites quickly, WWW experts suggest that these sites represent only about a third of the actual sites available. There is no comprehensive index or overall organization, so students must plan their searches carefully.

* For an introduction to the WWW, see Chapter 4.

- Computer commands and the use of keywords for subject searches that use the Web search engines have not been standardized; therefore, working with a variety of web browsers may be confusing. WWW users may find that working with a single search engine will be easier than trying to master all of them.
- Even those websites that are easily available are not always stable; URLs and even complete sites may change overnight, without warning, or they may be removed completely.
- Much of the information on the Web is superficial and general. For academic writers, the information provides a start, but just a start, to research. The general statements about topics on the Web must then be supported with facts, examples, experiences, and description that come from library sources such as books and journal articles, and other sources such as interviews, experiments, and surveys.

EXERCISE 8-K

1. Access the WWW, select a search engine and, using your keywords, locate 2 or 3 websites that contain information about your topic. Print helpful pages. Be sure that you have the complete WWW citation.
2. Evaluate how well or how poorly your keywords worked in locating WWW information about your topic. Discuss your evaluation with a small group of classmates.
3. Write end-of-text citations for each relevant WWW source.

Writing Assignment III

Although you may not have completed your research for your paper, turn in the following *draft* documents:

- an end-of-text reference list. Use APA style. **Note:** Remember that you cannot cite a reference unless you have used that reference in an in-text citation.
- a list of the titles of your nontext materials. For each visual that another author has made, write an end-of-text citation.
- completed Appendix (either your interview questions or your survey).

Evaluating Library Sources

Because most academic books are carefully reviewed by discipline-specific readers and by editors before they are published, readers can expect that the material is relatively credible and accurate. Similarly, most magazine (and newspaper) articles go through a rigorous process of peer and editorial review before they are published. Sources are checked; facts are checked and rechecked for reliability and accuracy. However, student writers are entirely responsible for verifying the facts and figures used in research writing. Therefore, good researchers will also evaluate the information from magazines and journals, using the criteria listed below.

GUIDELINES
for Evaluating Books and Journals

- What are the purpose(s) and who is the audience for the book?
- What is the scope of the material? (comprehensive? partial? limited?)
- What is the date of publication? (up-to-date? out-of-date? timeless?)
- What is the authority of the author? (An expert? What else has she or he written?)
- What is the credibility of the author? (biased? objective? too involved?)
- How helpful and relevant are the references? (quantity? quality? current?)
- How accurate is the information? (current? controversial? well supported?)

In addition, researchers must consider the relevance of the information for their topics. Is the information directly related? Can the material be used objectively? Is the level of formality appropriate for the audience?

EXERCISE 8-L

1. Use one of the sources you have identified for your research paper. With a partner, evaluate that source. Use the criteria in the **Guidelines for Evaluating Books and Journals.** Discuss your answers with your partner.
2. Which of the criteria do you think is most important? Why? Discuss your choices with your partner.
3. What other criteria can you and your partner add to the Guidelines?

EVALUATING WWW SOURCES

Anyone can put anything on the WWW. Some websites download published material from books and magazines/journals. As long as the articles are not cut, summarized, or otherwise changed, researchers can evaluate the material using the **Guidelines for Evaluating Books and Journals** above. If the material appears only in part, the reasons for the changes should be given.

However, much of the WWW information has not been reviewed, edited, or verified. The information can therefore be unreliable, incorrect, biased, and/or inaccurate. Opinions may be presented as facts, advertisements may be presented as research, and/or commercial websites trying to sell a product can resemble academic websites. The material may be very old and therefore incorrect; the site may even have been abandoned. There are also

- "vanity" home pages, those made just for the pleasure of those creating them
- sites in which the creator exhorts, preaches, or presents propaganda
- sites that contain pornography
- sites that may be ill-informed, racist, paranoid, and even dishonest.

In these cases, the information provided is at best not usable; at worst, it is inappropriate and even dangerous.

Because the Web is an unstructured information resource, it is a chaotic research resource. Therefore, readers must approach the Web with caution; evaluating WWW information is a complex task.

GUIDELINES

for Evaluating WWW Materials

Authority of the Website

- The *address* (the URL) of an information website usually ends in *.edu* (education), *.gov* (government), or *.org* (organization).
  - A commercial address ends in *.com*; newer URLs may use *.firm* or *.stor.*
  - The URL for a personal (individual) website usually has a tilde (~).
- The *sponsor* (an educational institution? a government agency?) should be listed. A postal address (not just an e-mail) for the sponsor, the server administrator, or the website designer can verify the legitimacy of the sponsor.
- The purpose(s) for the website by the sponsor or developer should be clear:
  - developed as a public service?
  - designed by an organization to gain members?
  - offered by a commercial sponsor? For what reason(s)?

Note: A commercial sponsor may support a website in return for advertising on the site. This does not necessarily mean that the website is of lesser value or has less credibility. But the ads must be clearly differentiated from the information content, and researchers must use other criteria to evaluate the website.

- The *copyright:* if the page is copyrighted, a copyright symbol (©) will appear; information should appear about the origin of the copyright.
- The *author* should be clearly listed as well as some indication of that author's qualifications about the topic. Read the material carefully to look for possible biases and hidden agendas.

Accuracy of the Website

Verify this information:

- Where was the material gathered?
- Are sources for any factual information clearly listed so they can be verified?
- Are the sources for nontext material clear, and is the nontext material clearly labeled and easy to read?
- If no sources are listed, determine whether the material is just unsupported opinion by checking another (printed) source.
- Is the information free of grammatical, spelling, and other language errors that can indicate a lack of quality control and accuracy?
- Is it clear who has ultimate responsibility for the accuracy of the content?

Relevance of the Website:

- Is the material current? Check
  - the original date of the material,
  - the date the material was placed on the site, and
  - the date of the latest site update/revision.
- Is the material directly related to your topic?
- Who is the target audience for the material? Is it appropriate for your audience?

EXERCISE 8-M

1. Use one of the WWW sources you have identified for your research paper. With a partner, evaluate that source. Use the criteria in the **Guidelines for Evaluating WWW Materials.** Discuss your answers with your partner.
2. How much information for verification is available for the WWW source? What is missing?
3. Which of the criteria do you think is most important? Why? Discuss your choice with your partner.
4. What other criteria can you and your partner add to the Guidelines?

Writing Assignment:
Writing the Abstract

When you have completed the draft of your research paper, reread the draft in order to write a 50–100 word abstract (summary) of the paper. To review summary writing, see Chapter 5, pp. 137–139. Also look at Student Samples 13 and 14 below.

Student Samples

Research Papers

On the following pages are parts of research papers written by students that demonstrate the writing conventions for each section of the paper. Important features of each sample are indicated in brackets.

TITLE PAGE

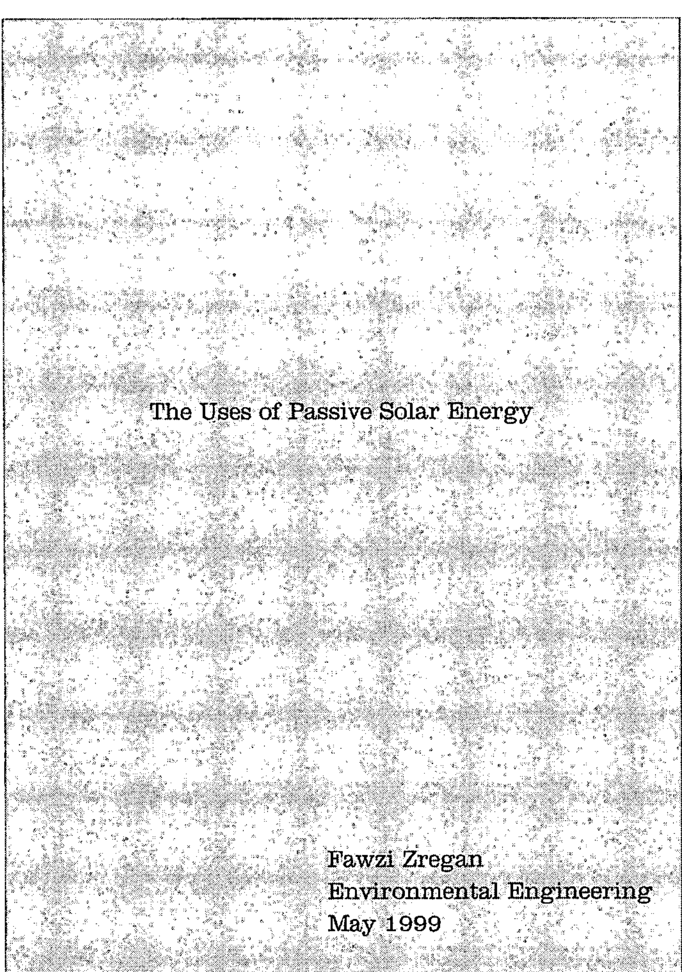
The Uses of Passive Solar Energy

Fawzi Zregan
Environmental Engineering
May 1999

13 STUDENT SAMPLE

ABSTRACT #1

[Title] *The Vocational Education Program in Bolivia*

[Introduction: report] This paper reports on a recent project for Vocational Education implemented in Bolivia during the past five years. The experimental project, based on a similar foreign program, was a failure because it was *[Writing forms: evaluation, problem-solving]* not adapted to Bolivians' needs. This report evaluates the failure of the original project, demonstrates that the basic tenets of the plan were positive, *[Conclusion]* and proposes adaptations to the project that will lead to a fine Vocational Educational system.

Maria Teresa Teran, **Bolivia**

ABSTRACT #2

The Effects of Carbon Monoxide

[Passive voice]

[Writing forms: explaining, persuading]

In this paper, the mechanism of carbon monoxide is described and the chemistry of carbon monoxide is presented. The most important aspect of carbon monoxide is examined: its possible catastrophic effects on the global environment. Some specific examples of these effects are discussed: on the human fetus and the heart, on vegetation, and animals.

Marilia dos Santos, **Sao Tomé**

OUTLINE #1

How to Improve Olive Harvesting in Libya

[Writing forms: explaining, problem-solving]

[Nontext materials]

[Methods of development: process, comparison-contrast]

[Techniques of support: facts, personal experience, physical description, examples]

[Concluding techniques: summary, recommendation]

I Introduction
- A. General information about olive trees
- B. Thesis statement of intent

II Background Paragraph
- A. Traditional methods of olive harvesting
  1. Hand-picking
  2. Natural drop
  3. Beating
  4. Hand-shaking
- B. Disadvantages of traditional methods

III Mechanical Harvesting
- A. Combing
- B. Beating
- C. Mechanical shaking
  1. Stem-shaking
  2. Main branches shaking

IV Chemicals for Helping in Mechanical Olive Harvesting
- A. Maleic hyrazide
- B. Ethylene releasing compounds
  1. Cyclohexamid
  2. Ethephon
  3. CGA 13586

V Conclusion

Ali Darrot, **Libya**

OUTLINE #2

Countertrade: The New Alternative in Latin America's Foreign Trade

[Writing forms: explaining, problem-solving]

I Introduction
- A. Brief description of Latin America's problem
- B. Countertrade as alternative

[Demonstration that the problem exists]

II Background Paragraph
- A. Concept of balance of payment
- B. Balance of payment difficulties in Latin America
  1. Deficits
  2. External debt

[Failure of previous solutions]

III Export as the principal income in Latin American economies
- A. Few commodities
- B. Export instability
- C. Effects of world market prices
- D. Scarcity of foreign exchange

[Proposal for solution] IV Adoption of new policies and strategies
- A. Bilateral trade
- B. Countertrade

V Countertrade
- A. Definition
- B. Forms
- C. Variables

VI Reasons for implementing
- A. U.S. companies' interest
- B. Advantages for Latin America

[Concluding techniques: summary, recommendation] VII Conclusion

***Hernan Perez,* Colombia**

TABLE OF CONTENTS #1

Biomarkers to Measure the Toxicology of Lead

***Mary Chanco,* U. S.**

18 STUDENT SAMPLE

TABLE OF CONTENTS #2

Computerized Inventory Control System Study

***Lynn Stonemark,* U. S.**

19 STUDENT SAMPLE

INTRODUCTION #1

The Application of Remote Sensing in Estimating Evapotranspiration

[Definitions] [Direct quotation with ellipsis; in-text citation]

Remote sensing is the "science and art of obtaining information about an object, an area, or a phenomenon through the analysis of data acquired by a device . . . that is not in contact with the object, area, or phenomenon under investigation" (Lilles & and Kiefer, 1997). It offers an excellent device to use in various fields: geology, forestry, water resources, engineering, and land use. Evapotranspiration is water lost from this earth's surface that man tries to study in order to control it. However, it is quite difficult to study and estimate the quantity of evapotranspiration from the very large earth's surface. Now a tool has been developed to solve the problems: remote sensing. This paper will discuss the advantages of remote sensing and will propose the use of remote sensing by the Ministry of Forestry in Thailand.

[Problem] [Thesis statement of intent] [Educated audience]

***Arthorn Boonsaner,* Thailand**

INTRODUCTION #2

THREE GRAND CHESS MASTERS

[Engages audience] [Limited background information] [Thesis statement of intent]

Chess, the game of kings and the king of games, is played by intelligent people; usually the more intelligent person wins. The story of chess is a long one; it includes the development of rules and the description of chess championships and champions. This paper will discuss the spread of chess around the world. Then it will describe three famous chess players: Theophilus Thompson, Alexander Alekhine, and Bobby Fischer.

***Esmaell Al-Hammad,* United Arab Emirates**

21 STUDENT SAMPLE

BACKGROUND PARAGRAPH #1

The History of Zaire's Independence

[Topic sentence] *[History]* *[Direct quotation; information inserted in brackets]* *[History]*

After independence, the Congolese changed their country's name from the "Belgian Congo" to the "Democratic Republic of Congo." However, "the country was ill-prepared for independence, though Patrice Lumumba tried hard to maintain cooperation between the various [political] parties" (Growther, 1983, p. 510). Each province formed its party, trying to be free from the central government when Lumumba was Prime Minister. Lumumba called for help from the United Nations, and they responded, but not in the way he wanted. So Lumumba asked the Soviet Union to cooperate. Unfortunately, his failure was due to his relations with the Soviet Union's leaders because the other political parties in the newly named Democratic Republic of Congo were against Communism.

***Mbembo (Ben) Bontutu-E-Kuma,* Zaire**

22 STUDENT SAMPLE

BACKGROUND PARAGRAPH #2

Tai Qi: The Chinese Superlative *Kung Fu*

[Extended definition, process] *[History]* *[Comparison and contrast]*

In Chinese, *Tai Qi* means "top, super, and unique." Practitioners of *Tai Qi* employ slow, controlled physical stances and motions while simultaneously breathing in fresh air and breathing out carbon dioxide during specific motions and stances. *Tai Qi* was created during the prosperous Tan Dynasty in 676. For more than one thousand years, it has been the leader among the various branches of Chinese *kung fu,* which is a martial art like boxing and wrestling. In contrast to *kung fu, Tai Qi* is more a spiritual exercise rather than physical action.

***Steven J. Tu,* Republic of China (ROC)**

23 STUDENT SAMPLE

BODY PARAGRAPH #1

Developing Creativity in the Pre-School Child

*[Topic sentence, **audience**]* *[Transitions]* *[Techniques of support: examples, facts]* *[Concluding sentence]*

Through class activities, the **teacher** can develop creativity by giving importance and value to what the child has made and by encouraging him to develop his own ideas and thoughts. For example, when the child paints a boat on the sea, the teacher could ask him what he has painted, what colors he has used, and why he has painted it. In this way, not only the teacher but also the child is evaluating and describing the product. Furthermore, if the teacher ascertains that a child is not happy with the task he has accomplished, the teacher can show him the value of the task. This will give the child security in his work and will allow him to further develop his creativity. Finally, the dual evaluation of the task by the teacher and the child will be constructive. The teacher can also suggest new ideas by asking the child if there is another way he can accomplish the task and by making the child aware of various alternatives available to him.

***Ana Paez,* Venezuela**

BODY PARAGRAPH #2, WITH TABLE

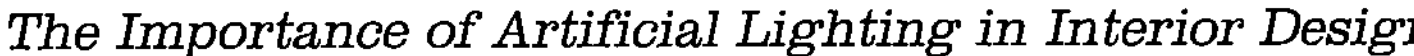

The Importance of Artificial Lighting in Interior Design

[Subheading] A. Color

[Methods of development: extended definition, cause-effect] *[Techniques of support: facts, examples]* *[Introduction to nontext material]*

Color is a quality of light reflected from an object by the human eye. When the light falls upon an object, some of it is absorbed. That which is not absorbed is reflected, and the color of an object depends upon the wavelength that it reflects. So light causes the different color cones, and the visible color phenomenon depends upon lightning. The most masterful color scheme can be ruined simply by leaving it in dullness or by washing it out with glare. On the contrary, artificial lighting can create new colors by softening or intensifying those colors the decorator used or by blending them harmoniously (Bradford, 1996). The repetition of colors and light reflection are shown in Table __, which indicates the effects of light on color.

[Table title, citation] Table __ *The Relation of Colors to Light (Bradford, 1996, p. 206)*

[Table organized from greatest to least percent]

Color	Reflection	Color	Reflection
White	85%	Dark Gray	15%
Ivory	75%	Olive Green	10%
Light Gray	65%	Dark Brown	5%
Yellow	60%	Dark Blue	5%
Tan	60%	Black	5%

***Jee S. Han,* Korea**

25 STUDENT SAMPLE

BODY PARAGRAPH #3, WITH REFERENCES

SOCCER INJURIES AND TREATMENT

[Heading] Common Soccer Injuries

[Sub-heading] Sprains

[Topic sentence] *[Audience: novice soccer players]* *[Purpose: to explain* how*]* *[Methods of development: process, cause-effect]* *[Double citation: first citation has no author]* *[Introduction to nontext material]*

The most common soccer injury is the sprain, a tissue injury that happens only in a joint where two bones connect. The players can sprain their wrists, knees, and elbows, but the most common sprain that soccer players face is the ankle sprain (Alen, 1995). This happens because of the forced starts and stops and the quick changes of direction that occur in the game. Sprains occur more frequently if the player wears cleated shoes (Conversation, 1986). When a player twists or sprains his ankle, the acronym RICE applies: immediately after the injury, the player should Rest (i.e., stop putting weight on the ankle). Next, put Ice on the injury for 30-40 minutes so that the cold will constrict the blood vessels, thus preventing additional swelling and pain. Third, the ankle should be wrapped snugly (i.e., Compressed) in order to decrease swelling. Finally, the player should Elevate the ankle so that it is above his heart; in that way, swelling and pain will also be decreased (*Preventative*, 1997; Roseberry, 1996). After 48 hours, heat should be used to increase blood flow, and therefore healing, to the injured area. Figure __ shows the four RICE steps for sprains.

References

Alen, G. (1995). The deadly reality of a soccer game. *McCleans*, 2, 27-29.

[No author; title used] Conversation with the Arabic Pele: Al-Mujalla. (Spring, 1986). *The International News Magazine of Arabia,* 31, 80–82.

[WWW source] Preventative care: Soccer injuries to children. (1997). [Online article]. Retrieved March 2, 1998 from the World Wide Web: http://www.montclair-ortho.com/prev~1.htm

[Unpublished thesis] Roseberry, A.G. (1996). The influence of lower body flexibility on athletic injury in male football and soccer players. Master's thesis, Colorado State University, Department of Exercise and Sports Science.

***Sultan Al-Hajri,* United Arab Emirates**

26 STUDENT SAMPLE

BODY PARAGRAPH #4: SCIENTIFIC WRITING

Laboratory and Field Experiments on the Control of the Whitefly

[Heading serves as topic sentence]

Materials and Methods

[Audience: professor]

[Description of experiment]

[Writing conventions: short paragraphs, long sentences, use of passive voice verbs]

Tomatoes were grown as host plants in 12.5 cm diameter pots containing methyl bromide-fumigated soil mixed with organic manure prior to experiments and maintained under favorable greenhouse conditions. Cultures of tobacco whiteflies were maintained in separate insect-proof cages in the greenhouse, usually on tomatoes, for use in establishing infestations, or as a source of eggs and immature whiteflies of known age.

Whitefly eggs and juvenile stages of known age were obtained every two to three days by successfully exposing groups of French beans in the secondary leaf stage for twenty-four hours to caged, ovipositing adults. Adults were then removed from the plants, without affecting the eggs, by gentle plowing. Then the plants were placed in a cage in a greenhouse free of adults, and the eggs and immature whiteflies were allowed to develop until they were ready to be used.

***Thabet Allawi,* Jordan**

BODY PARAGRAPH #5: TECHNICAL RESEARCH AND FORMULAS

Analyses in Basins Without Sufficient Data

[Introduction of equations]

Many studies have been made in order to develop empirical formulas expressing precipitation for various durations as a function of frequency. The formulas have the form:

[Writing conventions: equations numbered at right margin, then described and interpreted immediately below]

$$i = \frac{KTp^x}{t^n} \qquad (6)$$

$$tp = C_t\,(LLc)^{0.3} \qquad (7)$$

where L is the length of the main stream, Lc is the length between the mass center of the basin and the main stream, and C is a coefficient that varies between 1.35 and 1.65. For rains with a duration of tr = tp/5.5, Snyder found that the peak of the unit-graph was given by the equation:

$$Qp = \frac{CpA}{tp} \tag{8}$$

[Use of present tense] where A is the drainage area, Cp a coefficient that varies between 0.56 and 0.69. For the base time Snyder adopted the following equation:

$$T = 3 + 3\,\frac{tp}{24} \tag{9}$$

[Reference to previous formula] where tp was defined in equation (7).

With the unit-graph of a basin, the maximum discharge that can be expected for any rain of any frequency can be found. The accuracy of the [Conclusion] method depends on the accuracy in the evaluation of the constants.

***Eduardo Lopera,* Venezuela**

28 STUDENT SAMPLE

BODY PARAGRAPH #6, WITH FIGURE

Memory Management Techniques

[Heading] II. Techniques

[Subheading] A. Single Contiguous Allocation

[Method of development: process] This technique consists of assigning that part of the memory that is not occupied by the operating system to one job, if the space available is big enough for the job. Otherwise, it will be assigned to another space. Using this scheme, only one job can be processed at one time, so as we can observe, multiprogramming is not permitted. [Introduction to Figure] Figure __ shows a flow chart of the technique.

[Flow chart]

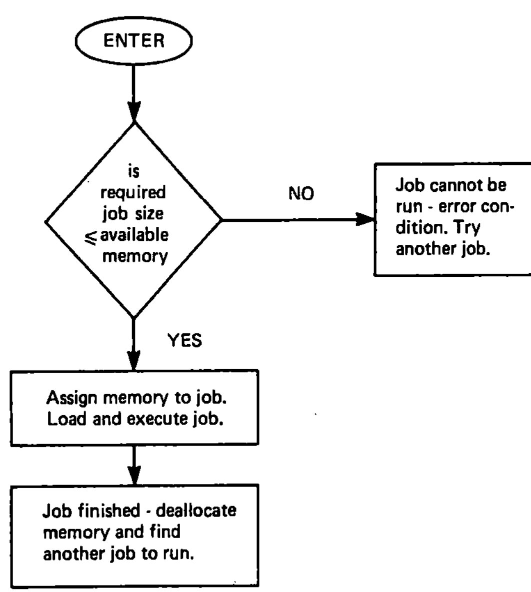

Figure __ *Flow Chart of Memory Management Techniques*

***Marysabel Alarcon,* Venezuela**

29 STUDENT SAMPLE

CONCLUSION #1

VITAMIN C

[Link to thesis statement] [Summary] [Recommendation] In 1932, Charles Glen King and W. A. Waught isolated vitamin C. Many scientists were very interested in this discovery and spent their careers researching it. Consequently, we now clearly know the chemical properties of vitamin C, the metabolic processes of vitamin C in our bodies, the functions of vitamin C for humans, the optimum amount of the vitamin for human needs, and the distribution of vitamin C in foods. Also, we know that megadoses of vitamin C can prevent us from getting some diseases, and that it is helpful in decreasing the severity of others, but that such megadoses may have side effects for some people. Further study is required to determine the effect of vitamin C on such diseases as cancer and stroke.

***An Tsai,* Republic of China (ROC)**

CONCLUSION #2: LONG RESEARCH REPORT

NUTRITION AND AGING

[Heading] Conclusion

[Link to thesis statement] [Summary] [In-text citations] [Solution] [Recommendation] [Prediction] Although many hypotheses of the causes of aging have been proposed, the biological mechanisms responsible for them remain largely unknown. Aging, a period in the lifespan, is not a disease or a sickness. But as man ages, disease often follows. Moreover, the increased number of older people has produced many medical, social, and economic problems (Bates, 1989; Li, 1995). The elderly therefore need others' assistance. In the near future, we must provide better medical care and better nutritional programs for the aging, or we risk a breakdown in society.

***Songchun Pak,* Korea**

APPENDIX #1: INTERVIEW QUESTIONS

Appendix __

Interview Questions: Intercultural Gestures

1. What gestures have you encountered in the U.S. that have surprised you? Which seem awkward or embarrassing for you? Why?
2. What body language have you encountered in the U.S. that has surprised you? Which seem awkward or embarrassing for you? Why?
3. What gestures and body language in U.S. culture are similar to gestures in your culture?
4. Please show me gestures and body language in your culture for

(a) come here/stay away!
(b) greetings
(c) signaling a waiter
(d) mourning/sadness
(e) not understanding
(f) maybe
(g) yes
(h) no
(i) OK
(j) goodbye

5. Please show me some of the facial expressions in your culture. For example, how much and what kind of
   - eye contact do people in your culture use to designate

     (a) interest
     (b) anger
     (c) surprise
     (d) disappointment

   - eyebrow movement do people in your culture use to indicate

     (a) suspicion
     (b) agreement
     (c) frustration

6. Please show me appropriate gestures and/or body language in your culture the would accompany the following expressions:

   (a) "I don't know"
   (b) "I can't hear you"
   (c) "This is delicious!"
   (d) "Get out of my way!"
   (e) "Oh, sorry: I forgot!"
   (f) "Your baby is beautiful!"
   (g) "Wait a second!"
   (h) "Good luck!"
   (i) "Thank you!"

***Molly Hand,* U. S.**

32 STUDENT SAMPLE

APPENDIX #2: SURVEY

Appendix __

POLLEN ALLERGY SURVEY

Directions: Please help us with an assignment in our first-year composition class by completing this short survey. You have been selected to take this survey because you suffer from pollen allergies.

When you finish the survey, please put it in the attached stamped, self-addressed envelope, and drop the envelope in any mailbox.

Class (Circle one): F S Jr Sr Grad Other Age: ______
Sex (Circle One): F M Major: ______________________

1. Please list your most severe pollen allergies.

2. How long have you known you had these allergies? (Check one)
   ____ less than a year
   ____ 1–3 years
   ____ 4–6 years
   ____ longer

3. Have your pollen allergies changed over time? (Check all that apply)
   ____ become more severe
   ____ become less severe
   ____ increased in number
   ____ decreased in number
   ____ begun earlier
   ____ begun later
   ____ lasted longer
   ____ lasted shorter
   ____ Other (please describe): ______________________

4. What have you used for the treatment of your pollen allergies?
   ____ OTC remedies
   ____ avoidance
   ____ injections
   ____ prescribed medicine
   ____ Other (please describe): ______________________

5. What is the most important factor in your decision about treatment for your pollen allergies?
____ cost ____ effectiveness
____ convenience ____ safety
____ Other (please describe): ________________________________
____

6. What have you found to be the most effective treatment for your pollen allergies?
____ OTC* remedies ___ avoidance ___ injections
____ prescribed medicine ___
____ Other (please describe): ________________________________
____

*OTC: over-the counter remedies such as Sudafed and inhalants

Other comments: ________________________________
____

THANK YOU VERY MUCH FOR YOUR TIME AND CONSIDERATION!

Melinda O'Doake, Martha Hurst, U. S.

REFERENCE PAGE #1

The Feminist Movement in Egypt

References

[Listed alphabetically by author's last name]

Basu, A. (Ed.). (1995). *The challenge of local feminisms: Women's movements in global perspectives.* Boulder, CO: Westview Press.

[Must be double-spaced]

Botje, H. (1986). Egyptian women advance. *World Press Reviews, 54,* 12, 30–32.

[Journal article]

Busha, H. (1985) Women under Arab legislation. *Women of the Whole World, 15,* 46–48.

Jayawardena, K. (1996). *Feminism and nationalism in the Third World.* London: Zed Books.

[E-mail interview]

Kassaby, O. (1998). Personal communication (April 2).

[Anthology]

Moghadam, V.M. (Ed.). (1993). *Identity politics and women: Cultural reassertions and feminisms in international politics.* Boulder, CO: Westview Press.

[Newspaper article]

Tolchin, S. & Tolchin, M. (1990). The feminist revolution of Jihan Sadat. *New York Times Magazine, 95,* 20–21, March 16.

Hana Al-Qemlas, Kuwait

BIRTH ORDER

References

[WWW sources: no authors; begin with title]

Birth order and your child. (1996, June 15). *PCGC Parenting Tips.* [Online article]. Retrieved May 3, 1998 from the World Wide Web: http://trfn.clpgh.org/orgs/pcgc/birthorder.html

[WWW sources: no authors; begin with title]

Birth Order Personality Inventory. *The birth order home page.* (1997, December 20) [Online article]. Retrieved February 2, 1999 from the World Wide Web: http://www.nxn.nwr/~cliffi/BOTEST.htm

[Personal interview]

Dinkins, M. (1998). Personal interview. (October 10)

[Older book]

Forer, L. K. (1976). *The birth order factor.* New York: David McKay Company.

[Student-designed survey]

Ishigami, Y. (1998). Birth Order Survey.

Kingsmen, L. (1990). *Effects of birth order.* New York: Soloman.

[Date of writer access]

[No punctuation at end of URL]

Morgan, V. (1997, October 1). Birth order. *Family front.* [Online article]. Retrieved March 8, 1999 from the World Wide Web: http://www.hhcn.com/family/1001/html

[Can divide URL at any slash (/) or period (.)]

Sutter, L. M. (1997, November 6). Birth order factsheet. [Online article]. Retrieved March 8, 1999 from the World Wide Web: http://www.ag.ohio-state.edu/~ohioline/hyg-fact/5000/5279.html

***Yashugi Ishigami,* Japan**

Chapter 9

Grammatical Explanations and Exercises

I have been frustrated in writing for years because I have problems with my grammar. I hate in-class writing because I usually make even more grammar mistakes, and sometimes my teachers cannot even understand my thoughts. Now I have begun to prioritize and study the grammar that interferes with communication. I think that in the future I will be a better writer.

Hong Yijang, People's Republic of China (PRC)

THIS CHAPTER PRESENTS some practical rules for academic writing. It is not a complete grammar review; instead, it is concerned with those problems most frequently encountered by ESL writers. Each explanation of a rule is followed by a brief exercise. If you need additional practice, consult a handbook of grammar that focuses on ESL problems, such as one of the following:

Azar, B. S. (1999). *Understanding and using English grammar. 3rd Ed.* Upper Saddle River, NJ: Prentice-Hall Regents.

Byrd, P. & Benson, B. (1992). *Applied English grammar.* Boston: Heinle & Heinle.

Byrd, P. & Benson, B. (1994). *Problem/solution: A reference for ESL writers.* Boston: Heinle & Heinle.*

Verb Problems

The selection of verb tenses and the problem of subject–verb agreement are difficult for writers because they must consider the tenses used in previous or succeeding sentences. In addition, writing conventions require specific verb tenses in different academic writing situations. For example, in the abstract of a research report, background information is usually written in present tense, while the actual research is usually described in past tense or present perfect tense; the methods of the research and the results are written in past tense, while the recommendations for future research are often written in present tense with modal auxiliaries.

For the academic reader, verb tense errors can be serious; they often interfere with communication. Below are diagnostic exercises concerning verb tense and verb tense agreement. By completing the exercises, you should be able to determine whether or not you have significant problems. If you need a thorough review, consult one of the handbooks listed above.

EXERCISE 9-A Write the correct form of the verb in each blank in the paragraph below.

Since I began ____________ (TAKE) this writing course, I ____________ (FEEL) that I ____________ (KNOW) less each day. Every night I ____________ (TRY) to ____________ (STUDY), but I ____________ (HAVE) adverse feelings against this subject. In fact, I ____________ (DO) not ____________ (LIKE) to write, even in my native language. Also, my major, electrical engineering, ____________ (HAVE) not ____________ (MAKE) it necessary for me to ____________ (WRITE) very much, so I ____________ (HAVE) not ____________ (HAVE) much practice. Even so, I still ____________ (COME) to class optimistic each day, and I ____________ (THINK), "Alfredo, you ____________ (CAN) learn to ____________ (WRITE) English. Your government ____________ (PAY) for you to ____________ (LEARN)." Then the teacher ____________ (PUT) the assignment on the

* To acquire any of the books suggested in this chapter, order through a bookstore or, with a credit card, from an online bookstore.

chalkboard, and my mind ______ (BEGIN) to ______ (REJECT) it immediately. I ______ (IMAGINE) myself at night ______ (TRY) to ______ (WRITE) something, and when the class ______ (FINISH), I think, "What in the world ______ (DO) I ______ (KNOW) about this terrible subject, writing? What ______ (CAN) I write? My vocabulary ______ (BE) so limited, and I ______ (CAN) not ______ (EXPRESS) my ideas well."

***Alfredo Chorro,* El Salvador**

EXERCISE 9-B Reread 2 to 4 of the student samples (SS) listed below. Underline the verb tenses used in each paragraph, and discuss those verb tenses with a small group of classmates.

1. How many different verb tenses are used in each of the paragraphs?
2. What questions do you have about the use of verb tenses in each paragraph?
3. Do you disagree with the use of any of the verb tenses? Why?
4. For one of the paragraphs, what other verb tenses might be used? How do you know?

Student Sample (SS)	Topic	Writer	Page
Chapter 1, SS 15	The octopus	Annick Burkhalter	22
Chapter 2, SS 12	Children of divorced parents	Roberta Scott	44
Chapter 2, SS 29	Effects of apartment living	Norlela Othman	60
Chapter 3, SS 11	Vitamin D deficiency	Saleh Saeed	84
Chapter 5, SS 17	Body paragraph #3		158

EXERCISE 9-C In the paragraphs below, many of the verbs have been changed so that they are incorrect in tense and in subject–verb agreement. Underline each of the verbs in the paragraphs; then correct the incorrect usage. Each paragraph contains at least twelve (12) errors.

In my country many customs still existing about the choice of a woman for me to married. Despite the influence of other cultures, especially American, the Latin American woman has always submit to the man. She has working in the home and take care of the children. The counsel that parents generally give their sons state that the chosen girl must to be pretty (if that is possible), kind, intelligent, and faithful, and she must came from a good family. Virginity is one of the most important requirements for her to being considered a good woman. She must also be obedient and possesses a certain level of culture if she is to be a successful wife and mother. Although some of these requirements are begin to disappear, the traditional woman in Latin American was still thought to be the best choice for a wife.

***Ramon Vega,* Colombia**

Teachers of foreign languages should to be extremely well-qualified in order to carried out their duties properly. In fact, a teacher must be possess a minimum of a graduate degree from a certified educational school or institute if he teach high school or below. Besides the academic degree, teachers should not considered teaching only as an occupation to earn money. They should also be interesting in teaching. It is not only necessary that teachers be knowledgeable in their major fields, but they should also being skillful as well. For example, the language teacher must knowed the target language well enough to be imitating by his students. Proficiency in the target language include four skills: understanding, speaking, reading, and writing. A teacher may also knew the linguistic facts of the language of the students in order understand the problems they will have while learn the target language. Furthermore, the teacher must be familiar with the audio-lingual techniques. Having all these qualifications will helped the students to learn correctly and quickly.

Abbas Al-Ballal, **Saudi Arabia**

PASSIVE VOICE

To test for passive voice, ask yourself: Can I add *by someone* or *by something* at the end of the sentence?

The room *was destroyed.* *(by someone or something)*
Fungi *were grown* for two weeks. *(by someone or something)*

Some English teachers believe that students should not use passive voice verbs because the passive voice slows down the sentence structure and causes the reader to tire easily. However, most scientific and social science academic writing uses the passive voice. In fact, passive voice is used frequently in both spoken and written English (this sentence, for instance, has a passive voice verb).

Passive voice can be useful

- *in social sciences writing,* when the agent (i.e., the person or thing performing the action) is unknown or unimportant.

  [We do not know who founded them, OR the founder is not important]

  Turkish coffeehouses, called "Kahuehane," *were founded* centuries ago.

- *in scientific and technical writing,* to describe technical processes and to report research procedures and results. Writing conventions require the agent(s)—the subject(s)—to use passive voice in order to be modest and objective.

  [What was done is more important that who did it]

  Choline and Vitamin B complex *were administered* to the rabbits; the effects of the elements on the animals *were* then *observed.*
  The results of the experiment *were analyzed.*

- *in reports about victims and disasters,* when the agent/subject is a victim. Passive voice is often used to describe disaster. Listen to a news broadcast: for an event in which a person suffers violence or catastrophe, passive voice conveys a sense of real accident, of the victim's helplessness.

  [The subject did not act, but instead was acted upon]

  She *was hit* by a car. *(by someone or something)*
  The child *is trapped* in the burning building.
  His brother *was kidnapped.*

As a general rule, use the passive voice only when you make the decision that it will be useful. That is, use passive voice (a) when it is expected, as in some scientific, technical, and social science academic writing, (b) when the agent (the person or thing performing the action) is unknown or unnecessary, or (c) when the subject of the sentence is a victim.

EXERCISE 9-D Change the passive voice in the paragraph below to the active voice. **Note:** You will probably have to rearrange parts of some of the sentences to create a coherent paragraph.

The prison had been escaped from by a man who had murdered six people without reason. Even though the prison had been judged to be the most secure in the country, the escape had succeeded because it had been carefully planned. A prison guard had been distracted; his gun was taken and he was hit on the head with the gun. Then the guard's uniform was put on. Next the heavy fence around the prison was climbed, and the barbed wire on the top of the fence was cut with a metal cutter that had been stolen from the prison repair shop. The river that surrounded the island was swum despite the frigid water, so the escape was completed. In the town near the prison, precautions were taken: doors were bolted, windows were locked, and children were called inside. Policemen from nearby towns were ordered to the area, and roadblocks were set up. Every car was thoroughly searched. Fortunately, the murderer was recaptured later that same day by the same policeman who had been knocked unconscious. The capture was performed when the murderer's gun was not able to be fired because it had become wet in the water.

***Lorel Birmingham,* U.S.**

ACTIVE VOICE VERBS

If you choose to use active voice verbs, try to use colorful, descriptive verbs. Make the subject of the sentence (the agent) perform. Make it do something. In the sentences below, the first sentence of each pair is written in the passive voice; the second sentence changes the verb to active voice, using verbs that are lively, interesting, and descriptive.

Thunder *was heard* in the mountains.
Thunder growled/grumbled/rumbled/crashed/snarled in the mountains.

The car *was driven* down Main Street.
The car careened/lurched/rattled/purred down Main Street.

REPORT VERBS

The verbs used in academic writing can help the reader understand the information better. Many essays and papers in your college/university classes will report information: describe a laboratory experiment, investigate a question, explain a concept, evaluate a product, solve a problem, argue about a controversy, etc.

[Passive voice] Birth order has been *described* as . . .
[First person, active voice] In this paper, I will *discuss* . . .
[Author giving results] The survey results *indicated* that . . .
[Note that] The results of the experiment *demonstrated* that . . .
[[Present tense] Authors in the magazine *Ebony examine* . . .

In addition, in many of your academic papers, you will need to report the ideas (and perhaps the actual words) of experts. That is, you will also use reporting verbs to introduce direct quotations and to paraphrase the ideas of others.

[Introduction to material]	Aguirre *maintained* that . . .
[Direct quotation]	According to Barnes, "The evidence *revealed* that . . ."
[Introduces paraphrase]	In a recent research report, the authors *recommended* that . . .
[Reported speech]	The graduate student *proposed* that . . .
[In-text citation]	A recent study (Gottfredson, 1997) *found* that
[Note that]	The results of a large-scale study *suggest* that . . .

Selecting reporting verbs carefully can show the reader the strength of the results and/or the evaluation of material by the writer.

Stronger Reporting Verbs	**Weaker Reporting Verbs**
found that	*suggest* that
recommended that	*indicated* that
demonstrate that	*proposed* that
predict that	*claim* that

Usually report writers use

- **present tense** when the information or results are widely expected or known by the readers.
- **past tense** when the information or results may be tentative (or not widely known or accepted).

Below are some commonly used verbs in research reports. Notice that the left columns (Reporting Results) contain verbs often used in reporting the results or effects of something. The verbs in the right columns (Other Reporting Verbs) are used more often to report information that is not directly related to results or effects.

Reporting Results		**Other Reporting Verbs**	
indicated	stated	described	alleged
suggested	noted	discussed	revealed
demonstrated	showed	presented	presumed
reported	found	explained	implied
investigated	claimed	maintained	proposed
predicted	asserted	examined	affirmed
recommended	observed	contended	argued
hypothesized	assumed		

EXERCISE 9-E

1. Which of the reporting verbs in the lists above are NOT followed by *that*?
2. Which of the words in the left columns (Reporting Results) are very strong? Which of those words are relatively weak?
3. Which of the words in the right columns (Other Reporting Verbs) are evaluative? That is, which have a positive or a negative meaning associated with them?
4. Using the introductory words and the reporting verbs below, write five partial sentences in your notebook. Be sure to (a) select the correct verb tense and (b) add an appropriate in-text citation indicated in each set of brackets [ ].

   A. In [book/article title], ________________ (*state*)
   B. [Author] (19__) ________________ (*imply*)
   C. Recent research ________________ (*affirm*)
   D. According to [author], ________________ (*investigate*)
   E. The percentage of ________________ (*show*)

5. Share your sentences with a partner. Discuss any questions you have about each other's sentences.

Parallel Structure

Parallelism is the repetition not just of ideas but also of grammatical structures and grammatical function. These structures can be simple (such as a repetition of a series of single related nouns), or more complex (such as a repetition of a series of phrases, clauses, or complete sentence structures). Balance is also inherent in parallelism: word balances with word, phrase with phrase, sentence with sentence. The result is rhythm within a paragraph that strengthens the coherence and emphasizes the ideas.

The rule for parallelism: if you have two or more similar structures in a sentence that perform the same grammatical function, they must be parallel.

[Relative clause, past tense] She was a woman **who** under**stood** children, **who** enjoy**ed** housework, and **who** worshipp**ed** her husband.

[Infinitive phrases + object] Michael wanted **to catch** a snake, **to put** it in a cage, and **to take** it to school.

[Preposition + object (phrase)] During spring break, the students traveled **to** Oregon, **to** California, and **to** Utah.

[Past perfect + reflexive pronoun + prepositional phrase] In order to pass his final examination, he **had** barricad**ed himself** in his room, (**had**) chain**ed himself** to his desk, and (**had**) buri**ed himself** in his books.

[If clause, if clause] **If we are to finish** this textbook, **if we are to have** a chance to finish, we must meet each day for at least two hours.

As these examples show, a single sentence containing parallel structures is often more effective and concise than a paragraph made up of a series of parallel sentences.

EXERCISE 9-F Correct the errors in parallelism in the following sentences. The first has been completed for you.

1. Rodney Stephens was the editor of the largest newspaper in the city, a diplomatic representative to Kuwait, and he invented many useful devices.

   Correction: Rodney Stephens was **the editor of** the largest newspaper in the city, **a diplomatic representative** to Kuwait, and **an inventor of** many useful devices.

2. Fertilizer is used to enrich the soil, to improve crops, and for making more food.
3. She took a shower, got dressed, smiled at the mirror, and her lipstick was checked.
4. It can be dangerous for one's health to diet continuously, to sleep all day, and not doing any exercise.
5. The weight of the airplane depends on its size and materials; the thrust forces are dependent on engine power.
6. The purpose of this paper is to show the dynamic state of the airfoil, how the lift force is generated, and how the air flow relates to both.

EXERCISE 9-G Complete the unfinished sentences below with at least three parallel structures. The first sentence has been completed for you.

1. **Raise** your right hand, . . .

   Raise your right hand, **place** your left hand *on the Bible*, and **repeat** this statement *after me*: "I swear to tell the truth, the whole truth, and nothing but the truth."

2. He was a criminal. He was a person who . . .
3. To win the spelling bee, she needed only to . . .
4. On Peggy's trip through Europe, she traveled to . . .
5. Dr. Lindstrom has contributed a great deal to this community: lecturing, . . .

6. Before you leave, please close the door, . . .
7. If your car will not start, try checking the battery, . . .
8. Since they moved into the house, they have painted all the rooms, . . .
9. The sports facilities are beautifully designed: modern, . . .
10. Those students are so lazy; all they do is watch television, . . .

Sentence Structure and Sentence Combining

Effective academic writing is strengthened by the use of sentences of varying length. Very short sentences, for emphasis, and long sentences, which often describe, are interspersed with sentences of ordinary length (the majority of sentences). The structure of individual sentences is also varied, including sentences with

- semicolons (to join short related sentences),
- coordinate conjunctions (to join two related sentences),
- an independent and a dependent clause (to show relationships between important and less important information), and
- parallel structures (to add rhythm and tone to the writing).

Sentence combining is not simply a language exercise; it is a skill to be practiced and integrated into the writer's style. Too many short sentences can result in a choppy paragraph. Too many long sentences may confuse the reader. Effective, coherent academic writing combines some short sentences with appropriate punctuation.

This section provides a diagnostic paragraph (Exercise 9-H), briefly reviews basic information about English sentence structure, and offers exercises to practice correctly forming and varying sentence structures.

EXERCISE 9-H For many ESL academic writers, the difference between a comprehensible and an incorrect sentence is often a matter of recognizing that English sentences are generally shorter and are punctuated differently than sentences in other languages. Read the paragraph below. Identify each sentence and insert the necessary punctuation.

About half a year ago in Nagasaki prefecture an American protector cut the nets and let dolphins that the fishermen had caught escape The fishermen were very angry and they brought a law suit against the American but at the trial the American said that the act was moral and legal because dolphins are very clever animals We must protect them he shouted Is what he said about dolphins true Yes but the American should have thought about the fishermen's lives The sea around Nagasaki prefecture is a good fishing ground and many fishermen make a living by catching the fish Also there are a lot of dolphins in that area and dolphins eat the fish which are the source of the fishermen's livelihood so the fishermen try to catch the dolphins in order to protect their business The American however only had a single thought the protection of the dolphins He didn't know how important fishing is for the Japanese.

***Keio Maeda,* Japan**

CLAUSES AND PHRASES

In order to combine sentences successfully, you must (a) understand the concept of phrases and clauses in English and (b) learn appropriate punctuation of combined sentences.

1. A **clause** is a group of words that must contain at least a subject and a verb. It can contain much more.

[One clause] Janet slept.
[One clause] While the thunderstorm roared
[Two clauses] While the thunderstorm roared, Janet slept.

2. An **independent clause** (IC) is a clause (i.e., a group of words with a subject and a verb) that can stand by itself; it is a complete sentence.

[One IC] I like painting.
[One IC] I am quite ignorant about the history of art.

3. A **dependent clause** (DC) is a clause that cannot stand by itself; it needs to be joined with an IC to become a complete sentence.

[One DC] Although I like painting, . . .
[One DC] After we completed the experiment, . . .
[DC, IC] Although I like painting, I prefer sculpture.
[DC, IC] After we completed the experiment, we wrote the report.

4. A **phrase** (ph) is a group of words that is missing a subject, a verb, or both.

[Two prepositional phrases] . . . in the back of the bedroom . . .
[Subject, but no verb] The man . . .
[Verb + modifier, but no subject] . . . swaying gently.

SENTENCE STRUCTURE RULES

In the examples of English sentence structure rules below, the independent clauses (ICs) are underlined, and the dependent clauses (DCs) are *italicized.*

1. A complete sentence must contain at least one IC.

[One IC] <u>Chinese cooking is easy.</u>

2. A sentence may contain one IC with many modifying words (e.g., adjectives, adverbs) and/or phrases.

[Ph, IC.] In making a Chinese meal, <u>Chinese cooking usually involves one or more meats and several colorful chopped vegetables.</u>

3. A sentence may contain several ICs.

[IC; IC, and IC.] <u>Stir-frying is one category of Chinese cooking</u>; <u>it is one of the most commonly used methods</u>, and <u>it is used both in restaurants and in home cooking.</u>

4. A sentence may contain one or more ICs and one or more DCs.

[Although *DC, IC; Ph, IC]* *Although the shapes of the pieces of meat can be thin slices, match-like sticks, or little cubes*, <u>the pieces need to be consistent in size</u>; in that way, <u>the meat will cook at the same rate.</u>

5. A sentence may contain one or more ICs and one or more DCs as well as modifying words and/or phrases.

[Ph, before DC, IC, and IC, DC, Ph] To cook delicious Kon Pao chicken, *before I make the sweet and sour sauce with soy sauce and oyster sauce,* I cut fresh chicken pieces into narrow slices along the grain and drop them individually into a very hot wok, and I stir them *until they are no longer pink,* usually about two to three minutes.

EXERCISE 9-I Identify each of the ICs in the sentences below by underlining the subject and the verb in each.

1. The name "stir-fry" reveals the method of cooking.
2. Simultaneous stirring and frying is quite a simple process.
3. For different kinds of meats, the cutting methods are closely related to the cooking and the texture of the meats.
4. The tenderness of the meats will be increased by the addition of a little starch prior to cooking.
5. The cook can either mix the starch and water in a bowl first, or he can sprinkle the starch directly on the meat.

***Hongyu Zhou,* People's Republic of China) (PRC)**

JOINING INDEPENDENT CLAUSES [ICs]

One way to vary sentence structures is to join two related independent clauses (ICs)—that is, two complete sentences. Each of the ICs is equal in importance in the joined sentence. There are two ways to join the ICs: using a semicolon (;) with an optional conjunctive adverb (called a "long word"), or using a comma and a required coordinate conjunction (called a "short word").

Joining ICs with a Semicolon

The semicolon (;) is placed between two ICs. The rules for semicolons:

1. The semicolon can be used only between two ICs that are related in content and in purpose.

[IC; IC.] The history of Indian classical dance dates back many centuries; it started even before the written language was known.

[IC; IC.] Ancient Indian story-tellers were accompanied by musicians to enhance their stories; they slowly started swaying to the music.

2. An *optional* conjunctive adverb (called a "long word") following the semicolon (and usually followed by a comma) can make the sentence more coherent by demonstrating the relationship between the two ICs. Figure 9-1 gives examples of "long words" and the relationships they demonstrate between ICs. Notice the comma that follows each "long word."

Additional Information	Contrasting Information	Cause-Effect Information
IC; moreover, IC.	IC; however, IC.	IC; therefore, IC.
IC; furthermore, IC.	IC; nevertheless, IC	IC; consequently, IC.
IC; in addition, IC.	IC; as a result, IC.	

Figure 9-1 *Examples of "Long Words" (Conjunctive Adverbs) Showing Relationships Between Two Independent Clauses*

Examples:	**Structure**	**Relationship**
Indian classical dance became a form of worship; **therefore,** it was performed only in temples.	*[IC; therefore, IC.]*	*[Cause-effect information]*
In the olden days, women were not supposed to be seen in public; **consequently,** Indian classical dance was performed only by men.	*[IC; consequently, IC.]*	*[Cause-effect information]*
Fortunately, the women could watch any public dance performance from specially created areas; **furthermore,** they could dance within the four walls of their homes for their own enjoyment.	*[IC; furthermore, IC.]*	*[Additional information]*

EXERCISE 9-J In the paragraph below, circle the semicolons used to join two ICs. In the sentences joined with semicolons, (a) underline the subject and the verb of each IC, and (b) put a box around the conjunctive adverbs (i.e., the "long words") that signal the relationships between the ICs. Then identify the relationships between each of the combined ICs.

Classical dancing was an art form that the royal princesses wanted to learn; however, they could not learn it from male teachers. Therefore, the teachers had to teach their wives, who could then teach the princesses. Even then public performances were still restricted to men performing at religious festivals; the only women who danced in public were street walkers. During the British rule of India, the royalty gradually lost its importance; consequently, the dancers began to lose patronage. The teachers then started teaching ladies from wealthy families. Later, after independence from the British, many women had learned to dance; moreover, they refused to abide by the age-old tradition of not being seen in public. Women from middle-class families started dancing at family functions like weddings; the dance form lost its worship value and became a form of entertainment.

Perlini Danegkar, **India**

Joining ICs with Commas and "Short Words"

A comma and a coordinate conjunction (called a "short word") are placed between two ICs that are related in content and in purpose. Figure 9-2 lists examples of the "short words" and the relationships they demonstrate between ICs. Notice the comma that precedes each "short word."

Additional Information	**Contrasting Information**	**Cause-Effect Information**
IC, ***and*** IC.	IC, ***but*** IC.	IC, ***so*** IC.

Figure 9-2 *Examples of "Short Words" (Coordinate Conjunctions) Showing Relationships Between Two Independent Clauses*

1. To join two ICs, use both a comma and a short word.

[Additional information]

Pasarmalam is a Malay term for "night market." The word *pasar* means "market," **and** the word *malam* means "night."

[Cause-effect information] Most of the freshly prepared food at the *pasarmalam* is cheap, **so** people prefer to buy their dinner there rather than at a fast food restaurant.

Note: To join an IC and a *phrase* (in brackets in the examples below), use just the "short word" without the comma.

The *pasarmalam* starts as early as 4 p.m. **and** [lasts as late as 2 a.m].
A variety of local delicacies are prepared in the open air **and** [sold to the hungry passersby].

EXERCISE 9-K Join the following sentences with a comma and a "short word" (a coordinate conjunction) or just a "short word." Explain your choice of the short word by describing the relationship between the parts of the sentence.

The stalls in the *pasarmalam* sell food, utensils, and garments. The utensil stalls are usually set up somewhere further down the road _______ traders display their merchandise. Some traders simply set up their merchandise on a mat by the roadside _______ arrange their merchandise on the mat. The stalls sell essential kitchenware _______ the prices are very reasonable. For instance, a frying pan costs only about myr $3, which is equivalent to US $1.20. Usually the shopper can find a large crowd at one stall with especially good prices _______ he will know which stall to hurry to. Sometimes the voices of bargaining can be heard clearly even from a distance _______ those voices are always filled with courtesy, not with challenge.

***Kai Meng Hoh,* Malaysia**

DEPENDENT CLAUSES

Words that introduce a dependent clause (DC) are called "subordinate conjunctions " (or "subordinating words"). Because the DC cannot stand by itself, it must be joined to an IC. In the joined sentence, the DC is a weaker, less important clause. Figure 9-3 shows some of these subordinate words and the relationships they show between the DC and the IC.

Cause-Effect Information	Contrasting Information	Time Information	Conditional Information
Because DC, IC. IC *because* DC.	*Although* DC, IC. IC *although* DC.	*After* DC, IC. IC *after* DC.	*If* DC, IC IC *if* DC.
Since DC, IC. IC *since* DC.	*Even though* DC, IC. IC *even though* DC.	*Before* DC, IC. IC *before* DC.	**Note** the many *time* subordinate words.
Note: There are no "additional information" subordinating words because the DC gives information of lesser, not equal (i.e., additional), importance.		*During* DC, IC. IC *during* DC.	
		While DC, IC. IC *while* DC.	
		When DC, IC. IC *when* DC.	**Note:** DCs can either precede or follow ICs.
	IC *until* DC.	*Until* DC, IC.	

Figure 9-3 *Examples of Subordinate Conjunctions*

Currently, one of the most serious economic problems facing the U.S. today is the ever-increasing cost of the prison system. The average cost of maintaining a prisoner is over $25,000 a year in state prisons, and the amount is even greater in federal penitentiaries. Moreover, the number of prisoners is growing because crime is increasing and courts are becoming stricter. Recent proposed solutions have included eliminating prison sentences for "white collar" crime until the prison population reaches manageable levels, making prisons more punitive by reducing comforts such as televisions and weight-lifting equipment for prisoners, and even requiring capital punishment for all criminals who have an odd social security number although this suggestion has not been widely accepted. However, I propose that the U.S. solve the problem by expanding graduate programs in universities. First, most graduate students can be supported for a mere $10,000 to $15,000 annually because they are not protected by the Constitutional clauses concerning "cruel and unusual punishment." Second, graduate students work without vacations, benefits, and even weekends; therefore, much of the research in the U.S. will be accomplished in less time. Third, because graduate students do not have social lives, or any additional time, crime should decrease substantially. Finally, prisoners surveyed indicated that they preferred jail to graduate school, suggesting that graduate school would be a greater deterrent to crime.

***R. J. Carter,* U.S.**

EXERCISE 9-L

1. In Student Sample 9 above, underline the subject and the verb of each IC; put a box around the semicolons and the conjunctive adverbs (the "long words") that signal the relationships between the ICs.
2. Put parentheses ( ) around the commas and coordinate conjunctions ("short words") that join two ICs.
3. Put brackets around the subordinate words that begin DCs in the paragraph.
4. Identify the relationships in purpose and content between each of the combined ICs and the combined ICs and DCs (*additional, contrasting,* or *cause-effect* information).

RELATIVE DEPENDENT CLAUSES

Another form of the dependent clause is the relative clause (RDC), which has an unusual formation in English. The relative dependent clause (RDC) modifies a noun or a noun phrase; it gives further information about the noun or noun phrase. The RDC replaces a noun or a noun phrase with a relative pronoun: the most widely used relative pronouns are *that, who,* and *which.*

1. In an RDC, a relative pronoun is substituted for a noun or a noun phrase in the IC. These relative pronouns become subordinating words that change an independent clause (IC) into a dependent clause (DC).

[Two ICs] South Africans buy many products. The products are imported.

[Relative pronoun] **that**

[IC + RDC] South Africans buy many products that are imported.

[IC] Petroleum products are the largest import in South Africa.

[IC] Imports of petroleum products are estimated at $2.5 billion.

[Relative pronoun] **which**

[Subject + RDC, +V + O] Imports of petroleum products, **which** are estimated at $2.5 million, are the largest import in South Africa.

2. The relative DC modifies a noun; therefore, it often occurs in the middle of an IC: after the Subject of the sentence and before the Verb and the Object.

[IC] Some nations are serious obstacles to a sanction policy.

[IC] These nations are economically dependent on South Africa.

[Relative pronoun] **that**

[with RDC] Some nations **that** *are economically dependent on South Africa* are serious obstacles to a sanction policy.

[IC] Other countries are also an obstacle to the success of a sanction policy.

[IC] These countries have sizable investments in South Africa.

[Relative pronoun] [with RDC] **that**

[Subject + DC + V + O.] Other countries ***that*** *have sizable investments* in South Africa can also be an obstacle to the success of a sanction policy.

3. In addition to *that, who,* and *which,* relative pronouns also include

whom *whose* *why* *when* *where*

These relative pronouns are used in other contexts as well, particularly as question words. The test for a relative pronoun that introduces a relative clause is that it (a) substitutes for another noun or pronoun and (b) forms a DC.

[Question word; not a relative clause] **Whose** government imposed the sanctions?

[RDC: whose replaces The United Kingdom] The United Kingdom, ***whose*** *government states that some sanctions are not effective,* believes that these sanctions will do more harm than good.

[Question word; not a relative clause] **Which** are the most important: military, political, or economic sanctions?

[RDC; which replaces economic sanction] An economic sanction to ban bank loans to the government, ***which*** *could have forced the government into compliance,* was not completely successful.

[Question word; not a relative clause] Do you know **where** South Africa is?

[RDC; which replaces South Africa] In South Africa, ***where*** *an apartheid government ruled for fifty years,* stimulated sanctions and boycotts from those who disapproved of that regime.

[RDC; which replaces military power] The arms embargo was meant to weaken South Africa's military power, ***which*** *exceeded that of all the neighbor countries together.*

EXERCISE 9-M Combine each set of ICs below to form a single sentence with an IC, an RDC, and perhaps another DC. Share your sentences with a partner. (The RDC for each combined sentence is in parentheses.)

A. The sanction against bank loans initially seemed to be working.
   (**which** initially seemed to be working)
   The sanction was unsuccessful because many countries used "back door" lending.

B. Many South Africans have found the trade embargo effective.
   (**who** have found the trade embargo effective)
   Many South Africans believe that the ban on luxury items has been the most successful.

C. In South Africa, many thought that sanctions must be upheld by all countries.
   (**that** must be upheld by all countries)
   Many thought the sanctions were the best solution for change.

D. Some countries did not impose sufficiently high sanctions to bring about change
   (**that** did not impose sufficiently high sanctions to bring about a change
   Some countries caused the sanctions to fail.

E. The military power exceeded that of all the neighbor countries together.
   (**which** exceeded that of all the neighbor countries together)
   The military power was ineffective in monitoring the sanctions.

EXERCISE 9-N

1. With a partner, reread the Student Sample 7 (p. 292). Underline with wavy lines three relative dependent clauses (RDCs) you find in that paragraph.
2. In the paragraph below, put a box around the semicolons and conjunctive adverbs (the "long words") that signal the relationships between the ICs. Circle the semicolons and the comma + short words used to join two ICs.
3. Identify the relationships in purpose and content between each of the combined ICs and between the ICs and DCs (*additional, contrast,* or *cause-effect* information).
4. Underline with wavy lines the relative dependent clauses.
5. Identify the relationships in purpose and content between each of the combined RDCs and ICs (*cause-effect, time, contrast,* or *conditional* information).

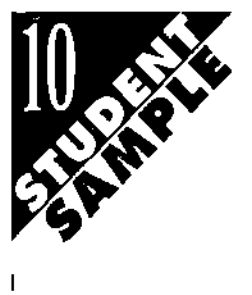

One of the few sanctions that proved to be effective is the diverted trade embargo, a sanction that focused its effects on the white minority more than on the black South Africans. Some European countries, for example, refused to ship luxury items, which were mainly consumed by the wealthy white minority, while others banned the import of goods mainly produced by South African whites. Unfortunately, sometimes the different policies among European countries weakened the embargo. Sweden, for instance, banned imports of fruits and vegetables; Norway, which has one of the largest fleets of commercial ships in the world, would not allow any of its ships to carry South African material, and other European countries followed other guidelines. In fact, for several years, Belgium banned vegetables from South Africa, but their $1.5 billion import of South African diamonds remained untouched.

***Marius Winger,* South Africa**

JOINING ICs WITH DCs AND RDCs

Relationships

1. A DC or RDC must be joined to an IC to make a complete sentence.

*[**When** DC + IC.] [Time information]*

When you are hiking in the wild, there are several ways to identify which direction is north.

*[IC + **when** DC.] [Time information]*

There are several ways to identify which direction is north **when** you are hiking in the wild.

*[**Which** RDC] [Additional information]*

One way to identify north, **which** takes a wristwatch, is to point the short hour-hand straight at the sun.

2. Subordinating words and their DCs can be used either first <u>or</u> later in the sentence.

*[**Although** DC ,+ IC.] [Contrasting information]*

***Although** using a compass is the easiest way,* you can also use the sun or the stars.

*[IC + **although** DC.] [Contrasting information]*

You can use the sun or the stars ***although** using a compass is the easiest way.*

3. The comma is used only when the DC is first.

*[**If** DC, + IC.] [Conditional information]*

***If** you have ever once been lost in the wilderness,* you are probably familiar with confusion and frustration.

*[IC + **if** DC.] [Conditional information]*

You are probably familiar with confusion and frustration ***if** you have ever been lost in the wilderness.*

*[**After** DC, + IC.] [Time information]*

***After** 15 minutes have passed,* you should mark the endpoint of the new shadow carefully.

*[IC + **after** DC.] [Time information]*

You should mark the endpoint of the new shadow carefully ***after** 15 minutes have passed.*

4. Punctuation (i.e., the use of commas) changes with the RDC, depending on whether the clause is restrictive (necessary for the complete meaning of the sentence) or nonrestrictive (additional information but not necessary for the meaning in the sentence).

[RDC information essential for meaning: no commas]

From the short hour-hand **that** is pointing directly at the sun, locate twelve on your watch and divide the distance from the short hour-hand in half.

[RDC adds nonessential information; use commas]

If you get lost at night**, which** might make you afraid**,** use the stars to help find due north.

EXERCISE 9-O Read Student Sample 11. Identify the subordinate (i.e., dependent) clauses and the relative dependent clauses (RDC) by <u>underlining</u> the subordinate words or the relative pronouns. Then describe the relationship between the DC or RDC and the IC in each sentence.

If I get lost during the daytime, which does not happen often, I must first locate north. One way is to find a stick that is about a yard long and a small stone. Then I find a place in the sunshine because I want the stick to cast a shadow. After I drive the stick into the ground, I place the stone at the end of its shadow. When 15 minutes have passed, I mark the endpoint of the "new" shadow carefully with a stone that is the same size as the first. Finally, I stand with my back to the stick and my heels on the two endpoints. I am now facing north.

***Chris Fogstad,* Norway**

Figure 9-4 is a review of the connectors and punctuation you can use to combine clauses (both ICs and DCs) and to identify relationships between those clauses:

Connectors	*Additional Information*	*Contrasting Information*	*Cause-Effect Information*
Coordinating Conjunctions (Short Words)	IC**, and** IC.	IC**, but** IC.	IC**, so** IC.

Connectors	*Additional Information*	*Contrasting Information*	*Cause-Effect Information*
Conjunctive Adverbs (Long Words)	IC**; moreover,** IC. **; furthermore,** **; in addition,**	IC**; however,** IC. **; in contrast,**	IC**; therefore,** IC. **; consequently,** **; as a result,**

Note: The use of the "long words" is optional.

Connectors	*Cause-Effect Information*	*Time Information*	*Conditional Information*
Subordinate Words (DC, IC) (IC DC)	**Because** DC**,** IC. **Although** DC**,** IC. **Even though** DC. IC **since** DC.	**When** DC**,** IC. **While** DC**,** IC. IC **before** DC. IC **after** DC. IC **since** DC. IC **until** DC.	**If** DC**,** IC. DC **if** IC. **Unless** DC**,** IC. ***Note:** DC can be the first OR a later clause.*

Connectors	*Additional Information*	
Relative Pronouns (RDCs)	. . . RDC . . . . . . **,** RDC**,** . . .	*[Restrictive clause; do not use commas]* *[Nonrestrictive clause: surround with commas]*

Figure 9-4 *Sentence-Combining Options for ICs, DCs, and RDCs*

Sentence Combining and Punctuation

Appropriate punctuation helps the reader; in addition, a change in punctuation can change the meaning of a sentence. For example, notice the difference in meaning between these two sentences; the difference is due entirely to the use of punctuation.

Woman—without her, man would be a savage.
Woman, without her man, would be a savage.

Read the short letters below and note the differences in meaning that are due to differences in punctuation.

I Dear John,
I want a man who knows what love is all about. You are generous, kind, thoughtful. People who are not like you admit to being useless and inferior. You have ruined me for other men. I yearn for you. I have no feelings whatsoever when we're apart. I can be forever happy—will you let me be yours?

Kirsten

II Dear John,
I want a man who knows what love is. All about you are generous, kind, thoughtful people who are not like you. Admit to being useless and inferior. You have ruined me. For other men I yearn. For you, I have no feelings whatsoever. When we're apart, I can be forever happy. Will you let me be?
Yours,

Kirsten

EXERCISE 9-P Read the related pairs of sentences in Student Sample 13. Use Figure 9-4 to help you join each pair in *two* ways. Rewrite the combined sentence if necessary. Be careful about the correct use of punctuation.

1. The discovery of the substance endorphins is attributed to Dr. Choh Hao Li in 1964. The significance of the discovery was not realized until a decade later.
2. In 1975, a group of scientists was trying to find a painkiller. They believed that the human body produced such a painkiller.
3. They found a protein that was synthesized within the body for its own use. That protein was Dr. Choh's mysterious protein.
4. The scientists named the protein "endorphin." The dictionary defines that word as "any group of peptide neurotransmitter occurring naturally in the brain and having pain-relieving properties" (p. 59).
5. Endorphins are extremely powerful. They are dozens to hundreds of times more potent than heroin.
6. Endorphins are concentrated in the brain along the area that controls the nervous system. They slow down or block the transmission of sensory information, especially pain.
7. People who exercise heavily do not feel pain when they stop. This is because of increased concentration of endorphins in their nervous systems.
8. This is known as the "endorphin high" for athletes. They enjoy the feeling.

K. Y. Chin, **Malaysia**

USING COLONS

In general, a colon (:) means "as follows." A colon indicates that what follows explains and/or emphasizes that which preceded the colon. Colons are used after an IC and before an IC, a DC, or a phrase.

Punctuation for the colon differs in two ways from other forms of punctuation: (a) the colon symbol is followed by two spaces, and (b) the colon symbol is put outside quotation marks (see the section on Quotation Marks below). Rules for colons are demonstrated in Student Sample 13.

1. Use a colon at the end of an IC (a complete sentence) to introduce and to emphasize a series: a list of three or more words, phrases, or clauses that are directly related in content and in purpose.
2. Use a colon after an IC to emphasize the point that follows.
3. The word(s), phrase(s), or clause(s) that follow a colon should be parallel (see the section on parallelism starting on page 288).

[IC, but IC: IC.] *Plantanos* belong to the banana family, but they differ in three ways: they are bigger, broader, and sweeter than bananas.

[DC, IC: IC.] If you use bananas instead of *plantanos*, the taste of the dish will differ: it will be flat, simple, monotonous, and graceless.

[DC, IC: phrase.] When *plantanos* are ripe, they have three characteristics: a softness, a yellowish color, and a slight sweet smell.

[DC, IC: phrase.] When you prepare *patacones*, you will need one special ingredient: coconut oil.

[DC, IC: IC.] If your first experience with cooking *patacones* is unsuccessful, I have one piece of advice: you should try again!

[DC, IC, but IC: IC, so IC.] After the *plantanos* are half-cooked in boiling water, take the pieces out of the water and remove the skin, but be careful: the *plantanos* are extremely hot, so they can cause serious burns!

[IC, so DC, IC: IC.] I prefer *patacones* that are not so oily, so when I finish frying the *patacones*, I perform a special process: I hold a slice between my hands, cover the piece with a paper towel, and press the towel on the *patacone* gently.

***Alejandro Valerio,* Costa Rica**

EXERCISE 9-Q Read the sets of sentences in Student Sample 14. Combine each pair of sentences by using a colon. In some cases, you will eliminate words or change the sentences. Then, with a partner or a small group of classmates, use Figure 9-4 (p. 298) to identify the independent clauses (ICs), the dependent clauses (DCs), the relative dependent clauses (RDCs), and the phrases (Ph) in each combined sentence.
Note: There are many correct ways to combine these sets of sentences.

1. There are several steps to prepare for the funeral service in Sri Lanka. The steps are informing the temple, arranging for embalming and cremation of the body, and turning all photos in the home to face the wall.
2. The head monk at the temple meets with the family of the deceased. He tries to share the sorrow of the family.
3. He begins by quoting the teaching of Buddha. "Death is as natural as birth, and no one on earth can hide from it."

4. I spoke with a close friend of Mr. Perl, the deceased. He told me of fun-filled days he spent with Mr. Perl at the Teachers Training Institute.
5. Mr. Perl's wife was very upset at the approaching cremation. She fainted several times.
6. After the coffin had been driven to the cemetery, it was put in a specially made structure. Typically, the structure is made with wood and paper because it burns easily.
7. Soon the whole structure was on fire. Huge flames reached the sky.

Yehan Wijesena, Sri Lanka

EXERCISE 9-R The following paragraphs are written in short, choppy sentences. Combine some of the sentences to increase the unity and coherence of the paragraphs. It may be necessary to rewrite some of the sentences. Use coherence devices (see p. 116), and appropriate punctuation such as commas, semicolons, and colons. Rearrange some of the sentences as necessary. Remember: there are several ways to combine the same set of sentences correctly.

Then share your combined sentences with a partner. Note the similarities and differences, and discuss any questions you have with your partner.

I Trips take Joseph Cancellare to Australia and India. The trips are to the field. Cancellare is a marine geologist. He studies characteristics in the field. The characteristics are chemical. The characteristics are physical. The characteristics are of marine aerosols. He studies their distribution. The distribution is over the ocean. He studies their impact. The impact is on conditions. The conditions are meteorological. The conditions are climactic.

II When I was in high school, I had many friends. I could divide my friends into two groups. One group was friends who were worried. They worried about the future. They worried all the time. They were good students. They were responsible. They were loyal friends. They didn't have too much time for friendship. The second group didn't worry about anything. They were fun-loving. They were poor students. They were often in trouble. They lived in the present. They lived for the present. They had time to spend with everyone. They had a lot of fun. They were very friendly.

III Nicaragua is a country. It is one of the countries in Central America. Central America is located on an isthmus. There are five countries in Central America. Nicaragua is in the middle of the isthmus. It is the largest of the countries in Central America. It is about 81,249 square miles. It is not as big as the United States. In comparison it is much smaller. But size is not so important. Nicaragua is beautiful.

USING QUOTATION MARKS

Quotation marks (" . . . ") in writing are used primarily to indicate direct speech; they are also used to indicate the titles of television programs, articles in magazines, and chapters in books, as well as to indicate the use of a special word or phrase.*

1. Most forms of punctuation (periods, semicolons, question marks) usually come before (i.e., inside) the final quotation marks. An exception is the colon (:), which usually goes outside the quotation marks.

* For additional information about how to use and to cite (i.e., reference) direct quotations, see Appendix A.

[Period inside quotation marks] If I asked my fellow students how much they had studied, the answer invariably was, "I haven't studied at all."

[Colon outside quotation marks] "This false modesty forces people to lie": so says the young author of a recent popular Japanese novel.

2. A pair of quotation marks (" . . . ") surrounds direct speech to indicate that the writer is using *the exact words* of the speaker.

3. Within a sentence, a comma usually precedes the direct quotation, AND the first word of the direct quotation is capitalized.

According to many Japanese, "Modesty is a great virtue."

When Japanese people give a gift to a friend, they typically say, "Just a trivial thing."

4. If a direct quotation is not introduced, a comma does not precede the direct quotation, AND the first word of the direct quotation is not capitalized. Notice that the period comes <u>after</u> the citation in parentheses.

The characteristic of modesty forces me to "interpret the hidden meaning" of what modest people say (Madono, 1997, p. 66).

Modesty has "a bad influence on some people's self-esteem" (Ishimira, 1998, p. 4) and, consequently, on their actions.

5. If you eliminate some of the words from a direct quotation, indicate their omission by using an **ellipsis**: three dots with a space between each dot (**. . .**). If an ellipsis follows or precedes punctuation, keep the punctuation: (. . . **:**) or (**,** . . .). *[Note: ellipses is the plural]*

[No comma before quotation] A definition of Japanese modesty might be "to pay one's respect to others **. . .**"

[Note comma and capital letter] According to Inkyo, "The Japanese sense of modesty **. . .** lowers peoples' self-confidence."

6. If you add or change some words in a direct quotation (to clarify meaning or to change verb tense), indicate this by putting those added words in brackets **[ ]**.

[Word added] As Mr. Kirabawa explained, "Originally, being modest meant showing those above one's **[**social**]** rank his lowly attitude or speaking about himself humbly."

[Word "me" changed to "her"] A sophomore Japanese student stated that she dislikes the concept of modesty because "it forces **[**her**]** to behave in ways that she finds uncomfortable" (Madono, 1997, p. 63).

7. For a direct quotation within a direct quotation, use single quotation marks (" . . . ' . . . ' . . .").

Mr. Kirabawa described his daughter's reaction: "When I attempted to explain my definition of modesty as humility, she said she believed modesty was **'**contrived humility,**'** not real humility" (1998, p. 2).

8. Enclose titles of television programs, of articles in magazines, and of chapters in books in quotation marks.

[Note italicized book title] In *Understanding the Japanese*, there is a chapter titled "Modesty: The Greatest Virtue."

[Note italicized magazine title] A recent issue of the American magazine *Vogue* contained an article about modesty in Japan: "Modesty: Respect or Insincerity?"

9. Enclose special words and phrases in quotation marks to demonstrate that you are speaking about the word, not simply using it in a sentence.

   In Japanese culture, the word "modesty" traditionally means having respect for others, but in today's Japan, the meaning has changed.

   [Note colon] She would usually say, "No, no, he is a bad son in comparison with your son": that was a "modest" answer, in her opinion.

   ***Miki Inkyo,* Japan**

EXERCISE 9-S Read Student Sample 15, and circle each set of quotation marks. Underline the examples of (a) eliminated material (ellipses) and (b) added material to the direct quotations.

What allows birds to fly so freely? According to Phillip Stegman, my ornithology professor, their wishbones, which are formed by "the two clavicles in birds [that] are usually fused together." Professor Stegman stated that this skeletal piece "provides an increased site of origin for the pectoral muscle . . . which probably evolved for this purpose." Contrary to what we would think, the wishbone (also called the "furcula") is not rigid but can spread due to "the coracoid displacement . . . and the extended wings via the pectoral muscles during the downstroke."

***Jacques Laine,* France**

EXERCISE 9-T Punctuate these sentences with appropriate use of quotation marks, commas, periods, and capitalization.

1. Jennifer asked what makes a person feel lonely
2. Marysabel she called come into the living room.
3. Please look up the meaning of lagniappe.
4. John Wayne received his only oscar for his performance in true grit.
5. Farrage said Fawzi, if you don't study for the TOEFL you will not improve your score.
6. On her t-shirt was written the title of a book: migrant education, harvest of hope

Diction

Being able to use the English language effectively will be very helpful for your academic writing. The use of a good English dictionary, a thesaurus (i.e., a dictionary of synonyms), and a vocabulary-building book will help you expand your vocabulary and learn to use that new vocabulary appropriately. Examples of such books include:

Dictionaries

The Newbury House Dictionary of American English (2nd Ed.). (1999). Boston: Heinle & Heinle.

The American Heritage English as a Second Language Dictionary. (1998). Boston: Houghton Mifflin.

Longman Dictionary of Contemporary English (3rd Ed.). (1995). Essex, England: Longman.

Thesauruses

Chapman, R. (Ed). (1992). *Roget's International Thesaurus* (5th Indexed Ed.). San Francisco: HarperCollins.

Laird, C. & Shannon, S. (Eds.). (1995). *Webster's New World Thesaurus.* New York: Pocket Books.

Vocabulary Building

Lichtenstein, E. (1997). *10-minute Guide to Building Your Vocabulary.* Indianapolis: Arco.

Mohr, C. & Goodman, D. (1996). *Building Vocabulary.* Princeton, NJ: Townsend Press.

Perry, D (1993). *College Vocabulary Building* (9th Ed.). Mesa, AZ: South-Western.

Problems with vocabulary can inhibit and hinder your writing. If you have difficulty spelling—and even if you do not—always use the SPELL CHECK program on the computer. If you prefer to review spelling rules as well, consult any grammar book or

Castley, A. (1998). *Practical Spelling.* San Francisco: Learning Express.

Meyer, J. N. (1997). *Vocabulary and Spelling Skills: College Students.* Upper Saddle River, NJ: Prentice Hall.

Note: You can also access many reference books on the World Wide Web.

PRECISION IN DICTION

In English academic writing, brevity, precision, and accuracy are the marks of a successful writer. In order to make your writing more precise, observe the following rules:

1. Try to avoid these words, or at least try to use them infrequently:

   A. ***There is, there are, there was, there were*** are usually unnecessary words.

   [Wordy] *There are* usually three forces acting on the airplane.
   [Better] Three forces act on the airplane.

   B. ***This*** (unless you follow it immediately with its referent) is vague and causes reader confusion.

   [Vague, confusing] *This* can be divided into four groups: wings, body, landing gear, and tail surfaces.
   [Better] <u>This structure</u> can be divided into four groups: . . . OR
   [Best] <u>The structure</u> of an airplane can be divided into four groups: . . .

   C. ***It***, especially at the beginning of a sentence, is usually unnecessary.

   [Wordy] *It was* Mr. Eastman *who* convinced me to major in psychology.
   [Better] Mr. Eastman convinced me to major in psychology.

   D. ***Very, nice*** are overused words that do not carry much meaning.

   [Lacks precise meaning] She is a very nice girl.
   [Better] She is bright, helpful, generous, and outgoing.

   E. ***You*** addresses the reader in a too-familiar way. Instead, use "I" if you are relating a personal experience, or the imperative (with "you" understood) if you are describing a process.

   [No: reader was not there] *You* could see the fireworks exploding in the night sky.
   [Better] I saw the fireworks exploding in the night sky.

[No: too familiar] First, *you* stir-fry the chunks of chicken.
[Better] First, stir-fry the chunks of chicken. OR
[Better] First, I stir-fry the chunks of chicken.

F. ***thing*** (including *something, everything, nothing*) is vague and forces the reader to "read between the lines," or do the writer's work. In the humorous selection below, notice the confusion of the description because of the frequent use of *thing.*

Things

The man stands by the horses, on each side of the *thing* that projects from the front end of the wagon, and then throws a tangled mess of gear on top of the horses and passes a *thing* that goes forward through a ring and hauls it out, and passes the other *thing* through the other rings and hauls it out on the other side of the other horse, opposite to the first one, after crossing them and bringing the loose end back, and then buckles the other *thing* underneath the horse and takes another *thing* and wraps it around the *thing* I spoke of before and puts another *thing* over each horse's head with broad flappers to it that keeps the dust out of his eyes, and puts the iron *thing* in his mouth, and brings the end of these *things* aft over his back after buckling another one around his neck to hold his head up, and hitching another *thing* on a *thing* that goes over his shoulders, and then takes the slack of the *thing* which I mentioned a moment ago and fetches it aft and makes it fast to the *thing* that pulls the wagon and hands the other *things* up to the driver to steer with.

2. Try not to begin a sentence with the same phrase with which you ended the previous sentence. This repetitious "echo" effect is unnecessary and slows the reader.

[Repetitious] A student should maintain a grade point average (GPA) of "B" *in his major field. In his major field,* a high GPA will assist him in getting a job.
[Better] A student should maintain a grade point average (GPA) of "B" in his major field because a high GPA will assist him in getting a job.

3. Try not to use unnecessary words. Wordiness slows the reader.

[Wordy] In my opinion, I think that an author when he is writing shouldn't get into the habit of making use of too many unnecessary words that he does not really need in order to put his message across.
[Better] An author should not use unnecessary words.

4. The humorous list below contains some other suggestions for writing effective academic prose.

Don't use no double negatives.
Verbs has to agree with their subject.
Never, ever be redundant; don't use more words than necessary; it's highly superfluous.
Kill all exclamation points!!!!
Avoid commas, that are not, necessary.
Contractions aren't a good idea.
Exaggeration is a billion times worse than understatement.
Never use a long word when a diminutive one will do.
Be more or less specific.
Last but not least, avoid clichés like the plague.

EXERCISE 9-U The sentences below are ineffective because they are imprecise. Eliminate any unnecessary words. Change passive voice to active voice unless there is a reason to use passive voice. Make each sentence as brief, precise, and accurate as you can. You may need to rewrite some of the sentences.

1. After removal of the old finish is completed, the next step is preparation for the new finish. Preparation for the new finish is perhaps the most painstaking step.
2. Those very big pointed things in Egypt were all built by men who were not free to choose.
3. There are several nice girls that I date.
4. One factor we should consider is how important a thing good water is to public health.
5. The radio he built was a beautiful thing.
6. There are fifty men who are trying out for the football team.
7. The terrain can be seen by obtaining a topographical map of the area one intends to cover. The area to be covered having been studied, the task is now what to carry within the pack.
8. There is a very nice girl in physics class who has a mind like a computer.
9. The best time to have a garage sale is on the weekends. Weekends are preferable because people are home more and have more time to spend at garage sales.
10. It was Senator Campbell who proposed the bill.
11. The thing we should consider is our budget.
12. The kind of rat that is brown in color is as supple in its ability to change its shape as a piece of rubber is.
13. There was a number of gate-crashers who managed to get into the concert.
14. A sentence ought not to have any words that are not entirely necessary, and for that matter, there should be no unnecessary sentences contained within a paragraph. This is true for the very same reason that a drawing, if it is to be a good drawing, should have no lines that are not completely necessary.
15. By September 23rd, pitchers should be ready to go into full practices. Practices are organized so that all baseball players can better themselves as individuals through the process of perfecting fundamentals. Fundamentals to work on as a pitcher are wind-ups, throwing drills, and good follow-throughs.

Confusing Words

Below are four sets of words that second-language writers often confuse. The rules are not complete; not all of the exceptions are given. Nevertheless, these rules should give you enough information to use them correctly in most of your writing.

1. **Another**: an adjective or pronoun used with a single referent (*an* other); used with a singular verb; never used with *the.*

   One reason Matthew passed the exam was that he studied very hard; *another* [reason] was that he had plenty of time to write his essay.
   One way to write effectively is to be precise. *Another* [way] is to be accurate.

   Other(s): an adjective (always singular) or a pronoun used with either single or plural referents; often used with *the.*

[Adjective is always singular]

Rafia could taste only cinnamon in the cake, but Maha said *the other* spices were allspice and cloves.

[Plural pronoun]

Rafia could taste only one spice in the cake, but Maha said *the others* were allspice and cloves.

[Singular pronoun]

Today the mailman delivered two letters. One envelope contained a bill, and the *other* held letters from my family.

[The *is optional*]

Today the mailman delivered a lot of mail. Some was from my family, but (the) *others* were bills.

2. **Especially**: adverb (*-ly*) meaning "very."

   Stephen was *especially* talented as a left wing in soccer.
   You're looking *especially* beautiful today.

   Special: adjective meaning "exceptional."

   Elisabeth gave us a *special* gift: a bowl that she had made in pottery class.
   For most children, their birthday is a *special* day.

3. **Interested/bored** vs. **Interesting/boring**:

   -ed form: past participle used as an adjective.

   "The interested class listened carefully" means that the class was interested IN SOMETHING or SOMEONE.

   -ing form: present participle used as an adjective.

   "The interesting class was filled with intelligent men" means that the class was interesting FOR SOMEONE or SOMETHING.

   Note: Both forms can be used correctly, but the meaning of the word changes with its use.

   "I am bored" (*with something:* means that you don't like it).
   "I am boring" (*to others:* means that they don't like you!)

   [Subject/agent felt negatively/positively about the object]

   I am ***interested* / *bored*** in Microbiology class.
   We were so ***bored*** with the movie that we left. (We didn't like the movie.)
   The class was interest***ed*** in her speech. (The class liked her speech.)

   [Subject/agent is the cause for the feeling]

   Microbiology class is *interest**ing**.* [for me]
   The movie was really *bor**ing**.* [for me]
   The class found her speech *interest**ing**.* [for them]

4. **Afterward, After that:** a time adverb and adverb phrase meaning "subsequently"; often *then* can be substituted for *afterward* or *after that.*

   After: a preposition that is followed by a phrase OR a subordinating conjunction that is followed by a dependent clause (DC); a time word meaning "following." *Then* cannot be substituted for *after.*

   Afterward, After that:

   [Then *can be substituted*]

   We went to the picnic; *afterward,* we went to my favorite disco.
   The cat meowed pitifully; *after that,* Lorel comforted her pet.

   After:

   [Ph, IC.] *After* the movie, we walked to the pizza parlor.
   [IC + DC.] We took the exam *after* studying for four days.

EXERCISE 9-V These sentences use one or more of the words on the previous page. Fill in the blanks with the correct word.

1. ______________ inventing "dry plates," George Eastman, the founder of Eastman Kodak, made photography a portable pastime by creating flexible film that could be rolled up and fitted into a ______________ camera.
2. One goal of the agricultural experiment is to determine the best fertilizer for wheat; the ______________ is to decide the amount of water necessary for proper growth.
3. It is difficult to learn statistical analysis, ______________ if you have never learned how to add or subtract numbers, or if you are ______________ with the subject.
4. Researchers at the University of Pennsylvania have demonstrated that a dieter should drink a cup of hot soup before a meal; ______________ his eating pace will be slower.
5. During your vacation, whether you go to the beach, to the mountains, or to ______________ place, you will be ______________ in resting, seeing friendly people, or engaging in ______________ amusements.
6. I wanted to read the book ______________ I saw the movie because the movie was so ______________.
7. Dermatologists say that sunlight is ______________ hard on the skin because it kills some cells and damages others.
8. Alfalfa is ______________ sensitive to pollution by ozone and sulfur dioxide. ______________ ozone lowers the resistance of the plant, the alfalfa dies of a fungus.
9. A new dairy farmer in Latin American has two ______________ problems. ______________ he has found the land he wants, he must choose a good herd of cattle. Then he must solve ______________ problem: getting the necessary financial help to operate his farm.
10. Although Turkish coffeehouses are very simply decorated, they have a ______________ atmosphere.
11. ______________ we left the museum, we went to ______________ place we were ______________ in ______________ we could order dinner.
12. We swam from one side of the lake to the ______________ because we were too _______ to stay on the shore.
13. Just before dawn we sneaked to nearby trees; ______________ we proceeded to ______________ bushes that were only a few yards from the fence.
14. In Argentina, it is necessary to test canned beans with ______________ litmus paper to measure the hydrogen content; this test is ______________ necessary if the container has been damaged.
15. The idea of escape depends on different conditions that vary from one culture to ______________.

Prepositions

English has more than 40 prepositions. The meanings of these small words are often difficult to remember, and their uses often seem arbitrary. Therefore, the appropriate use of prepositions can be extremely difficult. Below are two paragraphs to test your preposition proficiency.

EXERCISE 9-W Fill in the blanks in the paragraphs below with appropriate prepositions.

Natural selection can favor certain mutations and provide them with an advantage _________ survival. A trait _________ humans called sickle cell anemia offers an excellent example _________ how natural selection operates _________ favor of a genetic mutant. Sickle cell anemia is a condition caused _________ sickle-shaped red blood cells that _________ normal individuals are round. The outward manifestation _________ this anomalous condition is a reduced ability to carry oxygen _________ the muscles _________ the body. Because oxygen is essential _________ the proper functioning _________ muscles, individuals _________ sickle cell anemia become easily exhausted and sometimes delirious _________ exercise. However, one who is born _________ the sickle cell anemia trait is immune _________ malaria. _________ some regions _________ Africa where malaria seriously threatens survival, up _________ forty percent _________ the population exhibits the sickle cell trait. What ordinarily would be an undesirable mutation becomes a selective advantage _________ areas where malaria jeopardizes the viability _________ individuals.

***Kurt Bucholz,* U. S.**

The road soon narrowed and followed close _________ the base _________ the purple-green mountains. Hilary saw the beauty _________ the mountains, the colorful flowers and vines growing _________ the road's edge. Every tree and bush seemed alive _________ blossoms, a riot _________ color pressed _________ the shadowed backdrop. Riverwater lapped _________ the grassy banks, and a statue _________ the Christ figure stood quietly _________ a rose arbor. White walls stretched away _________ the entrance to *Quinta Christina*, and the narrow lane was paved _________ cobblestones. The house, built _________ white stucco, reflected its colonial architecture _________ an intricately carved facade. The cobblestone drive ended _________ a well-tended garden, wet _________ mist _________ a fountain that sent slender spires _________ water _________ the late afternoon air. _________ one side of the house a pebble-strewn path led _________ the stables, barely visible _________ the background. Overhead the sky was clear, a brilliant blue fringed _________ clouds that pressed _________ the mountains.

***Shannon Sayer,* U. S.**

Phrasal Verbs

Prepositions are used in verb particles, also called "phrasal verbs," and sometimes "two-word verbs" or "three-word verbs," such as

turn on	*break down*	*take off*	*grow out of*
turn off	*break off*	*take on*	*catch up with*
turn in	*break up*	*take out*	*watch out for*
turn out	*break in*	*take in*	*follow up on*

These verb particles are usually idiomatic: that is, they are used in less formal situations than in academic writing. Furthermore, the same two-word verb has different meanings in different contexts. For each of the verb particles, a more formal word or phrase should usually be used in academic writing.

Verb Particle	→	**More Formal**
give in	→	*agree*
give up	→	*surrender*
die out	→	*become extinct*
turn down	→	*decline*

Each grammar book suggested at the beginning of this chapter has a section about phrasal verbs.

Editing

Revision ("seeing again") is a process of writing in which you work to make your writing better by, for example, adding details and examples, changing the arrangement of sentences, removing irrelevant material, and reading your writing from your reader's point of view. **Editing** is a more discrete form of revision: instead of looking at the major parts of your paper, you look for errors in grammar and sentence structure, in spelling and vocabulary, that could interfere with your reader's comprehension.

Being able to identify and correct your own errors is a talent; unfortunately, many writers have difficulty identifying their own errors. In fact, it is usually easier to see errors in the writing of others than in your own writing.

For preposition use—and for some students, the even more difficult use of articles—find a native English speaker who will read your academic writing before you turn it in to your instructor. As you sit beside the native English speaker, she or he can tell you which prepositions (and articles) need correction. Of course, because you are the author, only you will make the corrections, but working with a native English speaker can increase your knowledge and decrease your anxiety with these troublesome parts of speech.

EXERCISE 9-X Below are sentences taken from student papers that contain many errors. Rewrite the sentences and correct each error. You may have to change spelling, sentence structure, diction, verb tenses, and/or punctuation. Try to make each sentence as clear, as correct, and as precise as you can. In the first sentence, the errors are underlined and corrected for you. **Note:** Some sentences have more than one error, and there are several ways to edit some of the sentences.

1. It is possible to solve your problems with only to have a little bit of peace, and a little meditation, and mental relaxation.

   Correction: Solve your problems with a little peace, a little meditation, and a little relaxation.

2. Escape is getting away from something harmful to oneself; for example, to run away from a treacherous dog.

3. I asked the taxi driver how long would it take to the airport, and he said that about half an hour.
4. Working outside the home help women to be sociable; so it would be helpful as an educational process.
5. When the student woke up he found the note, when he had read it he run to school to apologize for his mistake.
6. Realizing how important the writing class; I attend it this semester.
7. For example, young people don't have enough attention from his parents, the father is busy in his businessman meetings.
8. With most American food you don't lose time to prepared a dinner, because, you only put the food in the oven for 20 minutes at 400 F. and your dinner it is ready so you can use the time to study.
9. I am entitled to rights like self-satisfaction and a career; But now I don't want it because the responsibility take too much effort.
10. Each course usually have a large amount of material to be study and understood; that is seemes impossible to learned them in a week only.
11. I took Guilherme and put on him some warm dress, I don't need asked to him why he had ran away.
13. For some women is hard to combine efficiently the house work with a job, because many of they are pressure for time.
14. Because the TOEFL test you ability to listen, read, and to answer questions about what you listen and read about.
15. The Bong Lhang snake attacks the light of an automobile so you can see many of them are run over by automobile died on the streets.
16. Lacking calcium; for instance, the blood took the calcium from the tooths and bones.
17. In the evening Kuta Beach is very beautiful, I never missed the sunset, I just sat on the beach, listen to the soft breeze whispering a nice melody, enjoying the illumination of the sun.
18. For example, using a tractor to plow the land.
19. Often the powerful country help the repressed people to escape from a dictatorship however it dictates to them which system they must elect.
20. I was completely surprised when my roommate took off his clothes; and he stretched out on his bed.

EXERCISE 9-Y The paragraphs below have been changed so that they contain a variety of typical errors in spelling, sentence structure, and punctuation. Correct the errors, changing the sentences to improve clarity and precision.

Fourty year ago in Saudi Arabia there are no regular school but there are rings in the mosques and people learn in this ring some lesons about the Koran, Islam, read, and writting by the sheiks. Now there is much regular school for example there are seven University. The student in those school learned by the educational technology, and by the best teachers who from Saudi Arabia or from another countries. Those student learned science as chamistry bioloby physic but also literature, and history, and also mathematic and engineer and agriculture. in fact there is a very big defferent between past and present.

Abdullah Husain, **Saudi Arabia**

When you enter to my apartament in the north you will saw to front of you the sitting room which have a confortable rugs, TV, the lamps, stereo and many picture. On your left hand you see the dinning room which has a table about six chairs and besides you will saw to kichen which is a refrigerator, dishwasher, and the pots. In the southeast I had a bedrooms for my husband and I which have queen bed. In the southwest you will see a room to my childrens which have two bed and toys for my son. Among the dinning room and the first room you will find the restroom. In fact my apartament was very confortable.

Yolet Goitia, **Mexico**

There are many differences between American food and Persian food. The most of American foods contains meat, potatoes, and some time vegetables. Steak, hamburgers, and hot dogs is the favorite American meets. The American food is almost sweet, but not always. Even tomato sauce has sugar. And also crackers have sugar added. Also American added salt to food for example butter contain salt and vegatable oil. These kind of foods are made fast and takes less time to cook it. In the another hand the most Persian food consisting to rice mixed by many vegatable or meat for example Kabab and Cotelet. We don't put to sugar or very salt to the food. Instead we adding spices as cumin and thyme. Finally Persian food are make lower than American foods and take more time to cook.

Nahid Azadi, **Iran**

Color and temperature affect the soil productivity as the darker the soil in color, more absorption of temperature than the lightest color. When soil temperature be high that cause raise of water and hot temperatures which increase the water movement and the activity of the roots in order to absorb the water and the nutrition and the minerals from the soil. On the otherwise, the dark color soil means the high contents of organic matter and developed soil but the light colors soil like the sand means not contains organic matter and underdeveloped soil. However, the dark soil be more productive than light color soil due to the dark soil has high number of organic matter and minerals. Also the absorption temperature increase the soil reaction and decomposition of the organic matter which produce simple forms of minerals available for the plant absorption.

Mohamed Yacoub, **Libya**

Resources for Effective Editing Skills

For additional help in learning effective editing skills, consult one of these books:

Ascher, A. (1993). *Think about editing: A grammar editing guide for ESL writers.* Boston: Heinle & Heinle.

Byrd, P. & Benson, B. (1989). *Improving the grammar of written English: The editing process.* Belmont, CA: Wadsworth.

Fox, L. (1992). *Focus on editing: A grammar workbook for advanced writers.* New York: Longman.

Lane, J. and Lange, El. (1993). *Writing clearly: An editing guide.* Boston: Heinle & Heinle.

Raimes, A. (1992). *Troublespots: An editing guide for students (2nd Ed.).* Upper Saddle River, NJ: Prentice-Hall Regents.

Raimes, A. (1996). *Keys for writers: A brief handbook.* Boston: Houghton Mifflin.

Appendix

Citation

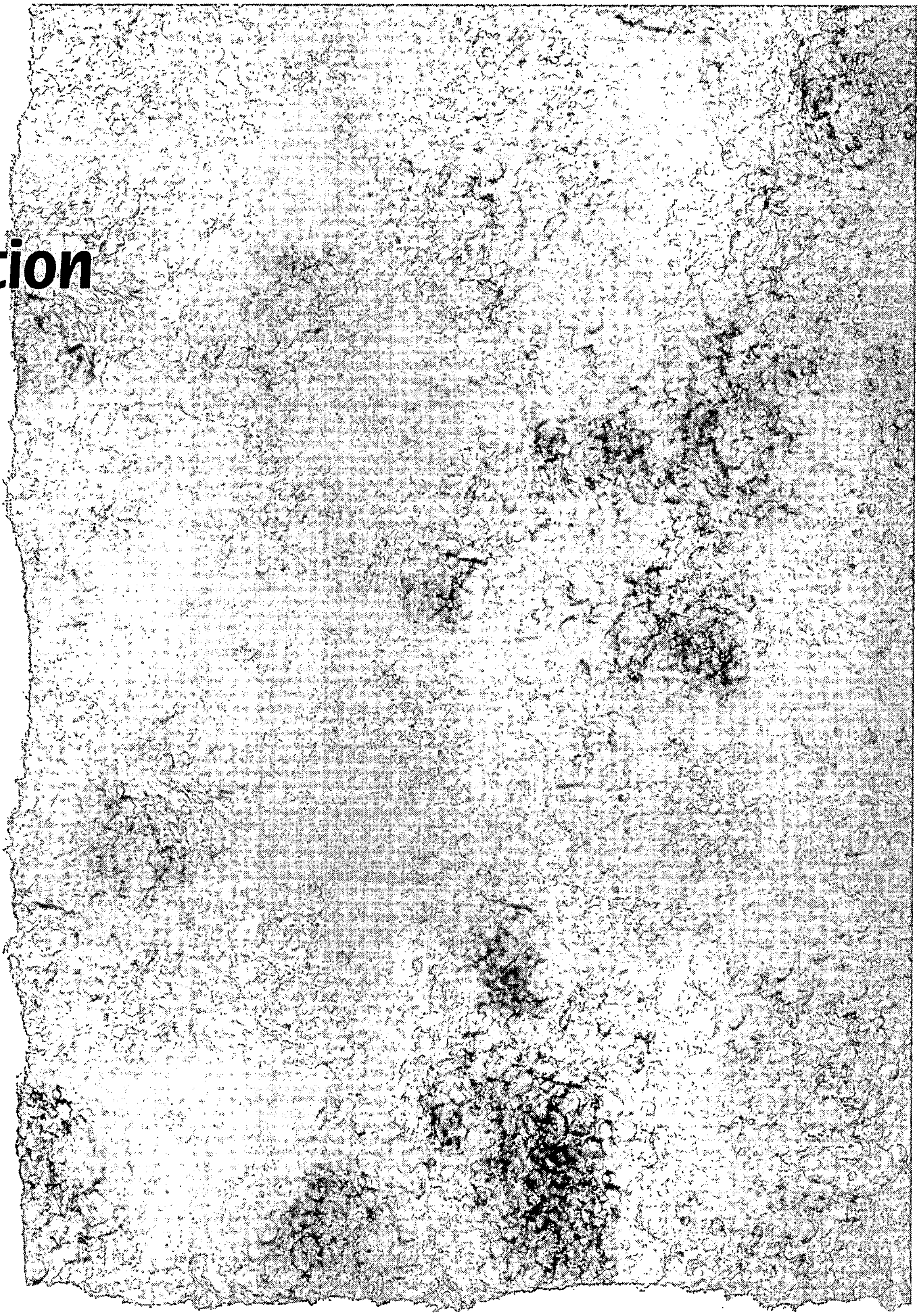

A CITATION (sometimes called a "reference") gives credit in writing to the author of an idea. A writer who uses (repeats) the ideas and/or the words of another author will cite that author twice: once in an abbreviated form in the body of the paper, and once completely at the end of the paper, on a separate page titled *References* (or *Bibliography*, or *Works Cited*).

Many styles of citation exist (see "Discipline-Specific Citation Styles" on p. 168, 323, and 325). But regardless of the citation style (format) you use, the same information is included to enable any reader to locate the cited material in a library or on the Internet.* Figure 1 displays the general information that is essential in all citations, and some specific information that is essential in different kinds of materials.

All citation formats
- author(s)
- year of publication
- title of material

Specific citation formats

Books	*Magazines*	*Internet/WWW*
• place of publication	• volume number	• complete date of WWW placement
• name of publisher	• issue number	• number of pages in the material
• inclusive page numbers		• WWW address
		• complete date of material retrieval

Figure A-1 *General and Specific Information Needed in Citations*

What to Cite and Why

Remember the two general rules for citing a source in U.S. academic writing:

- Authors *own* words and ideas; therefore, writers must give authors credit by citing (giving a reference for) each author's words and ideas used.
- Reference (i.e., cite) **any information that you did not know before you began the paper**.

Writers must cite a source for any fact or information that is not general knowledge. For example, a writer might know in general that freedom of the press allows newspaper reporters to print facts about a public official's abuse of power, but she or he might not know the source of that freedom, the legal differences between freedom of speech and libel, or the extent to which a reporter may keep his sources secret. When that writer locates the information, she or he will need to cite the source(s), to give credit to the author(s) of the material she or he discovers.

Note: Not citing sources can result in **plagiarism**, a serious offense in U.S. academic writing that can result in the writer failing the course or, worse, expulsion from his or her college/university.

In addition to the legal and ethical reasons for using citations in U.S. academic prose, there are several practical reasons:

* In the past, some academic writing used footnotes (a number in the text that referred to the complete reference at the bottom of that page) or, in longer material, end-of-chapter notes. Most academic citation styles no longer use footnotes. Informational footnotes, like this one—those that explain something additional in the text—are often used in academic writing.

Reasons for Using Citations in Your Writing

In-Text Citations
1. to give credit to the author who wrote the material
2. to lend credibility to the paper (i.e., to use an expert as evidence)

End-of-Text Citations
1. to help the reader find the material quickly and easily
2. to demonstrate to the reader the breadth, depth, and currency of the writer's research

In fact, while writers will not cite their own ideas, if they know some of the answers to their questions, they might cite a source they find in order to strengthen their credibility in the eyes of their audience.

General Rules for APA Format

In this textbook, you will learn the most widely used citation format in college/university undergraduate classes: **APA Style**. This format was developed by the American Psychological Association and is used in the social sciences and in some science disciplines. While you may not always use APA Style in your academic career, knowing APA Style will prepare you to switch with ease to another style/format if that becomes necessary. For a complete introduction to APA Style, consult the *Publication Manual of the American Psychological Association.*

APA FORMAT FOR IN-TEXT CITATIONS

Below are rules for APA in-text citations. An example follows each rule, and specific concerns are noted in small print.

1. If the **ideas of another author** are used in a sentence, and the author's last name is not identified in the sentence, the in-text citation includes the last name of the author and the year of publication. The citation can occur within the sentence OR at the end of the sentence.

   When the message from the foot is received, deposits of wastes in that part of the body will break up and allow oxygen to be sent to that area (Kunz, 1997).

   - in parentheses, the author's last name
   - comma between last name of author and the year of publication
   - period at the end of the sentence comes after the citation in parentheses.

   The combination of chemicals in a firecracker work together to cause the color, the design, and the explosion (Allen & Pope, 1997).

   - article has two authors; ampersand [&] between last names
   - authors + year of publication in parentheses

2. If the **ideas of another author** are used in a sentence, and the author's last name is identified in the sentence (e.g., According to Scott Burrell, . . .), cite just the year of publication immediately after the ideas.

   In one chapter in *Body Talk* (1994), Desmond Morris describes six different gestures used by people in cultures around the world to indicate "Hello!"

   - author identified and therefore already "given credit" in the sentence
   - therefore, the citation in parentheses does not contain the author's last name

   When I took Rebecca Oxford's Style Analysis Survey (SAS) (1992), I discovered that I was a visual learner.

   - author's name used in the sentence, so include only the year in parentheses
   - comma follows the first part of the sentence (DC, IC) after the citation, but a comma does not come before the citation

- abbreviation of the survey name put in parentheses immediately following the complete title of the survey

3. The **ideas and words of another author** are used in a sentence. Use direct quotation marks (" . . . ").* Then give the citation immediately following the quotation, as explained above, and give the page number where you found the quotation.

   Three other rules for using direct quotations:

   - Be sure you use the EXACT words of the author in a direct quotation.
   - If you eliminate one or more words, show the reader by using an **ellipsis**: three dots, with a space after each. *[Plural is ellipses]*
   - If you add one or more words (usually to clarify meaning or to change a verb tense), put those words in brackets [ ].

   According to Mary Ann Christison, "When students learn about MI, they become more confident learners" (1997, p. 13).

   - quotation marks indicate an exact use of the author's words
   - author identified in the sentence, so name does not appear in the parentheses
   - comma precedes direct quotation
   - first word of direct quotation capitalized because it begins the quotation
   - parenthetical citation follows the direct quotation immediately
   - p. = 1 page, and pp. = more than 1 page

   Birth order is defined as "the order of chronological birth of children" (Sulloway, 1996, p. 245).

   - quote involves only half the sentence
   - no comma precedes quotation
   - first letter of the quotation not capitalized because the quotation is part of the existing sentence
   - page number on which the quotation occurs must be included in the citation
   - the citation, in parentheses, comes before the period at the end of the sentence
   - comma between the year and the page number

   According to Professor Paul Mussen, an expert in child psychology, "Younger children [aged 4–6] are usually less cautious of their behavior. They tend to participate in . . . more dangerous activities and are more likely to take risks" (1997, pp. 33–34).

   - because the name of the author is identified in the sentence, only the year and the page numbers appear in parentheses
   - ellipsis indicates omitted words
   - additional information added in brackets [ ]

4. A **direct quotation of more than 40 words** (about three lines) must (a) be separated from the main text, (b) be indented 5 spaces, (c) have no quotation marks, and (d) have the citation *follow* the final punctuation.

   In his recent study on solar electricity, José Espinoza, an undergraduate electrical engineering major from Colombia at Colorado State University, gave a brief historical summary of solar electricity.

   > The phenomenon of solar electricity was first noticed at the end of the 19th century. It was known that an electrical current was produced when light was shone on an electrical cell. However, no one knew why this current was produced. Albert Einstein gave the

---

* For additional information and practice using direct quotations, see pages 286–287.

answer in 1920. He explained the photoelectric effect, which paved the road for the discovery of the photovoltaic effect. (1997, p. 12)

- author identified in the sentence before the quotation
- long quotation (64 words) separated from text
- left margin of quotation indented five spaces (one tab length)
- no direct quotation marks used
- citation follows final punctuation (period)

Over seventy people have now died nation-wide from hantavirus, a largely unknown illness until 1993:

> The current *Sin Nombre* [Spanish for "without a name"] strain of the deadly virus is transmitted by deer mice. The common house mouse and urban rats have not been found to carry the strain so far, but the Centers for Disease Control and Prevention in Atlanta caution that they believe more rodents than just deer mice may carry the virus. . . . Deer mice are the same size or slightly larger than house mice, but unlike gray house mice, they are bicolored, with a brown topside and white on the underside of their bodies. (Tri-City Pest Control, 1998, p. 1)

- no author identified in the previous sentence; no author given in the publication
- publisher given as author
- definition added in brackets [ ]
- ellipsis indicates omitted material

APA FORMAT FOR END-OF-TEXT CITATIONS

Below are the rules for APA format for end-of-text citations and typical examples from student writing. Also included are special notes to emphasize the details of each citation.

1. For **books:** general format for a book written by one or more authors:

→ Last name of author, First initial. (year of publication). *Title of the book.* Place of publication: Publisher.

Sulloway, F. (1996). *Birth order, family dynamics, and creative lives.* New York: Pantheon Books.

- first line indented five spaces (one tab length); subsequent lines at margin
- only the first letter of the first word in the title and all proper names capitalized
- the publication information for a book on the back of the title page
- state omitted from place of publication because city is easily recognized
- colon after place of publication

2. For **periodicals** (magazines and journals): An article in a magazine or journal has the following general format:

[Note multiple authors]

→ Last name of author, First initial(s), Last name of next author, First initial(s). (Year of publication). Title of article. *Title of magazine, volume number* (issue), inclusive page numbers.

Adams, B. N. (1997). Birth order: A critical review. *Sociometry, 35,* 411–438.

- author includes both first and middle name (so two initials)
- title of article capitalized only at the beginning of the title and the first letter of the first word after the colon
- period at the end of the article's title, then two spaces

- title of journal *italicized* (or it could be underlined)
- volume number included (found on the cover page of the magazine or at the bottom of the Table of Contents)
- comma between title of magazine and volume number

Kammeyer K. (1967). Birth order as a research variable. *Social Forces,* 46 (6), 71–80.

- indentation of first line, but all other lines begin at the margin
- double-spaced throughout
- title of journal: all main words capitalized (but not *and, the, a, of* etc.)
- no issue number given because pages are sequentially numbered throughout each year
- issues individually paginated, so issue number is necessary
- numbers for inclusive pages (but do not use "p." or "pp.")

Newman, L. S., Higgins, E. T., & Vookles, J. (1992). Self-guide strength and emotional vulnerability: Birth order as a moderator of self-affect relations. *Personality and Social Psychology Bulletin, 18,* 402–411.

- multiple authors format = Last, F., Last, F. ,& Last, F.
- ampersand [&] between last and previous author in multiple-authored material
- title of journal AND volume number italicized (or underlined)
- comma following issue number

3. For **chapters in edited books** or **articles in edited anthologies,** use an end-of-text citation that is similar to the format for magazines/journals. An article or chapter in a book/anthology edited by another person has this general format:

Last name of author, First initial(s). (year of publication). Title of article/ chapter. In F. Last (Ed.), *Title of book/anthology* [inclusive pages, i.e., first and last pages of the article/chapter]. Place of publication: Publisher.

Sakamoto, N. (1997). Conversational ballgames. In S. Reid, *Purpose and process: A reader for writers (3rd ed.)* (pp. 313–318). Upper Saddle River NJ: Prentice Hall.

- book title has only first word and first word after colon capitalized
- article appears **In + F. Last** (not Last, F.)
- title of book is preceded by a comma
- 3rd ed.: this book has been revised twice
- inclusive page numbers of article follow title of book in parentheses
- initials of state given after the name of the city (NJ) with no punctuation

Pollio, H. R. & Edgerly, J. W. (1996). Comedians and comic style. In A. J. Chapman & H. C. Foot (Eds.), *Humor and laughter: Theory, research, and applications* (pp. 215–242). New Brunswick NJ: Transaction Publishers.

- two authors of the chapter; two co-editors (Eds.) of the anthology
- has both a first initial and a middle initial listed for each author
- chapter appears **In** F. M. Last & F. M. Last
- multiple editors (Eds.) of the anthology format: **F. M. Last & F. M. Last**
- inclusive page numbers of article listed in parentheses ( ) immediately following title of the anthology

Citation of Internet (World Wide Web) Sources

The World Wide Web is under constant construction and change.* Even so, APA style for Internet sources is becoming standardized. For future changes and additions, consult

- the newest edition of the *Publication Manual of the American Psychological Association*
- the APA website: http://www.apa.org
- a website devoted to discussion of APA style formats: http://www.lib.usm.edu/userguides/apa.html

For **in-text citations** from the WWW, use the same APA form used for other sources. The examples and notes below demonstrate the in-text citation for WWW sources.

Dust allergies are the most prevalent (Edelson, 1997).

- writer is using the ideas, but not the words, of the author
- author is not identified in text; use (Last, year)

The whistles, clicks, and barks of dolphins, according to Zihlman and Lowenstein, "have a number of potential functions" (1998, p. 2).

- writer is using the ideas and the words of the authors in a direct quotation
- quotation is integrated into the sentence
- two authors are identified in the sentence, so the citation does not contain their names
- citation includes the year and the page number of the direct quotation

In contrast, **end-of-text citations** on the WWW are both similar to and differ from other secondary source materials. Similarities include:

- indentation of first line; no indentation of following lines
- author(s) forms: Last, F. OR for multiple authors, Last, F., Last, F.M., & Last, F.M.
- capitalization, punctuation, and italicizing of similar forms

For materials published in other sources (e.g., in a newspaper or magazine) and then loaded onto the WWW, the end-of-text citation will include some information about the published data as well as the additional WWW data: the title of the magazine/journal (italicized or underlined) and the month and year of publication. In addition, the WWW citation will include the necessary information to enable the reader to access that article on the WWW, such as the date the material was placed on the WWW and the **URL** (**U**niversal **R**esource **L**ocator): the WWW address.

The overall format for a WWW citation includes the following:

→ Last, F. (Year, Month Day of Publication or Placement of the Materials) on the WWW. *Title of document.* [Type of document described]. Retrieved Month Day, Year you accessed the material: complete URL

Eastman, M. (1994, May 2). *Sumo rituals.* [Online article]. Retrieved October 12, 1997, from the World Wide Web: http://www.Japansumosociety.org

- double-spaced
- URL (WWW address): note capitalization and punctuation carefully
  - general beginning (for most URLs): http://www.
  - individualized address must have capitalization and punctuation correct
  - last piece of address shows the kind of group (and maybe the country):

* For an introduction to the WWW, see Chapter 4, page 103ff. For additional information about evaluating and citing WWW sources, see Chapter 8, page 266.

> .com = commercial > .org = organization
> .hu = from Hungary > .mx = from Mexico

- bracketed [ ] information is a brief description of the material for the reader
- period after the brackets

Edelson, S. B. (1997, October 23). *Allergies.* [Online article]. Retrieved June 15, 1998, from the World Wide Web: http://www.ephca.com/ allergy/html

- author with first and middle initial
- date of publication or of material being placed on the WWW includes month and day
- title of material is italicized
- material is briefly described in brackets [ ] for the reader
- "Retrieved" introduces the date you accessed the material
- complete URL is not followed by a "dot" (period)

Zihlman, A. L. & Lowenstein, J. M. (1998, July 26). Dolphins sapiens: How human are dolphins? *Oceans,* July, 1997. [Journal article posted on the World Wide Web]. Retrieved April 20, 1999, from the World Wide Web: http://www. dolphins.sdsu.edu

- two authors, each with a first and middle initial
- comma after year and before month and day of placement on the WWW
- article previously published in a journal; month and year given
- brief description in brackets capitalizes first word, ends with period outside the brackets
- URL can be divided at the end of the line after the forward slash (/) or dot

PROBLEMS WITH WWW RESOURCES

Unfortunately, many WWW sources are incomplete. If the author's last name and first initial (Last, F.) are not available, use the first significant words of the title for the in-text citation; do not use insignificant first words such as *a, an, the, of, or.* Below are examples of (a) in-text citations and (b) end-of-text citations from incomplete WWW information.

[In-text] Children should always ride in the back seat of the car (Airbags, 1996).

- use of the first significant word of the title (see full titles below) because the author is unknown
- comma follows title

[End-of-text] Airbags a danger to small children. (1996, December 11). [Online article]. Retrieved on June 15, 1997, from the World Wide Web: http://www. mayohealth. org/mayo/9611/htm/airbags/htm

- use article title because the author is unknown
- brief description of the article in brackets

Note: To insert these end-of-text citations into the Reference page at the end of a paper, use the first significant word in the title of the article as a last name, and insert the citation alphabetically in the reference list.

Sample End-of-Text Reference Page

References

[Journal article] Allen, L. & Pope, G. (1997). Give me an "A.": July 4th displays get an explosive new look: Fireworks you can read. *Science World, 53* (2), 14–16.

[Online article, WWW] Boulet, J., Jr. (1997, June 15). *Pro and con—English pro.* [Online article].

Retrieved October 22, 1997, from the World Wide Web: http://www.online.com/procon/htm/englishpro.html

[Newspaper article on the WWW]

Chinoy, I. (1997, January 3). In presidential race, TV ads were biggest '96 cost by far. *The Washington Post*, B6. [Newspaper article on the World Wide Web]. Retrieved February 11, 1998, from the World Wide Web: http://ads.washingtonpost.com/wp-srv/national/longterm/campfin/stories/cf033197.htm

[Newspaper article]

Clair, R. (1997, March 20). Let there be light: Translucent door opens the foyer. *St. Louis Post-Dispatch*, D2.

[Magazine article]

Emerson, H. & Monmaney, T. (1988, September 26). The risk from radon. *Newsweek, 112*, 69.

[Edited book]

Glantz, M. H. (Ed.). (1994). *Drought follows the plow: Cultivating marginal areas.* New York: Cambridge.

[Journal article]

Holmes, S. E., Drutz, J. E., Buffone, G. J., & Rice, T. D. (1997). Blood lead levels in a continuity clinic population. *Journal of Toxicology: Clinical Toxicology, 35*, 181–186.

[Online article, WWW, no author]

Know what you're handling. (1998, August 5). [Online article for Pyro website]. Retrieved October 8, 1998, from the World Wide Web: http://php.indiana.edu/~flinn/What-every-pyro.html

[Journal article]

Krishnamurti, T. N., Correa-Torres, R., Latif, M., & Daughenbaugh, G. (1998). The impact of current and possibly future sea surface temperature anomalies on the frequency of Atlantic hurricanes. *Tellus: A Dynamic Meteorology and Oceanography, 50A* (2), 186–210.

[Foreign magazine]

Richard, M. (1991, October 31). Cohue au Palais de verre. *LeMonde*, 3.

[Textbook]

Smith, F. K. & Bertolome, F. J. (1986). *Bringing interiors to light: The principles and practices of lighting design.* New York: Whitney Library of Design.

[Article in edited Proceedings]

Watson, G. & Yamashita, T. (1997). Nearshore, wave and topographic effects in storm surges. In B. Came (Ed.), *Proceedings of the International Conference on Coastal Engineering* (pp. 1417–1430). Melbourne, Australia: Monash University.

Discipline-Specific Citation Styles

Undergraduate college/university classes will often ask you to use APA format. However, for some course assignments, students may be required to use another citation style such as MLA (Modern Language Association) or CBE (Council of Biology Editors).*

* For a list of some discipline-specific style manuals, and for an exercise to help you analyze the citation format in your major field, see page 168.

Usually the instructor will give specific written directions concerning the reference style; if not, ask your instructor (a) which citation format to use and (b) for an example of that format. Students in major fields must learn the citation format common to that field. Ask an academic advisor, another instructor, or the secretary in the department (a) what citation style is generally used and (b) where to find examples of that reference style.

Study the citation style carefully. As you analyze the format, consider the following:

All Citations

- Order of information: What comes first? Then what? And after that?
- Available information: What doesn't exist? What to do about it?

In-Text Citations

- Placement: Where to place the citation in the sentence?
- In-sentence use of author's name: What to put in parentheses of citation?

End-of-Text Citations

- Position on the page: What's indented? What's not?
- Spacing: Single or double (or something else, or a combination) for each citation? between citations?

In addition, writers must carefully study

- **Punctuation:** Where are the commas, the parentheses, the quotation marks, the periods, the colons, the brackets?
- **Capitalization:** What is capitalized? What's not?
- **Italicization or Underlining:** Use one or the other, but not both, for the same piece of the citation—they both mean the same thing.

Note: Within a single major field of study, there may be differences in citation styles. For example, your department may require one reference style, a respected journal in the field another, and a single instructor still another. It is therefore important for you to be aware of the requirements and to analyze different reference formats.

Below are examples of several citation styles. Remember that although these in-text citations and reference lists have come from student papers in various fields, the styles may not exactly represent the reference styles required by your department. Instead, they serve as possible examples for analysis. You must then investigate and analyze the formats in your department yourself.

English department

In-text

[Page number at end]

According to Roger Axtell (1990), "Cite your own personal experiences, or, if possible, of a mutually respected third party" (33).

References

[Book; last, complete first name; year at end]

Axtell, Roger E. *Do's and taboos of hosting international visitors.* New York: John E. Wiley and Sons, 1990.

[Journal article; quotation marks, italics, (year), colon]

Kimball, Geoffrey. "Men's and women's speech in Koasati: A re-appraisal." *International Journal of American Linguistics* 53 (1997): 30–38.

[Book; 2nd author's name reversed]

McFarlane, Evelyn and James Saywell. *If. . .(Questions for the game of life).* New York: Random House, 1995.

[Edited book]

Oe, Kenzaburo, Ed. *The crazy iris and other stories of the atomic aftermath.* New York: Grove Press, 1985.

Mondul Dul, **Cambodia**

Hydrology

[Et al. = *several authors;* a, b = *two different articles by the same authors]*

In-text

This cost analysis is based on the partial data obtained by Murphy et al. (1996a, b) on the solar pilot plants in Florida.

References

[Textbook]

Howe, D. (1998). *Solar desalination of water: An introduction.* New York: A.G. Smith.

[Journal article; note capitals]

Kettani, M. A. (1997). "Solar desalination with latent heat recovery," *Solar Energy* 12, 79–102.

[First of 2 articles, same authors, year]

Murphy, J., J. R. Irwin, and J. A. Eibling. (1996a). "Efficiency of solar distillation still," *Energy Engineering,* 21, 5, 112–116.

*[Second article, 1996**b**; note issue number]*

Murphy, J. J. R. Irwin, and J. A. Eibling. (1996b). "Solar desalination in connection with controlled environmental agriculture in arid zones," *Energy Conservation and Management,* 26, 1, 20–25.

[Research report: state document]

Taylor, M. F. (1998). "Field evaluation of solar sea-water stills," Report No. 243, Office of Saline Water, Columbus, Ohio.

***Muhammad Murad Alam,* Saudi Arabia**

Economics

In-text

Dornbush (1) states the gross national product (GNP) is one of the most important indicators in measuring economic progress.

References

[Book; note numbers, sequence]

(1) Dornbush, R., and S. Fischer. *Macro-Economies.* McGraw-Hill, New York, 1994.

[Federal government document; note capitalization]

(2) *Economic Report of the President.* Transmitted to the Congress, January 1999. United States Government Printing Office, Washington, 1989.

[Doctoral thesis]

(3) Jensen, E. R. The Sources of Aggregate Demand Disturbances: An Empirical Analysis. Unpublished thesis, University of Michigan, 1998.

[Magazine, no author]

(4) "Investments Today," *Money,* Vol. 15, May, 1996, 50–52.

***Indro Bachtiar,* India**

Chemistry

[Use of number in brackets for citation]

In-text

Many kinds of aromatic hydrocarbons can't be polymerized because the monomer is very stable [1, 2, 4].

Bibliography

[Journal article; note order of authors, year]

1. Ran, R.C., J. S. Jian, and S. Ji, Polymer-supported Lewis acid catalysts: Cationic polymerization, J. Mol. Catal, 1993, **21**, 203–210.

[Book; note commas]

2. Fraze, A. H., High temperature resistant polymers. Wiley, New York, 1994.

[Abbreviation of journal, boldfaced volume]

3. Stille, J. K., Supported chiral catalysts in asymmetric synthesis. J. Macromal. Sci. Chem, 1994, **121** (13–14), 1689–93.

[Article in edited book; note punctuation, sequence]

4. Corey, L. S., P. Hodge, and D. C. Sherrington, Synthesis and characterization of polymers. In Polymer-supported reactions inorganic synthesis (A. Recca, Ed.), Wiley, New York, 1995, 249–255.

***Pablo Etcheverry,* Argentina**

Fluid Mechanics

[And, not &; comma]

In-text

The inflow forecasting model carries out two distinct operations, the first being the creation of a series of natural runoff simulations from which can be extracted the second (Baines and Davies, 1990).

Works Cited

[Book; notice capitalization, no place of publication]

Baines, P. G. Topographic Effects in Stratified Flows. Cambridge University Press, 1995, 209 pp.

[Journal; sequence, punctuation]

Baines, P. G. "A Unified Description of Two-layer Flow Over Topography," J. Fluid Mech. **156** (1994), 127–167.

[Sequence of same author; underlining; research report number]

Baines, P. G. & Davies, P. A. "Laboratory Studies of Topographic Effects in Rotating and/or Stratified Fluids." Orographic Effects in Planetary Flows, Chap. 3, 233–299. GARP Publication No. **23**, WMO/ICSU, 1990.

[Abbreviated journal title, boldfaced issue number]

Kitabayashi, K. "Wind Tunnel and Field Studies of Stagnant Flow Upstream of a Ridge." J. Meteorol. Soc. Japan **65** (1989), 193–203.

***Yasser Raslan,* Egypt**

Electrical Engineering

[No comma]

In-text

These methods have been replaced by the Carnegie-Mellon University Vision Laboratory (Kanade 1993).

References

[Conference proceedings; single-spaced; no indentation

Chen, L. K. "A Fabry-Perot Interferometer System for High-Speed Velocity Measurement," *Proceedings of the SPIE—The International Society for Optical Engineering,* Vol. 2969, pp. 1050–57, 1997.

[Book; 2nd edition, sequence]

Craig, J. J. *Introduction to Robotics: Mechanics and Control,* 2nd ed. Addison-Wesley, San Francisco, 1995.

[Research report; notice capitalization, punctuation]

Kanade, T. "An Optical Proximity Sensor for Measuring Surface Position and Orientation for Robot Manipulation," Vision Laboratory, Carnegie Mellon University, Report No. CMC-RI-TR-93-15, 1993.

[Semicolon between multiple & reversed authors; Vol. *and* pp. *written]*

Zimbleman, D.; J. Burt. "Acquisition, Tracking, and Pointing X," *The International Society for Optical Engineering,* Vol. 2383, pp. 55–65, 1996.

***Zheng Ma,* People's Republic of China (PRC)**

GUIDELINES for Citation

1. Cite any information (electronic, audio, or print) that you did not know before you began writing.
2. When in doubt, cite it.
3. Even when paraphrasing or summarizing, if the idea(s) belong to another author, use a citation.
4. Unless you did the counting yourself, cite others' statistics and numbers.
5. In general, use quotation marks* when three or more *major* words of another author are used consecutively (do not count articles, prepositions, or conjunctions).

* For additional information about using quotation marks, see pages 301–302.

6. If you quote two or three sentences, use only one set of quotation marks (at the beginning of the first sentence and at the end of the last).
7. Direct quotations must be exact.
   - If you omit words in a direct quotation, use an ellipsis (three dots, separated by a space: . . .).
   - If you add words to a direct quotation, use brackets for those words [ ].
8. If a direct quotation is more than 40 words (about three typed lines), separate that quotation from the rest of the text:
   - begin the quotation on a new line
   - indent the direct quotation
   - do not use quotation marks
   - end the direct quotation with a period
   - add the citation after the period, in parentheses
9. It is not necessary to use a citation if the information is a fact that is known by most of your readers.

Using Citations

In U.S. academic prose, instructors prefer that student writers investigate the ideas of several authoritative sources rather than depend on just one or two sources. In other words, quantity is nearly as important as quality. Therefore, try to use more than one authoritative source in each paragraph; do not simply quote or cite the same author again and again.

In general, try not to use too many direct quotations; often, instructors prefer students' own words that are supported with the ideas (but not necessarily the direct quotations) of authoritative sources. In addition, instructors prefer that you summarize and synthesize your authoritative sources rather than list quotation after quotation. The reasons:

- If you cite the ideas of several authors, you indicate to your audience that you have read broadly as well as deeply about the topic.
- If you paraphrase, synthesize, and/or summarize the evidence from several authoritative sources, your ideas are substantially strengthened.

When you first use a direct quotation, and often when you use a source, introduce the author and/or the context of the quotation. Then follow the direct quotation by explaining exactly how the quotation fits into your specific argument and appeals to your specific audience. That is, in the same way you (a) introduce and (b) interpret nontext materials (see p. 109ff), you should introduce and demonstrate the relevance of your sources.

You may decide to use a direct quotation if the author's words are memorable or unique, or if the direct quotation will emphasize a very important point. If you decide to use a direct quotation, try to use a piece of the quotation in your own sentence. Use only the best pieces of the author's words; paraphrase (and cite) the rest in your own words for clarity and continuity.

Finally, remember that you do not have to make every decision about citation alone. You may consult a style manual, your instructor, the writing center on your campus, or a knowledgeable friend. With time and practice in the citation format and style of your major field, you will become more comfortable with the guidelines for citation.

Appendix B

Surveys

Survey 1

Perceptual Learning Style Preference Questionnaire

Joy Reid

Directions: This survey will show you how you prefer to learn English. Read each of the statements below. Then mark the appropriate box for each statement: that you Strongly Agree (**SA**), Agree (**A**), are Undecided (**U**), Disagree (**D**), or Strongly Disagree (**SD**). Mark only one box for each statement, the box that most accurately identifies your feelings about each statement as it concerns learning English. When you finish, use the scoring guide at the end of the survey to discover your learning style preferences.

Statements	SA	A	U	D	SD
1. When the teacher tells me the instructions, I understand better.					
2. I prefer to learn by doing something in class.					
3. I get more work done when I work with others.					
4. I learn more when I study with a group.					
5. In class, I learn best when I work with others.					
6. I learn better by reading what the teacher writes on the chalkboard.					
7. When someone tells me how to do something in class, I learn it better.					
8. When I do things in class, I learn better.					
9. I remember things I have heard in class better than things I have read.					
10. When I read instructions, I remember them better.					
11. I learn more when I can make a model of something.					
12. I understand better when I read instructions.					

Note: Teachers and students using this textbook have permission to use the surveys in this Appendix for class work. If the surveys are used for research purposes, please contact the survey designers for permission:
Joy Reid: jreid@uwyo.edu
Mary Ann Christison: mary.ann.christison@m.cc.utah.edu

Statements	SA	A	U	D	SD
13. When I study alone, I remember things better.					
14. I learn more when I make something for a class project.					
15. I enjoy learning in class by doing experiments.					
16. I learn better when I make drawings as I study.					
17. I learn better in class when the teacher gives a lecture.					
18. When I work alone, I learn better.					
19. I understand things better when I participate in role-playing.					
20. I learn better in class when I listen to someone.					
21. I enjoy working on an assignment with two or three classmates.					
22. When I build something, I remember what I have learned better.					
23. I prefer to study with others.					
24. I learn better by reading than by listening to someone.					
25. I enjoy making something for a class project.					
26. I learn best in class when I can participate in related activities.					
27. In class, I work better when I work alone.					
28. I prefer working on projects by myself.					
29. I learn more by reading textbooks than by listening to lectures.					
30. I prefer to work by myself.					

LEARNING STYLE PREFERENCES SELF-SCORING SHEET

Directions: There are 5 questions for each learning style category in this survey. The questions are grouped below according to each learning style. Assign each question you answered a numerical value as follows:

SA = 5 A = 4 U = 3 D = 2 SD = 1

Fill in the blanks below with the numerical value of each answer. For example, if you answered Strongly Agree (SA) for question 6 (a visual preference question), write a 5 (SA) on the blank next to question 6 below.

Example: Visual
6 - 5

When you have completed all the numerical values for Visual, add the numbers. Multiply the answer by 2 and put the total in the appropriate blank.

Follow this process for each of the learning style categories. When you are finished, the score at the bottom of the page will help you determine your major learning style preference(s), your minor learning style preference(s), and those learning styles that are negligible. See the next page for information about each learning style preference.

If you need help, ask your teacher.

Visual
6 - ____
10 - ____
12 - ____
24 - ____
29 - ____
TOTAL ____ x 2 = ____ *(Score)*

Tactile
11 - ____
14 - ____
16 - ____
22 - ____
25 - ____
TOTAL ____ x 2 = ____ *(Score)*

Auditory
1 - ____
7 - ____
9 - ____
17 - ____
20 - ____
TOTAL ____ x 2 = ____ *(Score)*

Group
3 - ____
4 - ____
5 - ____
21 - ____
23 - ____
TOTAL ____ x 2 = ____ *(Score)*

Kinesthetic
2 - ____
8 - ____
15 - ____
19 - ____
26 - ____
TOTAL ____ x 2 = ____ *(Score)*

Individual
13 - ____
18 - ____
27 - ____
28 - ____
30 - ____
TOTAL ____ x 2 = ____ *(Score)*

Major Learning Style Preference Scores: 38–50
Minor Learning Style Preference Scores: 25–37
Negligible: 0–24

EXPLANATION OF LEARNING STYLE PREFERENCES

Students learn in many different ways. The questionnaire you completed and scored showed which ways you prefer to learn English. In many cases, students' learning style preferences show how well students learn material in different situations.

The explanations of major learning style preferences below describe the characteristics of those learners. The descriptions will give you some information about ways in which you learn best.*

VISUAL Major Learning Style Preference

You learn well from seeing words in books, on the chalkboard, and in workbooks. You remember and understand information and instructions better if you read them. You don't need as much oral explanation as an auditory learner, and you can often learn alone, with a book. You should take notes of lectures and oral directions if you want to remember this information.

AUDITORY Major Learning Style Preference

You learn from hearing words spoken and from oral explanations. You may remember information by reading aloud or moving your lips as you read, especially when you are learning new material. You benefit from hearing audio tapes, lectures, and class discussion. You benefit from making tapes to listen to, by teaching other students, and by conversing with your teacher.

KINESTHETIC Major Learning Style Preference

You learn best by experience, by being involved physically in classroom experiences. You remember information well when you actively participate in activities, field trips, and role-playing in the classroom. A combination of stimuli—for example, an audio tape combined with an activity—will help you understand more material.

TACTILE Major Learning Style Preference

You learn best when you have the opportunity to do "hands-on" experiences with materials. That is, working on experiments in a laboratory, handling and building models, and touching and working with materials provide you with the most successful learning situations. Writing notes or instructions can help you remember information, and physical involvement in class-related activities may help you understand new information.

GROUP Major Learning Style Preference

You learn more easily when you study with at least one other student, and you will be more successful completing work well when you work with others. You value group interaction and class work with other students, and you remember information better when you work with two or three classmates. The stimulation you receive from group work helps you learn and understand new information.

INDIVIDUAL Major Learning Style Preference

You learn best when you work alone. You think better when you study alone, and you remember information you learn by yourself. You understand new material best when you learn it alone, and you make better progress in learning when you work by yourself.

Minor Learning Styles

In most cases, minor learning styles indicate areas when you can function well as a learner. Usually a very successful learner can learn in several different ways.

Negligible Learning Styles

Often a negligible score indicates that you may have difficulty learning in that way. One solution may be to direct your learning to your stronger learning styles. Another solution might be to try to work on some of the skills to strengthen your learning style in that "negligible" area.

---

* Adapted from the C.I.T.E. Learning Styles Instrument, Murdoch Teacher Center, Wichita, Kansas. Used with permission.

Survey 2

Student-Generated Inventory for Secondary Level and Young Adult Learners

*Mary Ann Christison's Students**

Directions: Rank each statement **0**, **1**, or **2**. Write **0** if you disagree with the statement. Write **2** if you strongly agree. Write **1** if you are somewhere in between.

Verbal/Linguistic Intelligence

___ **1.** I like to read books, magazines, and newspapers.
___ **2.** I consider myself a good writer.
___ **3.** I like to tell jokes and stories.
___ **4.** I can remember people's names easily.
___ **5.** I like to recite tongue twisters.
___ **6.** I have a good vocabulary in my native language.

Musical Intelligence

___ **1.** I can hum the tunes to many songs.
___ **2.** I am a good singer.
___ **3.** I play a musical instrument or sing in a choir.
___ **4.** I can tell when music sounds off-key.
___ **5.** I often tap rhythmically on the table or desk.
___ **6.** I often sing songs.

Logical/Mathematical Intelligence

___ **1.** I often do arithmetic in my head.
___ **2.** I am good at chess and/or checkers.
___ **3.** I like to put things into categories.
___ **4.** I like to play number games.
___ **5.** I love to figure out how computers work.
___ **6.** I ask many questions about how things work.

Spatial/Visual Intelligence

___ **1.** I can read maps easily.
___ **2.** I enjoy art activities.
___ **3.** I draw well.
___ **4.** Movies and slides really help me learn new information.
___ **5.** I love books with pictures.
___ **6.** I enjoy putting puzzles together.

Body/Kinesthetic Intelligence

___ **1.** It is hard for me to sit quietly for a long time.
___ **2.** It is easy for me to follow exactly what other people do.
___ **3.** I am good at sewing, woodworking, building, or mechanics.
___ **4.** I am good at sports.
___ **5.** I enjoy working with clay.
___ **6.** I enjoy running and jumping.

Interpersonal Intelligence

___ **1.** I am often the leader in activities.
___ **2.** I enjoy talking to my friends.
___ **3.** I often help my friends.
___ **4.** My friends often talk to me about their problems.
___ **5.** I have many friends.
___ **6.** I am a member of several clubs.

Intrapersonal Intelligence

___ **1.** I go to the movies alone.
___ **2.** I go to the library alone to study.
___ **3.** I can tell you some things I am good at doing.
___ **4.** I like to spend time alone.
___ **5.** My friends find some of my actions strange sometimes.
___ **6.** I learn from my mistakes.

---

* **Reprinted with permission** from Mary Ann Christison. First published in 1996, *TESOL Journal* 6 (1), 10–14.

Survey 3

Type A / Type B Personality Inventory

Joy Reid

Directions: Answer the questions below. Then discuss the Type A and Type B personalities. Which are you?

1. When you brush your teeth, do you always put the cap back on the toothpaste? Do you squeeze the tube in the middle, or do you fold it up from the bottom?
2. You are going to the airport to catch a plane. Do you leave your house early enough to arrive at least half an hour before boarding, or would you rather arrive just as the boarding of the plane begins?
3. Do you prefer to plan your free time, or do you prefer spontaneity?
4. When you leave your car or apartment, do you double check to make sure the windows are closed and the doors are locked?
5. How do your bureau drawers look? Are socks all matched and stored symmetrically, or does it resemble the aftermath of a tornado?
6. When you go to the grocery store, do you take a list? Do you follow the list?
7. Do you talk fast? Do you interrupt people when they are talking?
8. When you go to the library to do an assignment, do you proceed with a series of planned steps, or do you take the time to look for other interesting material?
9. Are you usually on time? Do people who are late irritate you? Is it hard for you to find time to do things (such as getting a haircut or exercising regularly)?
10. Do you usually do more than one thing at a time?

INTERPRETING YOUR RESULTS

Some psychologists have identified two personality types that exist along a continuum. People who have an extremely Type-A personality are usually high achievers who are very organized and very neat. For them, scheduling their time is exceedingly important; they are always on time, they make lists for efficiency, they often talk fast and interrupt others, and they often do more than one thing at a time.

In contrast, people who have an extremely Type-B personality are usually more relaxed about time; they value spontaneity, and they are often late. They are not very neat, they "take time" to enjoy things, and the often operate without a schedule.

Of course, most people are not extreme in their personalities. Instead, they are nearer the middle of the scale below. Given your answers to the informal survey, where do you belong on this scale?

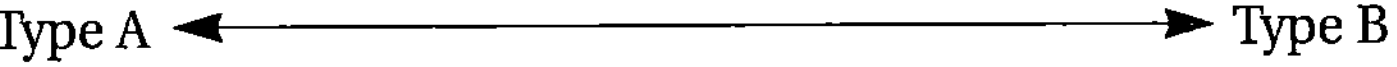

Appendix C

The Résumé and the Application Letter

A RÉSUMÉ, called by academics a **c**urriculum **v**itae (also called a "c.v."), is a formal summary of a person's background that is written in a clear and precise format. A résumé is often needed to accompany an application for admission to a college/ university or a graduate school, and it always accompanies any application for employment in the U.S.

Résumés in the U.S. require specific formats and styles, but they all contain the following information:

- **personal:** name, permanent address, and other contact information such as e-mail address and fax number
- **objective:** for a job or position that has been advertised/announced, the résumé begins with a concise, relevant statement of the applicant's objective
- **academic:** a summary of schooling, usually starting with the most recent college/university data, and listing backward
- **employment:** jobs held, either part-time or full-time
- **special talents or interests:** such as languages spoken, computer skills, honors received

The Résumé

Every year, more than a billion résumés are received by U.S. personnel (or human resource) directors. Of those résumés, about one in 245 leads to a job for the applicant. A personnel director faced with a stack of 100 résumés every day usually has less than one minute to skim each one and make an informed decision about the applicant, so the initial impression is crucial. Appearance and information help a résumé get attention; content, persuasion, organization, and relevant detail help the applicant get an interview. The *audience*—the person who reads the résumé—is introduced to the applicant by a single page of information, so that information must be clearly arranged and error-free.

The *purpose* of the résumé will influence the material and the arrangement of the document. For example, a résumé accompanying an application for graduate school admission would focus on previous education, any employment experience relevant to the proposed field of study, and any previous publications in the field.

In contrast, especially in job applications, the résumé should "sell" the applicant; that is, it must be persuasive. The résumé writer is not required to be modest; indeed, a résumé should "sell" his or her best qualifications to the reader. According to *NACE Spotlight* (November 17, 1997, vol. 20, num. 8), the top ten personal characteristics that employers seek in job candidates are

honesty, integrity	leadership skills	teamwork skills
communication skills	motivation, initiative	enthusiasm
flexibility	self-confidence	
strong work ethic	interpersonal skills	

USING ACTION VERBS

Résumés in the U.S., especially for young applicants, are expected to be about one page long. A résumé follows appropriate writing conventions and uses dynamic, concise language. If possible, it includes a variety of these résumé verbs.

acted	conducted	designed	formulated
administered	controlled	determined	guided
advised	coordinated	diagnosed	improved
applied	created	established	installed
analyzed	cultivated	expanded	introduced
clarified	defined	evaluated	investigated
completed	delegated	facilitated	managed

maintained	prepared	reorganized	supervised
negotiated	proposed	reviewed	trained
operated	provided	selected	translated
organized	recommended	solved	updated
performed	recruited	structured	wrote

STATING THE OBJECTIVE

Applicants should plan to write an individual résumé for each application, one that specifically targets the position and the company. The applicant tries to make a connection with the company and the company's needs, with the specific position being applied for: a management position with a major computer manufacturer, for example, or a position as a designer in a children's clothing company. Or the applicant describes his or her skills and abilities as they apply to a specific position: to apply skills in research design, data analysis, and report writing in a marketing research position, or to use social service training and administrative skills in a nonprofit organization.

RÉSUMÉ APPEARANCE

The résumé should be as clear, as clean-looking, and as appealing as possible. There is no one prescribed way to write a résumé, but it must be centered on the page with 1" margins, be neat and error-free, and be easy to read—usually with headings to guide the reader. The page should not be crowded with extra words, small print, too many fonts or formats, vertical or horizontal lines, or too much information. Instead, use an outline or block form, perhaps with bullets (•) to present the material; put the most important information first, and follow the **KISS** rule: **K**eep **I**t **S**hort and **S**imple. Use white space on the page effectively; use a 10–12 point font, and do not justify the right margins of the text. To print the résumé, use a laser printer with a new ribbon. Duplicate the résumé on white, cream, or gray high-quality paper with a clean, high-quality machine.

INFORMATION TO INCLUDE

[Formal language]

- name, address, other contact information
- objective (in a single sentence)
  - work-centered, not self-centered
  - what you can do for the employer
- experience: work history, employment, or professional experience
  - inclusive years (or months and years—no days) for each job
    - > no comma between month and year (e.g., February 1999)
    - > begin with most recent and work backward chronologically
  - job responsibilities, using past tense verbs
  - brief description of abilities, responsibilities, accomplishments for each job held; give fewer details for older or less relevant jobs
- education
  - degree(s) earned, using abbreviations (such as B.S., M.A.); include GPA (or major field average) if high, or honors and awards
  - begin with most recent and list backward
  - major and minor areas of study
  - include high school only if unique (such as Boston Latin or High School of Music and Art)
- other (if relevant)

professional training	special skills
professional memberships/affiliations	publications
licenses/certifications	military service
activities/interests/hobbies	languages

conference presentations | computer skills
related experiences | awards/honors

Do **NOT** include a date (this will appear on the cover letter), slang, any reference to salary, or contact information for references (or a statement that says "References Available on Request").

For additional information about writing résumés, access one of the following Internet addresses:

JobJungle	http://www.Jobjungle.com/how2.htm
Bowling Green State University	http://www.bgsu.edu/offices/careers/resume/res-wri.html
Edmund Stones The Write Résumé	http://www.i-connect.net/~resume

1 STUDENT SAMPLE

RÉSUMÉ FOR UNDERGRADUATE INTERNSHIP

[Contact information; single spaced]
[Place names spelled out in full; no abbreviations]

HANG (ALLEN) DU
Permanent Resident
2229 Coe Street #109
Port Angeles, Washington 98362
360-766-4504 (Home)
Email: hansdu@uwa.edu
Home Page: http://w3.uwa.edu/~hansdu

OBJECTIVE — To obtain a challenging summer internship related to computer software that allows for growth and an opportunity to contribute job experience.

EDUCATION — University of Washington, Seattle, Washington **GPA 3.918/4.0**
Port Angeles High School, 1996 **GPA 3.954/4.0**
53.5 credits earned toward B.S. in Computer Science/Engineering

HONORS/AWARDS — President's Honor Roll, Fall 1998, Spring 1999
Computer Science Development Scholarship, 1998–1999
Wal-Mart Competitive Edge Scholarship, 1998–1999
Trustees' Reception for University of Washington Outstanding Scholars, 1998

RELATED EXPERIENCE — **ACM Webmaster**, University of Washington, part-time, October 1997–present
- Updated local ACM homepage

HomePage Designer, June 1997–present
- Created Home Pages with HTML and JAVA

WORK EXPERIENCE — **Computer Programmer**, part-time, Sept. 1995–Sept. 1996
Henan University Affiliate High School, Kaifeng, China
- Programmed screen savers and developed education software

Computer Lab Assistant, October 1996–May 1997
Port Angeles High School
- Helped students learn Windows, Pascal, and DBASE

COMPUTER SKILLS — **Operating Systems:** DOS, VMS, UNIX, Win98, WinNT
Languages: PASCAL, JAVA, HTML, C, C++, VISUAL BASIC

LANGUAGES — Fluent in English and Chinese (Mandarin)

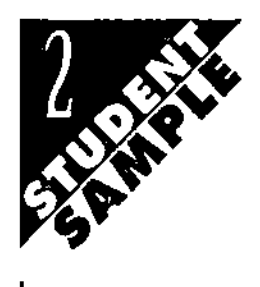

JOANN E. PEDERSON
1506 East Row Street
West Lafayette, IN 47907-1356
317-568-2527 (Home)
E-mail: jpederson68@aol.com

Objective

To utilize my work experience as I learn more about consulting with a diverse array of clients.

Education

B.S. in Management/Marketing, Purdue University, anticipated 5/99

Work Experience

FRESHMAN LIFE ASSISTANT, Purdue University, Office of Student Life — 3/96–5/97

Scheduled, counseled, and advised individual students
Organized and developed correspondence materials

PEER ASSISTANT COORDINATOR, Purdue University — 2/96–present

Developed and implemented existing program
Interviewed and selected applicants; organized training sessions

VISITOR INFORMATION CENTER HOSTESS, Purdue University — 2/96–present

DATA CLERK, Big Horn Rural Electric Company — Summers, 1990–1994

Developed and implemented monthly billing procedures for 1200 members
Developed topics and wrote articles for company newsletter
Produced newsletter on Macintosh using Pagemaker and Microsoft Works

INTERN: Congressman Craig Thomas, Washington, D.C. — 7/96–8/96

REPORTER, *Engineer Daily,* Purdue University daily newspaper — 9/96–6/97

- Developed and wrote columns pertaining to campus life
- Interviewed individuals, researched background, wrote news articles

Leadership Activities and Societies

- Student Representative, Director, Admissions Selection Board — 5/96
- Omicron Delta Kappa — 5/95–present
- Phi Kappa Phi and Beta Gamma Sigma — 5/95–present
- Delta Delta Delta, Public Relations Chair — 5/94–present
- Associated Students of the University of Washington Senator — 5/96–present
- University of Washington Honors Program — 5/94–present
- Mortar Board Senior Honorary Society
- Iron Skull Junior Honorary Society
- SPURS Sophomore Honorary Society

Honors and Awards

- Outstanding Junior in Department of Management/Marketing
- Purdue University Superior Student Scholarship
- National Collegiate Student Government Award
- Presidential Scholar

BHARAT R. ASHRA
18 Widgeon Way
Greenwich, CT 06830
(203) 622-8499
Email: 068320@aol.com

Highly experienced Foreign Exchange Trader with significant trading and private investment background. Successfully traded in difficult and illiquid market conditions. A self-motivated, adaptable, results-oriented team player with strong analytical, problem-solving, and decision-making skills.

EXPERIENCE

American Express Bank, Ltd., New York 1995–present

Director, Foreign Exchange Trader 1997–1999
Reported to chief trader, responsible for successfully trading Spot Sterling, Swiss and EMS currencies with minimum risk exposure to the bank. Discussed winning trade strategies with clients.

Helped management resolve clients' trade disputes
Worked with relationship managers to develop existing and new customers to market trade strategies
Analyzed market conditions and employed creative trading strategies, generating revenue while competitors lost profits

Customer Development and Marketing 1994–1995

Analyzed news breaks and market conditions to provide timely information to customers
Traveled on marketing trips to Far East to consolidate relationships with clients

Kanji Pitamber & Co., Bombay 1992–1994

Managing Partner, Foreign Exchange and Finance Brokers

Led a staff of 30 people to successfully manage the 60-year-old family business
Managed investment and real estate portfolios
Arranged private financing for small/medium businesses

Union Bank of Switzerland, New York 1985–1992
Foreign Exchange Trader, Spot, Forwards, Futures

Traded Spot Sterling
Managed Sterling book and assisted chief of Swiss book
Arbitrage between IMM Futures and Spot markets in Swiss, Sterling, and Marks

EDUCATION

MBA, Finance, Adelphi University, New York, 1985
B.A., Commerce, Business Administration, Bombay University, 1982

ONLINE RÉSUMÉS

Many U.S. companies have begun to accept résumés on the computer; indeed, some, like Boeing, want only online résumés. When this is the case, the application form is found on the website of the company. Usually, no application letter will be required. Instead, the applicant simply completes the online form.

Online résumés do not allow for individualization; they require a specific font, no boldfacing or italicizing, and only enough detail to fill the space allotted. In addition, because some of the online résumés will be computer-scanned rather than be read by a person, the applicant must use the **keywords** that the computer-scanner will identify. That is, the computer will scan, retrieve, and route online résumés to appropriate employment personnel based on the keywords the computer encounters. For example, if you are applying to an engineering firm, you should use specific terms in the job description (such as *real time data base design, computer-aided design, computer-controlled manufacturing, network management, licensed professional engineer*) as well as listing the needed skills (such as FORTRAN, C++, Windows NT on VME-based systems).

Even without allowing for individual creativity, online résumés require the basic rules: error-free, correct information; concise engaging detail; demonstration of the ability to (a) follow directions and (b) write well; and clear focus on the job description.

The Application Letter

The purpose of the application letter is to introduce the applicant and to ensure that the attached résumé will be read.* The letter is usually written in response to a specific job advertisement. To respond effectively, the applicant should do necessary research: access materials about the specific companies and positions for which the applicant is applying from the library and/or from the campus Career Services office. The applicant should also look up the website for the company and read the information carefully. In the application letter, the writer should mention positive aspects of the company to show the reader how interested the applicant is in the company.

The application letter must demonstrate excellent organizational and writing skills; it should be one page in length, error-free, and complete; and it should use a business-like tone and language. The letter should

- be addressed to a specific individual with correct title and address
- focus on the needs of employer
- highlight but NOT repeat the résumé
- explain skills clearly related to the specific job applied for
- emphasize specific positive, concrete accomplishments

Finally, the applicant should sign the letter in blue or black ink, put the application letter on top of the résumé, fold both into even thirds, slip both into the formally addressed envelope so that the letter comes out right-side-up, and seal the envelope.

Note: Other letter types in job hunting include the inquiry letter, which asks about possible vacancies or internships that have not been advertised or announced, and the thank-you letter, which follows an interview and expresses appreciation, establishes good will, and strengthens the applicant's candidacy for the position.

* For additional information about and practice with business letter writing, see pages 3–4.

[Permanent address; single spaced; date]

1506 East Row Street
West Lafayette, IN 47907-1356
January 13, 1999

[Reader's name, title, full address; block format]

Kristen Lindemann
Management Consultant
McKinsey & Company
291 Mohawk Trail
Bridgewater, New Jersey 08807

[Formal introduction]

Dear Ms. Lindemann:

[Statement of intent] *[Personal "link" to reader]*

I am interested in working as an intern for McKinsey & Company. Currently, I am a Presidential Scholar at Purdue University completing my junior year as a management major, and I obtained your name through the Presidential Scholar Alumni Directory.

[Double-space between paragraphs] *[Brief summary of persuasive information]*

Through my upper division course work, I have gained insights into management principles, and I would like to experience first-hand their translation into practice. Enclosed is a résumé detailing my work experience and extracurricular activities. As a Freshman Life Assistant, I am involved in troubleshooting and problem-solving processes for individuals, and I participate in the planning and implementation of projects for first-year students in this program.

[Additional special skills that match the position]

My computer skills have allowed me to publish the Freshman Life newsletter, and I have written for the Purdue student newspaper on a regular basis. As a consequence, I have learned to meet tight deadlines and still produce quality work. I look forward to many similar challenges and the opportunity to further develop my skills while helping your consulting firm.

[Appreciation; request for reply]

I would appreciate any information you have about internship possibilities. Thank you for your time and consideration. I look forward to hearing from you.

Sincerely,

JoAnn Pederson

JoAnn Pederson

515 E. Pershing, #346
Atlanta, Georgia 30034
September 20, 1999

Ms. Liz McGroary
Personnel Director
Quark, Inc.
1800 Grant Street
Austin, TX 75705

Dear Ms. McGroary:

[Formal language] Do you have a need for a tax expert in your finance department? If so, then please consider my application. I am currently taking courses to earn a Bachelor of Science degree in Accounting with concentration in tax research and tax preparation. I expect to graduate in May 2000 with a cumulative grade point average of 3.7/4.0. I will then be ready to step into a successful company and help create its future.

[Emphasizes accomplishments] *[Skills related to the specific job]* I have gained valuable experience by doing tax research for class projects and for business clients. While working for H&R Block, I prepared tax returns for individual as well as corporate clients. I developed a broad understanding of both state and federal tax requirements, and I acquired detailed knowledge of the Texas tax system when I filed use-tax returns for my RV rental company which has a branch office in Houston. I have worked with computer-based accounting since 1975, and I enjoy the challenge of updated and new software programs. I am a dynamic leader whose knowledge, skills, and abilities complement the Quark image.

[Focuses on needs of employer] I am willing to relocate and can make arrangements for an interview at your Atlanta office; I am also willing to fly to Austin for an interview. I will telephone you next week to discuss my application. Thank you for your time and consideration.

Sincerely,

Peggy Coffman

Peggy Coffman

Index

A

B

C

D

E

F

G

H

I

J

K

Q

R

S

T

U

V

W